Fear and Sanctuary
Burmese Refugees in Thailand

Hazel J. Lang

Fear and Sanctuary
Burmese Refugees in Thailand

SOUTHEAST ASIA PROGRAM PUBLICATIONS
Southeast Asia Program
Cornell University
Ithaca, New York
2002

Cornell Southeast Asia Program Publications
640 Stewart Avenue, Ithaca, NY 14850-3857

Studies on Southeast Asia No. 32

Printed in the United States of America

ISBN 978-0-87727-731-6

Cover: Photographs by Hazel J. Lang. Cover design by Judith Burns, Publications Services, Cornell University.

CONTENTS

MAPS

PREFACE

Thailand shares a long 2,401-kilometer stretch of border with Burma/Myanmar and has become a long-term host to a steadily growing flow of refugees fleeing from the neighboring war-affected borderlands. *Fear and Sanctuary* takes an in-depth look into the nature and causes of the Burmese refugees' displacement. It documents and conceptualizes the problem as a whole, addressing both the root and precipitating causes of displacement within Burma and the cross-border response in Thailand.

The book seeks to combine a detailed definition and analysis of the problem with a broader conceptual map. It is also a necessarily eclectic pursuit which garners perspectives from across academic disciplinary boundaries, weaving together insights from various literatures spanning several relevant disciplines, including international relations, "refugee studies" and international refugee law, political geography, anthropology, and a wide range of area studies writing on Burma and Thailand.

Field research for this book was conducted on several occasions between 1994-2000, in Thailand and in the refugee camps along the Thai-Burmese border between Sangkhlaburi in Thailand's Kanchanaburi province and Mae Hong Son in the north. My first visit to the border in December 1993 to the then-headquarters of the ethnic and pro-democratic opposition forces at Manerplaw, just inside Burma on the Moei (Thaungyin) River, introduced me to the some of the political intricacies of the Thai-Burmese borderlands and the refugees. For the Mon focus of this study, my primary locale then became the Mon border region where I settled into life at Pa Yaw (literally "border") camp, housing some four thousand refugees at the time. Pa Yaw was nestled deeply in the mountainous jungle, about fifty kilometers southwest of Three Pagodas Pass and contiguous with areas in Burma still controlled by the insurgent New Mon State Party (NMSP). The end of my first main stay there also coincided with the cease-fire agreement reached between the NMSP and the State Law and Order Restoration Council (SLORC) in June 1995, which also presaged the repatriation of the Mon camps back to Burma.

Burma or Myanmar? Whether to call the country "Burma" or "Myanmar" provokes controversy. It has now become customary to make a brief note on this matter, with a brief history of the name changes. After the takeover by the SLORC in September 1988, the official name of the country was changed from the post-1974 form of the "Socialist Republic of the Union of Burma" back to the "Union of Burma" (which was the original designation after independence from Britain in January 1948). Then in July 1989, the SLORC re-named the country the "Union of Myanmar," or "Myanmar Naing-Ngan" in a direct transliteration from the Burmese language. At this time, several other names, such as those of some large cities and administrative divisions, were also changed. For instance, among other changes, Rangoon became Yangon, Moulmein became Mawlaymyine; Tenasserim Division became Tanintharyi Division, and Pegu became Bago Division. The

United Nations and many governments subsequently recognized these name changes. (At the same time, Australia, the United States, and several European countries still refer to the name of the country as "Burma.") The problem with the name changes has become politically charged. While the SLORC/SPDC claims that it has simply reinstated the original names for the country, its political opponents in particular regard the changes as illegitimate. Opposition groups call for a boycott of the name "Myanmar" as a form of protest against the regime's human rights abuses and lack of consultation regarding the change. This rhetorical character of the country's name cannot be avoided and sometimes inspires passions. This book has retained "Burma" as a more familiar form. The term "Burmese" is used as a noun to refer to all the citizens of contemporary Burma and as an adjective, whereas "Burman" connotes the major ethnic group.

A note on the SLORC and the SPDC: The State Law and Order Restoration Council (SLORC) is the name of the twenty-one-member junta that assumed power on September 18, 1988, after the military's crackdown on the country-wide pro-democracy uprising. It claimed a temporary role for itself, as the name suggests, but the junta has remained firmly in power since that time. The SLORC established an administrative structure with Law and Order Restoration Councils (LORCs) at the state/divisional, district, township and ward/village-tract levels. On November 15, 1997, the SLORC was officially dissolved (and several members were "allowed to resign"—that is, certain corrupt members were purged). It was replaced with the nineteen-member State Peace and Development Council (SPDC). The original top four strongmen of the SLORC (Senior General Than Shwe, General Maung Aye, Lieutenant-General Khin Nyunt, and Lieutenant-General Tin Oo) each retained their positions in the newly reconstituted junta. Significantly, the nineteen-member SPDC is made up of senior military officers, which includes the commanders of each of the twelve military regions. The former LORCs were renamed Peace and Development Councils (PDCs).

I have so many people to thank for their support and advice in helping me to produce this book. I am especially grateful to the generosity and commitment of Desmond Ball, Jan Jindy Pettman, and Carl Grundy-Warr. My thanks also to Carolyn Nordstrom, Stephanie Lawson, Gail Craswell, Brigid Ballard, and Nancy Viviani. I greatly appreciate the meticulous attention and immensely helpful comments on an earlier version of the manuscript provided by Mary Callahan. It was a pleasure to work with Deborah Homsher of SEAP, who superbly edited this manuscript and who made the process of publishing it smooth and enjoyable.

I was privileged to have enjoyed the interaction and friendship of many wonderful colleagues and friends in the Department of International Relations at the Australian National University, including Liz Gardiner, Wynne Russell, Lesley McCulloch, Gavin Mount, Cindy O'Hagan, Craig Meer, Charles van der Donckt, Eric Chauvistré, Kim Ong, Johanna Sutherland, Anthony Langlois, Kathy Morton, David Cooper, Emily Rudland, Morten Pederson, and Ko Aung Myoe. Thanks also to Andrew Selth for many wonderful discussions on Burma. I appreciate the assistance I have received from Lynne Payne and Amy Chen from International Relations on computer and administration matters over the years. Keith Mitchell from the ANU Cartography Unit did a fine job on the production of the maps.

For the fieldwork in this book, I have an enormous number of people to thank. Many of those who so generously gave me their time and helped me so significantly cannot be named here. But you know who you are, and I thank you. The hospitality and kindness I have received on the Thai-Burmese border over the years has not only facilitated my research, but also showed me much about the possibilities for strength and generosity in the midst of adversity. I would like to thank members of the New Mon State Party, the Mon National Relief Committee, the Karen National Union and Karen Refugee Committee, the Karenni National Progressive Party, the Karenni Refugee Committee, the Shan Human Rights Foundation, and many others. I also appreciate the assistance from a number of independent Burmese observers. Thanks, too, to Alison Tate, Lyndal Barry, Mary O'Kane, Brenda Belak, Sittipong Kalayanee, Deb Stothard, Ko Soe Aung, Chao-Tzang Yawnghwe, Amanda Zappia, Marc Purcell, Annabel Anderson, Madoka Chase, Anelyn de Luna, Nai Banyikim, Daw Myint Myint Aye, Banyar Naing, Hongsar Channaibanya, and Min Win Htut. My appreciation is also extended to numerous organizations in Bangkok, including the Burmese Border Consortium, the UNHCR; to Panitan Wattanayagorn, Supang Chantavanich, and other colleagues at Chulalongkorn University; and to numerous other senior Thai officials and decision-makers in government agencies involved with refugee matters in Thailand. I would like to acknowledge the generous support of the Sir Edward Weary Dunlop Fellowship in Asia, administered through the Asialink Centre at the University of Melbourne, for funding the follow-up research on the future prospects for the refugees.

In addition to those friends mentioned above (and not mentioned!), I could not have lived without Julian Kelly, Felicity and Mark Donnelly, Donna Christie and Michael Bolt, Barb and Rog Kelly, Khin Ma Mar Kyi, Tracey Hind, Rosanne Monahan, Di and Rog Gabb, and the Hughes and Coombes families. Thank you also to Ranmal Samarawickrama, Sebastian Appenah, Fiona Stitfold, Kerrin Forster, and Peter Love for your support. Finally, this is dedicated to my beloved mother, Hannelore, who died in 1996, before she could see the final product of this undertaking with which I was always so preoccupied.

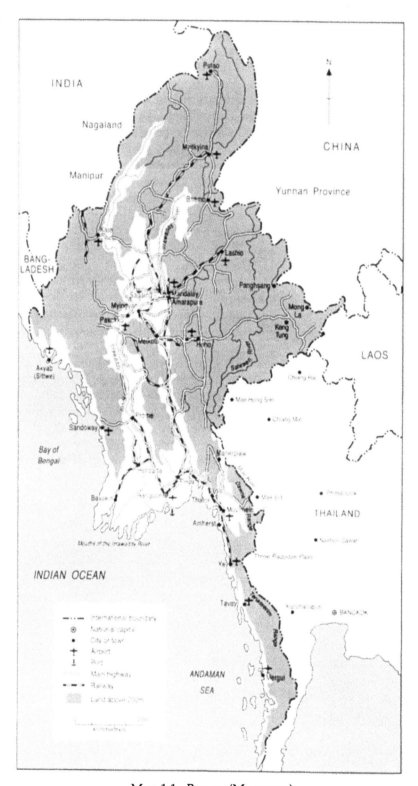

Map 1.1   Burma (Myanmar)

INTRODUCTION:
FEAR AND SANCTUARY

Refugees are defined by the fear they flee from and the sanctuary they seek. The growing problem of Burmese refugees encamped along the Thai border manifests dramatically the human insecurity prevailing in the neighboring borderlands. What has brought about the displacement of the Burmese refugees, and how are we to approach a comprehensive understanding of the nature and causes of this situation? This book defines and documents the problem as a whole, investigating how the predicament of Burmese refugees in Thailand is ultimately rooted in the patterns and consequences of war and conflict in Burma, as well as analyzing the manifold aspects of Thailand's cross-border response and the complexities of the borderlands' politics. Where do we begin?

Since independence in 1948, Burma has been plagued by an extraordinarily protracted internal war. After barely three months, the country was engulfed in a multifarious conflict between the central government in Rangoon and a plethora of anti-government rebellions. Long-running insurgencies fought by the Communist Party of Burma (1948–1989) and a large number of well-armed ethnopolitical organizations have threatened the central authorities throughout both the democratic eras (1948–58, 1960–62) and the long period of military domination (1962–present). Under successive governments, the *tatmadaw* (the Burmese armed forces) has fought back, always striving to make its counterinsurgency strategy more effective; it has emasculated or finally defeated many of its opponents only relatively recently. In the contested borderlands where insurgency and counterinsurgency have been waged, the war has increasingly penetrated into the midst of civilian life over the course of time. What this has involved, how this has occurred, and the consequences for the displacement of civilian populations are key concerns in this book.

Thailand, which shares a porous 2,401–kilometer stretch of border with Burma, has received steadily increasing flows of displaced persons from Burma's ethnic minority regions since the Karens established the first "semi-permanent" refugee camps in 1984. In terms of registered camp populations along the border, in 1984 there were less than ten thousand; by 1990, after the Karennis and the Mons had also set up their camps, there were 43,500; and by 1995 the number had grown to over 92,000 people. In 1996, the Mon camps were repatriated across the border, following the military cease-fire in June 1995. With their repatriation in view, this study takes the context and experience of the Mon refugees as a particular focus. In the year 2000, over 122,000 persons were registered in a string of border camps: these included some 94,000 Karens, over 18,000 Karennis, and a population of around ten thousand Mons in their resettlement sites just inside Burma. Some 1,700 Burmese students and political activists, who fled after the 1988 pro-democracy uprising, were also residing in a holding center in Ratchaburi province near Bangkok. In addition to these displaced persons who are registered in the camps, Thailand has also absorbed approximately 100,000 "hidden" Shans (particularly those displaced after the *tatmadaw*'s large-scale relocation program in central Shan state beginning in March 1996) who fled Burma with their extended families and now survive mainly in the illegal daily labor economy.[1] While the numbers and ethnic groups listed here provide one with an accepted profile of the Burmese refugee presence in Thailand, in fact these figures understate the problem.

There are also further undetermined numbers of displaced persons who move well beyond the camp structure on the border. As indicated, the above figures represent registered camp numbers alone. They do not include the displaced persons who either never enter, or who slip out of, the camp structure, managing to "disappear," undocumented and illegally, into the immigrant workforce beyond. According to representatives from Thailand's National Security Council and the Ministry of Labor and Social Welfare, in 1998 the majority of the estimated 750,000 undocumented migrants working in Thailand were from Burma.[2] It is also estimated that some twenty thousand Burmese women work in the commercial sex industry in Thailand.[3] These numbers are, of course, only one indication of the extent of continuing displacement occurring in the borderlands affected by war. Many more people remain internally displaced on the Burmese side of the border, too, completely hidden from view and stranded far from protection and relief.

AIMS AND SCOPE

This book undertakes an in-depth, multi-faceted study into the nature and causes of the Burmese refugees' displacement, displacement resulting from a conflict in which the ongoing struggles for control over the modern territorialized state have turned civilian populations into deliberate targets. While it devotes particular attention to the experience of the Mon refugees (1990-1996), it also seeks to reflect on the problem as it is played out more broadly. The aim is to conceptualize and document the predicament of fear and sanctuary structured around an analysis of the root and precipitating causes of displacement in Burma and the cross-border response to the refugee presence in Thailand. It is also hoped that a detailed analysis of the context and sources of the problem will help establish a basis from which to address future resolutions meant to solve such problems.

First, with a broad historical sweep, my argument will relate the root causes of the refugee situation to their long-term antecedents in the historical and political setting of Burma, antecedents which inform the context of contemporary civil war and ethnopolitical conflict. The next layer of inquiry addresses the more

---

[1] Personal communication, Shan Human Rights Foundation, Chiang Mai, March 14, 2000.

[2] Seminar, "Policy and Plans to Repatriate Undocumented Migrant Workers," Chulalongkorn University, Bangkok, March 13, 1998.

[3] Asia Watch/Women's Rights Project, *A Modern Form of Slavery: Trafficking of Burmese Women and Girls into Brothels in Thailand* (New York: Asia Watch/Women's Rights Project, 1993).

immediate nature and precipitating causes of civilian displacement in the conflict areas in order to determine conditions and patterns on the ground. Considering these two contextual components together will enable us to clarify the nature and causes of warfare that lead to displacement and refugee migration.

The book also seeks to characterize the nature of the Thai host response to the problem of cross-border displacement. How has Thailand responded and how have the wider borderlands' relationships influenced the story of sanctuary in Thailand? This analysis of sanctuary in Thailand not only examines the quality of refugee protection afforded as a necessarily "palliative" response, but also considers Thailand's borderland politics and the prospects for a sustainable resolution to the cross-border predicament there. An understanding of the Thai response to sanctuary is incomplete without substantive study of the changing politico-military realities of the borderlands context and of how these have infused and influenced the fortunes of refugees seeking sanctuary, and, indeed, the overall refugee predicament. In addition, the book examines the quality of refugee protection afforded to a quite distinctive group of urban-based asylum-seekers in Bangkok who fled Burma after the 1988 pro-democracy uprising. And, as considered below, this study of the situation of Burmese refugees in Thailand also allows for reflection on some of the key challenges confronting and redefining concepts of refugee protection in the international system today.

GLOBAL DIMENSIONS OF THE REFUGEE

The condition of "the refugee" illuminates significant aspects of the modern state and international relations between states. Essentially, this condition involves the rupture of the minimum relationship of protection, trust, and loyalty between the citizen and the home state.[4] The refugee is severed from the ties and duties of protection theoretically insured to citizens of the sovereign territorial state and forced to search for sanctuary elsewhere. The literal meaning of asylum is "freedom from seizure," which, as Atle Gahl-Madsen comments, presupposes some kind of protecting power.[5] In this same vein, Hannah Arendt regarded the predicament of refugees (and the stateless, in particular) as one characterized by a loss of humanity, for refugees are exposed to "the abstract nakedness of being human" when they can no longer rely on a state to insure their protection.[6] As T. Alexander Aleinikoff writes, "the modern world operates under the motto of a state for everyone and everyone in a state."[7]

The international refugee system was formulated to address the problems faced by (externally) displaced persons through the intervention of legal principles to which states can accede if they are committed to protect "genuine" refugees. The 1951 UN (United Nations) Convention on Refugees (and its companion 1967

---

4 Andrew Shacknove, "Who is a Refugee?," *Ethics* 95,2 (1985): 275, 277-278.

5 Atle Gahl-Madsen, *The Status of Refugees in International Law*, vol. 2 (Leiden: A. W. Sijthoff, 1972), p. 3.

6 Hannah Arendt, *The Origins of Totalitarianism*, 3rd. edition (London: George Allen and Unwin, 1967), p. 300.

7 T. Alexander Aleinikoff, "State-centred Refugee Law: From Resettlement to Containment," in *Mistrusting Refugees*, ed. E. Valentine Daniel and John Chr. Knudsen (Berkeley: University of California Press, 1995), p. 257.

Protocol) provides the universal legal definition in this regard.[8] Yet the limitations of modern international law, at the broadest level, prevail here, as they do elsewhere. That is, modern international law is essentially organized around the primacy of the state. Therefore, while international refugee protection law intrudes upon the domain of state sovereignty in a normative sense, no supranational will or enforcement mechanisms exist to support such law; the same is true of universal human rights law.[9] In other words, notwithstanding the important influence of international norms on refugee protection, in practice, state administrations are the final arbiters. This weakness in traditional international law has been described by Andrew Linklater, who notes that international law "granted sovereign states the right to decide how far to honour universal moral obligations: these were deemed to be imperfect duties (indeterminate and unenforceable) rather than perfect duties (stipulated in law and backed up by force)."[10] This is not to dismiss or diminish the relevance and impact of internationally accepted principles of refugee protection, but simply to note the challenge state sovereignty poses to protection in broad terms. This global dimension of asylum and refugee protection is played out and negotiated in many, various local domains around the world, one of which is the focus here.

Challenges of Displacement

In addition, the original 1951 UN Convention-based conception of a refugee fails to take into account several of the challenges and conditions of refugee displacement frequently encountered today. Major anomalies exist between the post-World War II (Cold War) European context in which the Convention was drafted and the evolving, contemporary realities of displacement, such as those confronted in the Thai-Burmese borderlands. For instance, contemporary wars and sociopolitical violence clearly present challenges for refugee protection that, in terms of both causes and responses, extend well beyond the original scope of the 1951 conception. Whereas the 1951 Convention defines a refugee as an individual personally engaged in a political controversy, most contemporary Burmese refugees are not fleeing a controversy in which they have been directly involved as

---

[8] The definition contained in the 1951 UN Convention stipulates that a refugee is someone who is: (i) outside his or her country of origin; (ii) in fear of persecution "for reasons of race, religion, nationality, membership of a particular social group, or political opinion," determined on an individual basis; (iii) and, owing to such fear, is unable or unwilling to avail him- or herself of the protection of that country. See United Nations Conference of Plenipotentiaries, *Convention Relating to the Status of Refugees (1951)*, Geneva. Chapter 1, Article 1A (2). Adopted July 28, 1951. Entered into force April 22, 1954.

[9] Richard Falk, Friedrich Kratochwil, and Saul H. Mendlovitz, "Tensions Between the Individual and the State," in *International Law: A Contemporary Perspective*, ed. Richard Falk, Friedrich Kratochwil, and Saul H. Mendlovitz (Boulder, CO: Westview Press, 1985), p. 473.

[10] Andrew Linklater, "The Evolving Spheres of International Justice," *International Affairs* 75,3 (1999): 480.

activists.[11] The authors of *Escape from Violence*[12] have outlined the changing orientation in a three-part typology that considers the causes of refugees' departures. The first "type" is the refugee as an activist, personally engaged in an activity that the state seeks to terminate; second, there is the refugee as a target, designated by the misfortune of belonging to a social or cultural group singled out for abuse by state power; and, finally, there is the refugee as a "mere victim," displaced by socio-political violence that is not necessarily directed at him or her as an individual, but which makes survival impossible in his or her own country. Aristide R. Zolberg, Astri Suhrke, and Sergio Aguaya point out that the first two categories (those of "activist" and "target") constitute the classic refugee "type" as recognized by the 1951 Convention. The third category ("victim"), however, extends beyond the 1951 definition, and the existence of this new type of refugee is a result of the contemporary prevalence of generalized violence, insecurity, and large-scale exodus. Obviously, the international refugee protection system has had to grapple simultaneously with various refugee problems, becoming involved not only with growing numbers of refugees, but also with more people who are not technically "refugees" in the formal Convention-based sense. The situation of Burmese asylum-seekers in Thailand fits into this latter category. Meanwhile, however, many other displaced people remain unprotected and entirely invisible to the agencies that compile international refugee statistics.

Any redefinition of the concept of a refugee must take into account the changing nature of war after 1945. The global trend towards violent internal conflicts (such as civil war and ethnopolitical conflict)[13] and the increasing prevalence of noncombatant civilian—as opposed to combatant soldier—casualties suffered in such conflicts are significant factors driving contemporary refugee flight and displacement. Today the traditional measures of war—such as numbers of battle-related deaths and calculations of losses incurred through inter-state conflicts—underestimate the impact of wars because an increasing share of international warfare is comprised of "low-intensity," often protracted,[14] internal conflicts. Moreover, a characteristic of "low-intensity," guerrilla warfare is that combatants tend to rely on non-combatants as part of their support system, a situation which serves to blur the boundaries between combatants and non-combatants.[15] In these

---

[11] Barry N. Stein, "The Nature of the Refugee Problem," in *Human Rights and the Protection of Refugees under International Law*, ed. A. Nash (Halifax: Institute for Research on Public Policy, 1988), p. 52; Gervase Coles, "Approaching the Refugee Problem Today," in *Refugees and International Relations*, ed. Gil Loescher and Laila Monahan (Oxford: Oxford University Press, 1989), pp. 374-383, 387.

[12] Aristide R. Zolberg, Astri Suhrke, and Sergio Aguayo, *Escape from Violence: Conflict and the Refugee Crisis in the Developing World* (New York: Oxford University Press, 1989), p. 30.

[13] For example, Wallenstein and Sollenberg note that, of the ninety-six conflicts recorded for the 1989-95 period, only five were clear-cut inter-state armed conflicts. Peter Wallenstein and Margareta Sollenberg, "The End of International War? Armed Conflict 1989-95," *Journal of Peace Research* 33,3 (1996): 356.

[14] As Myron Weiner notes, this is a distressing feature of ethnic conflict. Indeed several of the conflicts that produced refugees in 1969 (in Burma, Burundi, Ethiopia, Rwanda, Somalia, Sudan, and Tibet) were still continuing in the 1990s. Myron Weiner, "Bad Neighbors, Bad Neighborhoods: An Inquiry into the Causes of Refugee Flows," *International Security* 21,1 (1996): 24.

[15] Kay B. Warren, "Introduction: Revealing Conflicts Across Cultures and Disciplines," in *The Violence Within: Cultural and Political Opposition in Divided Nations*, ed. Kay B. Warren

kinds of settings, violence and fear are used as methods to establish control,[16] and the consequences for civilian populations necessitate inquiry and analysis if we are adequately to understand and address the causes of refugee displacement. The patterns of displacement in the Burmese borderlands are distinguished by features that typify "low-intensity" guerrilla warfare.

Further, after they have reached their cross-border havens, refugees are also intimately linked to their country's security problems—and, consequently, those of their host. This is because they frequently remain closely connected to the conflict from which they have fled, residing among, and identified with, combatants on one side in an ongoing war, a situation that politicizes and frequently complicates their sanctuary.[17] This is a characteristic of the border camps in Thailand.

The general pattern of international responses to asylum and refugee "solutions"[18] has also been in transformation in recent decades. Western approaches to refugee policy are no longer as likely to emphasize and focus on the status of "exiles" as was true during the Cold War, when discussion of refugees was influenced by "exile bias,"[19] that is, the notion that people were "voting with their feet" by seeking resettlement opportunities in the West. Now, in the post-Cold War era, consideration of asylum and refugees is more likely to focus on "compassion fatigue" and typical patterns of intolerance in the host countries, which could be summarized as "more refugees, less asylum." Into the 1990s, international discourse about the status of refugees has more often advocated

---

(Boulder, CO: Westview Press, 1993), p. 3; Timothy P. Wickham-Crowley, "Terror and Guerrilla Warfare in Latin America, 1956-1970," *Comparative Studies in Society and History* 32,2 (1990): 223-226.

[16] Carolyn Nordstrom, "The Backyard Front," in *The Paths to Domination, Resistance, and Terror*, ed. Carolyn Nordstrom and JoAnn Martin (Berkeley: University of California Press, 1992), p. 261. On the more general point of fear and control, Ruth Leger Sivard notes that "militarized government survives on fear-inducing tactics," citing the official use of violence against the public in Burma and noting that it is frequent. Ruth Leger Sivard, *World Military and Social Expenditures 1993*, 15th edition (Washington, DC: World Priorities, 1993), pp. 22-23. In the UN Development Program's *Human Development Report*, which charts ratios of military spending to social spending, and calculates numbers of human rights violations, and ethnic and religious conflicts, among other things, as indicators of human security, Burma was rated as a country "in crisis." For example, the report notes that military spending in Burma accounted for 35 percent of the total budget and 6 percent of the GDP; and arms made up more than a fifth of the country's total imports. United Nations Development Programme, "New Dimensions of Human Security," in *Human Development Report 1994* (New York: Oxford University Press, 1994), pp. 38, 42.

[17] On the connection between refugees and security in more general global terms, see Gil Loescher, *Refugee Movements and International Security* (London: Brassey's for the International Institute for Strategic Studies, 1992), pp. 41-48; and Myron Weiner, "Security, Stability, and International Migration," *International Security* 17,3 (1992/93): 106-110.

[18] The search for permanent solutions is contained in the 1950 Statute of the United Nations High Commissioner for Refugees (UNHCR). The conventional model of the three "durable solutions" for refugees involves voluntary repatriation, local integration, and third country resettlement. United Nations High Commissioner for Refugees, *The State of the World's Refugees: The Challenge of Protection* (New York and London: Penguin Books, 1993), p. 121.

[19] Coles, "Approaching the Refugee Problem Today," p. 387.

prevention efforts in countries of origin (a tendency of "source control bias"),[20] as well as promoting the concept of "temporary protection."[21] In the post-Cold War context of the 1990s, repatriation has become the predominant focus for refugee "solutions," and concerns about repatriations—specifically, concerns that repatriation of refugees is often accomplished precipitously or under pressure— have emerged as key issues. These challenges and re-orientations at the global level have highlighted the need to reaffirm international commitment to the fundamental minimum principles of refugee protection.

In essence, the fundamental standards of adequate refugee protection hold steady: they stipulate access to asylum and uphold the principle of non-*refoulement*, which prohibits the expulsion or return of refugees to the place where their lives or freedom are threatened.[22] This principle of non-*refoulement* has attained the status of customary international law, meaning that it applies irrespective of formal accession to the refugee instruments.[23] The centrality of the principle of non-*refoulement* to refugee protection has also, to some extent, helped to overcome the otherwise narrow scope of the 1951-protection regime. We will consider what this means in relation to most Burmese refugees, who qualify as predominantly non-"classic" refugees in terms of both the character of the warfare and their displacement inside Burma and the cross-border response in Thailand-based camps. Later in the book, in Chapter Seven, we will also examine the concerns of Burmese pro-democracy asylum seekers in Bangkok, who are notable because they fit the more "classic" definition of refugee. These activists provide a point of contrast to the displaced populations encamped along the border and pose different kinds of protection problems.

DEFINING THE BURMESE REFUGEES

In relation to the Thai-Burmese borderlands, then, a broader notion of the term "refugee" than that codified in the 1951 definition will be employed in this discussion to encompass persons forced to flee their homes due to fear, danger, and sociopolitical violence associated directly and indirectly with war. This usage accords with the *prima facie* definition of refugees commonly employed from the 1990s. *Prima facie* status is generally applied in situations where the large-scale movements of people fleeing violence make it impractical to determine the status of individual refugees.[24] This book contextualizes the substantive situation of the Burmese refugees, with a view to the larger framework of refugee protection principles, questioning the adequacy and quality of protection for this group of

---

[20] Aleinikoff, "State-centred Refugee Law," p. 258. See also, Adam Roberts, "More Refugees, Less Asylum: A Regime in Transformation," *Journal of Refugee Studies* 11,4 (1998): 375-395.

[21] On temporary protection, see Manuel Angel Castillo and James C. Hathaway, "Temporary Protection," in *Reconceiving International Refugee Law*, ed. James C. Hathaway (The Hague: Martinus Nijhoff Publishers, 1997), pp. 1-21.

[22] See UNHCR's Executive Committee, "General Conclusion on International Protection (No. 81 [XLVIII], 1997),"reproduced in *International Journal of Refugee Law* 10,1/2 (1998): 258.

[23] On legal aspects of the principle of non-*refoulement*, see Guy S. Goodwin-Gill, *The Refugee in International Law* (Oxford: Clarendon Press, 1996), pp. 137-155.

[24] UNHCR, Executive Committee of the High Commissioner's Programme, *Forty-fifth Session, Note on International Protection (Submitted by the High Commissioner*, "II. The Concept of International Protection," UN doc. A/AC.96/830, September 7, 1994), paragraph 27.

people who effectively fall outside the parameters of international protection in absolutely formal terms. On this point, James C. Hathaway writes that

. . . contemporary international refugee law is marginal to the protection of most persons coerced to migrate, who must rather accept whatever emergency assistance or limited resettlement opportunities are voluntarily made to them through various official and non-governmental initiatives.[25]

Today the majority of the world's displaced persons contend with this predicament in various forms. This particular study reflects on how the Burmese refugees have fared in this context; it will not focus so much on their exclusion from the formal system of refugee protection *per se*, but will look to see how the realities of displacement in this region relate to the broader normative frameworks and principles of international protection. The main focus here, however, is to analyze the refugee issue in view of the intricacies of the Burmese/Thai political context in which displacement and sanctuary are situated. A context-specific analysis, grounded in broad thematic reflections, allows for historically specific generalizations that are responsive to complex realities.[26]

In Thailand, defining "the refugees" is a delicate matter, and a note on terminology is needed. Since the late 1990s, official Thai parlance has referred to "displaced persons fleeing fighting" (not "refugees") and to "temporary shelters" (not "refugee camps"), and official pronouncements have repeatedly confirmed the Burmese refugees' official status as illegal entrants under Thai law. However, in practice, the Burmese are recognized as de facto "refugees" and as a group with genuine claims to asylum in the border camps. Bangkok's general policy approach has been to "accept and assist displaced persons on a humanitarian basis." The policy is to provide "temporary shelter," and it promises that Thailand will not repatriate asylum-seekers until the conditions allow them to return home safely. Furthermore, the Thai position says that before it is possible to return such displaced persons to their homes, officials in charge must communicate with the government of Burma to confirm that it is willing to cooperate in a future repatriation.[27] Thailand has now contended with a large, long-term refugee flow across its western border, and it is contemplating the future voluntary return of the refugees to their homelands. There are multiple layers to the machinations of Thai policy, and these are outlined in Chapter Four. Thailand is clearly vexed by the prospect of remaining an indefinite host to a protracted problem, as this particular policy statement reveals:

. . . the influx of displaced persons has entailed huge cost[s] for Thailand in terms of administration and personnel, environmental degradation,

[25] James C. Hathaway, "Reconceiving Refugee Law as Human Rights Protection," in *Human Rights in the Twenty-first Century: A Global Challenge*, ed. Kathleen E. Mahoney and Paul Mahoney (Dordrecht: Martinus Nijhoff Publishers, 1992), p. 660.

[26] Chandra Talpade Mohanty, "Under Western Eyes: Feminist Scholarship and Colonial Discourses," in *Third World Women and the Politics of Feminism*, ed. Chandra Talpade Mohanty, Ann Russo and Torres Lourdes (Bloomington and Indianapolis: Indiana University Press, 1991), pp. 67-69.

[27] Personal communication, senior policy and military officials, Bangkok, April 2000.

deforestation, and epidemic control and the displacement affected Thai villages as well as the psychological impact on the local population.[28]

PROCEDURE OF THE BOOK

As noted above, the book is thematically organized around the causes of refugee displacement in Burma and the responses to the flow into Thailand. Chapter Two examines the historical setting and underpinnings of ethnopolitical conflict and civil war in Burma, seeking to examine the long-term root causes of refugee displacement. In particular, it explores the ways in which ethnic difference has been manifested in state-minority relationships and politicized in the post-independence inheritance of modern day Burma. It also considers the militarization of ethnic identity in the course of insurgency and counterinsurgency in view of this inheritance. Chapter Three looks more closely into the nature and context of the more immediate conflicts precipitating civilian displacement. It takes the Mon experiences as its particular focus and examines how insurgency and counterinsurgency have had an impact on civilian lives and survival.

Conditions in Burma have precipitated the cross-border movement of displaced persons into Thailand. Chapters Four and Five undertake a critical consideration of the host response to the cross-border camps. Chapter Four discusses Thailand's overall response to the Burmese refugees since 1984, considering as well that nation's long history of hosting Indochinese refugees, while Chapter Five analyzes the shifting sanctuary provided by the Mon refugee camps (1990-96) in detail. These chapters consider the nature, policies, and politics of sanctuary, and reflect on the quality of protection in relation to the broader normative framework of international protection principles. Chapter Six elaborates on the context of cross-border sanctuary as it shifts according to some of the salient characteristics of the evolving politico-military borderlands' environment. Chapter Seven analyzes the Thai response in the urban setting of Bangkok, where a protection apparatus is in place, but where the political activism of these particular Burmese asylum-seekers has aroused political sensitivities and thus created problems having to do with their protection. Finally, Chapter Eight reflects, by way of the conclusion, on the meaning and consequences of these kinds of contexts for our understanding of the plight of the refugees and their future prospects.

---

[28] Surpong Posayanond, Director-General, International Organizations Department, Thai Foreign Affairs Ministry, "Thailand's Policy on Myanmar Displaced Persons: The Challenges of Humanitarian Assistance," *UNHCR Newsletter*, Regional Office for Thailand, Cambodia and Vietnam (March 2000): 6-7.

Map 2.1   Divisions and States of Burma

CHAPTER TWO

BURMA: HISTORY, ETHNICITY, AND CIVIL WAR

Burma as represented on a modern political map is not a natural geographical or historical entity; it is a creation of the armed diplomacy and administrative convenience of late nineteenth-century British Imperialism.

Edmund Leach, 1963[1]

ETHNICITY

Few states actually qualify as "nation-states," if by that term we mean a "state whose people share a strong linguistic, religious, and symbolic identity."[2] Most states are multinational or polyethnic in composition and, in that context, their élites are often concerned, in a variety of ways, with promoting the integration of pluralistic ethnic groups within their structures.[3] Post-colonial states have inherited arbitrarily imposed borders and institutions of colonial administration, as noted by Edmund Leach in the above epigraph, and found it necessary to deal with them.

Ethnic diversity may be peacefully accommodated or fiercely contested. While nationalist ideologies advocating anticolonial struggles have often downplayed ethnic differences in the pursuit of national independence, once independence has been achieved, the leaders of newly formed states have frequently demanded allegiance to the state without sufficient regard for formal recognition of the diversity. In some cases, the result has been violent ethnopolitical conflict and civil war. As Ted Robert Gurr shows in the "Minorities at Risk" project—a global survey of 223 politically active communal groups since 1945[4]—ethnopolitical conflict has prevailed on a wide scale, and the great majority of victims have been civilian noncombatants.[5] State building has entailed policies aimed at

---

[1] Edmund Leach, "The Political Future of Burma," *Futuribles*, Volume 1 (Geneva: Droz, 1963), p. 125.

[2] Charles Tilly, *Coercion, Capital, and European States, AD 990-1990* (Oxford: Basil Blackwell, 1990), p. 3.

[3] Anthony D. Smith, *The Ethnic Revival* (Cambridge: Cambridge University Press, 1981), pp. 8-10.

[4] Ted Robert Gurr, *Minorities at Risk: A Global View of Ethnopolitical Conflicts* (Washington, DC: United States Institute of Peace Press, 1993).

[5] Ted Robert Gurr, "Peoples Against States: Ethnopolitical Conflict and the Changing World System," *International Studies Quarterly* 38,3 (1994): 352.

assimilating various ethnic groups and restraining their collective autonomy[6]; in response, excluded ethnic groups have been mobilized, sometimes by armed force, against the state, and the state has fought back. State building has therefore rarely been achieved without coercion. Since Burma's independence, a pattern of authoritarian and nationalistic reliance on repression to restrain minority ethnic nationalism has prevailed,[7] and successive governments have primarily relied on military means to tackle the challenges posed by non-Burman indigenous peoples.

Anthony D. Smith defines an ethnic group, or *ethnie*, as "a named human population with a myth of common ancestry, shared memories, and cultural elements; a link with a historic territory or homeland; and a measure of solidarity."[8] More particularly, ethnonationalism involves the self-conscious assertion of a common form of identity derived from a combination of these features.[9] While ethnicity is often defined by a group's identification of itself, its meaning is also situated in external contextual realities.[10] Gurr notes that ethnopolitical conflict occurs where groups define themselves using ethnic criteria to make claims for their collective interests against the state (or other political actors).[11] Further, ethnonationalism as a form of political mobilization is a distinct product of the modern state in the sense that earlier systems of monarchical authority did not politicize ethnicity *per se*. The concept of ethnicity has shifted across historical circumstances, becoming more potent and germane to political mobilization in the modern grid of the territorial state and its bureaucratic machine.[12] As Smith also notes, a collectivity is molded in the dynamic context of particular political processes.[13] Ethnic identities, however they are centered, are always historically contingent, and groups assimilate or differentiate themselves over time as they respond with adaptive strategies to new social and political circumstances.[14]

As an overview of Burma's historical inheritance—essential to understanding the long-term root causes of refugee displacement—this chapter examines the historical setting and the underpinnings of ethnicity, ethnic conflict, and civil war

---

[6] Gurr, *Minorities at Risk*, pp. 135-136.

[7] Ibid., p. 66.

[8] In Smith's definition, the element of solidarity in ethnicity refers to a common sense of belonging that may be contrasted with pre-modern times when a given "ethnic population" often lacked this sense of ethnic belonging. For Smith's elaboration on each of these features, see Anthony D. Smith, "The Ethnic Sources of Nationalism," in *Ethnic Conflict and International Security*, ed. Michael E. Brown (Princeton: Princeton University Press, 1993), pp. 28-30.

[9] Smith, "The Ethnic Sources of Nationalism," pp. 34-37. See also, Walker Connor, *Ethnonationalism: The Quest for Understanding* (Princeton: Princeton University Press, 1994), pp. 89-117.

[10] Kumar Rupesinghe, "Governance and Conflict Resolution in Multi-ethnic Societies," in *Ethnicity and Power in the Contemporary World*, ed. Kumar Rupesinghe and Valery A. Tishkov (Tokyo: United Nations University Press, 1996), pp. 13-15.

[11] Gurr, "Peoples Against States," p. 348. See also, Ted Robert Gurr and Barbara Harff, *Ethnic Conflict in World Politics* (Boulder, CO: Westview Press, 1994), pp. 1-14.

[12] Smith, *The Ethnic Revival*, pp. 77, 136.

[13] Ibid., p. 76.

[14] Gurr, *Minorities at Risk*, p. 4; Charles F. Keyes, "Introduction," in *Ethnic Adaptation and Identity: The Karen on the Thai Frontier with Burma*, ed. Charles F. Keyes (Philadelphia: Institute for the Study of Human Issues, 1979), p. 6.

in Burma. Here we consider the concept of ethnic identity and its significance as they have shifted across the precolonial, colonial, and post-colonial polities in Burma. Some of the complexities underpinning the civil war, ethnopolitical conflict, and the "ethnocratic state" in Burma[15] are discussed, with a particular focus in the latter part on the response of the government, which has been dominated by the military since 1962. In addition to this wider overview, a brief historical background to the Mon insurgency is outlined. But first, we begin with a glimpse of Burma at the time of independence and review the problems faced by the newly independent republic.

The Contested State: Independence and the "Rangoon Government"

The newly independent state of Burma that emerged on January 4, 1948 began turbulently. From the very beginning, Rangoon was confronted by ideological and ethnopolitical challenges that rapidly developed into civil war, some of which persist to the present day. While the Burmese nationalists (under the British-led forces) fought in the wartime anti-Japanese resistance along with the communists and other ethnic forces,[16] this unity was short-lived. The newly independent parliamentary republic was engulfed by unrest within weeks of independence. The Anti-Fascist People's Freedom League (AFPFL)[17] government in the immediate post-independence period was dubbed the "Rangoon Government" because it exercised little control outside of Rangoon. Violence proliferated. A government document published in 1949 described the situation:

> Burma, today, admittedly stands internally torn by insurrections all over the country with large sections of the countryside under complete domination of the insurgents . . . The insurgents are not only disturbing the Constitution. They are threatening the very existence of the Union. They are undermining the Independence and the integrity of the State.[18]

Within barely three months of independence, the Communist Party of Burma (CPB)[19] had gone underground and begun its forty years of armed rebellion. By 1949,

---

[15] David Brown, *The State and Ethnic Politics in Southeast Asia* (London: Routledge, 1994), pp. 33-65.

[16] The Japanese occupation of Burma lasted from 1942-45. With the Japanese invasion of Burma, almost all the British administration fled to India. The country was left in Burmese hands, and was permitted to form a subordinate administration in August 1942 under Japanese control, becoming an "independent" country in the following year. See Andrew Selth, "Race and Resistance in Burma, 1942-45," *Modern Asian Studies* 20,3 (1986): 492.

[17] The AFPFL was formed in 1945 out of the national front of various organizations that rallied to fight the Japanese. Its stated goal was independence for Burma. Although technically a coalition party, from 1945 to 1958 the Socialist Party dominated. Mary P. Callahan, "Building an Army: The Early Years of the Tatmadaw," *Burma Debate* 4,3 (July/August 1997): 4-10. See also U Maung Maung, *Burmese Nationalist Movements 1940-1948* (Honolulu: University of Hawai'i Press, 1989), pp. 179-188.

[18] Government of the Union of Burma, *Burma and the Insurrections* (Rangoon: Government of the Union of Burma, 1949), p. 32.

[19] The CPB began its revolt at the end of March 1948. The majority "White Flag" faction was led by Thakin Than Tun. The underground "Red Flag" faction, led by Thakin Soe, was already

insurrection led by the Karen National Defense Organization (KNDO) had come within four miles of Rangoon (it temporarily seized Insein township before it was halted). Other important cities around the country, such as Mandalay, Maymyo, and Prome, as well as much of the delta, had fallen to insurgent control.[20] Mary P. Callahan notes that, according to one "official history," by 1949, 75 percent of towns in Burma had fallen to one insurgent group or another.[21] Smaller rebellions also broke out among the Mons, Pa-Os, Karennis, Kachins, and Muslim Arakanese. Numerous other armies, including various illegal, anti-state, anti-AFPFL, and quasi-legal paramilitary squads maintained by Cabinet members and other politicians, also roamed the country during this period.[22]

Callahan describes the time as a "swirling period of seemingly endless cycles of disarming, [and] re-arming the disenchanted."[23] The Burma Army organization, too, was in disarray, with increasing numbers of officers deserting to join the Communist, ethnic, or other paramilitary organizations opposed to the state.[24] While the forces of the Communist and Karen armies numbered around ten to fifteen thousand and ten thousand, respectively,[25] by the time General Ne Win assumed his position as Commander-in-Chief in February 1949, he commanded fewer than two thousand remaining government troops. Further, divisions and struggles were occurring within the Burma Army itself. By the end of 1951, however, some measure of stability was restored to the "old house with rotted supports,"[26] and the rebellions no longer threatened the central authority of U Nu's AFPFL government to the same extent. The survival of the "Rangoon Government" into the 1950s has been attributed to a combination of factors. These include disunity among various rebel groups; an end to "the war of spectacular gains and losses"[27] and the gradual government recapture of some KNDO headquarters and towns; the offer of numerous amnesties[28]; the government's successful mobilization of allegiance and establishment of networks for counterinsurgency under its local

---

in the field (beginning July 1946), after breaking away from the AFPFL in the midst of negotiations for the transfer of power from the departing British colonial administration.

[20] Hugh Tinker, *The Union of Burma*, 4th edition (London: Oxford University Press, 1967), p. 41. For an account of the KNDO's activities in Insein, see Bertil Lintner, *Burma in Revolt: Opium and Insurgency Since 1948* (Boulder, CO and Bangkok: Westview Press and White Lotus, 1994), Chapter 1. On the KNDO at this time more generally, see John F. Cady, *A History of Modern Burma* (Ithaca, NY: Cornell University Press, 1958), pp. 592-594.

[21] Mary P. Callahan, "The Origins of Military Rule in Burma" (PhD dissertation, Cornell University, 1996), pp. 311-312, 365.

[22] Ibid., p. 6. See also Mary P. Callahan, "The Sinking Schooner: Murder and the State in Independent Burma, 1948-58," in *Gangsters, Democracy, and the State in Southeast Asia*, ed. Carl A. Trocki (Ithaca, NY: Cornell Southeast Asia Program Publications, 1998), pp. 17-37.

[23] Callahan, "The Origins of Military Rule in Burma," p. 7.

[24] Ibid., pp. 311-324. See also Robert H. Taylor, *The State in Burma* (Honolulu: University of Hawai'i Press, 1987), p. 236.

[25] Lintner, *Burma in Revolt*, p. 79.

[26] U Nu, quoted in Callahan, "The Origins of Military Rule in Burma," p. 322.

[27] Tinker, *The Union of Burma*, p. 47.

[28] Amnesties were offered in 1948, 1949, 1950 and 1955, although the response was limited. Richard Butwell, *U Nu of Burma* (Stanford: Stanford University Press, 1969), p. 99.

and national Socialist Party leaders[29]; and, not least, the development of the *tatmadaw* (the Burmese armed forces) from a disorganized fighting force into an effective institution of control, one which has dominated the Burmese polity since the mid-1950s.

It was in this context, characterized by weak civilian government and the plethora of insurgencies challenging the state, that, by 1953, the *tatmadaw* emerged as a powerful centralized institution of control.[30] In the words of U Nu, the armed forces evolved from "stooges, without backbone, at the beck and call of this or that organization" into "dependable custodians of the Union."[31] Robert H. Taylor notes that although Burma's political doctrine and constitution subordinated the military to the civilian state, in practice the army leadership during the 1950s developed independent of civilian control, and civilian governments came to depend on the army for office.[32] Direct military involvement in business and economic activities was also established in the 1950s, beginning with the Defense Services Institute in 1950 (and institutionalized under the Union of Myanmar Economic Holdings Ltd. today). The military was first installed by the "coup" of 1958 and its authority confirmed during the *tatmadaw*'s subsequent "Caretaker Government" of 1958–60; it consolidated its authority more permanently in the period after the coup of 1962. Although the insurgency that marked the immediate post-independence era was checked by the early 1950s, and a degree of stability returned to Burma—so that widespread martial law was lifted in many areas—internal communist and ethnic insurrections continued throughout the democratic period. The threat of the US-backed Kuomintang (KMT), which retreated into northeastern Burma following the Communist victory in China in 1949, also provided impetus for the ascendancy of a strong *tatmadaw*.

Why the newly independent state was so challenged by ethnonationalist claims is a long and complex story. Certainly, the modern state as a single geopolitical entity was unable satisfactorily to accommodate the manifold layers of political, identity, and territorial claims and grievances of the various ethnic groups and their representatives. The colonial administration bequeathed to Burma a legacy of divisive political categories that exacerbated group differences in postcolonial politics. The colonial system had transformed previous political patterns of interaction, laying the groundwork for contestation between groups and investing ethnicity with meaning for political mobilization. This legacy contrasted with earlier patterns of precolonial rule, which were characterized by

---

[29] See Callahan, "The Origins of Military Rule in Burma," pp. 370-386. Callahan suggests that the re-establishment of national authority was mobilized by locally based and recruited, state-armed and authorized, village, town, and district militias faithful to the party. This eventually worked in favor of the government's reassertion of "at least nominal control over much of Burma proper." Ibid., pp. 381-382.

[30] Callahan also argues that the *tatmadaw* emerged in a privileged position among state institutions in this early democratic era because it was "significantly more centralized and institutionally capable of exerting influence over territories beyond the greater Rangoon area" than other national institutions in the country, namely the AFPFL and the bureaucracy. Ibid., p. 31.

[31] U Nu, quoted in Tinker, *The Union of Burma*, p. 326.

[32] Robert H. Taylor, "The Military in Myanmar (Burma): What Scope for a New Role?," in *The Military, the State, and Development in Asia and the Pacific*, ed. Viberto Selochan (Boulder, CO: Westview Press, 1991), p. 146.

patron-client allegiances in major competing political centers and were not generally charged with politicized ethnic allegiances, as such.

PRECOLONIAL ANTECEDENTS

Burma is often considered to be one of the most culturally and ethnically diverse countries in the world, comprising a rich cultural mosaic of peoples. But the construction of "ethnicity" as a cardinal claim of identity—and motivation for political mobilization—is a distinct product of the colonial and modern nation-state. As Benedict Anderson points out, "It is easy to forget that minorities came into existence in tandem with majorities—and, in Southeast Asia, very recently."[33] While a great variety of communal identities has always been evident throughout the territory now included in the domain of contemporary Burma, these identities were seldom organized under a single, unified sovereign power in the precolonial epochs. Rather, precolonial history featured a variegated pattern of competing power centers—including the Mon, Burman, Shan, and Arakanese kingdoms— whose "fields of influence were subject to frequent pulsation."[34] J. S. Furnivall captured the shifting course of Burmese history in his description:

> Until recently the inhabitants of the deltaic plains along the southern coast were Mons or Talaings . . . Formerly, their northern neighbors were the Pyus, but these were conquered and assimilated by the Burmese [i.e., Burmans][35] who came down into the plains about AD 600–800. By 1100 the Burmese had conquered the whole of Burma. Two hundred years later the Shans, cousins of the Siamese, broke across the eastern border, and the subsequent course of Burmese history is largely a tale of conflict between Burmese, Shans, and Mons, punctuated by wars with Siam and Arakan. In the event the Burmese gained the mastery, drove the Shans back to the eastern hills to rule petty states as vassals of their Burmese overlord, and subjugated, and in great part assimilated, the Mons. They also conquered the Arakanese.[36]

Some historians (writing from a Burman perspective) have identified a long-term historic tendency toward a certain degree of political centralization, economic integration, and ethnic homogenization under Burman influence.[37] The earliest "unification" occurred during the Pagan kingdom (1044–1287) in central Burma,

---

[33] Benedict Anderson, *The Spectre of Comparisons: Nationalism, Southeast Asia, and the World* (London: Verso, 1998), p. 318.

[34] Victor B. Lieberman, *Burmese Administrative Cycles: Anarchy and Conquest, c. 1580-1760* (Princeton: Princeton University Press, 1984), p. 227.

[35] Furnivall here uses the term "Burmese" as it was used before 1948, to mean ethnic Burmans; after 1948, however, the term "Burmese" was used to describe all the inhabitants of the Union.

[36] J. S. Furnivall, *Colonial Policy and Practice: A Comparative Study of Burma and Netherlands India* (New York: New York University Press, 1956), p. 12.

[37] See Victor B. Lieberman, "Reinterpreting Burmese History," *Comparative Studies in Society and History* 29,1 (1987): 161-194. Lieberman argues that polities periodically refined their administration in order to enhance the financial and military position of the state in competition with adjacent polities. See also, Taylor, *The State in Burma*, p. 24; and Ronald D. Renard, "Minorities in Burmese History," in *Ethnic Conflict in Buddhist Societies: Sri Lanka, Thailand and Burma*, ed. K. M. de Silva et al. (London: Pinter Publishers, 1988), p. 80.

beginning with Anawratha. In his conquest of Thaton in 1057, Anawratha not only gained mastery of the delta and access to the sea, but also literally carried off, adopted, and absorbed much of the culture from the Mon kingdom of Pegu, including its religion (the sacred scriptures and clergy of Theravada Buddhism), literature, and art.[38] The kingdom of Pagan collapsed in 1287 following the invasion by Mongol armies. For the next two and a half chaotic centuries, it endured repeated challenges until it was reduced to a political center of only local significance, while other kingdoms, such as the Mon, Shan, and Tai, gained strength. Later, Burman rule emerged at the height of the Toungoo Dynasty (1486-1597) and the Konbaung Dynasty (1753-1885) and wielded authority over a region loosely corresponding to modern Burma.

Burman suzerainty from the mid-sixteenth century to the early Konbaung era practiced direct, personal rule over the core or nuclear zone around the capital and over the zone of dependent provinces controlled by court-appointed officials; it maintained indirect rule over the peripheral zone of tributaries under the authority of hereditary rulers from various non-Burman backgrounds. During this period, from about the mid-sixteenth to the mid-eighteenth centuries, in particular, Burman monarchs extended their empire southward through conquest and moved into Lower Burma (the Mon kingdom of Pegu), gradually incorporating the southern districts into the northern-based polity. As noted, the result of political suppression was the substantial cultural and linguistic assimilation of the Mons; this was accomplished despite several Mon rebellions. Victor B. Lieberman writes that, during this period, increasing numbers of Mons changed their political allegiance by choosing to identify themselves as Burmans.[39] This pattern may be contrasted with the patterns of allegiance evident during the earlier Pagan period, during which "there was no attempt to stamp out the Mon culture . . . [o]n the contrary."[40]

In response to historical analyses that identify Burmans as a notably successful and dominant ethnic group in the precolonial era, certain scholars of Burmese history have questioned any retrospective casting of ethnicity as a reified political category in analyses of the region's precolonial history.[41] Lieberman in particular challenges the ethnic framing of historical Burman-Mon antagonism. The patterns of political authority in precolonial Burma, derived from patron-client relations, emphasized loyalty to patrons (whether they were the monarch, local princes, or military officials) and thus respected personalized authority rather than a politically defined form of ethnic or national allegiance. And because rule was based on personalized loyalty, this in turn favored autonomy and ethnic heterogeneity in administration at the local level. The royal court and its service people, too, were polyethnic. Such a cosmopolitan orientation was

[38] George Coedès, *The Making of Southeast Asia*, trans. H. M. Wright (London: Routledge and Kegan Paul, 1966), p. 113.

[39] In this regard, he interprets ethnicity as a badge of political allegiance. Lieberman, "Reinterpreting Burmese History," p. 181.

[40] Maung Tha Hla, "Ethnic Communalism in Thailand and Burma," *Journal of the Burma Research Society* 56,1/2 (1973): 36. See also G. H. Luce, "Mons of the Pagan Dynasty," unpublished lecture delivered at Rangoon University, January 2, 1950.

[41] See, for instance, Victor B. Lieberman "Ethnic Politics in Eighteenth-Century Burma," *Modern Asian Studies* 12,3 (1978): 455-482; Robert H. Taylor, "Perceptions of Ethnicity in the Politics of Burma," *Southeast Asian Journal of Social Science* 10,1 (1982): 7-22.

reinforced by the responsibilities inherent in Theravadan kingship, which emphasized the king's imperative to advance the spiritual welfare of his followers rather than to promote ethnicity as a sign of political identity.[42] Thus in Lieberman's view, the wars between Ava and Pegu, which have often been characterized as Burman-Mon wars, were not predominantly "racial" or "national" struggles, but were regional and dynastic conflicts in which the names "Burman" and "Mon" served as emblems of political loyalty to Ava and Pegu, respectively.[43]

The trend toward "ethnic homogenization" in the era of the classical polity, identified by historians such as Lieberman, was, however, a long and uneven process.[44] In the early period of Burman rule in Lower Burma, Mon cities such as Pegu and Syriam prospered under the Toungoo monarchs Tabinshwehti (r. 1531–50) and Bayinnaung (r. 1551–81). But as armies continued to capture and sack Mon cities, the once vibrant Mon culture was decimated to such an extent that it never fully recovered. Despite the Peguan revolt of 1740 against Ava rule (involving, as Lieberman admits, anti-Burman sentiment and ethnic polarization)[45] and the Peguan siege of Ava in 1752, at last the Burman forces did succeed in sacking Pegu and conquering all of Lower Burma. This was accomplished by 1757 under the renewed power of King Alaunghpaya's army. While some urban centers were partially restored in the seventeenth and eighteenth centuries, the surviving Mon population was more dispersed and agrarian than it had been previously, before the conquest.[46] Lieberman is reluctant to represent the conquest in terms of ethnicity as such, but he notes that Alaunghpaya's victory created the conditions for the further decline of Mon identity. Other contributing factors included Mon migrations to Siam and Burman migration into Lower Burma, the acceleration of Mon assimilation through the suppression of Mon culture and language, and a process of linguistic (re)identification of the population as Burman-speaking. The implication was that "[b]y 1810 the Burman cultural assault that began in

---

[42] During the Toungoo period (c. 1539-1752) the ruler of any non-Burmese territory could be admitted to tributary status by having the leader swear an oath of allegiance to royal patronage. This led to the tendency of regional loyalties to the patron rather than a sense of pan-ethnic consciousness. Lieberman, "Ethnic Politics in Eighteenth-Century Burma," pp. 459-466; Lieberman, *Burmese Administrative Cycles*, p. 60. See also, William J. Koenig, *The Burmese Polity, 1752-1819* (Ann Arbor, MI: Center for South and Southeast Asian Studies, University of Michigan, 1990), Chapter 3. For a detailed study of social organization in precolonial Burma, see Michael Aung-Thwin, "Hierarchy and Order in Pre-Colonial Burma," *Journal of Southeast Asian Studies* 15,2 (1984): 224-232.

[43] Lieberman, "Ethnic Politics in Eighteenth-Century Burma," p. 458. He argues that during the wars of the fourteenth and fifteenth centuries, satellites of Ava and Pegu switched allegiances with ease. Yet with the onset of Peguan revolt in 1740 and Alaungphaya's resistance that followed, polarization between "Burman" and "Mon" was particularly sharp, "perhaps because these were periods of maximum insecurity when people eagerly sought visible symbols of conformity amongst their neighbors in order to allay their anxieties." Nevertheless, he argues that the adoption of a particular ethnic identity did not become an indispensable prerequisite for political support. Ibid., p. 462.

[44] For a detailed history, see Lieberman, *Burmese Administrative Cycles*.

[45] Lieberman, "Reinterpreting Burmese History," pp. 192-193; "Ethnic Politics in Eighteenth-Century Burma," pp. 462-475.

[46] Michael Adas, "Imperialist Rhetoric and Modern Historiography: Lower Burma," *Journal of Southeast Asian Studies* 3,2 (1972): 182-183.

desultory fashion in the sixteenth century was well on the way to obliterating Mon culture."[47]

For the "hill peoples" in precolonial Burma, the practice of imperial administration in which royal authority diminished with increased distance from the capital meant Burman and Tai rulers claiming dominion over their areas did not attempt to establish direct or permanent control over upland peoples. Although rulers tried to collect tribute, and the highlands were often valued sources of trade and military manpower, a rugged, inaccessible topography and poor communications generally divided the highlands into various political and linguistic units living according to their own religious and cultural traditions under their own autonomous leaders.[48] While differences precluded the possibility of stable political integration, and Tai and Burman histories frequently stigmatized Karens, Kachins, Chins, and other animist hill peoples as "wild" and "barbaric,"[49] some degree of inter-group interaction with lowland Burma has always existed.[50]

In sum, identity and connections to the ruler in the precolonial polity were defined through a system of personal and regional identification with the monarch rather than through politicized ethnic allegiances conceptualized in majority-minority terms. The notion of indivisible, absolute sovereignty was absent in the classical polity, allowing local cultures and languages to flourish and permitting multiple, autonomous identities to coexist within an overarching suzerainty. Yet in the period since the sixteenth century, the Mons in Lower Burma have not always coexisted comfortably with the dominant polity in the manner suggested by this portrait of a diverse, and even tolerant, classical polity because their large distinctive kingdoms, culture, and language came under considerable attack and were suppressed by the Burmans in an attempt to assimilate them.

THE COLONIAL MATRIX

Undoubtedly the most rapid and dramatic change to the polity in Burma came with the advent of British colonialism. The imposition of the colonial system of authority eventually affected all aspects of social, political, and economic life and, subsequently, ethnic relations, with important legacies for the future independent Burma. British colonialism staked its claim on "Burma" by demarcating its borders around a territory and a population in the image and interests of the European nation-state. Colonial conquest quickly displaced

---

[47] Victor B. Lieberman, "Political Consolidation in Burma," *Journal of Asian History* 30,2 (1996): 167.

[48] Lieberman, *Burmese Administrative Cycles*, p. 131; Josef Silverstein, "Fifty Years of Failure," in *Government Policies and Ethnic Relations in Asia and the Pacific*, ed. Michael E. Brown and Sumit Ganguly (Cambridge, MA: MIT Press, 1997), p. 169.

[49] Lieberman, *Burmese Administrative Cycles*, p. 135.

[50] F. K. Lehman, "Ethnic Categories in Burma and the Theory of Social Systems," in *Southeast Asian Tribes, Minorities, and Nations*, ed. Peter Kundstadter (Princeton: Princeton University Press, 1967), p. 119. While making the general point about the political separation of hill regions in precolonial Burma, we need to be cautious about caricaturing hill cultures as discrete and isolated. As Edmund Leach demonstrated in his well-known article "The Frontiers of 'Burma,'" the frontiers separating petty political units within Burma were not clearly defined lines, but dynamic zones of mutual interest. Edmund Leach, "The Frontiers of 'Burma'," *Comparative Studies in Society and History* 3,1 (1960): 50.

indigenous territorial boundaries and personal monarchical authority in favor of the institutional grid of the colonial state.

There were three stages in the colonial annexation of Burma to British India between 1824 and 1886.[51] The first Anglo-Burmese war of 1824–26 ended in defeat for the Burmese and the first annexation of Burmese territory by British India. The Treaty of Yandabo compelled Burma to cede Arakan and Tenasserim, its two maritime provinces, to the British.[52] The second Anglo-Burmese war of 1852 resulted in the annexation of Pegu and Martaban, linking the whole of Lower Burma (the region of the Irrawaddy delta) to Tenasserim and Arakan and providing the British effective control over the trade of the entire country by sequestering the Ava (Mandalay) kingdom in Upper Burma from the sea. The third Anglo-Burmese war culminated in the annexation of Upper Burma to the Indian Empire in 1886. Notwithstanding significant indigenous resistance and renewed revolts in Lower Burma at the time, the British Indian empire now claimed the entire area of modern Burma as its own.[53]

British policy divided the country into two administrative systems, "Burma proper" and the "Frontier Areas." Burma proper comprised the regions of Upper and Lower Burma (corresponding to the nuclear and dependent provinces of the Konbaung state), and the Frontier Areas were composed of the surrounding uplands.[54] The mountainous border areas of frontier Burma covered nearly 50 percent of the total area and encompassed around 16 percent of the population. The colonial state imposed direct, centralized bureaucratic rule upon the area of Burma proper, the commercial heart of the country, while it remained distant from the Frontier Areas.

Furnivall has described the coercive transformation of traditional society and administration under colonial rule. He argues that, while in the early years the impact on social life of the British system of rule was negligible, by the time the Village Act was introduced in 1886, the Burmese system of local administration and social life had been broken down in Lower Burma.[55] The Village Act dismantled the traditional authority structure, based on circles of authority and influence, and focused on individual villages, each of which became "little more than a cog-

---

[51] Burman conquest to the west of Arakan in 1785, Manipur in 1813, and Assam in 1816 had led to contact and conflict with the British East India Company along their common frontier with British Bengal.

[52] Arakan was formerly the center of a flourishing rice trade; Tenasserim contained valuable teak and a trading channel with China and Siam. Furnivall, *Colonial Policy and Practice*, p. 24. For a detailed account of colonial administration in Tenasserim, see J. S. Furnivall, *The Fashioning of Leviathan: The Beginnings of British Rule in Burma* (Canberra: Department of Anthropology, Research School of Pacific Studies, The Australian National University, 1991), reproduced from the original in the *Journal of the Burma Research Society* 29,1 (April 1939); and Anna Allott, *The End of the First Anglo-Burmese War* (Bangkok: Chulalongkorn University Press, 1994).

[53] From 1886 until 1923, Burma was administered as a province of India, after which it became a separate colony and, in 1937, became a self-governing colony with foreign and military powers retained by the governor.

[54] Based on ethnic distinctions, the Frontier Areas encompassed the Kachin, Chin, Karenni uplands, the Karen Salween district, and the Shan plateau.

[55] Furnivall, *Colonial Policy and Practice*, pp. 42, 74-140.

wheel in the machinery for maintaining law and order and collecting revenue"[56] and an instrument of martial law.[57] Callahan expands on this point in her thesis, arguing that colonial rule in nineteenth-century Burma produced an institutional matrix organized around coercion.[58] Colonialism, therefore, not only reoriented traditional life and administration to accommodate its own particular geographical and administrative mechanisms of control, it also institutionalized an unequal relationship between military and civil authorities—favoring the military—that would influence the development of future military and civilian institutions in Burma.[59]

Colonial territorial division that separated Burma proper from the Frontier Areas exploited the topographical, historical, and cultural division of valley and hill peoples for the purposes of colonial control.[60] Colonial rule administered and defined the diversity rather than attempting to integrate everyone into a common political entity. Structured to administer closely the lowland populations[61] under direct rule while only indirectly governing hill peoples, this system furnished the administrative apparatus that would influence future conceptions of ethnicity. From the colonial perspective, the "frontier" populations presented no threat to colonial power,[62] and economic wealth was extracted predominantly from Burma proper. In this way, the Frontier Areas eluded the full force of the colonial state; and in the later years of annexation, interaction between the hills and plains was discouraged for military and political reasons. In the process of imposing different degrees of administration on lowland and hill peoples, colonial modernity began the institutionalization of ethnic categories.

Ethnicity was further institutionalized during the period of growth in self-government and politics between 1923 and 1941. When the parliamentary system was introduced in 1923, set up with self-governing institutions to parallel those in India, the hill minorities continued to remain separate. Comprising nearly half of the territory, the Frontier Areas were specifically excluded from the rest of Burma in the 1923 constitution; they were now designated as "Scheduled Areas" administered through a separate Frontier Service. The new legislature comprised mainly Burman members, but it contained a system of special and "communal" representation for Europeans, Anglo-Indians, Indians, and the Karens. This system continued when Burma was formally separated from India in 1935, though with

---

[56] Ibid., p. 75.

[57] Robert Taylor notes that while change was implemented gradually, by 1891 the old order was effectively gone, replaced by officially nominated local bodies known as circle boards. Taylor, *The State in Burma*, p. 86.

[58] Callahan, "The Origins of Military Rule in Burma," Chapter 3.

[59] Ibid., p. 86.

[60] Taylor, "Perceptions of Ethnicity in the Politics of Burma," p. 13.

[61] These were predominantly the culturally similar Burman, Mon, and Arakanese. In addition, significant numbers of Indian and Chinese migrants came to Burma in the nineteenth century.

[62] As the Burma Frontier Areas Committee of Enquiry itself later stated: "These hill areas contain more than 100 distinct tribes. The great majority, however, are too small to be of political importance and the four largest, Shans, Kachins, Chins and Karens, dominate more than 95 per cent of the Frontier Areas between them." Burma Frontier Areas Committee of Enquiry, *Report Presented to His Majesty's Government in the United Kingdom and the Government of Burma, Volume 1* (Rangoon: Superintendent, Government Printing and Stationery, 1947), p. 6.

some alterations: the number of seats in Parliament reserved for Anglo-Burmese and Chinese increased. While the colonial authorities claimed they were advocating the rights of minorities, the heavily weighted minority and special interest bloc prevented Burman representatives from commanding the majority of seats they might have been expected to gain.[63] This territorial and institutional division of authority had political implications for the character of Burmese nationalism. That is, in the struggle against colonial rule, nationalism was mainly advanced by the valley peoples of Burma proper.[64]

The anticolonial nationalist movement therefore emerged as essentially Burman in character. A tension in the key anti-colonial movement, Dobama Asiayone (the "We Burma" Association, committed to the achievement of full independence from the British), was expressed in its somewhat conflicting nationalist orientations. On the one hand, it made an inclusive appeal for independence for the whole of Burma, utilizing the discourse of the modern nation-state, and it opened its ranks to all Burmese, irrespective of ethnic background. On the other hand, however, it emphasized Buddhism and invoked particular cultural values such as Burmese language, literature, and the memory of the ousted monarchy.[65]

The tendency of the British armed forces in Burma to recruit from minorities (rather than Burmans) also influenced perceptions of ethnicity.[66] For instance, the Dobama Asiayone targeted indigenous minorities who collaborated with the British, thereby drawing ethnically demarcated boundaries around "nationalists" and "collaborators." The Karens, for example, were criticized for their cooperation with the British in their efforts to quell the Hsaya San Peasant Revolution of 1930-32, the 1936 student strike, and the 1938 general strike.[67] Japanese wartime occupation also disrupted the isolation of the Frontier Areas, and many minorities (especially the Karens and Kachins) joined the British, while Aung San and the Thirty Comrades of the national liberation struggle (initially) fought on the side of the Japanese Imperial Army. Ethnic divisions inherited from the British Burma Army—which included specifically Karen, Kachin, and Chin units—were perpetuated in the inception of the Burma Army (first as the Burma Independence Army, or BIA) in 1942.[68] John F. Cady notes that to the nationalist BIA, the Karens

---

[63] Furnivall, *Colonial Policy and Practice*, p. 169; U Maung Maung, *Burmese Nationalist Movements 1940-1948*, p. 8. Therefore, as Silverstein notes, "the evolution of self-government in Burma helped to foster and intensify ethnic pluralities and national disunity by emphasizing differences and by reducing the national power of the majority, through artificial institutional devices." Josef Silverstein, *Burmese Politics: The Dilemma of National Unity* (New Brunswick: Rutgers University Press, 1980), p. 29.

[64] Lian Kwen Fee and Ananda Rajah, "The Ethnic Mosaic," in *Asia's Cultural Mosaic: An Anthropological Introduction*, ed. Grant Evans (New York: Prentice Hall, 1993), p. 249.

[65] Selth, "Race and Resistance in Burma," p. 487; Clive J. Christie, *A Modern History of Southeast Asia: Decolonization, Nationalism and Separatism* (London and New York: I. B. Tauris Publishers, 1996), p. 59.

[66] See Tinker, *The Union of Burma*, Chapter 11. Callahan downplays the importance attached to colonial recruitment of ethnic minorities as a source of tension in the later colonial period because overall indigenous recruitment of Burmese was generally low. Callahan, "The Origins of Military Rule in Burma," p. 107.

[67] Ibid., p. 112.

[68] The Burma Independence Army (BIA) accompanied the Japanese Imperial Army into Burma in 1942. During the period of Japanese occupation, it was renamed the Burma Defense Army

were suspect due to their traditional pro-British alignment.[69] And then, with the outbreak of civil war in 1948, the unity of the armed forces was undermined, as some units came to identify as much with their own ethnic affiliations or factional leaders as with the central state.[70] Very quickly, under General Ne Win's leadership, new formations in the army were numbered rather than named, and ethnic associations thereby erased. Soon, recruitment from minority communities virtually ended, and the Burma Army came to assume a Burman-dominated character that contributed to the militarization of ethnic perceptions in Burma.[71]

The newly independent state inherited the legacy of ethnic plurality as (re)defined under colonial administration. While cultural plurality had prevailed in the precolonial era, personal monarchical authority did not set out to define and categorize the polity according to ethnic affiliation. Colonial rule did, however, with particular intentions in mind. As Sugata Bose suggests, the redefinition of ethnic plurality under colonialism contained an element in which "minorities came to be seen as only pawns in the endgame of colonial empires."[72] Bose argues that colonial modernity complicated the postcolonial inheritance of ethnic allegiances and perceptions in the following way:

> Through rigid classificatory schemes employed in colonial censuses and maps, the state made it harder to maintain peaceful coexistence of multiple social identities. Once colonial modernity had redefined "traditional" social affiliations, the way was open for the construction of divisive political categories that might deflect challenges of anti-colonial nationalists.[73]

How then did the postcolonial state in Burma respond to the legacy of colonial administration and ethnopolitical claims that came with independence? After the end of British rule, relationships between a variety of non-Burman indigenous groups and the demographically and politically dominant Burmans underwent a change in view of new political circumstances. That is, they were no longer invested with special status as they were under colonialism, and various (excluded)

(BDA) in August 1942 and the Burma National Army (BNA) in 1943. In July 1945, the British retitled the BNA as the Patriot Burmese Forces (PBF), and from late 1946 through 1947, it was reorganized and trained as a British-style infantry force. Robert H. Taylor, "Burma," in *Military-Civilian Relations in Southeast Asia*, ed. Zakaria Haji Ahmad and Harold Crouch (Singapore: Oxford University Press, 1985), pp. 18-19, 23.

[69] Cady, *A History of Modern Burma*, p. 439. For an historical perspective on the roots of the Karen-British "loyalist" relationship, see Christie, *A Modern History of Southeast Asia*, pp. 53-58.

[70] Robert H. Taylor, "Government Responses to Armed Communist and Separatist Movements: Burma," in *Governments and Rebellions in Southeast Asia*, ed. Chandran Jeshurun (Singapore: Institute of Southeast Asian Studies, 1985), p. 110.

[71] Josef Silverstein argues that this situation hardened the conviction of Burman civilian and military leaders that minority groups were bent on destroying the Union. At the same time, Burman domination of the armed forces reinforced minority perceptions that the Burma Army was determined to destroy them. Silverstein, "Fifty Years of Failure," p. 184.

[72] Sugata Bose, "Safeguards for Minorities Versus Sovereignty of Nations," *The Fletcher Forum of World Affairs* 19,1 (1995): 24.

[73] Ibid., p. 24.

ethnonationalist groups took up arms to demand political autonomy as peoples identified by their ethnic affiliations: Karen, Mon, and so forth.[74]

ETHNICITY AND MILITARY DOMINATION IN MODERN BURMA

As suggested, Burmese nationalism did not sustain a sufficiently inclusive discourse, nor did it practice ethnic plurality. In the post-independence era, non-Burman ethnic groups have consistently complained of a majoritarian, ethnic-Burman domination in centralized politics. There have been some attempts to accommodate plurality; for example, the civilian parliamentary period (1948-1958, 1960-62) embraced a nominal form of federalism. Since military rule was instituted in 1962, however, attempts to "unify" the country under a single territorial sovereignty have been more overtly ethnocratic in character.

The Panglong agreement, which was instituted in the year before independence (February 1947) and designed to guide the national integration of Burman and minority ethnic groups, advocated future ethnic equality and autonomy based on federalism. It outlined terms to regulate relationships between Burma proper and the major portion of the Frontier Areas for the interim period, until the enforcement of the new constitution, and it advocated the continued right to autonomy in internal administration for the Frontier peoples.[75] Leaders of the Shan, Kachin, and Chin ethnic groups ratified the agreement.[76] However, as Silverstein notes, the failure of the Karen and other minorities (such as the Chin of the Arakan Hill tracts, Naga, and Wa) to participate in the discussions and enter into the agreement weakened the claim that a foundation for the future of Burma existed for all.[77]

Burma's first constitution, drafted in 1947, established a federal structure of government and thereby attempted to incorporate ethnicity into the independence process. It sought to address the complex problem of how to construct a state in which formerly separate peoples were brought together into an administrative and territorial union, while at the same time retaining a nominal degree of autonomy where appropriate.[78] It contained provisions for special representation in the upper house of parliament and for three ethnically defined subordinate states (Shan, Kachin, and Karenni) and two special districts (Chin and Karen, with a provision for a future Karen state). Other minorities, however—such as the Mon

---

[74] Keyes, "Introduction," p. 6.

[75] Burma Frontier Areas Committee of Enquiry, *Report Presented to His Majesty's Government*, pp. 16-18. David I. Steinberg notes that the results of the Panglong conference were attributed to Aung San's high credibility with the minorities. He quotes Aung San's view that it would not be feasible to set up Burma as a "Unitary State," but rather: "We must set up a Union with properly regulated provisions to safeguard the rights of National Minorities." Quoted in David I. Steinberg, "Constitutional and Political Bases of Minority Insurrections in Burma," in *Armed Separatism in Southeast Asia*, ed. Lim Joo-Jock and Vani S. (Singapore: Institute of Southeast Asian Studies, 1984), p. 59.

[76] Under British census classification, the Mons, along with the Arakanese, were incorporated into the category of Burman.

[77] See Silverstein, "Fifty Years of Failure," pp. 176-177; and Martin Smith, *Burma: Insurgency and the Politics of Ethnicity* (London: Zed Books, 1993), pp. 77-80.

[78] Josef Silverstein, *Burma: Military Rule and the Politics of Stagnation* (Ithaca: Cornell University Press, 1977), p. 54.

and Arakanese, who lived among the majority Burmans in Burma proper—were not accorded special rights or privileges.[79] The right to secession was also outlined in the constitution, but it only applied to the Shan and Karenni states after ten years.[80] The Union thus began with a nominal federal structure that was politically incomplete. Taylor describes it as a form of "truncated federalism" that postponed difficult problems to be handled in the future through democratic politics.[81] Effective power remained with the central government, and many of the minorities were deprived of recognition.[82] In any case, at independence the AFPFL government was immediately overwhelmed with civil war and made vulnerable by a disintegrating army, particularly during the initial 1948–52 period.

By March 1962, postcolonial Burma's era of parliamentary democracy had ended. The limited federalism of the early state had not solved the turbulent problems of internal conflict. Despite the government's efforts, ethnic and communist insurgents fought on. In 1958 the *tatmadaw* had achieved more than sufficient political and military strength and grown to become U Nu's "dependable custodians of the Union." Confusion and instability resulting from the AFPFL-split and associated civil-military and intra-military rivalries[83] led to U Nu's fall from power and the resulting transfer of power to the Commander-in-Chief, General Ne Win, in September 1958.[84] In October 1958 the military assumed control of the country as the "Caretaker [*Bogyoke*] Government." Civilian government was emasculated. In this period of "constitutional authoritarian government,"[85] the transfer of power to Ne Win and his associates was aimed at restoring law and order and creating conditions for new elections, which were eventually held in 1960. The Caretaker Government's book, *Is Trust Vindicated?*, reflected with pride on the army's accomplishments, while expressing disdain for its civilian

---

[79] Silverstein, "Fifty Years of Failure," pp. 177-180.

[80] When the time for Shan secession came in 1957-58 and demands for Shan independence grew, the *sawbwas* (royal male rulers of the Shan states) came under great pressure to retire. The result was the forced renunciation of their rights at a ceremony in April 1959 in Taunggyi attended by Gen. Ne Win during the Caretaker Administration. However, as Callahan points out, U Nu had already sent the army to the Shan State as early as 1952 to displace some of the princes and set up an army administration, when the KMT began moving deeper into Burma. Mary P. Callahan, "Democracy in Burma: The Lessons of History," in *Analysis* 9,3 (1998): 14.

[81] Taylor, "Perceptions of Ethnicity in the Politics of Burma," p. 9. For further discussion of the early post-independence era, see Robert H. Taylor, *An Undeveloped State: The Study of Modern Burma's Politics*, Working Paper No. 28 (London: Department of Economics and Political Studies, School of African and Oriental Studies, University of London, 1983), especially pp. 19-30.

[82] See also, Silverstein, *Burma: Military Rule and the Politics of Stagnation*, p. 59; Smith, *Burma: Insurgency and the Politics of Ethnicity*, pp. 192-195; Taylor, "Government Responses to Armed Communist and Separatist Movements," p. 110.

[83] See Callahan, "The Origins of Military Rule in Burma." For a detailed analysis of the ruling party (AFPFL) split, civil-military, and intra-military tensions (field-staff axis of friction)—with emphasis on the latter factor—leading up to the coup, see ibid., pp. 468-511.

[84] Ne Win justified the takeover in a parliamentary speech: "The rebels were increasing their activities, and the political pillar was collapsing. It was imperative that the Union should not drown in shallow waters as it nearly did in 1948-49. So it fell on the armed forces to perform their bounden duty to take all security measures to forestall and prevent a recurrence." Bertil Lintner, *Outrage: Burma's Struggle for Democracy* (Bangkok: White Lotus, 1990), p. 34.

[85] Silverstein, *Burma: Military Rule and the Politics of Stagnation*, p. 76.

predecessor.[86] During a brief interregnum that lasted from 1960 to 1962, democratic rule under U Nu was restored, but the military assumed power more permanently in the coup of March 2, 1962. U Nu had promised in the election to address minority demands, but his "federal seminar," convened in mid-February 1962, was never concluded.[87] Instead, as Taylor writes, the army staged the coup against U Nu's government on the grounds that it "was conducting negotiations with minority leaders which would lead to the disintegration of the country."[88] Minority leaders attending the seminar were arrested.

General Ne Win's 1962 takeover formally installed military domination in the form of a military-backed Socialist government (firmly under his personal control, as "his word became law").[89] The bicameral parliament and 1947 constitution were dissolved, and a small military oligarchy called the "Revolutionary Council" (RC) ruled Burma until 1974.[90] Under the RC, all legislative, executive, and judicial power was conferred on General Ne Win as Chairman. The RC established the Burmese Socialist Program Party (BSPP) as its party and the isolationist "Burmese Way to Socialism" as its ideology. Military rule dismantled the (limited) federalist structure that had been designed to accommodate ethnicity and addressed ethnopolitical conflict by military means and a strong centralized state. In 1963, the RC sought to negotiate with leaders of the ethnic and communist insurgencies, but there was little constructive dialogue and warfare resumed. Representatives of various political and ethnic groups—some of which formed an alliance, the National Democratic United Front (NDUF)—came to Rangoon and held talks with Ne Win and the RC. Silverstein notes that there was no agreement on the definition and implementation of a cease-fire, and thus the first step toward ending insurgency could not be taken.[91] By the early 1960s, several additional groups had taken up arms in the Shan and Kachin states. The BSPP under Ne Win was declared the country's only legal political organization, while the many ethnic groups fighting for political recognition were deemed illegal.[92]

In 1974, the leadership of the BSPP (headed by U Ne Win, now retired as General) instituted a new constitution (later dissolved in 1988). In this constitution, there were concessions to demands for the establishment of additional Mon and Arakanese states and the reconstitution of the Chin Special Division into a state. In administrative terms, Burma (now the Socialist Republic of the Union of Burma) comprised seven divisions surrounded by seven named minority states. However,

---

[86] Callahan, "The Origins of Military Rule in Burma," p. 488.

[87] For further detail on this period and the Federal Movement, see Smith, *Burma: Insurgency and the Politics of Ethnicity*, pp. 195-197.

[88] Robert H. Taylor, "Myanmar: Military Politics and the Prospects for Democratisation," *Asian Affairs: Journal of the Royal Society for Asian Affairs* 29,1 (1998): 6.

[89] Ibid.

[90] The army ruled directly from 1962-71 through the Revolutionary Council and its subordinate state, division, and township councils dominated by military commanders. After 1971, the regime became nominally civilian in that the *tatmadaw*'s role was governed by the BSPP, "but the style and ethos of a military regime, as well as the leadership, remained largely unchanged." Ibid., p. 7.

[91] Silverstein, *Burmese Politics*, p. 233.

[92] Bertil Lintner provides a comprehensive summary of rebel armies and other anti-government groups in Burma in his *Burma in Revolt*, Appendix 3, pp. 421-437.

the formation of these states was merely an administrative exercise because, in practice, it did not correspond to a federalist form of minority representation. [93]

Under prolonged military rule, the trend toward a more centralized, "Burmanized," and militarized state was intensified. As indicated, the *tatmadaw* viewed itself as the sole legitimate force capable of bringing the country together, seeking "national unity" through a strong centralized, rather than federated, state. A military network radiating out from Rangoon would eventually gain control over all within the borders of Burma; in this way, the greatly diverse populations inhabiting its territory were treated as a single assimilable entity.[94]

The 1974 constitution maintained a cosmetic commitment to ethnic diversity, declaring that all groups had the right to preserve and protect their cultures, languages, and religion, provided that they did not undermine the unity and security of the state. It maintained that "state sovereignty must reside in the entire nation,"[95] effectively consigning ethnicity to political irrelevance and illegitimacy, except when it had to do with cultural practices. All citizens of the country were to share a common identity and loyalty. Burmese was the official language, although the qualified use of minority languages was permitted.

Elites in control at critical levels of state authority in the military, party, and other institutions were predominantly Burman. An increasingly ethnocratic and assimilationist state developed as the military made it increasingly clear that the national culture, its rule and policies, would be shaped by the numerically dominant Burmans.[96] As Cynthia Enloe has noted, "[n]ationalism, military professionalism, state building, and Burman communalism were tightly interwoven."[97] These interconnected factors, described by Enloe, created a notable division in government: ethnic heterogeneity characterizes the lower and middle echelons of government, while a striking level of ethnic homogeneity is found among élites in the upper levels.[98]

FIGHTING THE INSURGENTS: THE "FOUR CUTS" COUNTERINSURGENCY STRATEGY

After the failure of General Ne Win's peace parley in 1963, the regime continued to be confronted by a plethora of well-armed communist and ethnic insurrections in the central delta and border regions. In the mid-1960s, the *tatmadaw* responded by devising a new counterinsurgency strategy. This was a component in its broader development of a military doctrine and strategy designed

---

[93] Steinberg describes this as "titular administrative symmetry" between the Burman and minority regions. Steinberg, "Constitutional and Political Bases of Minority Insurrections in Burma," pp. 63-64.

[94] Curtis N. Thomson, "Political Stability and Minority Groups in Burma," *The Geographical Review* 85,3 (1995): 274.

[95] Taylor, *The State in Burma*, p. 303.

[96] For further discussion on the process of "Burmanization," see Silverstein, *Burmese Politics*, Chapter 10.

[97] Cynthia Enloe, *Ethnic Soldiers: State Security in Divided Societies* (Harmondsworth: Penguin Books, 1980), p. 138.

[98] Ibid., p. 18.

to suppress internal insurgency; this doctrine focused on unconventional, anti-guerrilla warfare rather than on repelling invasion by an external force.[99]

Officially endorsed in 1968, and still in operation today, the strategy is known as *Pya Ley Pya* or the "Four Cuts" strategy. Fundamentally, the strategy aims to cut the insurgents off from their support system, which is usually linked to the civilian population ("denying water to the fish"). Typically, such civilian support systems help to provide food supplies, funding, intelligence, and recruits to insurgents. The fourth "cut" is often referred to as "cutting off the [insurgent's] head" (or "putting the fish onto the chopping board").[100] With some local adaptation, the strategy was modeled upon the recommendations and examples found in the literature and reports of counterinsurgency elsewhere; for example, it adopts the tactic of establishing "resettlement villages" (supervised by around-the-clock "security committees") developed by Sir Robert Thompson in defeating communist insurgency in Malaysia.[101] In the context of counterinsurgency in Burma, the "Four Cuts" is essentially a military strategy of "base denial" to the insurgents in the context of guerrilla warfare, as outlined in the discussion at the *tatmadaw* Conference in 1968:

> In essence, the insurgents are waging a protracted war based on guerrilla warfare . . . They operate by relying on people's support . . . It is evident that villages are becoming insurgent strongholds and hide-outs. They infiltrate villages and breed hardcore cadres. Through these hardcore cadres, they control the villages. Then, in the next stage, these villages are turned into base areas. It is very difficult for our troops [the *tatmadaw*] to operate in these areas.[102]

In Burma, the displacement and resettlement of villages into strategic areas under army control has been routinely employed to cut the insurgents from their civilian support system. Old villages in the operation zones were burnt down, along with their food supplies, and rice was distributed at the new location. In this way, the government could maintain surveillance and prevent any "leakage" of rations to guerrilla soldiers. All villagers remaining behind were treated with suspicion as insurgents and risked heavy punishments. New villages were built outside the operation zones, and army encampments constructed, with villagers required to

---

[99] For the first comprehensive study of the development of the *tatmadaw*'s counterinsurgency policy and program against the Communist Party of Burma (1948-89), based on extensive archival sources held in Burma, see Maung Aung Myoe, "The Counterinsurgency in Myanmar: The Government's Response to the Burma Communist Party" (PhD dissertation, Australian National University, 1999).

[100] This is a frequent comment made by the ethnic oppositions in reference to counterinsurgency strategy. Smith, *Burma: Insurgency and the Politics of Ethnicity*, p. 259. It seems that, to some extent, this is also the *tatmadaw*'s intended meaning. Maung Aung Myoe indicates that it is to make the people "cut off the insurgent's head." Maung Aung Myoe, "The Counterinsurgency in Myanmar," pp. 192-193.

[101] See Robert Thompson, *Defeating Communist Insurgency: Experiences from Malaya and Vietnam* (London: Chatto and Windus, 1966). Maung Aung Myoe, "The Counterinsurgency in Myanmar," p. 213.

[102] Discussion from the Regional Command HQs at the 1968 Tatmadaw Conference, cited in Maung Aung Myoe, "The Counterinsurgency in Myanmar," pp. 192-193.

serve on day- and night-shifts as guards against rebel attack.[103] As a counterinsurgency tactic, the use of tight population control and surveillance, which effectively severs the people from the guerrillas, is crucial because it provides "the establishment of a solid security framework covering the whole population living in the villages and small towns of a given area."[104]

In conjunction with the Four Cuts strategy, the map of Burma (divided into five regional military commands in 1968) was shaded in three distinct colors: black for areas completely controlled by insurgents, brown (or grey) for areas contested by both sides,[105] and white for "free" areas, where the government has full control. The objective is to "clear" each insurgent-held area systematically until the map becomes entirely white.[106] In the counterinsurgency literature, an area is declared "white" when the threat of insurgent re-infiltration is removed and the area is "won" for the government.[107] Thus, in its overall counterinsurgency program, the *tatmadaw* was concerned not only with "the elimination of insurgents" facilitated by the Four Cuts strategy, but also with the building of "white areas" (areas "free of insurgents") and, finally, "hard-core" areas (government strongholds).[108]

The Burma Army developed an operational structure to support the Four Cuts strategy that entailed a "division of labor": garrison duties were handled under the geographically organized framework of regional commands and mobile assault operations under the Light Infantry Division (LID) system.[109] Battalions operating under the regional commands were generally engaged in "cleaning up the insurgent activities and consolidation of base areas," whereas battalions under the LIDs were "strike forces in operations."[110] With the introduction of the LID system in mid-1966, special mobile "strike forces" were formed specifically to combat communist and ethnic insurgencies.[111] In terms of military structure, the LIDs were directly connected to the General Staff office in Rangoon rather than to the

---

[103] For a description of the *tatmadaw*'s application of the Four Cuts strategy *vis-à-vis* the communist counterinsurgency program in the Irrawaddy Delta, Pegu Yoma and the Northwest regions, for instance, see ibid., pp. 212-215.

[104] Thompson, *Defeating Communist Insurgency*, p. 121.

[105] That is, a "brown" area is where both the opposition still operates and the government has "a security presence." Maung Aung Myoe, "The Counterinsurgency in Myanmar," p. 220.

[106] Smith, *Burma: Insurgency and the Politics of Ethnicity*, p. 259.

[107] Thompson, *Defeating Communist Insurgency*, p. 113.

[108] Maung Aung Myoe, "The Counterinsurgency in Myanmar," pp. 194, 219.

[109] Maung Aung Myoe, *Building the Tatmadaw: The Organisational Development of the Armed Forces in Myanmar, 1948-98*, Working Paper No. 327 (Canberra: The Strategic and Defence Studies Centre, Australian National University, 1998), p. 23.

[110] Maung Aung Myoe, "The Counterinsurgency in Myanmar," p. 200.

[111] The first LID—the 77th LID—was established in June 1966 at Pegu. In 1967 and 1968, two more LIDs were formed, the 88th (at Magwe) and 99th (Meiktila). This was followed in the mid-1970s by the 66th (Prome), 55th (Aungban), and the 44th (Thaton) in the latter half of the 1970s; and two others in the period leading up the SLORC regime, the 33rd (Sagaing) in the mid-1980s and the 22nd (Pa-an) in 1987. The 11th (Indaing) was formed in 1988 and the 101st (Pakokku) in 1991. LIDs were also called upon to quell serious civil uprisings in the major population centers (such as was performed in Rangoon by the 77th LID during the "U Thant" disturbances in 1974, and by the 22nd and 33rd LIDs in August and September 1988). Andrew Selth, *Transforming the Tatmadaw: The Burmese Armed Forces since 1988* (Canberra: Strategic and Defence Studies Centre, Australian National University, 1996), p. 40.

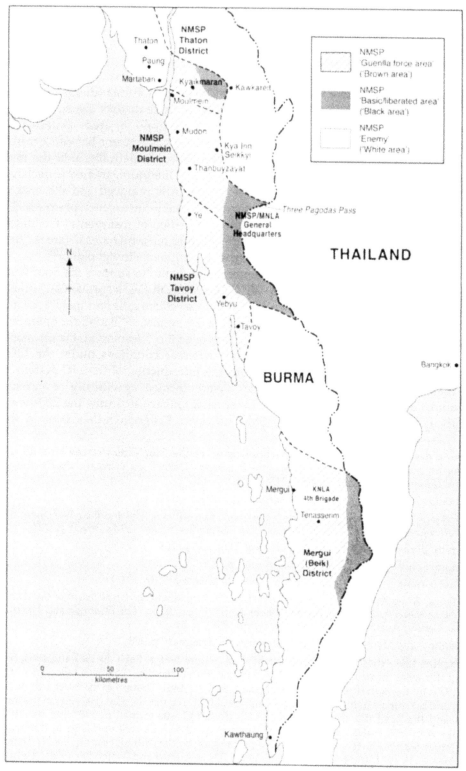

Map 2.2   New Mon State Party Districts, 1990

regional commands. Martin Smith argues that this arrangement was carried out deliberately so that the strike troops could be brought into an area with "few qualms about local sensibilities."[112]

Initially the *tatmadaw* concentrated on the strategically important regions of central Burma and the delta in order to secure bases for future operations.[113] From 1966–1975, the *tatmadaw* focused its efforts on the Communist Party's best-organized bases in regions of the Irrawaddy Delta and the Pegu Yoma (CBP headquarters were located in the Pegu Yoma from 1958-1975).[114] The Irrawaddy Delta had also been a base area for other groups, such as the ethnic Karen National Unity Party (KNUP) allied to the CPB's front, the National Democratic United Front (NDUF).[115] By May 1974, the *tatmadaw* declared the Delta a "white area," and the CPB headquarters in the Pegu Yoma was finally destroyed in March 1975, subsequently isolating the CPB in the northeast border region. By 1975, therefore, the *tatmadaw* had "cleared" central Burma of insurgency.[116]

Insurgencies were subsequently pushed into the borderland regions of the country. However, in its application of the Four Cuts strategy to these border regions, the Burma Army met with new difficulties. Guerrilla armies in the more remote mountainous areas had their own means of "back-door" escape and supply lines, in addition to their civilian support bases.[117] Opposition control of the border areas conferred on them distinct geographical advantages. For instance, the ethnic insurgent forces along the Thai-Burmese border benefited from the thriving black market trade. This was during the RC and BSPP era of socialist isolation, from 1962 to 1974, during which time Burma's own production of consumer goods and imports was decimated, and domestic shortages led to the development of a flourishing system of black marketeering and smuggling. Contraband from Thailand flowed across the border, and—beginning with a cadre led by KNU leader Bo Mya in the mid-1960s—rebel groups along the Thai-Burmese border set up their own lucrative "toll gates" through which goods were taxed. Numerous such gates were also established by the Mon, Karenni, and Shan oppositions. As Bertil Lintner writes, the collection of taxes from this enormous unauthorized trade and links with Thai merchants and military authorities provided non-communist insurgent groups with money to buy new US-made arms and ammunition and other supplies through

---

112 Smith, *Burma: Insurgency and the Politics of Ethnicity*, p. 260.

113 Maung Aung Myoe, "The Counterinsurgency in Myanmar," p. 233.

114 According to Maung Aung Myoe, the *tatmadaw* undertook nine major operations in the Pegu Yoma from December 1966 to March 1975. This mountain range was of vital strategic importance, with vast forest, agricultural, and population resources; the tropical rainforest which was home to the CPB headquarters provided perfect terrain for guerrilla warfare; they also enjoyed communications with a far-reaching regions throughout Burma. There were six *tatmadaw* operations in the Irrawaddy Delta (January 1969 to May 1974). Maung Aung Myoe provides extensive details of these *tatmadaw* operations, including "village resettlement programs" and other successful applications of the "Four Cuts" strategy. See ibid., pp. 215-221, 224-230.

115 The delta also provided a transit area for the shipment of arms and ammunition by both the CBP and the NDUF from the Thai-Burmese border to their bases. Ibid., p. 215. For further detail on this period, see also Smith, *Burma: Insurgency and the Politics of Ethnicity*, pp. 262-272.

116 The government then set about building "white" and "hardcore" areas. Maung Aung Myoe, "The Counterinsurgency in Myanmar," p. 331.

117 Smith, *Burma: Insurgency and the Politics of Ethnicity*, p. 261.

Thailand.[118] Furthermore, as discussed in Chapter Six, Thailand was willing to cooperate in this trade because it appreciated the geo-strategic "buffer" role that the various non-communist ethnic armies provided against the spread of communism in the region.

Thus, from the mid-1970s, when the counterinsurgency campaigns turned to the large frontier regions, each year the Burma Army launched dry-season offensives against the borderland armies and the civilian populations under their control. However, as Andrew Selth notes, the effectiveness of its attempts to isolate and wear down insurgents' forces was hindered by inferior fighting capabilities.[119] Analysis of the Burma Army in the period prior to 1988 shows that a number of significant military obstacles hobbled their operations, including the army's possession of obsolete heavy equipment, their weak logistics and communications systems, shortages of transportation, fuel, ammunition, and spare parts, and an inadequate number of skilled troops.[120] Soldiers in the Burma Army also faced many hardships in the rugged, malarial jungles of the border regions. There were usually no roads, and troops often moved on foot. They needed to travel lightly and rapidly (their progress through the territory was commonly facilitated by the forced recruitment of civilian porters) because in mountainous terrain "long baggage trains are an invitation to ambush."[121] Under such conditions, the *tatmadaw* was left to tackle insurgent strongholds individually, with one or two large-scale operations per year. They typically mounted annual dry-season offensives against insurgent strongholds, conducted through the fixed garrison regional commands, supplemented by the mobile rapid deployment of Light Infantry Battalions (LIBs) drawn from the Light Infantry Divisions. Yet when the monsoon season approached, they generally fell back to secure positions, for they were unable to hold captured territory through the wet season.[122] Moreover, they were usually confronted by better-equipped and trained guerrilla opponents who, in contrast to the Burma Army, were operating with the support of the local populations.

Meanwhile, civil war widened the gap between the state and non-state protagonists in the conflict. For the government, the insurrections were a constant threat to "national unity." For the ethnic forces, the government was an institution set on their annihilation; this conviction reinforced ethnic identification among insurgent organizations. For the civilian populations inhabiting these contested areas, neutrality was impossible because local residents were implicated as supporters of the rebels. In this way, civilians were inescapably caught up in the conflict. Their experiences of suffering and the general militarization of everyday

---

[118] Lintner, *Burma in Revolt*, pp. 180-181.

[119] Selth, *Transforming the Tatmadaw*, pp. 47-48.

[120] See ibid., pp. 6-7, 45-48. Further, up until the late 1980s, insurgent organizations had signals intelligence capabilities to match those of the *tatmadaw*—and hence were kept informed of the *tatmadaw*'s preparations and operations. See Desmond Ball, "SIGINT Strengths Form a Vital Part of Burma's Military Muscle," *Jane's Intelligence Review* 10,3 (1998): 35-41.

[121] Frank S. Jannuzi, "The New Burma Road (Paved by Polytechnologies?)," in *Burma: Prospects for a Democratic Future*, ed. Robert I. Rotberg (Washington, DC and Cambridge, MA: The World Peace Foundation/Harvard Institute for International Development and Brookings Institution Press, 1998), pp. 203-204.

[122] Ibid., p. 204.

life often also served to reinforce (or force) an affiliation with the ethnic armed insurgency. This issue is the specific focus of the next chapter.

In the mid-1980s, counterinsurgency offensives waged against the ethnic groups along the Thai-Burmese border became increasingly large-scale. Until the expansion and modernization of the armed forces under the SLORC (State Law and Order Restoration Council), which took place after 1988, ethnic armies maintained superior military capabilities and continued to enjoy *de facto* governmental control in the border territories (the "liberated areas") which they held. After the mid-1980s, however, they began to face government campaigns of greater intensity that would, over the following years, wear them down and increasingly drive them out of their strongholds.[123]

In the dry season of 1983-84, the government launched its most intensive counterinsurgency offensives in southeastern Burma to date. While in the past the Burma Army had always retreated with the monsoons, this time it was resolved to maintain military pressure throughout the coming monsoon season. Notwithstanding the difficulties encountered by the army in cutting insurgent supply lines, attacks and systematic military harassment of civilian populations in these areas occurred. According to Smith, the *tatmadaw* behaved as a "marauding, conquering army," and civilian dislocation in rural ethnic communities became endemic.[124] Sizable populations were relocated, and increasing numbers of people lived in a state of emergency, periodically fleeing ahead of government forces before returning home when conditions permitted. Smith describes a scene of devastation in some of the Karen Areas by 1988 around the Dawna Range near the Thai border: "Dozens of villages had been burnt down, crops confiscated, and fields destroyed. Several thousand villagers had been moved into new 'strategic villages' on the plains to the west, while over twenty thousand Karen refugees had crossed into Thailand."[125]

The SLORC Takes Over: Consolidating Military Control

The *tatamadaw* has been historically suspicious of democratic civilian-based politics, a suspicion evident in its "national security" ideology. An official government publication describes the *tatmadaw*'s quest for national unity in these terms:

> What did the Tatmadaw do at the time of the four political crises of 1948, 1958, 1962, and 1988? Had the Tatmadaw kept itself aloof in those days, the country would have been destroyed four times over. Had the Tatmadaw not

---

123 Referring to the government's intensification of military campaigns against the Karen National Union, a report in the *Far Eastern Economic Review* in 1984 commented: "it looks as if the government is now preparing to crush the economic lifeline of the rebels and shatter the Karen insurgency at all costs." Paisal Sricharatchanya, "This Year's Big Push," *Far Eastern Economic Review*, May 10, 1994, p. 45.

124 Smith, *Burma: Insurgency and the Politics of Ethnicity*, p. 397.

125 For details of the movement of *tatmadaw* forces into the KNU's hitherto untouched northern strongholds, see ibid.

taken over power, particularly in 1988, the Union would now be in shambles, and bloodshed would have continued.[126]

When the SLORC regime was installed on September 18, 1988, it claimed only a temporary role, as the name suggests.[127] However, in practice, it set about consolidating long-term military control of the country. Taylor comments that, unlike General Ne Win's Caretaker government in 1958, the SLORC has shown little willingness to abandon power—instead it resembles the Revolutionary Council that held power between 1962 and 1971, "working to create the institutions which will embed themselves and their military successors in power for many years to come."[128] After taking power, the SLORC junta suspended the 1974 constitution and furnished itself with full executive authority. The junta established its formal administrative structure with Law and Order Restoration Councils (LORCs) at the state/divisional, district, township, and ward/village-tract levels, although the military regional commanders exercised informal authority over nearly all local and provincial affairs throughout the seven states and seven divisions of the country. The SLORC was officially dissolved on November 15, 1997, reformulating itself as the State Peace and Development Council (SPDC).[129]

In seeking to maintain dominance, since 1988 the regime has substantially expanded, modernized, and diversified the capabilities of the armed forces. The Burma Army (by far the largest and most powerful component of the *tatmadaw*) has expanded in size from 170,000 in 1988 to some 370,000 troops in 2000.[130] This increase of around 200,000 soldiers in ten years is described by one scholar as a "breakneck" recruitment, which carries with it organizational and other

---

[126] Nawrahta, *Destiny of the Nation* (Yangon: News and Periodicals Enterprise of the Ministry of Information of the Union of Myanmar, 1995), p. 23. (This is an official government publication.)

[127] For instance, an official publication on the role of the *tatmadaw* in Burma writes: "the Tatmadaw was not going to keep hanging onto power for a long time...[it] was not seizing power . . . it had formed only a temporary administration in discharge of its historic duty" [i.e., "to protect national solidarity and sovereignty"]. A Tatmadaw Researcher, *A Concise History of Myanmar and the Tatmadaw's Role, 1948-1988*, Vol. 1 (Yangon: News and Periodical Enterprise of the Ministry of Information of the Union of Myanmar, 1991), p. 153.

[128] Taylor, "Myanmar: Military Politics and the Prospects for Democratisation," pp. 7-8.

[129] No major policy shifts as such occurred in this change, and the former LORCs were simply renamed Peace and Development Councils. In the transformation, however, a number of former SLORC members were "allowed to resign," thereby purging a substantial number of notably corrupt members who were then required to report to the National Intelligence Bureau for investigation. Another dimension to the reorganization of the SLORC into the SPDC was an attempt by the central junta leadership further to curb the large political and military bases, havens for lucrative and illicit activities, which had been exploited by the military commanders since 1988.

[130] Andrew Selth, *Burma's Order of Battle: An Interim Assessment*, Working Paper No. 351 (Canberra: Strategic and Defence Studies Centre, Australian National University, 2000), p. 10. On the rationale for expansion under the SLORC, see Andrew Selth, "The Armed Forces and Military Rule in Burma," in *Burma: Propsects for a Democratic Future*, ed. Robert I. Rotberg (Washington, DC and Cambridge, MA: World Peace Foundation/Harvard Institute for International Development and Brookings Institution Press, 1998), pp. 91-96.

consequences for the future.[131] With its operational capabilities in the field also substantially enhanced, the army is not only larger, it is also more widely distributed, more mobile, and able to sustain itself in operations longer and at a "higher tempo" in the field than hitherto.[132] A huge expansion of the regime's military intelligence capabilities was undertaken in the 1990s, aimed at both eliminating political dissent among the civilian population and maintaining loyalty and unity within the ranks of the *tatmadaw*.[133] In the period since the SLORC, the *tatmadaw* has also enhanced its signals intelligence capabilities to strengthen dramatically its operations against the insurgency groups whose equipment and methods could now be outmaneuvered.[134] Since 1988–1989, China has been Burma's closest diplomatic ally, major intelligence partner, and foremost arms supplier (providing the regime with military equipment amounting to the value of perhaps US$3 billion).[135]

The Burma Army, with its expanded forces and improved capabilities, has consequently waged larger and more effective counterinsurgency offensives against its ethnic insurgent opponents in the borderlands. In particular, it has placed greater emphasis on logistics, and the traditional pattern of dry-season offensive and wet-season retreat has been abandoned. Now, drawing on scores of new battalions (both garrison and mobile), in conjunction with its various coordinating facilities,[136] the Burma Army has become strong enough to sustain itself logistically and remain in an area as long as necessary, regardless of the season. Whereas previously it moved into an area, wreaked havoc, and departed, it has developed capabilities that allow it to position itself in an area, fan out, and launch attacks from there. Further, it has gained increased control of the countryside by laying landmines in the jungles and forcing people to use the roads. Local people (armed oppositions and civilian populations alike) are consequently left with less time to prepare themselves for government attacks and then flee them, as they did in the past.[137] In addition, beginning with the 1991–92 dry-season offensive, the *tatmadaw* enhanced its logistical support for the army by improving roads and airports, building heliports, and expanding warehouses

---

131 Mary P. Callahan, "Cracks in the Edifice? Military-Society Relations in Burma since 1988," in *Burma/Myanmar: Strong Regime, Weak State?*, ed. Morten B. Pedersen, Emily Rudland, and R. J. May (Adelaide: Crawford House Publishing, 2000), p. 44.

132 William Ashton, "Burma's Armed Forces: Preparing for the 21st Century," *Jane's Intelligence Review* 10,1 (1998): 30.

133 Callahan, "Cracks in the Edifice?," p. 48. On the intelligence apparatus, see Andrew Selth, "Burma's Intelligence Apparatus," *Intelligence and National Security* 13,4 (1998): 33-70.

134 See Desmond Ball, *Burma's Military Secrets: Signals Intelligence (SIGINT) from 1941 to Cyber Warfare* (Bangkok: White Lotus, 1998).

135 Ibid., pp. 219-220. Although the regime's relationship with China has been the most important by far, it has also developed a number of other notable secret partnerships with Singapore, Israel, and Pakistan. See Andrew Selth, *Burma's Secret Military Partners*, Canberra Papers on Strategy and Defence No. 136 (Canberra: Strategic and Defence Studies Centre, Australian National University, 2000).

136 There are the five Regional Operations Commands (ROCs). Also, there are eleven Military Operations Commands (MOCs), and fourteen Tactical Operations Commands (TOCs) to manage regional garrison infantry battalions. See Selth, *Burma's Order of Battle*, pp. 10-11; and Maung Aung Myoe, *Building the Tatmadaw*, p. 56.

137 Interviews, Bangkok, March 1998.

adjacent to opposition-held territory. In this way, it was able to shorten its own supply lines and conduct its operations year-round. Now it could remain in an area (sometimes sustaining large numbers of casualties) in order to consolidate gains before undertaking additional offensives.[138]

"National Consolidation": The Cease-fire Strategy

The regime's brand of state nationalism advocates "national unity" and "national consolidation." In practice, "national consolidation" has entailed aims and achievements such as the "renunciation of armed insurrection" and the "return of armed groups to the legal fold," both of which the regime has professed and publicized widely in the state-run media and on billboards around the country.

The SLORC began negotiating cease-fire agreements with its former rebel opponents after the collapse of the CPB in 1989, when a number of breakaway ex-CPB ethnic forces (such as the Wa and the Kokang groups in the Northeast) "returned to the legal fold." A host of other ethnic insurgencies subsequently entered into cease-fire arrangements with the government: by 1995, the New Mon State Party was the fifteenth group to agree to a cease-fire. The architect of the cease-fire strategy was the SLORC's Secretary 1 and Chief of the Directorate of Defense Services Intelligence (DDSI), Khin Nyunt (then Brigadier-General). In 1993, Lieutenant-General Khin Nyunt toured the country for this purpose, targeting in particular those groups operating along the Thai-Burmese border, extending invitations for "peace talks" to the KNU, the NMSP (New Mon State Party), and the Karenni National Progressive Party (KNPP). In 2000, the major non-cease-fire groups remained the KNU, the KNPP (whose March 1995 cease-fire deal collapsed within three months), the Shan State Army (South), and several other smaller forces (which include various splinter factions). The regime has, however, claimed substantial successes in its "peace efforts" since the SLORC took power, as shown in a 1996 publication of the Ministry of Defense's think-tank, the Office of Strategic Studies:

> As the fruit of the State's effort for the reconsolidation of national unity, fifteen armed underground groups are now participating in the development activities of the nation hand-in-hand with the Government (*Tatmadaw*). Due to the State's policy and the correct measures taken, armed insurgency within the country is nearing the vanishing point . . .
>
> The change of heart exhibited by the armed groups of national races and their return to the legal fold is an unprecedented and spectacular accomplishment for internal peace known only during the time of the State Law and Order Council leadership.[139]

---

[138] Jannuzi, "The New Burma Road," p. 204.

[139] Colonel Kyaw Thein, "An Analysis of the Return of the Armed Groups of National Races to the Legal Fold and the Renunciation of Armed Insurrection," in *Symposium on Socio-Economic Factors Contributing to National Consolidation* (Yangon: Ministry of Defense and Office of Strategic Studies, 1996), pp. 196-197.

The government has paraded each group that accepts a cease-fire agreement before the media to represent yet another victory for the process of "national consolidation."[140]

Yet, at the same time, the government's call for "peace" (in practice, military cease-fires) has been accompanied by devastating counterinsurgency offensives. Since the 1991–92 dry season mentioned above, the government has been able to conduct concurrent campaigns along the borders of Thailand, Bangladesh, and India.[141] Along the Thai border, it aimed to destroy key insurgent strongholds and gain control of the border. Major offensives have been conducted in its Southeast (Mon and Karen states, Tenasserim division), Eastern (southern Shan state), and Northeast (northern Shan state) Regional Commands. Thus, the goal of "national consolidation" has been pursued with unprecedented military force.

Those who hope for long-term reconciliation in the country must note with trepidation that the SLORC's achievement of "peace" has been pursued by narrow military means. That is, the regime has imposed its military aims and vision on the country—it aims to compress diversity into a single territorial entity—without attempting any political negotiation that might ameliorate factors that underlie the conflict. Instead, the militarization of ethnicity since independence in Burma has been met with the militarized suppression of ethnic mobilization, a process that has been reproduced throughout Burma's post-independence history.

The final stage of the government's counterinsurgency program has involved the widespread relocation of villages under the direct control of the *tatmadaw,* coupled with the promise of infrastructural "development" programs in the border areas.[142] By 1995, the *tatmadaw* had extended its control over the increasingly war-weary ethnonationalist forces in the once rebellious peripheries as it had never done before, reaching into areas virtually all along the Thai border.

In sum, the politico-military scene in 1995 was dramatically different from that in 1962, when military rule was installed. In 1962, Ne Win's government was confronted with manifold insurrections which it could not successfully resolve with political negotiations. Then, by 1968, the government endorsed the Four Cuts strategy and began working to cut links between insurgent forces and their civilian bases; in this way, it succeeded in "clearing" central Burma by the mid-1970s, pushing the civil war and its own counterinsurgency campaigns into the border regions of the country. The *tatmadaw* fought on while the oppositions—the Communist Party and ethnic insurgencies—survived thanks to superior military capabilities, the support of their civilian bases, and substantial benefits derived from their extensive control of the border areas. However, the government's large-scale offensives along the eastern borderlands from the mid-1980s into the 1990s

---

[140] Referring to the fifteen cease-fires, the *New Light of Myanmar* stated in 1997, for example: "Under the present State Law and Order Restoration Council, one flower of peace after another has been won at everyone's astonishment for mother Myanmar to wear." *The New Light of Myanmar,* March 8, 1997.

[141] Selth, *Transforming the Tatmadaw,* p. 59.

[142] For this latter task, the SLORC formed the Ministry of Progress of Border Areas and National Races in September 1992. The government's Border Area Development Projects (BADP) express its "goodwill" towards those groups returning to the "legal fold." Lt. Col. Thein Han, "An Assessment of the Formulation and Implementation of Border Areas Development Project Strategies," in *Symposium on Socio-Economic Factors Contributing to National Consolidation,* pp. 223-231.

marked the beginning of growing *tatmadaw* gains into formerly rebel-held areas and the progressive emasculation of ethnic insurrection. Increasingly, the counterinsurgency operations and protracted conflict have dislocated civilian populations, creating internal displacement and driving greater numbers of people in search of a cross-border haven in Thailand.

The consequences for civilian displacement arising from this changing politico-military scene are the specific focus of the next chapter. The examination of the impact of war on civilian populations is drawn from the experiences of Mon refugees on the Thai border. The patterns of displacement and forced migration thus reflect the experiences of civilians living in and fleeing from the Mon areas of Mon State and Tenasserim Division in southeastern Burma, which were once predominantly "rebel-held" under the control of the NMSP. In order to provide a necessary background to the discussion of civilian displacement in the next chapter, the following section summarizes the history of the Mon insurgency and its various features.

THE STORY OF THE MON INSURGENCY

As noted earlier, since the destruction of the last Mon kingdom at Pegu in 1757, Mon cultural survival has been under threat. During this period of nearly 250 years, unknown numbers of Mons were submerged into the predominant Burman culture, while others fled to neighboring Thailand, where they were largely assimilated into the local population. The colonial publication *Races of Burma*, compiled in 1933 by the British Indian Army, refers to the "disappearance" with "obliterating swiftness" of the Mons.[143] The term "Talaing"—meaning "to tread"—applied by the Burmans to the Mons and sometimes used by colonial scholars pejoratively, designates the Mons as the "downtrodden."[144] Mon ethnic nationalists since the late-colonial period responded to this threat by generating historical consciousness and attempting ethnic revival. On the eve of independence for Burma, Mon nationalists mobilized ethnic awareness in order to participate and stake a claim in the structure of the new state.

Once flourishing as a great Indianized civilization of Southeast Asia, the kingdoms of the Mons, and their influence, extended at various times from present day Lower Burma (Thaton, Martaban, Pegu) to Thailand and the western borders of Cambodia (the Dvaravati and Haripunjaya kingdoms in the Menam basin), long before the rise of the Burmese and Thai states. Linguistically Mon-Khmer speakers, Mons are classified as a sub-group of the Austroasiatic language stock, and theirs was the earliest of the successive migration movements to descend from the north (southwest China) and settle in the deltaic plains of Lower Burma. G. H. Luce notes that the Mons were pioneers in the cultivation of rice and beans.[145] While the significance of the historical role and influence of the Mons is widely acknowledged, many of their ancient monuments and much of their literature have been destroyed. The Mons enjoyed a few key periods of independence: from the

---

[143] Major C. M. Enriquez, *Races of Burma (Handbook for the Indian Army)*, 2nd edition (Delhi: Manager of Publications [Government of India], 1933), p. 35.

[144] Robert Halliday, *The Talaings* (Rangoon: Government Printing, 1917), p. 3.

[145] G. H. Luce, "Mons of the Pagan Dynasty," unpublished lecture delivered to the Rangoon University Mon Society, January 2, 1950, p. 1.

ninth century in Pegu until the destruction of the Mon kingdom of Thaton under Anawratha in 1057; during the reigns of kingdoms founded at Martaban and then Pegu after the fall of the Burman kingdom of Pagan to the Mongols (1287-1539)[146]; and again, from 1740–1757, after which date the Burman King Alaungphaya extinguished the last Mon kingdom at Pegu.

After the Burman conquest of Thaton in 1057, the court at Pagan adopted key cultural elements of Mon civilization, in particular Theravada Buddhism and the Mon script (derived from Sanskrit) for use with the Burmese language. Mon prisoners taken back to Pagan "taught the Burmese their literature, their art, and, above all, their script."[147] The Burman kingdom of Pagan and the Mon kingdom of Pegu became two key protagonists striving for ascendancy during the centuries of Burmese history to follow. But since 1757, no new Mon kingdoms have arisen, and the Mon population has been concentrated in eastern Lower Burma, from Moulmein southward to Tavoy, along the shore of the Gulf of Matarban in the northern portion of the Tenasserim panhandle. Their location in areas along the Thai border placed them between the historically hostile Thai and Burman kingdoms and in the path of the routes used for invasions by these respective armies. Mons were frequently recruited as troops and informers by the Thai, and substantial numbers of Mons also fled to Thailand in the wake of warfare between the Mon and Burmans.

When Burma gained independence in 1948, the political and cultural aspirations of the Mons were not addressed, in spite of their attempts to put their "seven-point demand" for Mon rights before the British Governor and interim AFPFL government in 1947.[148] Under U Nu's AFPFL government, the Mons were not granted political and institutional rights as a separate identity within the Union, though they were granted certain privileges: the government permitted Mon language training in primary schools in Mon-populated areas, an annual cultural display, and a general movement in support of Mon cultural revival. However, U Nu considered that, culturally, "the Mons and the Burmans [were] inseparable," in the sense that "the two peoples have mixed so closely that their culture has become common property."[149] He stressed the need for a stable and strong Union, suggesting that "the Mons may be able to contribute to the strength of the Union, and the Union may be able to contribute to the strength of the Mons."[150] U Nu nonetheless promised in the 1960 election campaign to create an ethnically

---

146 Martaban was abandoned and their capital was moved to Pegu in 1369 after invasions by Thai kingdoms on the rise to the east. This period was punctuated by wars, such as those between Pegu and Ava, struggles in which the Shan chieftains of the eastern plateau and the Arakanese of the western coast also became involved at times.

147 George Coedès, *The Indianized States of Southeast Asia*, ed. Walter F. Vella, trans. Susan Brown Cowing (Canberra: Australian National University Press, 1975), p. 150.

148 The perception of Nai Shwe Kyin, chairman of the AFPFL Thaton district at that time, is that the leadership was afraid of resurgence in Mon national consciousness; that, should rights be accorded to the Mons, the "Burmanised Mons would reclaim themselves as Mon." Conversations with Nai Shwe Kyin, President of the New Mon State Party, Pa Yaw, Thailand, May-June 1995.

149 U Nu, "Promotion of Mon Culture," in *Forward with the People: Translation of Selected Speeches of the Hon. U Nu, Prime Minister of the Union of Burma, Delivered on Various Occasions Between 19th February 1953 and 1st June 1954* (Rangoon: Ministry of Information, Government of the Union of Burma, 1955), p. 15.

150 Ibid., p. 20.

designated state for the Mons, along with the Arakanese. From 1962, however, General Ne Win annulled any small concessions granted to the Mons under U Nu and banned the Mon cultural revivals and cultural displays permitted under U Nu. According to Nai Shwe Kyin, Ne Win claimed that "Mons and Burmese are inseparable because Burmese are Mon-blooded, so separate ethnic rights need not be given to the Mons."[151] Further, as noted above, the struggle for ethnic identity and its suppression became entrenched in a protracted process of militarization during the Ne Win era. As with many spheres in Burmese society, even seemingly benign activities connected with the movement for the preservation and promotion of Mon culture and literature were forced underground. Mon Buddhist monasteries served as sanctuaries for Mon literature and language; and Mon was the language used and taught in basic schools in completely insurgent-held or "liberated areas." A nominal Mon State was created, along with the Arakan and Chin states, in the BSPP's new constitution of 1974, but both the wording of the constitution and the assimilationist practices of the regime ensured that the nominal ethnic states "possessed no political or administrative sovereignty or autonomy."[152]

An awareness of this history and geography has permeated the post-independence Mon insurgency. A talk with any Mon revolutionary leader or soldier, for instance, elicits a condensed account of Mon history, of lost culture and civilization, and assertions of the determination to fight for its restoration. The armed resistance has also articulated a distinct territorial dimension, as indicated in this interview with the NMSP in 1967:

> Our aim is to reclaim the traditional and historic homeland of the Mon people which was conquered by the Burmese in 1757 and which did not receive its own rights after independence from Great Britain in 1948. Our aim is to establish a sovereign state, unless the Burmese government is willing to permit a confederation of free nationalities.[153]

In newly independent Burma, Mon armed insurrection began in March 1948 with the formation of the Mon National Defense Organization (MNDO). The MNDO cooperated with the Karen National Defense Organization in the occupation of Moulmein in August of that year. It was declared illegal and blacklisted on January 30, 1949.[154] The Karen and Mon insurgencies had, in August 1948, agreed to a pledge to "struggle jointly for the attainment of Mon and Karen states."[155] Over the years, a number of Mon cultural, political, and armed organizations have existed. In 1953, the various groups were brought together under the Mon People's Front (MPF). When, in 1958, the U Nu government proposed in principle the formation of separate Mon and Arakan States in the Union, the MPF entered into a cease-fire agreement on July 19. In the publication of Ne Win's military 1958-60 "Caretaker"

---

[151] Conversations with Nai Shwe Kyin, President of the New Mon State Party, Pa Yaw, Thailand, May 1995.

[152] Taylor, *The State in Burma*, p. 303.

[153] October 15, 1972 document reprinted in New Mon State Party, "The New Mon State Party, Answers to Questionnaire on Mon Freedom Movement," pamphlet (Bangkok, 1985).

[154] From New Mon State Party, "Basic Political Policy and Constitution, 1992," December 15, 1992.

[155] New Mon State Party, "Answers to Questionnaire," p. 10.

administration, *Is Trust Vindicated?*, the Mon insurgency was largely dismissed as consisting of "outlaw gangs" and *dacoits* (bandits) with little more than a few troops remaining.[156] However, on the day after the July 19 surrender of the MPF (with over a thousand members)[157] and the imprisonment of Nai Aung Tun and other leaders, disaffected former-MPF members under the leadership of Nai Shwe Kyin and Nai Dhamma Nay formed the New Mon State Party (NMSP) to continue the struggle.[158]

The NMSP formed its armed wing—the Mon National Liberation Army (MNLA)—in 1971. Various armed groups were in operation in Mon-populated areas in the period between 1958 and 1971, but the numbers were generally very small. This was a period of development for the NMSP. At the time of Ne Win's peace talks in 1963, for instance, armed supporters of the NMSP amounted to only one hundred troops;[159] yet by 1971 this number had grown to one thousand, approximately equal to the number of Mon troops fighting in 1958.[160] While different small armed groups continued to operate throughout the 1970s, the NMSP, as the political wing, and the MNLA, as the armed wing, formed the main Mon revolutionary armed force operating in Burma. The basic structure of the NMSP comprises a Congress held at not more than three-year intervals, in which both a Central Committee (with twenty-seven full members and five others) and an Executive Committee (made up of nine members, who make policy and decisions) are elected. Across this structure three main departments exist: party affairs (organization and alliance relationships), military, and administration.[161] The war office of the MNLA is regularly reviewed at the NMSP Congress.

The Mon armed struggle—and the nationalist movement more broadly—has drawn maps depicting the old Monland. At first, the NMSP laid claim to an area incorporating the five districts of Pegu, Thaton, Moulmein, Tavoy, and Mergui in Lower Burma. After its association with the National Democratic Front (NDF) from 1976, however, the NMSP has, since its second congress, officially dropped separatist aims and agreed to the more moderate demand for a democratic federal union.[162]

---

156 Government of the Union of Burma, Director of Information, *Is Trust Vindicated?: A Chronicle of the Various Accomplishments of the Government Headed by General Ne Win During the Period of Tenure from November, 1958 to February 6, 1960* (Rangoon: Director of Information, Government of the Union of Burma, 1960), p. 20.

157 Batdanta Palita, *The Mon Leaders and the Golden Jubilee of Mon National Day*, pamphlet (Bangkok: February 19, 1997) (published in Mon language).

158 Nai Shwe Kyin has been president from 1958-1981, and from 1987 to the present. There was a split in the party between 1981-1987, at which time Nai Non La became president of the largest faction. The NMSP entered into a cease-fire agreement with the State Law and Order Restoration Council in June 1995.

159 The NMSP entered these peace talks as a member of the National Democratic United Front (NDUF), an organization allied with the Communist Party of Burma at the time.

160 Smith, *Burma: Insurgency and the Politics of Ethnicity*, p. 222.

161 The administration department comprises committees in spheres of foreign affairs, health, education, finance, economics, justice, and relief. Since the cease-fire in 1995 between the NMSP and the SLORC, the NMSP has opened a fourth department to undertake liaison with the Burmese government in the cities.

162 Personal communication with Central Committee members of the New Mon State Party, Thailand, 1995.

As with the other ethnic insurgencies in Burma, the NMSP/MNLA has controlled various areas of territory in the rural borderlands where Mon villages are concentrated. These areas have come under the direct administration of the NMSP, which has functioned as the *de facto* authority in these places, administering, taxing, and defending its areas. Those rural areas in which it has been active include portions of the various NMSP districts in the following townships: the "black areas" (or, in NMSP parlance, "basic areas") within Yebyu, Ye (southern Ye, an area spanning from the coast across to the Thai border), and Thanbyuzayat; and the "brown areas" (NMSP "guerrilla areas") of Mudon, Kya Inn Seik Kyi, western Kawkareik, and Bilugyun Island west of Moulmein. After September 1988, over one thousand students and activists fleeing the crackdown on the pro-democracy uprising arrived in NMSP-controlled areas to join the movement and undertake military training. Then, on February 12, 1990, the NMSP's headquarters on the Thai border, just to the north of Three Pagodas Pass, was overrun by the Burma Army. According to the cease-fire agreement reached between the NMSP and SLORC in June 1995, the NMSP retained control in twelve selected base areas, some of which were designated as temporary (this was true in Mergui district in the south). And, as indicated earlier and elaborated in later chapters, since 1992–93, the overall build-up in the deployment of *tatmadaw* troops in southeastern Burma has been remarkable.[163]

CONCLUSION

Historical insight into contemporary issues of ethnic conflict and civil war in Burma is essential to understanding the root causes of civilian displacement in the conflict areas of the country's peripheries. This chapter has reflected on the historical formation of the nation of Burma as it exists today, with particular reference to the politics of ethnicity and the modern state in the context of military rule since 1962. It has considered how the notion of ethnicity has shifted across the polities of the precolonial, colonial, and postcolonial periods, culminating in the turbulence of the immediate post-independence period and resulting in protracted civil war since that time.

Cultural difference has existed across historical epochs, but it was not subject to politicization in the classical polity as it has been in the era of the modern nation-state, when cultural difference is associated with the concept of ethnicity. In the precolonial period, the patron-client character of monarchical sovereignty generally permitted ethnic heterogeneity (without the need for political mobilization of ethnic identity). At the same time, the case of the Mons may be regarded as somewhat exceptional because their once historically autonomous culture and civilization were gradually suppressed and incorporated by powerful Burman monarchs intent on conquest and expansion of their kingdoms. Contemporary Mon ethnonationalism manifests a strong identification with, and political mobilization of, the historical memory of the Mon culture, homeland, and

---

[163] For instance, in 1995 there were fifteen battalions operating in the Ye to Tavoy area alone: LIBs 401-410 (MOC 8); IB 25 (based at Tavoy), LIB 273 (Tavoy/Kanbauk), LIB 343 (Ye), LIB 106 (Maw Kanin), and IB 61 (Ye). With three to four hundred troops per battalion, this amounts to some five thousand *tatmadaw* troops in this region. Personal communication with New Mon State Party (individuals' names confidential), Sangkhlaburi, Thailand, 1995.

former kingdoms, and their loss. I have provided an outline of the Mon ethnic rebellion as an historical background to the discussion of displacement in the next chapter, which is based on experiences in the Mon border areas.

Colonialism in Burma, as elsewhere in Southeast Asia, imposed on this region an administrative apparatus and boundaries modeled in accord with European political geography, and these laid the groundwork for communal and ethnic divisions following independence; this was the inheritance Burma received from Britain. In this inheritance, ethnic difference, manifested in majority-minority terms, was politically charged and mobilized. At independence, ethnopolitical and ideological conflict prevailed, and since that time, the state policies, particularly under military-dominated regimes since 1962, have attempted to restrain ethnic minorities' demands for autonomy by means of a strong, centralized military apparatus.

While colonial rule contributed to the politicization of ethnicity and the mobilization of ethnic allegiances in opposition to the state, five decades of civil war have thoroughly militarized ethnic claims and their suppression. Insurgency/counterinsurgency warfare has widened the gap between the antagonists, with the civilian population caught in the middle. On the one hand, the central government has consistently emphasized the unrelenting threat of "disintegration" posed to the state by the rebellions; on the other, leaders of ethnic forces have viewed the military regime as bent on their cultural and political destruction. Coercion and military conflict have only hardened the antagonism. Civil war has developed to such an extent that ethnonationalist struggles have come to emphasize not only political and cultural claims, but, more recently, human rights abuses suffered by civilian populations inhabiting areas of conflict.[164] Meanwhile, the regime in Rangoon continues to reiterate the military view of the problem, a view which aims politically to "consolidate" (or homogenize) the population. This view invests the *tatmadaw* with the historic responsibility—as the primary "defender" of the country's independent spirit—to protect and defend national unity and state sovereignty. The military regime established by the SLORC junta in 1988 (and perpetuated by its successor, the SPDC, after November 1997) has expressed its objectives as the pursuit of the "three main national causes": "non-disintegration of the Union," "non-disintegration of national unity," and the "perpetuation of sovereignty."[165]

In his epigraph at the beginning of this chapter, Edmund Leach notes that Burma is a "creation of the armed diplomacy and administrative convenience of late nineteenth-century British Imperialism." This legacy has persisted into the contemporary era, and many of the civil conflicts stemming from it remain unresolved. The following chapter moves on to examine the implications of protracted civil war for civilian populations, since in Burma it is civil war that provokes refugee migration.

---

[164] An explicit discourse of human rights in the ethnic struggles, however, is very recent. This point is explored in the next chapter.

[165] The three main national causes are widely publicized in daily newspapers, magazines, and billboards across the country. For example, see "Situation of Nation, Tatmadaw Clarified to Military Officers, Other Ranks," *The New Light of Myanmar*, February 20, 1998. The government's publication, *Destiny of the Nation*, describes these "three national causes" as "the basis of the Tatmadaw's concepts and beliefs." Nawrahta, *Destiny of the Nation*, p. 102.

The SLORC's "Three Main National Causes." Government signboard, Three
Pagodas Pass town, Burma, 1995. Photo: Hazel Lang

"Welcome into the Legal Fold, NMSP." Government signboard, at the town market
in Three Pagodas Pass, Burma, 1995. Photo: Hazel Lang

New Mon State Party/Mon National Liberation Army, Women's Army Unit. On parade, near Three Pagodas Pass, 1989. Photo: NMSP

New Mon State Party/Mon National Liberation Army. Celebration of the Forty-Eighth Mon Revolutionary Day, at their camp near Tavoy. Photo: NMSP

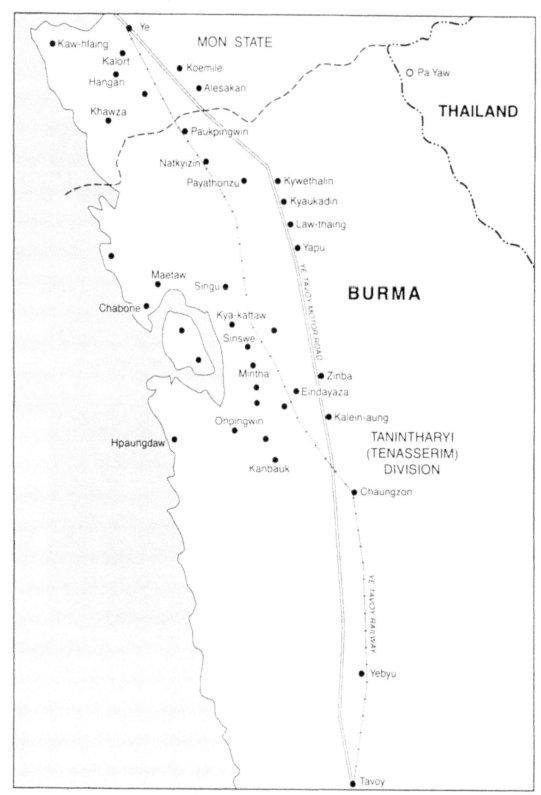

Map 3.1   Mon Region West of Pa Yaw

CHAPTER THREE

WAR AND CIVILIAN DISPLACEMENT

The tradition of the oppressed teaches us that the "state of emergency" in which we live is not the exception but the rule.

Walter Benjamin, 1968[1]

INTRODUCTION

Refugee migration needs to be considered in the context of the larger processes of politico-military conflict that produce it. In the contested borderlands of Burma, civil war has fundamentally involved entire civilian populations because insurgency and counterinsurgency have blurred the boundaries between combatants and noncombatants. In many ways the civilian population has become the "battlefield" of the conflict.

In global terms, throughout the twentieth century, the ratio of noncombatant civilian war victims to combatant victims has steadily increased, so that noncombatant casualties now typically outnumber combatant casualties. During World War I, over 90 percent of casualties were combatants; by World War II, over half the casualties were civilian, while today, over 90 percent of war-related deaths are civilian.[2] The target of war has shifted to civilians, with obvious consequences for dislocation and forced migration. Low-intensity guerrilla warfare is characterized by the overlap of combatant, noncombatant, and support system in a shared social and geographic space.[3] In this context, the boundary between combatant and noncombatant is blurred, and the civilian population becomes the military target of counterinsurgency campaigns. Civilians figure as collective, rather than individual, targets of a campaign to cut the rebel armies from their civilian base. In the process, they come under universal suspicion as "rebel sympathizers." In the Burmese borderlands, civilians inhabiting those areas where insurgent forces are active (the designated "black" and "brown" areas discussed in the previous chapter) are the targets. In this regard, the civil war has

---

[1] Walter Benjamin, "Theses on the Philosophy of History," in *Illuminations*, ed. Hannah Arendt, trans. Harry Zohn (New York: Schocken Books, 1968), p. 257.

[2] Mohammed Bedjaoui, *Modern Wars: The Humanitarian Challenge: A Report for the Independent Commission on International Humanitarian Issues* (London: Zed Books, 1986), p. 25. See also, David Turton, "Introduction: War and Ethnicity," in *War and Ethnicity: Global Connections and Local Violence*, ed. David Turton (San Marino: Center for Interdisciplinary Research on Social Stress and University of Rochester Press, 1997), p. 3; and Walter C. Clemens, Jr. and J. David Singer, "The Human Cost of War: Modern Warfare Kills More Civilians Than Soldiers," *Scientific American* 282,6 (June 2000): 56-57.

[3] Timothy P. Wickham-Crowley, "Terror and Guerilla Warfare in Latin America, 1956-1970," *Comparative Studies in Society and History* 32 (1990): 225.

generated substantial dislocation and displacement as fear and violence have come to destabilize everyday life and survival. Not only are civilians cast under universal suspicion, their very response—fear and flight from their villages—serves to further reinforce their status as suspects.

A study of the war, focused on civilian displacement, shows the ways in which insurgency and counterinsurgency have embroiled civilian populations and exposed them to danger, with consequences for forced displacement. This chapter contextualizes and addresses the conditions on the ground in order to gain a fuller understanding of the more immediate precipitating causes of displacement and subsequent cross-border movement. I will argue that civilians have not only had to suffer the immediate consequences of direct armed hostilities, but that they have been entrenched in a broader cycle of suspicion and fear and the consequences of militarized surveillance in their areas.

The perspectives of the refugees themselves and their stories of everyday life in their villages provide data that illuminate the causes of civilian displacement. In attending to refugees' stories, I subscribe to Michel de Certeau's notion that attention to the "practice of everyday life"[4] provides a valuable source and site for analysis. Much of the research in this chapter is based on extensive interviews conducted in 1995, in one locale along the Thai-Burmese border: the Mon refugee camp at Pa Yaw (literally "border"), some fifty kilometers southwest of Three Pagodas Pass and just inside Thailand's Kanchanaburi province. The camp itself was cleared from dense jungle in mountainous terrain; seven months of monsoon season each year isolate it from Thai towns and facilities. Pa Yaw was populated by Mon people who had fled their homes from the "black areas" of the contiguous rural border region of Burma, predominantly in Ye and Thanbyuzayat townships in Mon State, and Yebyu and Tavoy townships in Tenasserim Division. Smaller numbers of Karen and Tavoyan villagers, and others from farther afield, also resided at Pa Yaw.

The majority of the people had fled from their villages in areas which, at the time, were under the full—or in some cases diminishing—control of the NMSP (New Mon State Party); in the Tenasserim Division region, the NMSP often acted in league with other armed oppositions, including the Karen National Liberation Army and the smaller Tavoyan armed front, the Meik-Dawei United Front. In 1995, these townships and village tracts in Mon-populated, NMSP-controlled areas were located within the jurisdiction of the *tatmadaw*'s Southeastern Regional Command (Mon and Karen States, Tenasserim Division) with its Infantry Battalions (such as IB 61 based at Ye) and a growing number of mobile forces of Light Infantry Battalions (with LIBs 401-410, 343, and 106 active in the Ye to Tavoy region) assigned to the area.[5] The Mon region opposite Pa Yaw, which incorporated Ye and Yebyu townships, in particular, was one of the main black areas, or NMSP "base areas," targeted by the *tatmadaw* in the early 1990s; in some places these "black areas" reached from the coast to the border. Most of the

---

[4] Michel de Certeau, *The Practice of Everyday Life*, trans. Steven F. Rendall (Berkeley: University of California Press, 1984).

[5] In 1996, the new Coastal Regional Command was established, covering the geographic area of Tenasserim Division, headquartered at Mergui. Some twenty-eight local battalions in Tenasserim Division formerly under the Southeastern Regional Command were incorporated under the command of Major General Thira Thura Sit Maung. Robert Karniol, "Burma Creates Improved Regional C2 Structure," *Jane's Defence Weekly*, May 29, 1996, p. 12.

Women at Pa Yaw Refugee Camp, 1995. Photo: Hazel Lang

Pa Yaw Refugee Camp, 1995. Photo: Hazel Lang

villagers were farmers, while others were typically fisher-people, shopkeepers, and traders. The overwhelming majority had fled to Pa Yaw as a final resort, generally after several years of continuing their struggle for survival at home and/or living as internally displaced refugees in the jungles nearby. Most, too, were "waiting" in Pa Yaw for peace so that they could return to their areas. Villagers also maintained a steady flow of communication with their home regions, often using peripatetic fellow villagers, Mon soldiers, or the ox and cattle traders as information sources. (See Map 3.1)

INSURGENCY, COUNTERINSURGENCY, AND CIVILIANS AS TARGETS

Both insurgency and counterinsurgency blur the soldier/civilian distinction. Insurgency blurs it because guerrillas derive support from their civilian base as a necessary part of their struggle. Also, guerrilla struggle is posited as a form of "people's war," "authorized from below," which can unfortunately place the civilian population at risk or even "invite" the enemy to attack.[6] According to the guerrillas, a whole people is mobilized for war, and the enemy is "not at war with an army but with a nation," an assertion that raises crucial questions about the risks of war that result from "the intimacies of the struggle" to which people are exposed.[7] The guerrillas are eager to assert their alliance with the people, and counterinsurgents are eager to sever it, largely because counterinsurgents recognize that the civilian base is so crucial for the opposition guerrillas. Thus, counterinsurgents are inclined to assume that civilians in contested areas have allied themselves with the rebels. While it may be in the interests of the counterinsurgency forces generally to insist upon the soldier/civilian distinction so that guerrillas can be isolated from the civilian population[8] and their struggle delegitimized, in practice the distinction is dangerously blurred for civilians in the throes of war.

In practical military terms, guerrilla ("little war") warfare as practiced by the insurgents tends to rely on small-scale, mobile, ambush and retreat tactics. There is usually no clear distinction between frontline and rear areas. This means that the support of the civilian base is crucial for providing information and for other physical support. So in counterinsurgency, it is precisely this civilian support base that is targeted for pacification or destruction in order to defeat the armed opposition. The scholar Donald Snow compares typical insurgent and counterinsurgent strategies:

> . . . the government remains under siege as long as the insurgency exists as a military force. Whereas insurgents may eventually succeed by avoiding defeat and simply outlasting the will of the government to resist, counterinsurgents can only win by the *total* military defeat of the insurgents . . .[9]

---

[6] Michael Walzer, *Just and Unjust Wars: A Moral Argument with Historical Illustrations* (New York: Basic Books, 1977), pp. 179-180.

[7] Ibid., pp. 180, 186.

[8] Ibid., p. 186.

[9] Donald M. Snow, *Uncivil Wars: International Security and the New Internal Conflicts* (Boulder, CO: Lynne Rienner Publishers, 1996), p. 80 (emphasis added).

As described in the previous chapter, the *Pya Ley Pya* or "Four Cuts," counterinsurgency strategy in Burma was designed for this purpose—to suppress insurgency by cutting the insurgents off from their support system (food supplies, funding, intelligence, and recruits) linked to the civilian population. Rather than a campaign to "win hearts and minds," as with some other counterinsurgency wars, it has been enacted more simply to gain and maintain control over entire segments of a population. Counterinsurgency targets are not simply the "rebel" soldiers; the war is also deliberately aimed at civilian noncombatants perceived as the primary source of support for the rebels. In the process, civilian communities are harassed and punished for their perceived sympathies and support for the guerrilla movement. Some areas will be subject to depopulation, as the government attempts to cut out all possible suppliers of rebels. In other contested areas, the population itself will remain the target. Fear serves as a key tactic of control, and the ultimate aim is to undermine resistance and political will and thereby achieve "victory" not merely on the battlefield, but through the fear suffered by civilians who have become deliberate targets.[10]

Militarized surveillance and violence by government forces in guerrilla warfare settings is described as "low-intensity" conflict.[11] But, as Carolyn Nordstrom notes, this terminology obscures the "total war" character of this kind of violent conflict, because it fails to acknowledge the fact that in a so-called "low-intensity" conflict, civil and political society as a whole—rather than the competing military forces—constitutes the strategic target.[12] In writing about counterinsurgency in Mozambique and Sri Lanka, Nordstrom describes such warfare as "dirty war," for in such conflicts civilian noncombatants, in addition to the combatants, are deliberate targets for terror (as the generalized opponent).[13] In Burma, too, designated rural ethnic populations have been routinely regarded as collaborators with the ethnic political groups that oppose the government, and attempts to cut the links have brought about substantial dislocation. One local community member described this phenomenon in the following way:

> . . . the local people always run when the SLORC troops come. They have no faith or confidence in the Burmese army because their experiences have shown that whenever they come, their properties are looted, their houses burnt. . . sometimes there is killing—executions, extra-judicial executions. The Army arrests whomever they think is a supporter of the insurgency movement, and

---

10 Carolyn Nordstrom, "The Backyard Front," in *The Paths to Domination, Resistance, and Terror*, ed. Carolyn Nordstrom and JoAnn Martin (Berkeley: University of California Press, 1992), p. 261.

11 Low-intensity conflict refers to the intensity of armed conflict as measured by the low number of battle-related deaths. Stockholm International Peace Research Institute, *SIPRI Yearbook 1997* (Oxford: Oxford University Press, 1997), p. 19. See also, Loren B. Thompson, "Low-Intensity Conflict: An Overview," in *Low-Intensity Conflict: The Pattern of Warfare in the Modern World*, ed. Loren B. Thompson (Toronto: Lexington Books, 1989), pp. 2-6.

12 Carolyn Nordstrom, *Warzones: Cultures of Violence, Militarisation and Peace*, Working Paper No. 145 (Canberra: Peace Research Centre, Research School of Pacific and Asian Studies, Australian National University, 1994), p. 14.

13 Nordstrom, "The Backyard Front," pp. 261, 266. See also, Nordstrom, *Warzones: Cultures of Violence, Militarisation and Peace*.

they interrogate through torture to extract a confession. In the process the victim might die. In that way people have died. Innocent.[14]

Suspicion of, and the use of terror against, civilians is most intense in the "black areas." To recapitulate briefly, the tri-color map produced by the *tatmadaw* in the late-1960s for its Four Cuts strategy involved "white" areas (meaning these were entirely controlled by the government; examples would be urban and semi-urban areas where insurgency groups could not operate openly); "brown" areas (disputed by both sides, so that people live part-time under opposition and part-time under government forces' control); and "black" areas (effectively controlled and administered by the opposition, and therefore the most fiercely contested). Black areas were, and continue to be, designated as "free-fire" zones. Civilians living in these zones are collectively regarded as potential insurgents or sympathizers, and government troops are sanctioned to shoot anyone at will. Such areas may sometimes change with developments in the fortunes of competing sides in the war, but in those areas where insurgencies continue to be active (black and brown areas), civilian communities live under the shadow of ongoing suspicion and consequent danger.

Civilians Under Suspicion

In these circumstances, it becomes impossible for civilians to live as neutral bystanders: insurgency and counterinsurgency insure that during the course of their day-to-day lives, they are caught up in the war to varying degrees. While, of course, some villagers actively participate in assisting and even becoming guerrilla soldiers, others would simply prefer to get on with their daily lives and stay out of the conflict. In those areas where guerrillas are active and where the opposition has secured military control with a *de facto* administration, they have always relied on and obtained the support of the villagers, support which takes the form of new recruits, intelligence gathering, or moral and physical support. (Some guerrilla forces often coerce recruits and demand support, too.) In the course of any counterinsurgency campaign, however, the blurred status of the "uninvolved civilian and the possible collaborator"[15] affects the local communities as a whole, often bringing grave consequences to individuals who may or may not have been directly involved in supporting the guerrillas. Ordinary villagers are frequently caught for interrogation and torture although they are innocent, uninvolved people. Given that "rebel supporter" status is imposed on entire communities, it becomes impossible to sustain the distinction between "civilian" and "rebel" at all. A former village leader who fled to the Thai border illustrated this predicament when he described his capture by a group of government soldiers from the Light Infantry Battalion who were operating in his area as he cut bamboo on a farm near his village. Because he had remained on the farm rather than returning to his village each evening, he was accused of collaborating with the Mon guerrillas also

---

[14] Interview with Mon refugee, Sangkhlaburi, Thailand, August 24, 1995.

[15] Kay B. Warren, "Introduction: Revealing Conflicts Across Cultures and Disciplines," in *The Violence Within: Cultural and Political Opposition in Divided Nations*, ed. Kay Warren (Boulder, CO: Westview Press, 1993), p. 3.

operating in the area.[16] After questioning, his explanation was rejected, and he was taken away to be tortured at the local military base. He described his response to his predicament in the following way:

> As a village headman in a conflict area, I dared not refuse to meet with either the Burmese troops or the Mon guerrillas when they demanded me to. I had to relate to both sides and tried to stay neutral between the two warring parties, as it could be more dangerous for me otherwise . . . After my release, I fled from the village in fear of further abuses by the local Burmese military.[17]

Following active fighting between government and ethnic opposition forces, government soldiers tended to visit nearby villages in order to punish local inhabitants. The logic is that the rebel soldiers *must* have received support and assistance from these people. Village leaders may be forced to lead the way to suspect enemy soldiers, and if they are unwilling or unable to do so, they may be tortured. In the period subsequent to such armed skirmishes (which have taken place up to several times a month), infuriated troops take revenge on local villages with systematic "punishment," including the raiding and burning of villages. Sometimes money is also demanded as compensation for government troops killed in battle.

The steady stream of orders signed by military officers of the Burmese army serving in contested areas provide further illustrations of what happens to civilians under suspicion in such cases. For example, the widely issued "night curfew" order exemplifies how the military typically fails to distinguish between ordinary villager and suspected collaborator. The following is quoted from one such order issued to a Mon village in November 1994:

410th Light Infantry Battalion, Letter No. 100/1/head-3
To: Chairman, Village Law and Order Restoration Council—Village.
Subject: Issuance of order for the locality.
The Villagers living within this area must obey all the following orders.
(a)   They must not run away from the Tatmadaw troops. If they do they will be shot and arrested.
(b)   Those villagers who are found serving as messengers/informers for the insurgents will be subject to the severest punishment.
(c)   Villagers must not travel from one village to another at night.
(d)   Villagers who stay on their farm must not keep foodstuff for more than one meal. If any extra food is found it will be confiscated or destroyed.
(e)   Only one person is allowed to stay on each farm at night. If more than one person is found they will be regarded as insurgents and as such will be subject to legal actions by the Tatmadaw.

---

[16] It has been quite common for villagers deliberately to remain on their farms, remote from the village, due to fear of being captured and made to serve as porters in addition to fear of other abuses (including frequent army demands for taxes and fees). One farmer interviewed in Pa Yaw reported that, as the situation in his village deteriorated, people were increasingly forced to remain secretly on nearby farms. In his case this meant he had to allow the foliage to grow high and to eliminate his crowing roosters in order to conceal any signs of human activity. Interview, farmer, Pa Yaw, June 22, 1995.

[17] Interview, farmer, Pa Yaw, June 22, 1995.

. . . The village headman must inform in advance each member of their respective village community of all the details of this order and must ensure that all members of the village community obey this order.
Those who fail to obey will be punished forcefully.
Signed Commander, 410th Light Infantry Battalion.[18]

"Night curfew" orders are one form of militarized surveillance—and a "legal" basis for punishment if disobeyed—used to intimidate and discipline a civilian population suspected of links with the opposition. A further, more subtle, means of controlling the population at night is the command (frequently issued as a written order) that villagers use candles or flames, rather than battery-operated torches, to light their way. This serves not only to make people more visible, but it also exacerbates a person's vulnerability (particularly for women), since the candle or flame can be blown out at will by a soldier.[19] Other forms of more blatant terror, torture, and killings have also occurred, recounted graphically in the pages of numerous human rights documents.[20]

FEAR

In her studies of war in rural Guatemala, Linda Green describes fear as a "motor of oppression"[21] and an "invisible violence."[22] Every Mon refugee whom I interviewed on the border referred to fear in various manifestations. In the areas under suspicion and targeted for attack noted above, fear pervaded everyday life, producing a sense of constant threat. Fear is an "invisible violence" because it is used as a pervasive tool of militarized control. It is important in this regard briefly to highlight why and how fear functions as an important component of violence and the root causes of civilian displacement in Burma (as elsewhere). The answer to the question, "why study fear?," is offered in Elaine Scarry's eloquent study, *The Body in Pain*: " . . . while the central activity of war is injuring and the central goal of war is to out-injure the opponent, the fact of injuring tends to be absent from strategic and political descriptions of war."[23] A number of scholars reflect this concern that conventional descriptions of war fail to note a wide range of injuries,

---

[18] Obtained from the Mon National Relief Committee, Sangkhlaburi, Thailand. Other orders have explicitly stated: "if . . . we see any villagers . . . outside the village, we will shoot them on sight." Copies of orders, which have been collected at substantial risk to the local informants, are kept with local human rights documentation groups in Thailand.

[19] Interviews with refugees, Pa Yaw, May-June 1995.

[20] See reports prepared by several United Nations bodies, including the UN Commission on Human Rights and its Special Rapporteur on the situation in Myanmar (reports submitted since 1992); the General Assembly (since 1991); and the good offices of the Secretary-General (since 1993); as well as regular reports by international non-governmental organizations such as Human Rights Watch/Asia and Amnesty International; and the documentation repositories of various local human rights organizations, such as the Karen Human Rights Group, the Mon Information Service, the Karenni News Agency for Human Rights, and the Shan Foundation for Human Rights.

[21] Linda Green, "Fear as a Way of Life," *Cultural Anthropology* 9,2 (1994): 236.

[22] Linda Green, *The Routinization of Fear in Rural Guatemala*, Occasional Paper No. 2 (Saskatchewan: Department of History, University of Saskatchewan, 1995), p. 1.

[23] Elaine Scarry, *The Body in Pain: The Making and Unmaking of the World* (New York: Oxford University Press, 1985), p. 12.

both physical and mental, suffered by non-combatants. Green, for example, questions "the way in which human aggression has been traditionally approached from a distance, ignoring the harsh realities of people's lives."[24] Certain dilemmas face the researcher who studies fear, for that person must take care to research and write about it responsibly, such that further pain is not inflicted,[25] or that victims are not "infantilized."[26] The points I wish to make here are that fear has served to destabilize everyday life and livelihoods in communities under attack in any "internal" war and that the fear suffered by civilians functions as an effective component of counterinsurgency warfare itself.

Not only does fear reinforce a sense of constant threat and insecurity, it also increasingly blurs the distinction between civilian and rebel in the conflict, serving to perpetuate the cycle of running and suspicion in free-fire zones (where government forces are sanctioned to shoot indiscriminately those suspected of collaborating with or assisting the opposition). In other words, since the people almost always run away when the government troops come, the view that the villagers are potential insurgents and rebel supporters is reinforced *because* they run away. A local Mon observer described the process in this way:

> Because the villagers always run away when the Burmese army troops arrive, that is why the Burmese troops in turn think, confirm, that the villagers are rebel supporters—because they run away. It is a vicious circle.[27]

In this way, fear and one response to fear—running—serve to entrench civilians further within the destructive processes that typify insurgent warfare.

"Always running," an expression used by one Pa Yaw villager, becomes a regular part of life, bringing with it an additional high price. Flight leaves village properties open to looting, crops open to destruction before they can be harvested, and stragglers vulnerable to seizure and/or abuses. The way in which people flee their village may vary from situation to situation, but a pattern can be discerned in their stories. A general scenario might involve the following:

When a village hears news of the imminent arrival of government troops—on their way to collect porters to transport military supplies, for instance—village men would generally flee ahead of the others and hide in the jungle until the troops had departed again. Meanwhile, the women would often gather with neighbors and friends, ready to answer the soldiers' questions, such as "where are your husbands?"; "did you offer food to the [rebel] Mon soldiers?"; "we've heard you had Mon soldiers staying in your house with you, is that true?"; "you don't like us, do you?," and so forth.[28] In preparation for such occasions, individuals routinely kept a small bag or *longyi* (piece of traditional clothing) permanently packed along with emergency supplies such as rice, fish paste, etc., ready for escape. In the men's absence, and often because of their absence, women remain exposed to other forms of punishment by government troops. One method of "arranging" for the men's

---

[24] Green, "Fear as a Way of Life," p. 228.

[25] See Scarry, *The Body in Pain*, p. 13.

[26] Veena Das, "Anthropological Knowledge and Collective Violence," *Anthropology Today* 1,3 (1985): 238.

[27] Interviews, Sangkhlaburi, August 1995.

[28] Interviews, Pa Yaw, May-June 1995.

return, for instance, is to order the women to sit in the hot sun (in the company of armed guards) all day without protection, until someone capitulates and calls the men to return.[29] Women have also been exposed to more serious violence, including rape. Rape is cited as a common tactic of warfare. In addition to constituting a heinous individual act against individual women, rape is a "state-generated act of war"[30] that often serves as exemplary punishment to the entire community. Although it may not be an explicitly stated military policy, rape has been used as a mainstay terror tactic to punish a community more broadly for perceived sympathies with the insurgents and to demonstrate the soldiers' domination over a civilian community collectively.[31]

PATTERNS OF CIVILIAN DISPLACEMENT

We have identified the oppressive dynamic of fear and how the cycle of violence embedded in "low-intensity" warfare produces civilian dislocation. The immediate precipitating causes of displacement that have driven people from their homes arise out of this context, and typically involve direct fighting, the requisition of forced labor, coercive financial demands, and the forced relocation of villages. While, again, stories and data noted here are drawn from experiences in the Mon areas, they resonate with stories from other areas of conflict in Burma more generally, though many of the events will vary from locale to locale, village to village, and person to person. But overall, the forms of violence reportedly experienced in the Mon areas resemble, procedurally and thematically, forms of violence encountered elsewhere in the border areas.

The perspective here is drawn from the reported experiences of civilians under threat of attack by counterinsurgency forces, although this is not to claim innocence for the insurgency forces. As noted above, insurgents militarize civilian communities and expose them to the risks of war; and insurgents also commit crimes. A focus on state-generated terror and counterinsurgency strategies, therefore, does not automatically grant innocence to the non-state/insurgent opposition groups in the war. Insurgent groups, too, have committed atrocities.[32] However, these have mostly been confined to attacks on their combatant enemy opponents (or on traitors

---

[29] Ibid.

[30] Cynthia H. Enloe, *The Morning After: Sexual Politics at the End of the Cold War* (Berkeley: University of California Press, 1993), p. 60.

[31] Dorothy Q. Thomas and Regan E. Ralph, "Rape in War: Challenging the Tradition of Impunity," *SAIS Review: A Journal of International Affairs* 14,1 (1994): 86-87. See also Carolyn Nordstrom, *Rape: Politics and Theory in War and Peace*, Working Paper No. 146 (Canberra: Peace Research Centre, Research School of Pacific and Asian Studies, Australian National University, 1994); and Wickham-Crowley, "Terror and Guerrilla Warfare in Latin America," pp. 230-233 (examining the incidence of rape by government troops in the context of guerrilla warfare).

[32] There is currently very little open source information available on crimes committed by insurgent forces in Burma. However, some insurgent groups have a long history of selected acts of sabotage and terrorist attacks on crucial infrastructure and other installations. For example, the SLORC's official publication, based on a 1989 press conference by Brig.-Gen. Khin Nyunt, entitled *The Conspiracy of Treasonous Minions Within the Myanmar Naing-Ngan and Traitorous Cohorts Abroad* (Yangon: Guardian Press of the News and Periodicals Enterprise, Ministry of Information of the Government of the Union of Myanmar, 1989), is filled with documentation of just such acts (obviously published in order to discredit its opponents).

within their own ranks). Insurgents have not often terrorized the general civilian population—not least because they must rely on the civilians' moral and physical support. The characteristic overlap between guerrilla movements and their civilian support base clearly means that the civilian population as a whole is a crucial ally, rather than a target of terror, for the guerrillas. Timothy Wickham-Crowley's study of terror and guerrilla warfare in Latin America, for instance, concluded that terror used by government troops was "vastly greater" than that used by guerrillas, noting that some guerrillas have succeeded virtually without terror, and where guerrilla terror has been employed, it has been generally far more selective than government terror.[33] Similarly, civilian refugees from Burma demonstrated an overwhelming fear of the counterinsurgency forces that accused them of collaboration with the rebels. The reason for their terror is clear. As described above, counterinsurgents deliberately target civilian populations.

Civil wars, internationally, generate contending images of non-state and state parties, and each party, typically, feels itself to be justified in its actions and unfairly maligned by its critics. Bernard Nietschmann argues that "non-state" insurgent or "nation" (meaning ethnonationalist or indigenous) forces are often misrepresented in a state-centric bias as "rebels," "terrorists," and so forth, as a means of legitimating the state's action to "annex their identities" and "incorporate their lands and resources."[34] On the other hand, state forces have consistently noted that allegations of human rights abuses are exploited and exaggerated for use as a political tool by opposition groups. Nevertheless, the general observation in this sensitive area is that insurgent groups do not match the scale of operations, goals, or tactics that are typically mobilized and employed by government forces. A report in 1995 to the United Nations Human Rights Commission by the Special Rapporteur on Burma focused on this problem of perspective and possible bias:

> The Special Rapporteur is aware that sometimes reports of arbitrary killings tend to be exaggerated or distorted, that there are cases of good treatment of villagers and captured insurgents by the Tatmadaw soldiers, that there is evidence that the Government is trying to discipline those soldiers who have committed serious human rights violations . . . and that the insurgents also commit serious violations of human rights from time to time. However, the Special Rapporteur cannot deny, in view of so many detailed and seemingly reliable reports, that violations appear to be committed consistently and on a wide scale by the soldiers of the Myanmar Army against innocent villagers (particularly those belonging to the ethnic minorities) in the form of summary

---

[33] In addition, the guerrillas, unlike the army, established as a permanent presence in an area "will have the information necessary to sort out 'offenders' (informers and spies) from the 'faceless' peasantry." Wickham-Crowley, "Terror and Guerrilla Warfare in Latin America," pp. 216-217.

[34] Bernard Nietschmann, "The Third World War," *Cultural Survival Quarterly* (Special Edition on "Militarization and Indigenous Peoples") 11,3 (1987): 5; and Bernard Nietschmann, "The Fourth World: Nations Versus States," in *Reordering the World: Geopolitical Perspectives on the Twenty-first Century*, ed. George J. Demko and William B. Wood (Boulder, CO: Westview Press, 1994), pp. 225-242.

or extrajudicial executions and arbitrary killings which occur in the contexts of forced labor, rape, forced relocation and confiscation of property.[35]

In more recent times, it has been a strategy of armed opposition groups and their allies consciously to elicit support and sympathy for their cause internationally by reporting the atrocities of government forces, thereby invoking a specifically human rights agenda aimed at delegitimating a government's counterinsurgency program.[36] Indeed, those who wish to understand such conflicts must take care as they assess reports that may be "ideologically freighted and tendentious."[37] Hurst Hannum notes that human rights non-governmental organizations are reluctant to condemn or highlight "defensive" killings by "minority militants."[38] In addition, on occasion the sides are not clear-cut when roaming bandits or *dacoits* take advantage of the situation and create chaos in the villages for their own gain.[39] Keeping these cautions in mind, I consider some of the key elements of civilian displacement in the context of counterinsurgency warfare.

The Precipitating Causes

The four main (overlapping), precipitating causes of civilian displacement typically involve: (1) the raiding of villages, which includes the seizure of food, livestock, and other properties, interrogation, torture, and even killing of villagers; (2) the continuing imposition of coercive financial demands for various taxes and "fees," extortion, and ransom; (3) the requisition of forced portering for the military, as well as other forms of forced labor; and (4) the forced relocation of villages. Civil war has meant that most villagers have come to experience a combination of these factors as a part of daily life. Columns from *tatmadaw* battalions on duty in an area typically visit a village two or three times a month (if they have not already moved into an area and set up a local camp).[40] Once in the village, the troops simply pass through, or they stay. When they stay overnight, they either order the inhabitants to provide them with food, or they seize it from them. It is also not unusual for the soldiers to shoot at and kill livestock, such as chickens, pigs, and cows, in the village even if they do not intend to eat these animals, because they aim to eliminate potential food sources—including paddy stacks and granaries—for rebel troops suspected of operating in the

[35] United Nations Commission on Human Rights, *Report on the Situation of Human Rights in Myanmar, Prepared by the Special Rapporteur, Mr. Yozo Yokota*, UN doc. E/CN.4/1995/65, January 12, 1995, paragraph 102.

[36] Nigel Rodley, "Can Armed Opposition Groups Violate Human Rights?," in *Human Rights in the Twenty-first Century: A Global Challenge*, ed. Kathleen E. Mahoney and Paul Mahoney (Dortrecht: Martinus Nijhoff Publishers, 1992), p. 316.

[37] Wickham-Crowley, "Terror and Guerrilla Warfare in Latin America," p. 202.

[38] Hurst Hannum, *Autonomy, Sovereignty, and Self-determination: The Accommodation of Conflicting Rights* (Philadelphia: University of Pennsylvania Press, 1990), p. 12.

[39] Interviews, Pa Yaw, May-September 1995.

[40] Mon villagers noted that the populations in their villages of the outer rural areas were declining as more people moved either to the camps in Thailand and beyond or to stay with relatives and friends in "safer" villages and the larger towns in "white" areas.

area.[41] Clothes, valuables, and other possessions are often stolen from villages by the soldiers in the process. It is also customary for soldiers to take up residence for a couple of nights in the center of the village. In addition to "coming for a meal" and destroying potential food sources for the rebels, the Burmese army may raid and harass villagers in order to get information about the insurgents; such harassment frequently involves beatings, detention at the local camp, and sometimes more serious abuses. Villagers working at nearby farms are susceptible to more serious abuses because the farms are regarded as easily accessible to the guerrillas. This Mon refugee living at Pa Yaw tells of a common scenario involving periodic visits to a village by local *tatmadaw* soldiers:

> They [the soldiers] used to come two or three times a month. They'd steal chickens, steal pots, plates, knives, and other valuable things. What they saw they took. From me they took three sacks of rice. If they couldn't carry something, they'd throw it into a well. You couldn't stop them, you couldn't do anything.[42]

More serious violence by government troops involves torture and killings. Extrajudicial, summary, or arbitrary executions have been reported, usually associated with specific incidents of alleged collaboration with rebels. Villagers who live in close proximity to an insurgent ambush on government troops have been subject to "revenge" killings for such attacks. Further, the logic of running ahead of oncoming troops can also reach a deadly conclusion as troops open fire on fleeing villagers. Torture has been inflicted with the aim of punishing alleged rebel sympathizers in order to gain information on their activities. Elaine Scarry argues that torture is used as a convincing spectacle of power by the torturers as a means of control through "the conversion of real pain into the fiction of power," and that torture is often used because the reality of that power is so highly contestable.[43] The use of torture as a tool of war can backfire. It has been shown that persistent human rights violations on a widespread scale can have the opposite effect of the intended pacification of a population (a central aim of counterinsurgency), for it can serve to generate resistance and make people willing to fight.[44]

Although there are always going to be good individual soldiers, the general behavior of the counterinsurgency troops in the villages has been characteristically reckless. A local Mon human rights commentator has argued that it is indeed in the interests of the military authorities at the center to allow a large degree of recklessness in the field and the villages. That is, when the troops on the ground act with virtual impunity—without being restrained by sufficient disciplinary measures and without adopting procedures that enable civilians to

---

[41] Interview with family from Chaung Pyar village, Ye Pyu township, Pa Yaw, June 1995. The local *tatmadaw* soldiers were from the LIB 404 operating in the area.

[42] Interview, Pa Yaw, June 23, 1995. The village once comprised around 150 families, but became smaller (with some forty families) as increasing numbers had fled. The Burmese army's LIB 406 was operating in their area at the time.

[43] Scarry, *The Body in Pain*, p. 27.

[44] Carolyn Nordstrom, "Creativity and Chaos," in *Fieldwork Under Fire: Contemporary Studies of Violence and Survival* (Berkeley: University of California Press, 1995), pp. 142-148; Hazel Lang, "Women as Refugees: Perspectives from Burma," *Cultural Survival Quarterly* 19,1 (1995): 55.

have their grievances seriously addressed—recklessness itself is condoned (or even used as a "strategy") by the central authorities: "in that way the soldiers will stay in the army . . . they can do a lot."[45] Nigel Rodley points out that the less sophisticated the security force (in terms of training, material support, and motivation), the greater its propensity to commit grave human rights violations.[46]

The second major factor that has served to undermine the survival of local civilian communities has been the imposition of a steady stream of coercive financial demands in the form of fees and taxes. In the absence of government control in the black areas, the military, via its local battalions in the field, has been used to collect fees and taxes by force (however sporadically).[47] This has been occurring in the context of a generally erratic, underdeveloped, and impoverished economy. These taxes and fees have been levied for a number of purported uses, ranging from infrastructure development (taxes for roads, railways, and other projects); village quotas of paddy (at times also requested for army consumption by the local company or battalion commander); "porter fees" (paid to the *tatmadaw*, with the understanding that this money will enable the government troops to hire porters and make it unnecessary for them to draft the taxpayers themselves as frontline porters); other miscellaneous fees to local army camps in cash or provisions; and other fees, whose purposes are a mystery to the citizens themselves. Examples of written orders demanding such fees include:

> To: Village Head.../Subject: You must send us money for porter fees./ Regarding the above subject, send porter fees from your village to #338 Light Infantry, Column #2, on August 7, as soon as possible without fail. If you fail to do so for any reason, you will face the consequences./Column Commander, #338 Light Infantry, Column 2.[48]

> Come and pay the servants' fees to the Army column at Ko-Mile village not later than November 20 (without fail)./ Company Commander, No. 3 Company, 343 LIB.[49]

For villagers, the government's demands are burdensome not only because they are costly, but also because such taxes are levied in a coercive way, because associated demands for labor in lieu of payment often follow, and because a villager's refusal or inability to pay may well result in punishment. These financial demands generally compound other hardships suffered by villagers outlined above. Thus, in the Mon areas where large-scale offensives have not been waged since the early 1990s, people have cited the persistent harassment, abuses,

---

[45] Interview, Sangkhlaburi, August 1995.

[46] Rodley, "Can Armed Opposition Groups Violate Human Rights?," p. 297.

[47] Those villages in the black areas (NMSP base areas, in many parts of Ye and Yebyu townships, for instance) were, in the past, generally "protected" from the financial demands of the Burmese army. Those villages located in brown areas, however, were subject to taxes and fees from both sides.

[48] Order obtained from Karen area by the Karen Human Rights Group (KHRG), dated August 5, 1993. The KHRG, established in 1992, is a small, independent field-based organization that collects raw data documenting human rights violations in opposition-held areas of Burma.

[49] Order obtained from Mon area by the KHRG, dated November 10, 1994. Ko-mile is the "nine mile" work site along the Ye-Tavoy railroad, Ye township, Mon State.

and threats to their livelihoods—rather than active combat alone—as major reasons for displacement and flight to the border camps. It is the militarized setting in which these demands occur that has fundamentally destabilized villagers' livelihoods. The problem is expressed in this vignette, told by a farmer from a village in Yebyu township:

> We want to work as we wish; live in peace, eat in peace . . . and we don't want to starve, to suffer. We work so hard to survive; yet whatever we earn is taken away from us.
>
> We tie up our pig at our house and then it is taken away and eaten up . . . then when you complain and ask for money for it, they send you to the village head and then the village head has to collect the money for it from the villages to pay him, and we [as the owners] have to also pay. So it becomes a continuous cycle. In the end, the responsibility comes back to you; [that is], you have to pay for your own pig. [he laughs][50]

After prolonged periods of struggle, many of the poorer, landless villagers are compelled to flee when the financial obligations—combined with fear, repeated demands for forced labor, and other abuses—undermine their ability physically to survive at home.

The third key precipitating cause of displacement is the military's practice of forcing villagers to act as unpaid porters or laborers for its own benefit. These practices are widespread and routine, exacting a heavy toll on life and survival throughout almost all of the border region. One can hear many stories of such abuses in the Thailand-based refugee camps. Very few villagers living in the contested areas—particularly among the poorest—avoid conscription as porters or as corveé laborers for the army. Not only do civilians suffer the immediate perils of conscription (abuse, disease, etc.), but when conscripted, they are prevented from working for their livelihoods on their farms and fields at home.

The Burmese army and the insurgent groups both use porters in the border areas. The general practice of the opposition groups resembles the colonial British practice of requiring Burmese villagers to help transport supplies from one village to the next. Both insurgent and counterinsurgent groups conscript people, and villagers have been burdened by many years of such demands. However, refugees fleeing the Mon areas report that they have suffered most from the systematic, large-scale demands of the counterinsurgency forces. This makes sense given the divergent logistical demands of government and guerrilla opponents and the nature of the latter's civilian base. While guerrilla forces live among the local people, the *tatmadaw* troops do not; and it is the *tatmadaw*, with its logistical problems, that requires large numbers of porters to move around. The discussion here is therefore centered on the practices of the counterinsurgency forces.

There are several "types" of forced porters used by the Burmese army. These include "operations" porters (usually used in large numbers for military operations and large-scale offensives), "permanent" porters (written orders are issued for people to go to local military bases), "emergency" porters (for short-term tasks),

---

[50] Interview, Pa Yaw, August 28, 1995.

and "porters of opportunity" (people simply seized at random by patrolling troops).[51]

Villagers are routinely used as frontline porters of supplies and ammunitions for the *tatmadaw*. They often endure harsh physical conditions and exhaustion as a result of long days of trekking over rugged terrain (inaccessible to vehicles) bearing heavy loads (an average of thirty kilograms for men, and twenty for women, when they are used). Porters receive little water, food, medicine, or opportunity for rest, and they are subject to the whims of armed "supervision." The porter's saying goes: "If you can't walk, you die. You walk, you live." Many a porter has witnessed or heard about the mistreatment or death of a fellow porter.[52] Many a porter has told of occasions when a weak or sick companion has been left behind to die, cast down a mountain side, or shot.[53] In addition to physical struggle across harsh terrain, porters are also subject to more blatant abuses at the hands of the soldiers for whom they carry.

As mentioned above, the physical dangers involved in portering are accompanied by wider threats to a villager's livelihood, and hence, survival, for portering disrupts daily household labor, such as the harvesting of crops, earning a living, and so on, thus compounding the cycle of insecurity. Further, the very fear of seizure for portering fuels the pattern of running, dislocation, and impoverishment. Conscription of porters has thus been a key factor entrenching the cycle of civilian displacement. Communities become impoverished as able-bodied people are either seized for portering, forced to pay high fees (ostensibly in lieu of physical service), or prompted by fear to run and hide ahead of troops en route to collect them. Some do avoid the physical hazards of portering through the regular payment of porter fees, but this often leads to impoverishment. Those unable to pay themselves free of portering duty often flee the village.[54] In some instances, as recounted in this man's story, people are confronted with overlapping demands for money and labor:

> The people in Paukpingwin village [Ye Pyu township] were normally required to pay two hundred *kyats* per household per month to the local Burmese military—the 406th LIB—as a regular portering charge. Besides this . . . the village was required to contribute six, seven . . . or sometimes up to fifteen men weekly as portering labor for the local Burmese troops on their regular patrols in the area. Any household which could not contribute its own labor when so required by the authorities must hire a substitute for it at . . . three thousand *kyats*. Despite its regular collection of all these portering taxes and labor from the village, the local Burmese military still sometimes seized people in the village at random and extorted money from the captured villagers. Before I left the village, about ten men in Paukpingwin had been seized at random like this by the local 406th battalion and then had to pay five hundred *kyats* each to the local military authorities for their respective releases.[55]

---

[51] Karen Human Rights Group, "Summary of Types of Forced Portering," KHRG No. 95-13, April 11, 1995.

[52] Interviews, Pa Yaw, May-September, 1995.

[53] Ibid.

[54] Ibid.

[55] Committee for the Promotion of People's Struggle in Monland, "Regular Use of Forced Labour/Porterage," unpublished field report, Sangkhlaburi, August 15, 1995.

In addition to being conscripted for military portering, villagers have been widely commandeered to perform other forms of forced labor. These range from overtly military-related work, such as guarding roads and bridges, the construction of local military camps, and service in those same camps, to construction or repair work on large-scale infrastructure development projects, such as roads, bridges, and railways, and small-scale commercial projects for the army, which often involved agricultural work. Villages receive a steady flow of written orders for "free labor," "voluntary labor," "government servants," and so forth, accompanied by the regular warning that "if you fail, it will be your responsibility" (with variations in expression). Forced labor imposes hardships on people both due to conditions at the work sites—where workers are required to spend long hours, bring their own food and tools, endure beatings for "laziness," and sometimes suffer even more serious abuses—and due to the deprivation they suffer when frequent and arbitrary demands for their labor make it impossible for them to continue working to support themselves. Work sites have also been used for the recruitment of porters of opportunity. Villagers report that sometimes people were arbitrarily "arrested" and taken to work as porters for the military directly from the work site.[56]

While forced or corveé labor is a widespread practice in Burma,[57] the Burmese authorities have consistently denied the use of forced labor, arguing that there is a long tradition in Burmese and Buddhist culture of "donating labor" for the benefit of the community. The official view on the matter often conflates the substantive issue of "donating labor" with historical and religious traditions in Burma:

> Voluntary service in the interest of the community is a deep-rooted and ancient Myanmar tradition. It is based on our view that man cannot exist in splendid isolation . . . and that to succeed in life, a human being must strike a balance between what is good for self and what is good for all . . . Since the beginning of their history, the Myanmar people have demonstrated this strong community spirit and service. We willingly give of wealth, time, and labor for the welfare of the people in [the] community.[58]

The tradition of voluntary labor was practiced as part of the social, political, and economic system in early monarchical Burma,[59] and the need for it continues in the contemporary setting today. In the context of the military state today, however, the tradition of "voluntary labor" has been manipulated on a large scale. Demands for labor are essentially coercive, abuses occur at work sites, and livelihoods are often severely disrupted due to frequency of demands. The most blatant abuses occur with forced recruitment for frontline portering, but the

---

[56] Interviews, Pa Yaw, June 1995.

[57] See UN General Assembly, *Human Rights Question: Human Rights Situations and Reports of Special Rapporteurs and Representatives. Situation of Human Rights in Myanmar. Note by Secretary General*, Fifty-second session, UN doc. A/52/484, October 16, 1997, paragraphs 50-68.

[58] *Myanmar Perspectives* 3,12 (December 1997). Accessed online at www.myanmar.com/gov.perspec/12-97/tra12-97.html [April 2, 1998].

[59] See Ko Ko Maung, "Benchmarks and Forced Labour," *Thai-Yunnan Project Newsletter* 29 (June 1995): 5.

widespread coercive requisition and use of "voluntary labor" on infrastructure and other development projects is also destabilizing.

A typical order for forced labor may read as the following, although orders vary in their content according to local circumstances. In the black areas, orders are frequently issued directly by the frontline battalion operating in the area:

Frontline #406 LIB/ Column 1 HQ/ To: Chairman/Secretary [of village]./ For railway construction, we have to have a discussion with the chairman and secretary. Therefore, come yourselves to Nat Gyi Zin camp. We give you your chance to come on 15-11-94 without fail . . . If you really work on behalf of the village people, you must come without fail. If you fail, it will be your responsibility./ If you don't come because you are afraid of Mon rebels, we Army must show you that we are worse than Mon rebels. That's all./ [signed for Column Commander, Nat Gyi Zin camp.][60]

The largest infrastructure project using forced labor in southeastern Burma has been the 110-mile (177-kilometer) Ye-Tavoy railway, running parallel to the Andaman Sea from Mon State's southernmost town of Ye to Tavoy in the capital of Tenasserim Division. Construction began in October 1993, and the project was divided into four parts: the section from Tavoy to Yebyu, from Yebyu to Kalein Aung, from Kalein Aung to Nat Gyi Zin, and from Nat Gyi Zin to Ye.[61] It is estimated that during the 1993–94 dry season alone, between 120,000 and 150,000 people were conscripted to work on the railway,[62] "supervised" by the Burmese army's LIB numbers 343, 407, 408, 409, 410, and IB number 61. Each family in the region was required to work on the construction (and subsequently the repair) of the railway, performing work ranging from clearing foliage to preparing and leveling the ground to crushing stone to cutting and laying sleepers and rails. Tens of thousands of local villagers were affected during the period 1993–98, though construction was officially completed in early 1998 and, beginning in 1996, the government began a new system of employing the local military in construction work for this particular project.[63] The majority of men, women, and sometimes

---

[60] This order is dated November 9, 1994. Original collected and translated by the Karen Human Rights Group, May 2, 1995. This particular order was issued for the construction of the Ye-Tavoy railway, which commenced in October 1993. In the black areas, "presents" (in the form of bullets) are known to have been enclosed along with such orders (as a threat in the event of non-compliance).

[61] According to local sources, conscripted labor was organized through seven "control centres"—Paupingwin, Kibun, Nat Zyi Zin, Paya Thone Su, Yapu, Kyanor, and Zimba. Committee for the Promotion of People's Struggle in Monland, "Ye-Tavoy Railway Construction," Bangkok: n.p., April 1994.

[62] Local labor was conscripted from seven townships in Mon State and Tenasserim Division: Ye, Thanbyuzayat, and Mudon in Mon state, and Yebyu, Tavoy, Launglon, and Thayet Chaung in Tenesserim Division. Committee for the Promotion of People's Struggle in Monland, *Newsletter* 2,3 (October 1994).

[63] Since 1996, Burmese authorities have changed their recruitment system to involve explicitly its "Tatamadawmen," probably as a means to enhance the government's image in light of growing international condemnation of its use of forced labor and to align more closely the *tatmadaw* with the development of the country. A March 1998 article in the *New Light of Myanmar* makes much of this latter image, which refers to the Ye-Tavoy (Dawei) railway as "built with the strength of the Tatmadawmen." *New Light of Myanmar*, March 29, 1998, p. 1.

children staying in the Mon refugee camps in Thailand were affected by forced labor in their areas (many of these people also worked on the Ye-Tavoy railway). Some were subjected to physical abuses at work sites, while others were deprived of their livelihoods due to frequent conscription and/or associated financial payments demanded in lieu of labor. The impact of forced labor was also exacerbated by growing militarization in these areas. The growing presence of the Burmese army along the railway route, for instance, had implications for military control over the area more generally; that is, infrastructural development served as a means for the *tatmadaw* to augment control and "secure" the area.

The fourth precipitating cause of displacement has been the relocation of villages. By relocating village populations into areas they control, the Burmese Army aims to sever links between insurgency forces and their support bases. Relocation also provides a "free labor" pool for infrastructure construction and military portering. Relocation has been a key tactic of the Four Cuts strategy, affecting a large number of communities in Burma, both in government-controlled areas and contested areas. Populations living in the contested areas where the government is gaining control typically receive written orders to vacate an area by the local LIB or IB and are threatened with punishment for failure to comply. Forced relocation produces multiple hardships, including abuses associated with the order to move, as well as economic deprivation due to loss of land, agricultural production, and food stocks, which are largely destroyed. The accompanying military surveillance and the general dislocation often convinces villagers to flee the area. If villagers do not comply with the government's demands that they relocate, they are likely to experience intimidating visits by troops, the burning of their houses, and exemplary punishment of selected persons in the village.[64] Forced relocation has produced substantial internal displacement as people flee to nearby jungle areas, "safe" villages closer to the towns, or across the border.

INTERNAL DISPLACEMENT

Forced relocation and other forms of military harassment have brought about substantial dislocation, much of which results in internal displacement as people are compelled to flee quietly, in small groups of a few families and/or individuals. While in Burma internal displacement has been widespread—estimated at between half a million to one million persons[65]—the internal movement from conflict areas has not been characterized by visible, large-scale migrations. As a report by the UN Commission on Human Rights has noted: "people

---

[64] Interviews with Mon refugees, Sangkhlaburi, August 1995.

[65] This figure of one million relates to the problem of internal displacement and forced relocation, and no independently verified statistics are available. United Nations Commission on Human Rights, *Internally Displaced Persons: Report of the Representative of the Secretary-General, Mr. Francis M. Deng, Submitted Pursuant to Commission on Human Rights Resolutions 1993/95 and 1994/68, (Further Promotion and Encouragement of Human Rights and Fundamental Freedoms, Including the Question of the Programme and Methods of Work of the Commission: Human Rights, Mass Exoduses and Displaced Persons: Internally Displaced Persons)*, UN doc. E/CN.4/1995/50, February 2, 1995, paragraph 85 (Myanmar).

. . . flee in absolute silence, not wishing in most instances to be identified as displaced, in order to avoid persecution and fearing execution."[66]

From the perspective of international agencies dedicated to protect refugees, the internally displaced are at a substantial disadvantage because they remain within the borders of their own country. In international law and politics, state sovereignty means that the primary responsibility for protection and assistance to internally displaced persons rests with the territorial state and its national protective mechanisms. Yet, as noted by Francis M. Deng—the Special Representative assigned to the problem of internal displacement, appointed by the UN Secretary-General in 1992—it is precisely in the setting of internal wars, when the civilian population is likely to be intermittently governed by contesting state and non-state forces, that responsibility for protection is undermined.[67] In view of this and the lack of a formal, effective international framework of responsibility for their protection, Internally Displaced Person(s) (IDPs) can be largely invisible to an international audience.

Due to the character of internal displacement, IDPs remain in adverse conditions, close to the perils that uprooted them from their homes. They remain vulnerable to attack, outside the physical shelter and assistance of the cross-border camps, and what's more, the victim population may be perceived by the national authorities "not as citizens meriting protection and assistance, but as part of the enemy, if not the enemy."[68]

In Burma, insecurity caused by the civil war has often left a common mark, as villages are reduced to a skeleton population with only the financially able and elderly remaining. As the prospects for survival have worsened, increasing numbers of people have fled to the border camps in Thailand and beyond. But, as suggested above, cross-border refuge has usually been the last resort, and cross-border migration is only the "tip of the iceberg," as this story illustrates:

> I arrived here [the refugee camp] in the middle of April. We couldn't stay in our village anymore . . . So we hid in the jungle, and then I couldn't do my work . . . If I worked all day I could only get food for one day, and I have a big family. I couldn't stay with them because I always had to run. I slept in the jungle for four months . . . I couldn't pay, and I couldn't run from the soldiers, so I couldn't stay in my village. I brought my whole family with me. I've never been here before, I'd only heard about this place.[69]

---

[66] United Nations Commission on Human Rights, *Situation of Human Rights in Myanmar*, Fifty-third session, UN doc. E/CN.4/1997/64, February 6, 1997, p. 11.

[67] Francis M. Deng, "Internally Displaced Persons," *International Journal of Refugee Law* 6,2 (1994): 293. The appointment of the Representative of the Secretary-General on Internally Displaced Persons (IDPs) was made in July 1992, at the request of the Commission on Human Rights to address the international political and legal aspects of the internally displaced (including the compilation of legal norms and a working definition to protect IDPs). See, for instance, United Nations Commission on Human Rights, *Internally Displaced Persons, Report of the Representative of the Secretary-General, Mr. Francis Deng, Submitted Pursuant to Commission on Human Rights Resolution 1995-57*, Fifty-first session, UN doc. E/CN.4/1996/Add.2.

[68] Francis M. Deng, "Internal Displacement: A Global Overview," paper presented to the Workshop on Internal Displacement in Asia, Bangkok, February 22-24, 2000, p. 4

[69] Karen Human Rights Group, "Ye-Tavoy Railway Area: An Update," KHRG Report No. 95-26, July 31, 1995.

AFTER THE CEASE-FIRE

The NMSP-SLORC cease-fire agreement reached in June 1995 was a small step toward the alleviation of the precipitating causes of civilian displacement. As discussed in the next chapter, the cease-fire is a necessary (but in itself insufficient) component of progress in the resolution of the civil war. For those who flee, it has meant respite from the more blatant fears and dangers associated with direct armed hostilities. In other words, more extreme abuses and atrocities against civilians have come to an end with the cease-fire. The civilian population is no longer the collective "battleground" of competing militaries and the target of counterinsurgency *per se*, as before.[70] The old practice of raiding villages on a periodic basis has ended, and the previous dramatic, chaotic pattern of fear and flight has also ceased, resulting in a "calmer" post-cease-fire situation. In other words, the villagers no longer suffer from the Army's assumption that they must be rebel sympathizers or collaborators. On the other hand, other precipitating factors of civilian displacement continue, notwithstanding the end of active combat in the Mon cease-fire areas. As the Burmese army moves further into previously rebel-held areas, establishing camps in various villages in order to consolidate a permanent presence and control in the border areas more generally, the growing presence of *tatmadaw* troops allows for a more pervasive and direct means of control, and further opportunities to exploit the labor and demand the "services" of the local population. In those areas where the Burmese army is present (and especially where it has not achieved full control), the recruitment of forced labor continues as a means to consolidate military surveillance. Hence, other precipitating causes of displacement identified in this chapter—including the numerous financial demands, forced labor, and portering—continue to varying degrees even in cease-fire areas.[71]

In the post-cease-fire period, therefore, government troops are able to reach populations in some of the former NMSP-controlled areas (with the exception of specified zones within the terms of the cease-fire) where battalions have set up camps to consolidate their control. An order issued by the 61st IB in August 1995, for instance, illustrates this access:

(1) Though the New Mon State Party has entered into a cease-fire agreement with the Government, our 61st Battalion still has to undertake the responsibility of regular patrol in the south and the north of Ye so that we can ensure our full control of the area./ (2) Moreover, our Battalion has to keep its troops fully organized to prevent the Karen [KNU, Karen National Union] insurgents' infiltration into the area . . . [72]

---

[70] Civilian populations, however, continue to remain under implied suspicion in areas where non-cease-fire groups are active (in particular those villages accessible to the KNU).

[71] Interviews, Sangkhlaburi, March 1998. This point is taken up in Chapter Five in an assessment of the cease-fire *vis-à-vis* the repatriation of the Mon refugees in 1996.

[72] This order was given to the local village Law and Order Restoration Councils (LORCs) in the villages of Ye Township, Mon State, August 1, 1995. Obtained and translated by the Mon Information Service, Bangkok, July 1997.

Therefore, the Burmese Army continues to levy fees and conscript villagers for labor,[73] and people continue to suffer impoverishment and dislocation. The poorer inhabitants from the outer rural areas (where the opposition was previously most active) continue to live in hiding from such demands, while others move between "two homes," one on their farm and the other in one of the border refugee settlements under NMSP jurisdiction.[74] Further, these populations are not excluded from continued front-line portering demands. During the *tatmadaw*'s 1997 dry season offensives against the KNU, for example, an estimated total of thirty thousand civilian porters were conscripted from areas mainly in Tenasserim Division, Mon and Karen States.[75] Financial demands were also imposed on many of these civilians in lieu of physical service. In these circumstances, the poorest people suffer especially, and only those with sufficient resources are able to survive.

HUMAN INSECURITY

In conclusion, both insurgency and counterinsurgency movements have implicated entire populations in the civil war. The cycle of insecurity was embedded in the nature and consequences of "low-intensity" warfare. In the context of insurgency, because civilians served as the crucial support base of guerrilla warfare, they became identified with the rebellions. In this regard, the overlap of combatant, noncombatant and support system was fraught with danger for civilians. Civilians became the deliberate targets of counterinsurgents' military campaigns for this reason. Typically, in this kind of warfare, the state forces deliberately target the civilian population because they define these civilians as potential collaborators or sympathizers. In counterinsurgency, where differentiation between combatant and noncombatant is so often blurred, the civilian villager will often suffer grave consequences, regardless of whether he or she has been actively allied with the insurgents. In such wars, villagers are collectively cast under a shadow of permanent suspicion by the military.

There are two major points to highlight from the study of war and civilian displacement in the Mon border areas of Burma. The first is that the cycle of fear and running has generated its own consequences for civilian displacement: that is, in the areas studied, the very act of running in fear served to reinforce the suspicions of the counterinsurgency troops from whom the civilians were fleeing.

Second, in the war-zones of the Burmese borderlands, it is not only direct armed hostilities that have led to insecurity and displacement. Civilians have at times been caught in the cross-fire, but they have also been routinely displaced by the ongoing process of militarized surveillance and control occurring in their areas.

---

[73] In 1997, the United Nations General Assembly noted this phenomenon: "It has been reported that the Myanmar army has substantially increased its permanent porters in the border regions. This in turn has led to an increase in non-front-line forced labor for the military, such as non-front-line portering and courier duties; building, maintaining and guarding military roads and bridges; sweeping roads for mines, and building and servicing military camps and farms." United Nations General Assembly, *Situation of Human Rights in Myanmar. Note by Secretary-General*, Fifty-second session, UN doc. A/52/484, October 16, 1997, paragraph 59.

[74] Interviews, Mon National Relief Committee, Sangkhlaburi, March 1998.

[75] Ibid. See also United Nations General Assembly, *Situation of Human Rights in Myanmar*, paragraph 57.

Sometimes a village has become a battleground, at other times a pool for the coercive recruitment of porters and laborers, as well as a setting for financial exploitation. The pattern of displacement, whether associated with direct hostilities or other factors discussed above (and it is often both), has undermined the security of everyday life, resulting in impoverishment and the destabilization of civilian livelihoods. Many have been displaced by the intersecting factors of fear and impoverishment. Further, although the gradual emasculation of the opposition insurgency and the concomitant gains of the Burmese army have resulted in a "calmer" situation (because active combat has decreased), this has not alleviated the key underlying sources of fear and impoverishment that produce civilian displacement. A large proportion of dislocation has resulted in internal displacement that is small-scale, largely invisible, and located close to the perils creating it. However, over time, steady streams of people from the eastern borderlands of Burma have journeyed to the Thai border and beyond. It was estimated in mid-1993, for instance, that in the Mon areas alone between two hundred and three hundred men, women, and children a day were crossing the border into Thailand: a regular flow of forced migration.[76] As one villager put it: "We are like ants, traveling away from our trouble to a safe place. We left everything behind to be safe."[77] The following chapters explore the politics and fortunes of refugee sanctuary in Thailand.

---

[76] Committee for the Promotion of People's Struggle in Monland, *Newsletter*, August 1993.

[77] Interview, Pa Yaw, June 1995.

CHAPTER FOUR

SANCTUARY IN THAILAND

INTRODUCTION

The previous chapter has shown the way in which patterns of civilian displacement are affected by the distinctive characteristics of a conflict effectively fought out between the combatants on a "battlefield" constituted of civilian populations. As war has encroached further into the midst of civilian life in more of the border areas, people have lived closer to the edge of survival, and with survival increasingly precarious within Burma, growing numbers of people have fled across the border into Thailand as a last resort. Because there is a long and porous border between the two countries, Thailand has provided ample opportunity for sanctuary. Adding to the large flows of displaced persons who have fled into Thailand from the Indochinese states since 1975, the asylum seekers from Burma's eastern minority borderland regions became new kinds refugees in an ever-fluid Thai landscape.

These next three chapters now turn to an analysis of the nature, policies, and politics of sanctuary in Thailand. This chapter provides an overview of Thailand's evolving response to the displaced persons encamped along its Burmese border, a response that was initiated on a "semi-permanent" basis with the establishment of Karen camps in 1984 (and, subsequently, Karenni and Mon camps in 1989 and 1990). It views Thailand's politics and policy repertoire in the broader context of its long and remarkable history as a refugee host. An account of the Thai response to the first organized camps along the border in 1984 is provided, followed by a review of the burden Thailand sustained as a result of protracted, Cold War-infused Indochinese refugee migrations; these refugees preoccupied Thailand in the mid-1980s. The framework of refugee protection in Thai law and policy is also outlined, and I discuss the key institutional players at the policy and ground levels, hoping to map the constellation of refugee policy and practice in Thailand.

A formal apparatus of refugee recognition *per se* has been absent in Thailand. It is not a signatory to the 1951 UN Convention on Refugees or its companion 1967 Protocol, and asylum-seekers are technically designated as "illegal immigrants" under national law. So how have the refugees fared in this situation? By definition, refugees not only lack the legal protection that ought to be provided by their country of origin, but also suffer the vulnerability that results because they are perceived as "uprooted" in their host country and are often pressured to return home. International refugee law was formulated to remedy this "gap" in protection through intervention. Yet, as noted in the introduction to this book, the 1951 UN Convention-based protection system—the central instrument of international refugee law—defines formal refugee status in a manner that ignores the larger realities of protection needs today. As James C. Hathaway remarks, "international refugee law as traditionally conceived and implemented can simply no longer be counted on to meet the needs of the world's refugees."[1] As a result of the law's inadequacy, it has become increasingly necessary for nations to adhere, voluntarily, to basic, minimum standards of international protection. The normative framework of refugee protection as it functions today is underpinned by the principle of non-*refoulement*—the principle that persons will not be forcibly returned to their country of origin where they are at risk or in danger, both at the border and within the territory of the receiving state.[2] Because the scope of the 1951-protection system is so narrow and inadequate, the principle of non-*refoulement*—together with the willingness of states to be more or less flexible concerning asylum-seekers in practice—comprises the key element of refugee protection today. Thailand has been a haven to over one million asylum-seekers since 1975 and has demonstrated such flexibility in practice. But how has the formal position of asylum-seekers as "unrecognized refugees"[3] affected the status of refugees in Thailand? What else has been going on in the story of refugee sanctuary in Thailand?

THE BURMESE BORDER REFUGEE CAMPS IN 1984

Until 1984, identifiable long-term refugee camps were absent on the Thai-Burmese border. Before the first semi-permanent cross-border camps were established in Tak province by the Karens in 1984, the porous Thai borderland was always a temporary home to small flows of people periodically displaced by seasonal fighting, people who typically returned to their villages when the situation allowed.[4] While some settled in Thailand in search of work or a better and more peaceful life—under Thai legislation those displaced persons who

---

[1] James Hathaway, "Preface," in *Reconceiving International Refugee Law*, ed. James Hathaway (The Hague: Martinus Nijhoff Publishers, 1997), p. xxix.

[2] The principle of non-*refoulement* is contained in Article 33 of the 1951 UN Convention on Refugees. It has attained status as customary international law, binding on even those states that have not ratified the 1951 Convention/1967 Protocol. In principle, it applies to a broad class of refugees and asylum-seekers, irrespective of their statutory status as refugees. See Guy S. Goodwin-Gill, "Asylum: The Law and Politics of Change," *International Journal of Refugee Law* 7,1 (1995): 6-7.

[3] This term is borrowed from Aristide R. Zolberg, Astri Suhrke, and Sergio Aguayo, *Escape from Violence: Conflict and the Refugee Crisis in the Developing World* (New York: Oxford University Press, 1989), p. 30.

[4] For instance, in 1975, a population of an estimated eight thousand Karen crossed the Salween River into Thailand at a point known as Pa Daeng, receiving emergency assistance from church organizations arranged by the Karen National Union. But over the following two to three years, many of the people returned to the Burma side of the border (with some remaining in the immediate borderland area). The Karen relief operation was formalized in 1980 with the establishment of the Karen Christian Relief Committee, which later expanded to become the Karen Refugee Committee in 1985. See Burma Ethnic Research Group, *Forgotten Victims of a Hidden War: Internally Displaced Karen in Burma* (Chiang Mai: Friedrich Naumann Foundation, 1998), p. 28. Thailand's response to displaced persons from Burma in 1977 (such as guidelines from the Ministry of Interior to governors in the border provinces concerning the refugees) is briefly discussed in Albert D. Moscotti, "Current Burmese and Southeast Asian Relations," *Southeast Asian Affairs 1978* (Singapore: Institute of Southeast Asian Studies, 1978), pp. 87-88.

arrived before March 19, 1976 are permitted to register and stay in Thailand[5]—most were intent on returning home. The host response in the period prior to 1984 was generally characterized by informal local hospitality; the borderlands' forest provided sufficient materials and food for people to sustain themselves, and these resources were complemented by intermittent assistance from missionary organizations working in the area.[6] The character of this seasonal, small-scale cross-border movement reflected the earlier patterns of war in which the *tatmadaw* retreated with the monsoon.

However, as noted in Chapter 2, from the time of the dry-season of 1983–84, the *tatmadaw* intensified its counterinsurgency operations against the main ethnic insurgent strongholds along the Thai border. They aimed to drive rebel forces and civilians from the area, strangle their funding from the lucrative black market border economy (trade and taxes), and establish a presence right on the Thai border. The Burmese army launched successful offensives against the Karen National Union (KNU) in the northern area of the Dawna range, beginning in January 1984 with the capture of the Karen National Liberation Army's (KNLA) base of Mae Tha Waw and continuing in February with attacks further south on KNLA camps and trading/tax gates at Klerday and Maw Pokay on the banks of the Moei River, and also Mae La, Wangka, Phalu, and as far south as Three Pagodas Pass. The capture of Mae Tha Waw effectively cut KNLA supply lines running from north to south,[7] although, despite protracted fighting, government troops failed to capture the latter bases (with one brief exception, for the KNLA and New Mon State Party bases at Three Pagodas Pass were controlled by the army from May 5-7).[8] As a result of this dry-season offensive and the heavy fighting that ensued, the KNU border economy suffered a serious shortfall of revenue, and the once thriving black market areas north of Mae Sot were reduced to rubble. This was the first time that the Burmese army maintained a presence throughout the rainy season along the Moei River on the border.[9] In contrast to the dry-season-offensive/wet-season-retreat pattern that characterized the army's actions in the past, this time government troops continued to fight into the wet season in the areas of KNU strongholds north of Mae Sot.[10] The KNLA launched a wet season counter-offensive in August 1984 and succeeded in dislodging the Burmese army (although Mae Tha Waw was not recaptured until October 1988), gradually opening its gates

---

[5] According to one source, in March 1976, the Ministry of Interior registered 41,762 displaced persons from Burma, with more than thirty thousand living in the two provinces of Chiangrai and Kanchanaburi. Court Robinson, *Double Vision: A History of Cambodian Refugees in Thailand* (Bangkok: Asian Research Center for Migration, Institute of Asian Studies, Chulalongkorn University, 1996), p. 3.

[6] Jack Dunford, "The Thai-Burmese Border: The Need for Humanitarian Assistance," unpublished paper presented to the Australian Council for Overseas Aid (ACFOA) Burma Seminar, Sydney, May 28, 1993, p. 1.

[7] Burma Ethnic Research Group, *Forgotten Victims of a Hidden War*, p. 24.

[8] Bertil Lintner, "Backs to the Wall," *Far Eastern Economic Review*, September 6, 1984, p. 28.

[9] Almerigo Grilz and Gian Micalessin, "Letter From Wangkha," *Far Eastern Economic Review*, November 1, 1984, p. 90.

[10] It was estimated that troops from the *tatmadaw*'s 44th and 66th LIDs numbered up to five thousand in this area. Paisal Sricharatchanya, "This Year's Big Push," *Far Eastern Economic Review*, May 10, 1984, p. 45.

to the black market trade once again. But from this time, the *tatmadaw* waged counterinsurgency campaigns of growing intensity.[11]

When in February 1984 some nine thousand Karen refugees fled into Tak province, the story of the "semi-permanent" refugee camps on Thailand's western border began. The initial Thai response was a simple humanitarian gesture that granted temporary sanctuary to the refugees; the Thai government hoped that the situation was indeed temporary and that when the fighting died down, people would, as in the past, promptly return to Burma. The local attitude toward the refugees was also generally sympathetic, given the continuity of ethnic Karen communities across the border and the local Thais' involvement in trade with the Karens from Burma.[12] In February, the Thai Ministry of Interior (MOI) invited the umbrella group of the voluntary agencies working with the Indochinese refugees in Thailand at the time, the Coordinating Committee for Services to Displaced Persons in Thailand (CCSDPT),[13] to provide emergency assistance to the displaced Karens. Under the umbrella of the CCSDPT, a small consortium of NGOs forming the Burmese Border Consortium (BBC) agreed to provide assistance. The BBC set up a "CCSDPT Karen Subcommittee," which convened its first meeting in April 1984, and in turn the BBC provided assistance through the Karen Refugee Committee (KRC) formed by the Karens to administer the refugee population. This administrative pattern subsequently applied to other new relief organizations as they were established in 1989 (the Karenni Refugee Committee) and 1990 (the Mon National Relief Committee).[14] Within the camps, there was a system of indigenous administration—with village heads, committees, and sections—reflecting the traditional structure of village management within Burma.

The relief effort in 1984 operated initially on a month-by-month basis, as the MOI wanted to restrict aid to essential emergency provisions so that new arrivals would not be "drawn" to Thailand and those already present would not be tempted to stay longer than necessary.[15] But with the arrival of the monsoon season that year, and since the Burmese army was not retreating in the usual way with the wet season, it became clear that the Karen refugees would not be in a position to return safely to their homes in Burma as usual.[16] It was estimated that only 15 percent of their rice crops could be planted in time for the beginning of the rainy season.[17] A longer-term stay needed to be negotiated with the local and Bangkok authorities. The Karen refugee administrators gained approval from the Governor of Tak

---

[11] For a detailed account of counterinsurgency in the various districts of Karen areas, see Burma Ethnic Research Group, *Forgotten Victims of a Hidden War*, pp. 23-34.

[12] Dunford, "The Thai-Burmese Border," p. 2. See also Ananda Rajah, "Ethnicity, Nationalism, and the Nation-State: The Karen in Burma and Thailand," in *Ethnic Groups across National Boundaries in Southeast Asia*, ed. Gehan Wijeyewardene (Singapore: Institute of Southeast Asian Studies, 1990), pp. 102-133.

[13] The CCSDPT was established at the request of the MOI in 1975 as the official NGO coordinating body for all agencies authorized by the Royal Thai Government to implement refugee assistance programs in Thailand. The CCSDPT is directly answerable to the MOI.

[14] In 1990, the CCSDPT Karen Subcommittee became the "Burma Subcommittee."

[15] Coordinating Committee for Services to Displaced Persons in Thailand, "Karen Emergency: Notes on a meeting in Mae Sot, August 10, 1984," unpublished meeting minutes.

[16] Letter from CCSDPT Karen Subcommittee to Director of Operations Center for Displaced Persons, Ministry of Interior, August 14, 1984.

[17] Ibid.

province to establish basic camp facilities, on the explicit understanding that, when the situation permitted, the people would return immediately to Burma. However, while Tak provincial authorities permitted consolidation of the various temporary camps in the area, the Bangkok-based authorities decided differently. A meeting on November 16 between the MOI, the military, and the Thai Ministry of Foreign Affairs revoked the Tak decision, and the Tak Governor was instructed to order all Karens to return to Burma within thirty days. In addition to concerns about the future costs of humanitarian assistance, anxieties were expressed that the Karens would try to establish permanent logistical bases for the resistance.[18] As it transpired, this instruction was not strictly implemented in practice, and there was room for negotiation and accommodation. But this decision did demonstrate Thailand's reluctance (discussed in the next section) to become host to a new, potentially burdensome, displaced population encamped along its western border; this reluctance was intensified by the fact that the Thais had already taken on a heavy Indochinese refugee burden.

While attention in 1984 was mainly centered on the Karens, a population of approximately six thousand displaced Mons fleeing from conflict in the Three Pagodas Pass base area also crossed into Thailand. Although the establishment of the Mon National Relief Committee (MNRC) is generally associated with the larger movement of displaced persons following the fall of the New Mon State Party (NMSP) headquarters at Three Pagodas Pass in February 1990 (described in the next chapter), it was in fact first formed in response to the needs of this earlier 1984 cross-border population. The Mons had fled in advance of an attack in mid-November, following the outbreak of heavy fighting around the border area of Three Pagodas Pass.[19] The Thai Border Patrol Police (BPP) and the local army permitted civilians—but not combatants—to cross to the Thai side, and representatives from the MNRC approached the CCSDPT and requested its members to provide relief to displaced persons sheltering haphazardly in thatch structures and under trees over a ten-kilometer stretch of area between the border and the Songkalia River.[20] Unlike the situation of the Karens, however, the Mon situation in Thailand in 1984 elicited a single relief gesture that was not expanded until the establishment of the Mon camps in 1990.

From the perspective of the host country, refugees may be regarded as a visible diplomatic liability and potential source of tension between the "sending" and "receiving" states. Although in practice the Bangkok authorities took a relatively accommodating approach, since they permitted the Karen camps to remain in 1984, traces of diplomatic and military tensions associated with the presence of the camps were evident from the time of their establishment. Referring to both the Karen and Mon camps, for instance, the MOI noted in December "that the Thai Government has considered the provision of assistance to the Karen and Mon based on humanitarian principles, while at the same time keeping in mind the

---

[18] Coordinating Committee for Services to Displaced Persons in Thailand, "Notes on a Meeting Regarding Karen Situation, November 16, 1984," unpublished meeting minutes.

[19] It was reported that approximately eight hundred *tatmadaw* troops attacked the Karen and Mon bases at Three Pagodas Pass, led by the 77th LID. "Burmese Poised to Strike at Karens, Mons," *The Nation Review*, November 29, 1984, p. 3.

[20] Coordinating Committee for Services to Displaced Persons in Thailand, "Notes of Meeting of Mon Displaced Persons in Kanchanaburi Province," unpublished meeting minutes, December 13, 1984.

diplomatic relations between the Thai and Burmese authorities."[21] For the displaced civilians, their implied association with the Karen and Mon insurgencies was imported into the cross-border setting, and this made the Thai authorities nervous about the diplomatic repercussions of hosting Burma's anti-Rangoon "insurgents." Thus, even while extending physical sanctuary, official Thai policy has always stressed the temporary and minimal nature of its humanitarian commitment and has emphasized the imperative to "prevent these minorities from engaging in any activities which may affect Thai-Burmese relations."[22] Thailand's official position from the time of the establishment of the refugee camps on the Burmese border has reflected this concern. However, in practice, there has been more than sufficient space for negotiation, flexibility, and accommodation outside the parameters of formal policy pronouncements.

At the time of their inception, however, the Burmese refugee camps were, to a large extent, overshadowed by the immense and protracted Indochinese refugee situation on Thailand's Cambodian and Laotian borders. Since 1975, when the exodus from the Indochinese states began, Thailand had became host to over one million refugees.[23] In 1984, therefore, Thailand's political anxieties and resources were necessarily channeled into managing these Indochinese refugees, a situation that was embedded in wider, regional, Cold War politics. Therefore, while the Thai authorities were anxious to avoid a new and complicated refugee problem on the Burmese border, Thai refugee policy was preoccupied with the Indochinese refugees. The following section reviews the nature of Thailand's response to the Indochinese refugees in order to establish a comparative basis for understanding the nature of the Thai response to the Burmese refugees.

THAILAND'S INDOCHINESE REFUGEES

Thailand has a long history of providing refugee sanctuary,[24] but the volume of the refugee inflow from the Indochinese states of Cambodia, Laos, and Vietnam, which began in 1975, was unprecedented. Thailand not only took on the heaviest portion of the Indochinese refugee burden because of its status as a first asylum country, accepting by far the largest population of any ASEAN state, but it was also involved in the wider drama of the Cold War power rivalries and realignments being played out on its border. By the mid-1980s, the huge relief apparatus established for the refugees on the Thai-Cambodian border had become crucial to perpetuating the cycle of war in Cambodia, for it supported the resistance against the Vietnamese-backed Heng Samrin regime in Phnom Penh.[25] Thailand was confronted simultaneously by the difficulties involved in pursuing its own

---

[21] Letter from Operations Center for Displaced Persons, Ministry of Interior to the CCSDPT, Bangkok, December 25, 1984 (unofficial translation).

[22] Kachadphai Burusapatana, Deputy Secretary of the National Security Council, "Displaced Persons and Illegal Immigrants," Presentation to Workshop on the 1951 Convention Relating to the Status of Refugees, Cha-am, Thailand, November 6-9, 1992, (unofficial translation), p. 10.

[23] Valerie O'Connor Sutter, *The Indochinese Refugee Dilemma* (Baton Rouge: Louisiana State University Press, 1990), p. 99.

[24] For an account of the period between World War II and 1975, see Neptnapis Nakavachara and John Rogge, "Thailand's Refugee Experience," in *Refugees: A Third World Dilemma*, ed. John Rogge (Totowa, NJ: Rowman and Littlefield, 1987), pp. 269-281.

[25] Zolberg et al., *Escape from Violence*, pp. 172-173.

political and strategic interests in a conflict sustained by external patrons, and by a massive, protracted humanitarian crisis.

In the first 1975–78 period, approximately 228,000 displaced persons arrived in Thailand. The largest numbers at this time migrated from Laos, the first wave comprising mainly highland Hmong people who had fought the North Vietnamese and Pathet Lao alongside the United States and who were fleeing the Pathet Lao, who captured Vientiane in May 1975. An estimated 150,000 people crossed into Thailand in the first two years alone,[26] and in 1978 further movements of large groups of predominantly lowland Lao from the urban areas of the country also fled, citing Vietnamese expansionism.[27] Approximately 34,000 Cambodians fled into Thailand during the takeover of Phnom Penh by the Khmer Rouge, which stretched from early 1975 to early 1979; by 1979, following the Vietnamese invasion of Cambodia, half a million Cambodians had fled to the Thai border.[28] The first wave of Vietnamese refugees (1975–77) fled following the surrender of South Vietnam to the Viet Cong in April 1975 due to their close connection with the South Vietnamese government and its American allies. The mass exodus of Vietnamese "boat people"—these were predominantly Sino-Vietnamese and other minorities considered to be "undesirables"—beginning in mid-1978 followed. The second wave of Indochinese refugees, from 1978–82, brought migration from these Indochinese states to a peak.

Because the situation raised the specter of a large-scale emergency developing, and because the exodus coincided with a series of disastrous "pushback" efforts on the part of receiving states,[29] the refugee problem gained international attention at the Geneva Conference on Indochinese Refugees convened by the United Nations' Secretary General on July 20-21, 1979. Attended by sixty-five states, the conference resulted in a "burden sharing" arrangement which assigned and formally instituted interrelated obligations to the countries of origin, first asylum, and eventual resettlement.[30] For Thailand, as a major first asylum country, the principles of "first asylum" and non-*refoulement* for refugees arriving by either land or sea were emphasized, coupled with the recognition, in view of resettlement commitments from the United States and other resettlement countries, that Thailand would not have to bear the long-term burden of asylum.[31] Overall, ASEAN countries and Hong Kong agreed that they would continue to offer temporary first asylum on the condition that resettlement countries honored their commitments at a sufficient rate in order to prevent the refugee population from escalating. Moved by both

---

[26] Arthur C. Helton, "Asylum and Refugee Protection in Thailand," *International Journal of Refugee Law* 1,1 (1989): 23.

[27] Lynellyn D. Long, *Ban Vinai: The Refugee Camp* (New York: Columbia University Press, 1993), p. 40.

[28] United States Committee for Refugees, *Cambodians in Thailand: People on the Edge* (Washington, DC: USCR, 1985), p. 7.

[29] The most infamous incident occurred in June 1979 at Preah Vihear, creating an international outcry. Over the course of several days, between 43,000 and 45,000 Cambodians who had crossed into Thailand were bussed four hundred kilometers north to a remote location on the northeast border, and pushed down a steep mountainside thick with landmines and the Vietnamese army. The Thai government had grievously violated the basic tenet of non-*refoulement*.

[30] Helton, "Asylum and Refugee Protection in Thailand," p. 24.

[31] Ibid.

humanitarian and foreign policy interests, the United States emerged as a leader in the relief aid effort and resettlement.[32]

The Vietnamese invasion of Cambodia at Christmas 1978, which installed the People's Republic of Kampuchea (PRK) government in Phnom Penh, came at the moment of a dramatic Cold War realignment of power relations, bringing the US together with China and the Khmer Rouge in opposition to Vietnam and the Soviet Union. This realignment would have an impact on the Thai-Cambodian border crisis over the next fifteen years. The war in Cambodia was supported and sustained by powerful international coalitions of external patrons. China supported the Khmer resistance through Thailand. The US and ASEAN supported Sihanouk and the non-communist forces, also through Thailand. The USSR supported and supplied the Vietnamese. The PRK government in Phnom Penh, not recognized by the UN General Assembly[33] and therefore ineligible for development aid, relied on assistance from Vietnam, the USSR, and the communist countries of Eastern Europe.

In addition, the traditional Thai-Vietnamese rivalry for influence in the Cambodian buffer state came into play. The Thai army began supporting the resistance in 1979, when the Thai government regarded the Khmer resistance as its own best defense against Vietnamese expansionism.[34] The activities of the Khmer Rouge in its string of military bases up and down the border—used for routine guerrilla attacks on PRK bases and stockpiled with large amounts of Chinese weaponry—were supported by a special, semi-covert unit of the Royal Thai Army, Task Force 838, whose role it was to facilitate the military activities of the resistance.[35] With Thai interests aligned in this way, Thai cooperation in the humanitarian relief effort along its own border was clearly motivated by support for the Cambodian resistance itself. Indeed, from the crucial initial phase of the conflict (1979–80), the refugee apparatus contributed to the insurgency against the Vietnamese-backed PRK.[36] From the perspective of Thailand and its international allies, therefore, the refugee populations acted as a military buffer against Vietnam. The political and strategic matrix in which the refugees lived meant that they were "political pawns" in the conflict.[37]

Living as political pawns bore heavily on the lives of the displaced Cambodians. The borderland was a violent place in which people were exposed to frequent artillery fire, forced conscription, and other abuses; shelter in the refugee camps was seriously compromised by proximity to the war. Further, those Cambodians who remained on the border for any amount of time found it increasingly difficult to return home, since they were identified with the resistance. The treachery of everyday life in the refugee camps mirrored the treachery of the war. There was massive corruption in the distribution of UN rice by the camp leaders, who used this food supply to further their own personal and

---

[32] O'Connor Sutter, *The Indochinese Refugee Dilemma*, p. 95.

[33] The General Assembly voted in September 1979 to allow the Khmer Rouge's Democratic Kampuchea to retain its seat at the UN as the "legitimate" state replacing the PRK.

[34] Lindsay Cole French, "Enduring Holocaust, Surviving History: Displaced Cambodians on the Thai-Cambodian Border, 1989-1991" (PhD dissertation, Harvard University, 1994), p. 70.

[35] Ibid., p. 27.

[36] Zolberg et al., *Escape From Violence*, p. 173.

[37] See Josephine Reynell, *Political Pawns: Refugees on the Thai-Kampuchean Border* (Oxford: Refugee Studies Program, Oxford University, 1989).

political standing.[38] Meanwhile, thousands of others lived in the interstices of the borderland outside the UNHCR (United Nations High Commission for Refugees) holding centers in Thailand, "trapped in the narrow war zone of the Thai-Cambodian border."[39] By the peak of the refugee crisis for Thailand (1980-81), over a million Cambodians had been drawn to the Thai borderland. Between 1982 and 1985, there was a seasonal pattern to border life, with six months of dry-season (November to April) in which the resistance camps on the Thai border came under Vietnamese attack, so that civilians routinely abandoned them during this season,[40] and six months of wet-season retreat. In early 1985, however, military campaigns by the Vietnamese/PRK army pushed the Khmer resistance forces and an accompanying 230,000 border Cambodians into Thai jurisdiction.[41] In the past, Thailand had routinely prevented such people from entering, but on this occasion the dynamic of the war had changed. In response, a new arrangement was made for this border population, as they were housed inside Thailand under the auspices of the United Nations Border Relief Operation (UNBRO, 1982-1991), separate from the UNHCR-run refugee camps (of which Khao I Dang was the main camp). The UNBRO arrangement theoretically separated border civilians from the military, a situation that provided a relatively safer environment for the provision of humanitarian aid. But the camps continued to be run internally by civilian administrators from each of the resistance factions. Inhabitants in the UNBRO camps were fenced in and guarded by the patrolling Thai Task Force 80 Rangers, who often involved themselves in the internal affairs of the camps.[42]

Thailand had political motivations for providing sanctuary, but its readiness to offer assistance was partly undercut by ambivalence, for clearly the situation imposed a burden on the nation. The scale of the problem was enormous; as the Secretary General of the National Security Council (NSC) pointed out at the 1979 Geneva Conference, "for each displaced person that leaves Thailand, two new ones enter the country."[43] Faced with a massive humanitarian burden, Thailand was emphatic about its resolve to maintain its role as a country of *temporary* first asylum; third country resettlement and repatriation were the cornerstones of Thai policy in this respect.[44] As noted by Arthur C. Helton, the Thai authorities reacted with apparent compassion in some instances and with callousness in others.[45] Further, Thailand was not only burdened with a massive humanitarian crisis, but because of its proximity to the conflict, the war itself often spilled over its border, threatening its own citizens. The presence of Khmer "refugee warriors" in the border camps obviously "invited" Vietnamese attacks, and these attacks were not

---

[38] French, "Enduring Holocaust, Surviving History," p. 24.

[39] United States Committee for Refugees, *Cambodians in Thailand*, p. 13.

[40] French, "Enduring Holocaust, Surviving History," p. 25.

[41] United States Committee for Refugees, *Cambodians in Thailand*, p. 16.

[42] The Task Force 80 was then replaced in 1988 by a specially trained paramilitary unit under the Thai Military Supreme Command called the Displaced Persons Protection Unit (DPPU). Helton, "Asylum and Refugee Protection in Thailand," p. 35.

[43] Robinson, *Double Vision*, p. 44.

[44] Karen Jacobsen, "The Response of Third World Governments to Mass Influxes of Refugees: A Comparative Policy Analysis of Thailand and Zimbabwe" (PhD dissertation, Massachusetts Institute of Technology, 1992), Chapter 4.

[45] Helton, "Asylum and Refugee Protection in Thailand," p. 21.

always confined to Cambodian territory. Thousands of Thai villagers were displaced by the ongoing disruptions.[46]

Thailand's host response to the displaced persons is generally characterized as one of "humane deterrence." Introduced in 1980 and practiced for the next decade, "humane deterrence" mandated a "closed door" policy to Cambodian, Vietnamese, and Laotian entrants alike.[47] Fashioned to deter new arrivals, "humane deterrence" as a policy offered refugees "indefinite detention in austere camps, denial of all but essential services and maintenance, and deferral or denial of access to third country resettlement processing."[48] In Thailand's official parlance, the term "displaced persons" applied only to pre-1979 arrivals, while post-1979 arrivals were called "illegal entrants" or "illegal immigrants." However, in practice, as Vitit Muntarbhorn notes, those detained in government-directed camps were generally exempted from the application of immigration law and were accorded temporary refuge, with the understanding that they would eventually be subject to resettlement in third countries or repatriation.[49] Following the Paris Peace Agreement, signed on October 23, 1991, which placed Cambodia in the hands of the UN Transitional Authority in Cambodia (UNTAC), the UNHCR took over responsibility of the Cambodian border camps from the UNBRO, in preparation for one of the largest logistical operations of repatriation undertaken by the UNHCR hitherto.[50] Spurred by recognition that a growing number of Vietnamese refugees were pouring into camps and that, simultaneously, third countries were adopting more restrictive resettlement policies (as a result of "compassion fatigue"), the UN sponsored a second international conference on Indochinese refugees in Geneva in June 1989, resulting in the Comprehensive Plan of Action (CPA), signed by seventy-seven states. In the words of the UNHCR, the CPA was "a package of measures intended to reduce the flow of economic migrations from Vietnam while providing protection to those who had a valid claim to refugee status."[51] The CPA instituted a screening process—those "screened in" were eligible for third-country

---

[46] For instance, the UNBRO provided relief to some 55,000 affected Thai villagers, displaced by the above-mentioned dry season offensive of 1984-85 alone. Office of the Special Representative of the Secretary General of the United Nations for Coordination of Cambodian Humanitarian Assistance Programmes (OSRSG), *Cambodian Humanitarian Assistance and the United Nations (1979-1991)* (Bangkok: United Nations, 1992), pp. 28, 44.

[47] Vitit Muntarbhorn, *The Status of Refugees in Asia* (Oxford: Clarendon Press, 1992), p. 129.

[48] O'Connor Sutter, *Indochinese Refugee Dilemma*, pp. 102-103. "Humane deterrence" became the general policy adopted by host states throughout Southeast Asia and Hong Kong. See further, Dennis McNamara, "The Origins and Effects of 'Humane Deterrence' Policies in Southeast Asia," in *Refugees and International Relations*, ed. Gil Loescher and Laila Monahan (New York: Oxford University Press, 1989).

[49] Vitit Muntarbhorn, *The Status of Refugees in Asia*, p. 139.

[50] Between March 30, 1992 and April 30, 1993, more than 365,000 Cambodians returned to their homeland. United Nations High Commission for Refugees, *The State of the World's Refugees: The Challenge of Protection* (London: Penguin, 1993), p. 104.

[51] United Nations High Commission for Refugees, *The State of the World's Refugees: In Search of Solutions* (Oxford: Oxford University Press, 1995), p. 208. For further detail on the CPA, see Stern A. Bronee, "The History of the Comprehensive Plan of Action," *International Journal of Refugee Law* 5,4 (1993): 534-543; and Arthur C. Helton, "Refugee Determination under the Comprehensive Plan of Action: Overview and Assessment," *International Journal of Refugee Law* 5,4 (1993): 544-558.

resettlement and those "screened out" were to be repatriated to their country of origin, with no provision for local assimilation—which finally closed in June 1996.

An overview of the Indochinese refugees' situation highlights their position as political "pawns" in the wider Cold War drama. As a humanitarian and political problem for Thailand, the regional Cold War context in which the conflict was fought—and in which the refugees were located—was of key significance. Thailand provided large-scale humanitarian aid to the camps on the Cambodian border, in particular, in order to support the broader military and ideological opposition to growing Vietnamese power in Cambodia and Southeast Asia. Reflecting the Cold War climate, refugee "solutions" were originally oriented towards resettlement in the West; they thereby exploited Indochinese refugees as potent symbols of foreign policy and implied a condemnation of the situation—that is, Communism—in the country of origin. The emphasis then shifted toward greater restriction of entry and resettlement options ("humane deterrence" and "compassion fatigue"), and, finally, to a preference for repatriation.[52]

The Contrast with Burmese Refugees

The refugee situation on the Burmese border contrasts markedly with the situation of the Indochinese refugees summarized above. The refugees there have obviously fallen outside the wider embrace of Cold War affiliations and of any large-scale and politically manipulated humanitarian relief infrastructure; what's more, their situation has not been influenced by a dramatic "internationalization" of a locale, as was true for Indochinese refugees. Instead, the humanitarian relief effort on the Thai-Burmese border has been a relatively low-key, low-publicity affair, managed and negotiated by local refugee committees and their NGO counterparts, in striking contrast to the highly institutionalized Indochinese camps teeming with expatriate relief personnel.

Until the mid-1990s, Thai security arrangements in Burmese refugee camps were also comparatively low-key, in contrast with conditions in Indochinese camps, which were surrounded by large barbed wire enclosures and heavy Thai surveillance. In addition, the village-style character of the camps on the Burmese border largely preserved the traditional lifestyle of the displaced persons, most of whom had fled from their homes in the immediate contiguous border regions. On the Burmese border, however, this more low-key, "localized" response, and the original minimal relief structure, were conditioned by the expectations of Thailand that this was the only acceptable arrangement permitted.[53] The MOI regulations concerning the management of humanitarian relief have required that the expatriate staff be kept to a minimum, civilian camp inhabitants provisioned with supplies consistent with basic living standards in the border areas, and that aid-

---

[52] For a discussion of the general change in refugee policy in the post-Cold War era, in which the commitment to asylum by affluent states has been diminished in favor of the containment of forced migration in countries and regions of origin, see Andrew Shacknove, "From Asylum to Containment," *International Journal of Refugee Law* 5,4 (1993): 516-533.

[53] MOI Regulations, as of May 31, 1991. Burmese Border Consortium, "Appendix B," in *Burmese Relief Programme Report for Period January to June 1997* (Bangkok: Burmese Border Consortium, 1997).

dependency be minimized and self-sufficiency promoted, with no publicity.[54] The Thai government accepted the relatively non-intrusive consortium of voluntary agencies to work in the Burmese camps on this low-key basis largely because, as observed above, it was eager to prevent diplomatic "misunderstanding" with its Burmese neighbor.[55] This system functioned in the absence of the large-scale "refugee warrior" phenomenon that marked the situation for Indochinese refugees in the 1980s, and it did not involve the manipulation of humanitarian aid to support resistance fighters, a practice commonly employed by Thailand along on the Thai-Cambodian and Thai-Lao borders. This is not to say, however, that ethnic insurgent combatants did not regularly move in and out of the refugee camps between Burma and Thailand and that rice and relief supplies did not in some proportions "leak" across the border to insurgent bases. There was neither the scale nor the opportunity for major corruption in the distribution of relief in the Burmese camps, and the refugee camps in themselves were not critical bases to the war. Until the late 1980s, the ethnic armies' secure control of substantial areas of the border territories within Burma, undergirded by its many successful economic ventures, meant that the refugee camps were not needed, and so did not function, as a support base for "refugee warriors" to the extent that the Indochinese camps did. (The nature of the Thai-Burmese borderlands' context is more specifically explored in Chapter Six.)

POLICY MACHINATIONS

Officially, refugee sanctuary in Thailand has been negotiated outside the formal parameters of international refugee law. As noted above, the Royal Thai Government (RTG) is not a signatory to the 1951 UN Convention on Refugees or its companion 1967 Protocol, and under national law, asylum seekers in Thailand are technically "illegal immigrants." In strictly formal terms, legal refugee protection, and even the term "refugee," does not exist in Thailand. While Indochinese arriving in Thailand prior to 1979, and some of the earlier immigrants who arrived even before this time, were recognized as "displaced persons," subsequent arrivals have been designated as "illegal immigrants." The official designation in law of "displaced person" (*phu opphayop*) relates to a clause in the "Regulations Concerning Displaced Persons from Neighboring Countries" issued by the Thai Ministry Of Interior on April 8, 1954. Here, according to the MOI, a "displaced person" is someone "who escapes from dangers due to an uprising, fighting, or war, and enters in breach of the Immigration Act."[56] Because they enter Thailand in breach of the Immigration Act, "displaced persons" are all *prima facie* illegal

---

[54] The guidelines from the Ministry of Interior include specific reference to this aspect on the Thai-Burmese border: "The NGO must be a small agency whose objectives and activities are in line with Thai government policies. There is to be no publicity about the provision of assistance." Chalerm Phromlert, Deputy Permanent Secretary of the Ministry of Interior, "Information from the MOI Regarding Policies for NGOs dealing with Refugees and Displaced Persons in Thailand," unpublished statement, Bangkok, May 23, 1994, p. 1.

[55] Interview, Khun Wannida Boonprarong, Chief, Displaced Persons and Illegal Immigrant Affairs Subdivision, Ministry of Interior, Bangkok, Thailand, March 9, 1998.

[56] Vitit Muntarbhorn, "Law and National Policy Concerning Displaced Persons and Illegal Immigrants in Thailand," unpublished paper (Bangkok: Institute of Asian Studies, Chulalongkorn University, undated), p. 7.

immigrants.[57] This sentence outlines the meaning of "displaced person" as formally defined by the Thai government, but in general parlance the term "displaced person" has often been used to refer to pre-1979 Indochinese and the subsequent populations of Indochinese and Burmese refugees alike. (While such people are designated as "illegal immigrants" according to these categories, it is obviously inappropriate to refer to people who have fled war in such terms.)

Asylum-seekers in Thailand today enter in violation of the 1979 Immigration Act[58]; by law they are "aliens" without Thai nationality, valid passports, or visas. Penalties for illegal immigration under the 1979 Act include repatriation (section 54) and imprisonment and fines (sections 62 and 81). The large Indochinese camp populations were, in practice, exempt from these provisions if they remained within the camp setting; those outside the camps were often difficult to monitor, and the enforcement of the law depended on the actions of provincial officials.[59] Of course, the sheer volume of persons made a tight web of control impracticable. The same characteristics have proved to be true for Burmese camps: the legal status of the refugees tends to be uncertain and strict control of the camp populations difficult. And, although in legal terms Burmese refugees are illegal immigrants, popular and (sometimes policy) parlance refers to them more loosely as "displaced persons," or even "refugees."

The Royal Thai Government is not a signatory to the 1951/1967 UN refugee instruments. However, when it became apparent that asylum seekers fleeing the Indochinese states would continue to flow into the country in large numbers that exceeded its resources to manage, Thailand formally requested assistance from and signed an agreement with the UNHCR in July 1975.[60] Pursuant to a June 1975 Thai cabinet decision, the MOI established the Operations Center for Displaced Persons, which has continued to work closely with the UNHCR and the CCSDPT over the years. The Cabinet decision of June 1975, however, expressed reluctance concerning the admission of refugees, pointing out that displaced persons were not desirable, were to be met with "preventive and retaliatory measures," and, where this was not possible, were to be detained in camps.[61]

Moreover, Thailand has not succumbed to pressure to accede to the UN's 1951 Convention/1967 Protocol. It has argued that non-participation in the agreement permits the government greater flexibility in its response to refugees and that, in view of the large refugee burden confronted by Thailand, the standards of the full obligations contained therein are too high and therefore unrealistic and unacceptable.[62] That is, if Thailand cannot fulfill the full obligations of the instruments, argues the Ministry of Interior, then it should not sign the

---

[57] Ibid.

[58] Immigration Act 1979, *Royal Thai Gazette*, 33/17-18, 20, 30 (June 30, 1979), English translation.

[59] Vitit Muntarbhorn, "Law and National Policy Concerning Displaced Persons and Illegal Immigrants in Thailand," p. 9.

[60] See Jacobsen, "The Response of Third World Governments to Mass Influxes of Refugees," p. 168.

[61] Ibid., p. 169.

[62] Interview, Khun Wannida Boonpracong, Chief, Displaced Persons and Illegal Immigrant Affairs Subdivision, Ministry of Interior, Bangkok, March 9, 1998.

Convention.[63] According to the MOI then, the vital question is not whether Thailand should or should not be a signatory. This is because (1) it considers the Convention's definitions and obligations, which originated in Europe, to be inappropriate to practical Thai realities; (2) it is already a member of the UNHCR Executive Committee (since 1975); (3) it has exercised considerable flexibility in immigration law in practice; and (4) it has demonstrated its commitment by admitting refugees for over twenty years.[64] These factors may be persuasive in view of the shortcomings of the 1951 UN Convention, with its narrow definition of "refugee" and individualized determination of cases, and, hence, its inapplicability to many refugee realities around the world. Nevertheless, international refugee protection remains formally unrecognized in Thailand. What has been the alternative?

Again, Thailand has been clearly reluctant to accede to the 1951 Convention in its present form. The gap in the formal legal protection of refugees, which would have been covered if Thailand were signatory to the Convention, is necessarily addressed by a reliance on the continuing humanitarian "goodwill" of the host authorities, and their affirmation of and adherence to basic protection principles (that is, admission and non-*refoulement*).[65] The office of the UNHCR in Bangkok points out that where the Convention and Protocol do not apply, the UNHCR Statute does.[66]

Further, the Thai perspective has evolved towards a growing acceptance of the UNHCR role on the Burmese border. In 1994, the populations in the camps along the border were accepted as *prima facie* refugees, and the UNHCR was given permission to undertake more frequent periodic visits to the border (albeit in an observer capacity).[67] According to the UNHCR's regional representative in Bangkok, the Royal Thai Government's approach to UNHCR had shifted: while in the early 1990s it showed mere "toleration" for the UNHCR's rather infrequent monitoring role, by the mid-1990s it had switched to official "acceptance."

Finally, in the first half 1998, Thailand formally accepted an enhanced, "permanent" role for the UNHCR on the Burmese border for the first time.[68] This

---

[63] Ibid.

[64] Ibid.

[65] For a discussion by the UNHCR on this problem of non-accession in general terms, including in relation to major countries of asylum, see UNHCR, Executive Committee of the High Commissioner's Programme, "Note on International Protection," Forty-fifth session, UN doc. A/AC.96/830, September 7, 1994, paragraphs 21, 38, 42, 68.

[66] Interview, UNHCR Protection Officers, Regional Office of the UNHCR, Bangkok, March 1998.

[67] Interview, Ruprecht von Arnhim, UNHCR Regional Representative, Bangkok, September 18, 1995.

[68] Nussara Sawatsawan, "Ogata Accepts Invitation," *Bangkok Post*, July 25, 1998. The UNHCR described its role as one in which "UNHCR field-based protection staff will advise the Government of Thailand in establishing criteria for refugee status determination procedures to ensure that groups of asylum-seekers fleeing conflict, or the effects of conflict, will be permitted temporary protection in camps in Thailand. UNHCR will provide assistance as required, to relocate camps at risk of incursion further away from the border, and, in collaboration with the Government, will conduct comprehensive and verifiable registration exercises and monitor the civilian character of the camps." UNHCR Funding and Donor Relations, East Asia and the Pacific, *UNHCR 1999 Global Appeal—Thailand/Myanmar*. Accessed online at www.unhcr.ch/fdrs/ga99/tha.html [March 21, 1999], p. 3.

new agreement between the Thai government and the UNHCR, effective from July 1998, arose out of both the deterioration of borderlands' security (exemplified by cross-border attacks on the Karen refugee camps since 1995, which will be discussed in Chapter Six) and out of Thailand's desire to work towards the resolution of what had become a long-term, protracted refugee problem. The shifting context of the war on the Burmese side of the border meant that Thailand was confronted with a refugee situation that looked different from the way it had in the past, especially prior to 1995. Expectations for a spontaneous and speedy return of the displaced persons could no longer be entertained, and the issue was becoming more difficult to deal with informally.[69]

After the UNHCR became officially operational along the border in 1999 (with field offices in Kanchanaburi, Mae Sot, and Mae Hong Son), it undertook a major refugee registration exercise in the border camps, in conjunction with the Thai Ministry of Interior. In addition to recording the bio-data of each household member, the exercise also recorded demographic information, such as the refugees' places of origin within Burma. On a computer-generated map produced by the UNHCR in early 2000, the data indicated numbers of refugees and their places of origin by township district. The agency also worked with Thai authorities to formalize refugee admissions procedures, including the establishment of Provincial Admissions Boards in the border provinces and the construction of reception buildings in several camps.

Players in Burmese Refugee Policy and Practice

Overall, as noted earlier, Thailand's basic approach to the Burmese refugees has been to grant *prima facie* asylum so long as it is low-key and the humanitarian gesture does not endanger national security or politically interfere with good relations between Bangkok and Rangoon. A simplified outline of the institutions engaged in this web of refugee policy and practice in Thailand is offered below.

Refugee policy making and implementation extends across a number of key civilian and military agencies. These include the National Security Council, the Ministry of Interior, the Border Patrol Police, the Ministry of Foreign Affairs, and the Thai military. The National Security Council (NSC, established in 1959) is the highest and most powerful civilian decision-making body directly concerned with refugee policy. As Panitan Wattanayagorn notes, in the past (prior to 1992), when the military was dominant, the NSC did not play a significant role in security policy. Previously, it articulated "an official concept of national security in accordance with the military's thinking." Today, however, the NSC is the "central institution for coordinating and integrating development in the border areas."[70] The primary function of the NSC is to act as advisor to the Prime Minister and the cabinet on national security policy, and it is the key coordinator (and sometimes mediator) at the policy level between various ministries on military, economic, internal, and foreign policies. It also has specialist subcommittees that

---

[69] Interview, Khun Wannida Boonpracong, Chief, Displaced Persons and Illegal Immigrants Affair Subdivision, Ministry of Interior, Bangkok, March 9, 1998.

[70] Panitan Wattanayagorn, "Thailand: The Elite's Shifting Conceptions of Security," in *Asian Security Practice: Material and Ideational Influences*, ed. Muthiah Alagappa (Stanford: Stanford University Press, 1998), p. 439.

regularly meet on the issues, particularly issues concerning "illegal workers" and "displaced persons fleeing fighting," both matters considered by the NSC to be significant for Thailand.[71] The NSC comprises nine ex-officio members and is headed in formal session by the Prime Minister (as Chairman). Other Council members include the Deputy Prime Minister (Vice Chairman), Ministers of Defense, Interior, Foreign Affairs, Finance, Transport, the Supreme Commander of the Armed Forces, and the Secretary General (who has cabinet rank and is under direct supervision of the Prime Minister). When required, senior government officials (usually at the Permanent Secretary level) are invited to attend meetings. Organizationally, the Office of the NSC comes under the Office of the Prime Minister and comprises the Office of the Secretary and Divisions 1-7, of which Division 2 has responsibility for refugees.

The Ministry of Interior (MOI) is the key civilian ministry responsible for policy implementation. It wields bureaucratic control over the Police Department (land and marine police, as well as the Border Patrol Police, BPP), the Immigration Division, provincial governors, and district officers—each important in overseeing refugee affairs on the ground. The MOI is responsible for overseeing the security and administration of those camps not directly "up against" the border (that is, three kilometers distant from the border and beyond) and for coordinating with various agencies on matters of change (such as repatriations and the relocation of camps).[72] As noted earlier, voluntary agencies assisting the refugees are directly answerable to the MOI. The BPP serves as the full-time policing element of the MOI, principally responsible for border patrol and a range of interdictory functions, such as dealing with drugs, smuggling, banditry, illegal immigration, the periodic flows of refugees, and so forth, and also performing a light infantry and intelligence-gathering role.[73] The BPP's paramilitary police units are responsible for security on the immediate border, sometimes as a joint force with the Royal Thai Army and the Thahan Phran (paramilitary rangers). The BPP was established in 1953, with the support of the US-CIA (Central Intelligence Agency) and under the patronage of the Thai king, to gather intelligence and maintain security in the remote border regions of the country. It has developed into a "powerful, multipurpose force" and "the primary armed institution responsible for the security of the Thai kingdom's lengthy international borders."[74] During the 1970s, it played a key counterinsurgency role against the Communist Party of Thailand (CPT). Although the BPP is organizationally allied to the Police Department, it is largely autonomous nationally and in many of its field operations; in the event of external incursion, it comes under the direct operational control of the military's Supreme Command Headquarters.[75]

The role of the Ministry of Foreign Affairs (MFA) involves liaison and coordination with external players and international organizations. The MFA has

[71] Interview, Director, Division 2, National Security Council, Bangkok, March 10, 1998.

[72] Interview, Khun Wannida Boonpracong, Chief, Displaced Persons and Illegal Immigrants Affairs Subdivision, Ministry of Interior, Bangkok, March 9, 1998.

[73] Robert Karniol, "Briefing: Thailand," *Jane's Defence Weekly*, September 9, 1995, p. 40.

[74] Thomas Lobe and David Morell, "Thailand's Border Patrol Police: Paramilitary Political Power," in *Supplementary Military Forces: Reserves, Militias, Auxiliaries*, Volume 8, ed. Louis A. Zurcher and Gwyn Harries-Jenkins (Beverly Hills: Sage Publications, 1978), pp. 153, 160.

[75] Ibid.

less direct influence or impact on the fortunes of refugee affairs than these other agencies. From 1975, the MFA was directed by the Thai cabinet to act as liaison with resettlement countries, sending countries, and international organizations in matters involving the Indochinese refugees. During the period of the large Indochinese refugee caseload in Thailand, this ministry was generally supportive of the refugees, for it was influenced by its international constituency and "the need to garner international approval of Thailand's handling of its refugees." [76]

While the NSC is the most powerful policy maker and coordinator at the policy level, the Royal Thai Armed Forces—and the Royal Thai Army, in particular—are the most powerful players on the ground. Clearly, the refugees and the border areas are sensitive, high-priority security matters for Thailand, making the army the strongest and most important player in practice. The Army's Commander in Chief and other senior officers are frequently the most outspoken authorities on refugee issues at the national level, and the army is ultimately in charge of major events, such as relocations of refugee camps and repatriation on the ground. Major decisions in this regard remain in the hands of the military.[77] The Burmese border comes under the First, Third, and, to a smaller extent, Fourth, regional Army Areas. Several special task forces operate as readily deployable combat forces along the border[78]; military intelligence and Special Forces also conduct specialized operations along the border; and covert functions are also carried out by the NSC and National Intelligence Agency (NIA) as civilian agencies.[79] The Mon refugees, considered in the next chapter, have been the responsibility of the Ninth Infantry Division, based in Kanchanaburi, with its large borderland jurisdiction covering Kanchanaburi, Ratchaburi, Petchaburi, and Prachuab Khirikhan provinces under the First Army Region.[80] The special task force within the Ninth Division, known as "Surasri," has specifically sought to coordinate refugee and border matters at the local level. The BPP companies operating along this part of the border come under its Division 13, headquartered at Kanchanaburi.[81]

---

[76] Jacobsen, "The Response of Third World Governments to Mass Influxes of Refugees," p. 163.

[77] Interview, Khun Wannida Boonpracong, Chief, Displaced Persons and Illegal Immigrants Affairs Subdivision, Ministry of Interior, Bangkok, March 9, 1998.

[78] These task forces, such as the Naresuan Task Force in the Third Army Region and the Surasri Task Force in the First Army Region, are drawn from the army's operational units and are quite substantial in size (larger than battalion size, up to regiment size). Several other joint military-civilian units also operate along the border, drawing on personnel from the Border Patrol Police, Thahan Phran, and the air force. See further, Karniol, "Briefing: Thailand"; and Anthony Davis, "Thailand Tackles Border Security," *Jane's Intelligence Review*, March 2000, pp. 30-34.

[79] Karniol, "Briefing: Thailand," p. 40.

[80] The Ninth Division was established in 1971 and was long regarded as a "special unit" and an "important division" that enjoyed a close relationship to the Chief of the Army in Bangkok. Until recently, the Ninth Division was directly subordinate to the Commander in Chief of the Royal Thai Army, but this autonomy was reduced in 1992 and it is now answerable to the Commander of the First Army region. *Matichon*, "9th Division Command Changes Discussed," June 7, 1994, pp. 1, 3 in FBIS-EAS-94-145, July 28, 1994, pp. 93-94.

[81] In organizational terms, Division 13 at Kanchanaburi comes under BPP Region 1. Division 13 has seven companies: 131, 132 (Kanchanaburi), 133 (Phanom Thuan), 134 (Sangkhlaburi), 135 (Thong Pa Phum), 136 (Sai Yok), and 137 (Suan Phung).

While this offers a sketch of the key structures and institutions involved with refugees in Thailand, in truth it is frequently difficult to chart clearly the path of refugee policy and practice. For example, although the following comments relate directly to Indochinese refugee policy, they highlight the significant variability and fluidity which equally applies to policies that affect the Burmese refugees:

> While it is possible to track Thai policy without great difficulty, one should bear in mind the fact that its application varies from group to group, from area to area, and from time to time. Although national policymakers may lay down the rules, at the local level application of those rules becomes much more nuanced, depending upon the attitude of local authorities . . .
>
> Indeed, the Thai case suggests . . . while the official policy has been to prevent or deter refugees from entering Thailand, in practice hundreds of thousands have managed to enter and have been granted temporary asylum. By contrast, where there are policy directives at the ministerial level to loosen the stringent policy towards refugees, some local administrators may act at times in contradiction of that relaxation . . . In a manner, a swinging door has emerged, whereby words are not necessarily matched by action and vice versa.[82]

CONCLUSIONS

Bordered by politically troubled countries, Thailand has been a long-term host to a vast number of displaced persons as a country of first asylum. Although this burden has produced a significant degree of "refugee fatigue," and Thailand has resisted formal recognition of asylum-seekers as "refugees"—with post-1979 Indochinese and the contemporary Burmese border populations alike officially regarded as "illegal immigrants"—it has extended sanctuary in practice. The character of sanctuary on the Thai-Burmese border has contrasted substantially with the character of sanctuary typically found on the Thai-Cambodian and Thai-Laotian borders during the 1980s, when that refugee situation was affected by Cold War conflicts and alliances and everyday life distorted by the large-scale, highly institutionalized (and massively corrupt) relief apparatus in place there. On the Burmese border, the string of comparatively low-key, village-style camps, managed by indigenous camp committees and served by a non-intrusive relief effort, has managed to preserve basic village structure and lifestyle, and, unlike the earlier situation along the Cambodian and Lao borders, third-country resettlement has not been the preferred option or solution for these refugees. Instead, displaced Burmese populations have lived in a state of prolonged suspension in their host country, waiting for the opportunity eventually to return to their homes in a safe, sustainable post-war environment. In this way, the character of the camps on this border has been socially and politically more appropriate to such circumstances.

In formal terms, the displaced persons sheltered along the Thai-Burmese border have lived at the margins of international protection, technically unrecognized as refugees. However, this unrecognized status did not have an

---

[82] Public Affairs Institute, *Indochinese Refugees*, pp. 22, 30, quoted in David W. Harris, "The Indochinese Refugee Problem in Thailand: A Political Analysis" (PhD dissertation, George Washington University, 1994), p. 22.

adverse impact on their sanctuary, for in practice Thailand maintained a flexible approach that accommodated the people safely, in accord with international refugee principles. Indeed, Thailand has demonstrated just such flexibility as should be required by states in the context of the limitations of the original 1951 refugee system. The various refugee communities and their representatives negotiated their stay with a constellation of host authorities, and this worked well so long as basic protection principles were upheld. By the late 1990s, sanctuary for Burmese asylum-seekers encamped along the border was necessarily accommodated in Thai policy. However, the realities of the shifting political context in which sanctuary is negotiated may place the priority of refugee protection in danger. As the next chapter shows, this occurred in the case of the Mon refugees who sought refuge in Thailand from 1990 to 1996.

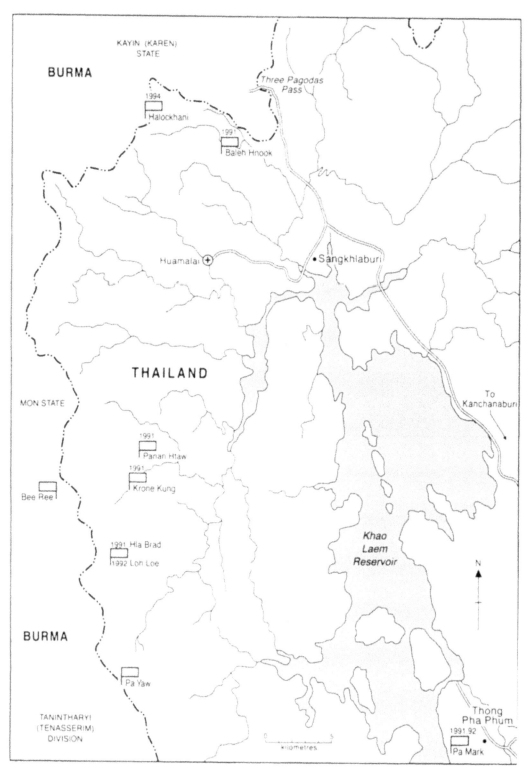

Map 5.1   Location of the Mon Refugee Camps, 1990–1996

CHAPTER FIVE

THE MON REFUGEES IN THAILAND, 1990-1996

INTRODUCTION

In its extensive role as a host to asylum-seekers, Thailand has demonstrated flexibility and an overall adherence to the norms of refugee protection. But within the story of the Thai response to the non-Burman indigenous refugees encamped along its western border, the chapter of the Mon refugees and the politics of their repatriation presents an exception to this record. Sanctuary for the Mons ended with their return to Burma in 1996, pursuant to the cease-fire between the New Mon State Party and the SLORC reached in mid-1995. The repatriation of the residents of the Mon camps may have removed their burdensome presence from Thai jurisdiction, but their plight remains an unfinished story, which raises important questions having to do with their protection status and security.

The case of the Mon refugees suggests that the "refugee solution" applied for this group of people emphasized repatriation as a goal in itself, configured within particular political vicissitudes, rather than attempting to forge a durable solution and insure human security. The politics surrounding the Mon refugees in Thailand show how their sanctuary was negotiated in conditions of a diminishing welcome, manifest first in relocations and insecurity of refuge, and culminating in their removal from Thai territory in 1996. Not only were the Mon refugees increasingly unwelcome inhabitants in the Thai borderland, their presence along an imprecise and ambiguous boundary became the impetus for a re-mapping exercise that served to exclude them from Thai jurisdiction altogether.

The Fall of Three Pagodas Pass

In February 1990, the *tatmadaw* captured the important Karen National Union (KNU) and New Mon State Party (NMSP) military strongholds and black-market trading gate at Three Pagodas Pass, sending some ten thousand people from the area into flight across the border.[1] The New Mon State Party/Mon National

---

[1] The population residing at Three Pagodas Pass had grown steadily since the mid-1980s. The intensification of counterinsurgency campaigns in the border areas resulted in the movement of Mon and Karen civilians into the village there. Several hundred students and activists also arrived as members of the All Burma Students' Democratic Front (ABSDF) after the military crackdown on the pro-democracy uprising in September 1988. For instance, among the ABSDF battalions formed along the Thai-Burmese border, numbers 101 and 102 were located in NMSP-controlled territory. About two hundred ABSDF soldiers coordinated with the MNLA during

Liberation Army (NMSP/MNLA) headquarters, located close to Three Pagodas Pass, fell to the government on February 11.[2] Both sides suffered casualties in the fighting, although *tatmadaw* casualties were thought to be higher.[3] The offensive involved fighting "day and night," and eventually forced the Mon National Liberation Army (MNLA) to withdraw from the Three Pagodas Pass village. Some NMSP officials contend that, on this occasion, the *tatmadaw* gained substantial military advantage in its approach to the stronghold because it was allowed to advance via Thai territory.[4] At the same time, the capture of Three Pagodas Pass by the Burmese army was not free from conflict with Thai authorities. A boundary dispute soon erupted in relation to the immediate territory around the "three pagodas" at the Pass, with Burmese troops attempting to remain on the Thai side following their capture of the base, claiming that demarcations on their British colonial map indicated this area belonged to Burma.[5] (This area has since remained a key site of boundary dispute between Thailand and Burma.)

NEGOTIATING SANCTUARY

The estimated ten thousand displaced persons living in makeshift jungle shelters in February 1990 were soon organized into five main camps on the Thai side of the border. These camps were Krone Kung, Panan Htaw, Baleh Hnook, Hla Brad, and Day Bung.[6] The newly revived Mon National Relief Committee (MNRC)[7] contacted the Coordinating Committee for Services to Displaced Persons (CCSDP) for assistance, reporting their immediate emergency and medical needs; subsequently, permission to operate the camps was granted by the Ministry of Interior in Bangkok. The Sangkhlaburi district officer also accepted the displaced persons, but on the condition that they return to Burma once the fighting died down

---

the fighting in February 1990. Fighting in the area continued after the government capture of the base, as the MNLA troops waged guerrilla campaigns against government troops at their former headquarters, attempting to cut supply routes of local *tatmadaw* units and to destroy other government infrastructure in the area. However, this time the Burmese army was in a position to consolidate control over its newly captured territory. In addition, some two hundred local Thai nationals also evacuated the area.

[2] The offensive was undertaken by a combined force of one thousand troops from the 31st, 101st and 106th Infantry regiments under the supervision of the No. 2 Tactical Operations Command from the Southeastern Military Command. "Further Reportage on Capture of Mon Headquarters," broadcast by Burmese state-run radio, February 13, 1990, recorded and translated by the Foreign Broadcast Information Service (FBIS), *Daily Report: Southeast Asia*, FBIS-EAS-90-030, p. 32.

[3] The New Mon State Party, "The New Mon State Party's Military Statement Ending February 1990," unpublished statement obtained from the NMSP.

[4] These officials point out that it would not have been possible to pursue the strategy (attack from the rear) without prior Thai knowledge and a "blind eye"—alleging that the *tatmadaw* was assisted by a Thai timber merchant (operating in the area under a SLORC-sanctioned concession) through their concealed transportation of troops into Mon-controlled territory. Ibid. See also "Mon Base Overrun in Fierce Fighting," *Bangkok Post*, February 12, 1990, p. 3.

[5] "Burma to Seek Talks on Three Pagodas Dispute," *The Nation*, February 28, 1990.

[6] These were in addition to Pa Yaw, about fifty kilometers southwest of Three Pagodas Pass, where an older small Mon community was already living.

[7] The MNRC was at first closely aligned with the NMSP. However, over the years it established itself as an independent specialist relief committee, separate from the NMSP.

and it was safe. However, a steady flow of new arrivals continued to appear in the Thai border area; for instance, an additional 2,500 were added to the camp populations in April 1990.[8] The cross-border movement of newly displaced persons continued, but the overall numbers of inhabitants in the Mon camps did not increase dramatically over time. Rather, people have moved about, often "disappearing" further into Thailand to join the ranks of illegal migrant workers; the MNRC counted four thousand such persons in May 1990.[9] People also kept in close contact with peripatetic villagers and traders regarding the unfolding situation in their home villages, remaining well-informed about activities in their areas and the possibilities for return.

While the initial response by Thai authorities to the Mon refugees was sympathetic, refuge required constant renegotiation. Over the period 1990-1996, the Mon camps in the borderland of Kanchanaburi province were faced with declining prospects of sanctuary, manifested in repeated orders for camp relocations implemented by local military authorities, orders which seemed to be motivated by a desire to return the refugees to Burma.[10] In 1991, there were eight Mon camps in Thailand with a total population of twelve thousand. In addition to the initial five camps named above, three new camps were established, at Pa Yaw (where a small population was already domiciled), at Pa Mark near Thong Phaphum in Kanchanaburi province, and at Prachuab, considerably further south in Prachuab Khirikhan province. (The Pa Mark camp was however closed down in May 1993, and the people moved to Pa Yaw.) (See Map 5.1.)

Relocating the Camps

The precarious situation facing refugees in the Mon camps in Kanchanaburi province was made evident by a series of relocations. The first relocation order from the local authorities in Sangkhlaburi district was issued as the monsoon season began in June 1991. This was for Day Bung camp, housing some 2,500 people, just west of Three Pagodas Pass. The Day Bung camp was relocated farther from Three Pagodas Pass during the peak of the monsoon; refugees were moved to Hla Brad (a camp about forty kilometers southwest) and other camps. It was difficult to move in monsoon conditions, with the rivers swelling with fast-flowing currents, making it dangerous for the young and infirm to cross. Nevertheless, the people made their way through the muddy jungle by various means, including on foot, and by boat, truck, and buffalo cart. The next relocation order issued by the Sangkhlaburi district authorities came during the following dry season, and it imposed an April 1992 deadline. This time, Baleh Hnook camp, with over a thousand inhabitants, was moved away from the Three Pagodas Pass area and relocated to the southwest, to the Pnang Tor camp. Baleh Hnook was a known support base for the NMSP/MNLA and was cleared from the Pass area for that reason. The decision-

---

[8] Mon National Relief Committee, *Monthly Report April 1990*, unpublished document.

[9] Mon National Relief Committee, *Monthly Report May 1990*, unpublished document.

[10] From the perspective of refugee administration, amongst those areas along the Thai-Burmese border host to the various refugee camps, the reception of the Mon camps, under the authority of the Royal Thai Army's Ninth Infantry Division, was regarded as the "coolest" and most problematic. Personal discussion with the Coordinating Committee for Services to Displaced Persons in Thailand (CCSDPT), Bangkok, September 1995.

making process concerning relocations may have seemed elusive, since the local district and military authorities each pointed to the other as the chief policy maker, but when the people were due to move, the predominant authority of the Royal Thai Army's Ninth Infantry Division proved incontrovertible. As one refugee worker commented in relation to the decision-making process: "No one ever says [who makes the decisions]. The district will say it is the army, the army will say it is the district. When they want the people to move, they send in the border police with guns."[11]

Relocations of Panan Htaw and Krone Kung camps were also completed by April 1992. If one takes into account the population relocated from Baleh Hnook, then some five thousand people, total, were moved during this period and resettled at Loh Loe (formerly called Hla Brad),[12] which forms part of a large area of mountain and jungle terrain straddling the Thai and Burmese jurisdictions. The refugees were initially notified that they would have to settle on the Burma side of the mountain, but this was successfully resisted by the MNRC. Those in charge of Krone Kung received permission to remain at their site, operating the boat station and hospital, through the rainy season, but when the time to move came, they were moved quickly; in one afternoon, the border police came, fired into the air, and cleared the camp (most of the refugees were sent to Loh Loe). By that time, Loh Loe had become the largest refugee camp on the Thai-Burmese border, containing eight thousand people and spanning three kilometers. Loh Loe was considered a very suitable site for a camp, with sufficient security, fresh water, forest resources, and convenient dry and rainy season transportation routes to Sangkhlaburi town and district hospital facilities. New schools (including a Mon high school), four monasteries, and two hospitals were built, and in May the population rose to ten thousand. The regular weekly deportations of illegal immigrants trucked from Thailand's immigration detention centers (IDCs) periodically added to the population; in April and May alone, 838 deportees (from a variety of backgrounds, including Mon, Burman, Tavoyan, and Muslim Arakanese) were delivered to Loh Loe.[13]

No sooner had the people arrived at Loh Loe than they faced further removal. Under orders from the Ninth Infantry Division, they were told to move by April 15, 1993.[14] They were ordered to move either to a new site right on the border at Halockhani, in *tambon* Nong Lu, still in Sangkhlaburi district, or to the existing camp at Pa Yaw, but both places were problematic. Pa Yaw was secure, but extremely isolated, being inaccessible by land for seven months of the year during the monsoon (June-December), far from the district hospital and Sangkhlaburi facilities, and with barely sufficient water supply at the site for one thousand people in the dry season. These problems notwithstanding, 1,500 people were relocated from Loh Loe to Pa Yaw by March 1993. Halockhani was problematic due to its proximity to the local Burmese army outpost, located approximately one hour's walk from the camp site; thus the refugees were being moved to a more

---

[11] Ibid.

[12] Some NMSP administration was located there at the time. (This was previously a headquarters site for Nai Shwe Kyin's faction of the NMSP.)

[13] Mon National Relief Committee, *Monthly Report May 1992*, unpublished document.

[14] Mon National Relief Committee, *Monthly Report December 1992*, unpublished document.

dangerous place. The majority of the Loh Loe population was moved to Halockhani.

The physical removal of the population of refugees housed at Loh Loe was not completed until the end of the dry season in 1994, though the threat of relocation had loomed from the time of the camp's inception. In August 1992, Thai district officials in Sangkhlaburi suggested the Mons "might prefer to return to Three Pagodas Pass,"[15] and offered to provide boat transportation for the purpose; but the Mons made no attempt to move. Later in the month, the BPP (Border Patrol Police) established barracks to accommodate twenty border police officers within Loh Loe camp, whereas previously they had maintained a routine checkpoint half way between the camp and Sangkhlaburi to monitor and "tax" camp residents moving to and from the camp. The MNRC was concerned about the BPP domiciled in their camp because they found their presence intimidating.[16] The MNRC expressed concerns in its December 1992 *Monthly Report*: "We, the Mon in Thailand, humbly beg the Royal Thai Government to reconsider any decision to relocate the families of Loh Loe and kindly to accept their existence in this camp. We ask for nothing except security for our children and your compassion in our plight." The MNRC chairman, abbot Pra Wongsa Pala, also appealed to Thai Prime Minister Chuan Leekpai to reconsider the decision to relocate Loh Loe and "kindly accept their current existence in the camp."[17] But in January 1993, the MNRC was informed that it would have to move, and this order was backed by a written statement referring to the NMSP as a "Mon terrorist gang" who forced the refugees to remain at Loh Loe against their will.[18]

Following a meeting held on February 16, 1993 at the Sangkhlaburi district office between representatives from the MNRC, the NSC, the army's Ninth Division, and the BPP, an agreement was negotiated stating that Thailand would indeed allow the Mon refugees to stay until the situation in Burma enabled a safe return. In the meeting, it was noted that the authorities sympathized with the plight of the refugees, but that government policy mandated the return of the refugees when the situation permitted.[19] A later meeting between the MNRC and the Ninth Infantry Division in September of that year at the Sangkhlaburi district office, however, reversed hope for further agreement between the MNRC and Thai authorities. In breach of the February agreement, the relocation order was reinstated. On October 6, 1993, an initial group of 139 Mon villagers was sent to the site at Halockhani, but the group resisted orders to clear the area on the Burmese side of the border and returned to that spot by October 13.[20] A small Mon settlement at the site on the Thai side of the border, located outside the refugee camp or relief purview, had earlier been ordered by district authorities to move to the Burmese side, and their camp was subsequently burnt by the local elements of the Ninth Infantry Division to ensure departure. These villagers moved and set up

---

[15] United States Committee for Refugees, *Refugee Reports* (Washington, DC: USCR 1992), p. 11.

[16] Visit to Loh Loe camp, February 1994.

[17] Letter from MNRC Chairman, Pra Wongsa Pala, to Prime Minister Chuan Leekpai, Royal Thai Government, December 1992.

[18] Mon National Relief Committee, *Mon Refugees: Hunger for Protection in 1994* (Bangkok: MNRC, 1994), p. 33.

[19] Interviews, Mon National Relief Committee, Sangkhlaburi, August 1995.

[20] "139 Refugees Unwilling to Cross over into Burma," *Bangkok Post*, October 11, 1993.

a small village across the border, at the site of what was later to become the Halockhani refugee camp. Further discussions followed concerning the question of relocation, resulting in the issuance of a statement by the National Security Council affirming that the people could remain in Thailand. But visits by the Ninth Division into Loh Loe camp in late December presaged the subsequent forced relocation; not long after, the government imposed a deadline of April 30, 1994 for the emptying of the Loh Loe camp. People began their move in January. The majority—over six thousand at the time—undertook the thirty-five-kilometer northward journey through the jungle to Halockhani, and smaller numbers traveled to Pa Yaw.

A confluence of rationales motivated the Thai government to relocate the Loh Loe camp. Clear or decisive explanations of these rationales were not provided, but it was possible to extrapolate from the wider context. At a local level, Colonel Nimit Maliyaem, Deputy Commander of the Ninth Infantry Division, noted concern about the destruction of the local borderland forest environment by refugee settlements: "That's why we had to order the relocation, to protect our forests."[21] This statement accorded with Thai regulations meant to alleviate the environmental impact of the camps on its forests. At the same time, it seemed clear that the issue of control, rather than environmental protection, was paramount for the Thai. Because the Loh Loe camp was isolated and had good access to roads and rivers, Thai officials were apprehensive about the ability of the camp inhabitants simply to "disappear" into Thailand. Loh Loe was said to be difficult to control, as Colonel Nimit explained at the time: "There are so many ways to sneak out of Loh Loe . . . from the pier [at Krone Kung] . . . they are free to go anywhere in the country. This makes it difficult for us to keep the Mon refugees in place."[22] Also, the links between the refugee camp and the NMSP—involving the transfer of food and other relief supplies from the camp to the NMSP across the border—was identified as problematic, especially since public knowledge of this relationship threatened Thailand's delicate diplomatic and business relationships with the Burmese government. Thailand was unwilling to be accused by Burma of "supporting the rebels." In the interview cited above, Colonel Nimit touched on this point: "The Mon refugees are allowed to stay on Thai soil due to humanitarian reasons only . . . Our government has built a strong relationship [with Burma] . . . and this is not to be destroyed."[23]

Overall, the series of site-to-site relocations served to emphasize the temporary status of the Mon camps. Rather than isolated incidents, the removals were components of a pattern in a wider climate of instability that came to characterize sanctuary for the Mon refugees in Thailand. The refugee population was inevitably at the mercy of the host authorities' decisions, and relocations served as a ready mechanism of control.

A DIMINISHING SANCTUARY: THE CASE OF HALOCKHANI

The relocation of the Mon refugees to Halockhani confirmed the sense that the Mon refugee camps in Thailand provided an insecure sanctuary. Questions regarding

---

[21] "Mon Refugees in Fear after Receiving Marching Orders," *The Nation*, October 12, 1993, p. 3.

[22] Ibid.

[23] Ibid.

safety plagued the new site. The MNRC considered Halockhani to be located too near danger and therefore unfit for a large refugee population since it was situated only about an hour's walk (four kilometers) from the local outpost of the Burmese army at Three Pagodas Pass. Concern about the location of Halockhani was expressed to the UNHCR (United Nations High Commission on Refugees) in Bangkok, which responded with reassurances that the population was "not in any immediate danger."[24] The UNHCR also reiterated the long-standing position of the Thai authorities that, in the event of an attack by the Burmese army, the residents of the new site would be allowed to move further into Thai territory.[25] Further into Thai territory? These responses failed to acknowledge that the position of Halockhani on the border was unclear and ambiguous. In fact, the camp site was soon entangled in a conflict sparked by the re-appropriation of an uncertain boundary, with implications for the refugees.

As recently as 1993, the Halockhani site was considered to be located in Burma, though now it seemed that the site, according to the Thai authorities, was "*on the border*."[26] In practical terms, the designation "on the border" permitted the continued delivery of humanitarian relief supplies and access to the refugees, an important consideration in view of Thailand's own prohibition against providing any cross-border assistance to the border areas inside Burma. This odd designation also enabled the population at Halockhani to maintain a *prima facie* status within the UNHCR mandate as refugees. Yet the refugee population at Halockhani inhabited an ambiguously defined space straddling a disputed part of the boundary. The uncertainty of the boundary, therefore, produced confusion with respect to whether the relocation to Halockhani was in fact a forced return (*refoulement*). Technically, the designation of the site as "on the border" meant, according to the Thai authorities, that the people in Halockhani had therefore not been forcibly repatriated across the border; this interpretation was accepted by the UNHCR. Following the succession of relocations that appeared directed toward cross-border return, however, the population at Halockhani appeared to be placed in a precarious refuge.

Out of Danger?

The concerns expressed by the MNRC about the proximity of Halockhani to the *tatmadaw*'s base were realized when soldiers from the 62nd Infantry Battalion (IB) attacked the refugee camp on July 21, 1994, and the entire population of over six thousand fled across the Thai checkpoint in torrential monsoon conditions.

On the morning of July 21, at 7:30 am, some one hundred troops from the 62nd IB, stationed at Three Pagodas Pass, arrived without warning and occupied a section of Halockhani at the western edge of the camp (the Plat Hon Pai section, housing about five hundred people), where they arrested sixteen camp leaders for interrogation. Later that morning, the troops set off toward the main camp, collecting some fifty men for use as "shields," but were prevented from reaching it by an ambush staged by MNLA soldiers. (The MNLA was aware of the movement

---

[24] Letter from UNHCR to Jack Dunford, Chairman, Burmese Border Consortium, CCSDPT, Bangkok, February 22, 1994.

[25] Ibid.

[26] Ibid.

of the Burmese troops and the possibility of attack because it had intercepted prior radio communications.) The retreating Burmese troops seized sixteen men as hostages and torched Plat Hon Pai.[27] Halockhani's six thousand inhabitants then fled unimpeded across the BPP checkpoint (an outpost of Company 134) at Ban Ton Yang,[28] where they set up a makeshift "settlement." The local authorities extended hospitality to the people in the immediate flurry of the attack, though a deadline for their return was soon introduced.

A number of different motives were suggested to explain the Burmese army's attack on the camp. One theory claimed that the 62nd IB was retaliating for a local incident that had occurred a month earlier. In this incident, which took place late at night on June 20, two *tatmadaw* soldiers had approached this same section of the camp, frightening a refugee couple who suspected that they were *dacoits* (bandits), resulting in an exchange of gunfire between the conflicting parties. In this exchange, the man shot one of the soldiers with his hunting rifle, and the soldier was found dead in the morning. (His G4 rifle was taken away to the Forestry Department of the NMSP.) According to a village leader, the soldiers from the 62nd IB visiting Plat Hon Pai on the morning of July 21 demanded to know whether there were guns in the village, probably because they hoped to discover the dead soldier's G4 rifle, which had gone missing the month before. A second theory, proposed by MNRC and the NMSP sources, maintained that the attack and seizure of the hostages was an organized effort (carried out in conjunction with the Southeastern Regional Command in Moulmein) to capture and intimidate village leaders, teachers, and health workers residing at Halockhani because they were regarded as NMSP sympathizers.[29] Adding to the debate, the Thai Ninth Infantry Division's commander, Major-General Chalong Chotikakham, essentially dismissed both these theories, noting that the Burmese soldiers from the 62nd IB entered the camp in search of weapons (and when no weapons were handed over, burnt down several houses in anger) and in order to conscript porters (referring to the men taken hostage).[30] The raid on the camp was also explained as part of the Burmese army's effort to demonstrate their power in the general area through which the Yadana gas pipeline to Thailand would run.[31]

The Halockhani residents themselves, rather than pausing to debate the precise motives for the attack, simply fled the camp in fear.

---

[27] Mon National Relief Committee, "Emergency Report of Mon National Relief Committee," unpublished statement, July 22, 1994.

[28] "Large Ethnic Group Flees Across Burmese Border," Radio Thailand Network (in Thai), Bangkok, recorded and translated by the Foreign Broadcast Information Service (FBIS), *Daily Report: Southeast Asia*, FBIS-EAS-94-141, July 22, 1994, pp. 50-51.

[29] Mon National Relief Committee, *Mon Refugees*, p. 9.

[30] "Army Official Calls Mon 'Illegal Immigrants,'" *The Nation*, August 27, 1994, p. A4.

[31] Ananda Rajah, "The Halockhani Incident and the Redefinition of a Boundary Issue between Burma and Thailand," *Boundary and Security Bulletin* 2,3 (1994): 94-95.

Immigration Detention Center deportees from Bangkok make their way to Halockhani camp on the border, 1994. Photo: Mon National Relief Committee

Temporary shelter at "New Halockhani" camp, July 1994.
Photo: Mon National Relief Committee

Thai border checkpoint at the Halockhani refugee camp (with Border Patrol Police outpost on the left). Photo: Hazel Lang

Boundary marker, Halockhani refugee camp (the Burmese side).
Photo: Hazel Lang

Bordering On Return

Local Thai authorities soon initiated attempts to return the people who were uncomfortably sheltering under blue tarpaulin and bamboo at the muddy new site, dubbed "New Halockhani," on the Thai side of the border checkpoint. At the height of the monsoon season, living conditions were difficult, with health troubles such as diarrhea, respiratory diseases, and malnutrition on the rise. Compounding the difficulties was the weekly arrival of additional illegal immigrants repatriated from the IDCs (Immigration Detention Centers) in Bangkok and Kanchanaburi, which together deported about four hundred people each week. This flood of hungry people strained already dwindling supplies at "New Halockhani." In spite of the dangers which had been confirmed by the July 21, 1994 attack, Thailand continued to pressure the Mon refugees to return to "old" Halockhani. On July 25 the Sangkhlaburi District Officer informed the MNRC that the refugees would not be permitted to remain in Thailand in any manner whatsoever.[32] Following a meeting between the MNRC and the BPP, an August 10 deadline was issued, and it was agreed that the BPP would be required to block access to the site if the deadline was contravened. However, the August 10 deadline passed, and the people remained. Ongoing appeals and representations were made by the MNRC to the local authorities, but the order to return held. In addition, at this time the Thai Ninth Infantry Division denied the UNHCR access to the camp.

Once the August 10 deadline had passed, the camp was officially sealed off, and refugees were categorically ordered to return to the old site. The Ninth Division instituted a blockade on basic supplies (including medicines and water) and on visitors (including the MNRC, the UNHCR, and news reporters). The rice store was, however, already stockpiled in preparation for the rainy season, and conditional access was granted to MSF doctors and the Burmese Border Consortium.[33] A combination of personnel from the BPP and local provincial police was used to block access to New Halockhani. Meanwhile, the fear of return on the part of the Mons was fueled further by news obtained by the BPP from intercepted military communications indicating that sporadic fighting between the *tatmadaw* and MNLA troops was occurring in the area. (Acting on this information, the BPP, on August 11, even instructed the camp to remain silent and extinguish all fires and lights.)[34] Unconvinced that they would be secure if they returned to Old Halockhani, the refugees defied orders and opted for the precarious shelter at New Halockhani.

The local authorities now extended the deadline to August 25. This announcement was accompanied by a statement from Deputy Secretary General of the NSC in Bangkok, Khachadpai Burusapatana, declaring the Mon population to be "illegal immigrants" who were required to return immediately once the situation went back to "normal." Khachadpai noted:

---

[32] Mon National Relief Committee, "Confidential Report of the Mon National Relief Committee, July 24, 1994," unpublished statement.

[33] Interviews with the CCSDPT and the MNRC, Sangkhlaburi and Bangkok, 1995.

[34] BurmaNet News, "Special Report from Inside Halockhani Camp." Received online from reg.burma@conf.igc.apc.org [August 13, 1994].

We regard them only as illegal immigrants. It is well known that this is Thailand's policy. Whenever there is fighting in Burma, there are always refugees fleeing across the border into Thailand at Mae Hong Son, Tak, and Kanchanaburi . . . When the situation returns to normal, we send them back to a safe area . . . The Mon are no exception. We cannot accept them as refugees.[35]

Responding to the Mons' refusal to move, the Thai government intensified its efforts to enforce their return. It was reported that troops from the Ninth Infantry Division and rangers were brought to the site to assist the BPP with repatriation.[36] Visitors to the camp were required to obtain prior written permission from the Ninth Infantry Division in Kanchanaburi. The officer in charge of border affairs at the Supreme Command Joint Operation Center in Bangkok, Lieutenant-General Sanan Kajornklam, also flew into the area. On August 22, a press conference was held with the *tatmadaw* commander of the 61st IB (which, in July, replaced the 62nd IB at Three Pagodas Pass), Colonel Tin Kyaw, in which he reassured his audience that it was now safe for the refugees to return to the original Halockhani site. Also, it was reported that a "guarantee" against any further attacks had been obtained from Colonel Tin Kyaw in earlier discussions between officers from the Ninth Infantry Division and the 61st IB.[37] Further, under instruction from the National Security Council, a detachment of rangers arrived and a Thai flag was erected at the outpost, apparently as a form of "protection" for the Mon refugees.[38] Despite these many reassurances, the August 25 deadline passed like the others, and the MNRC's chairman, Pra Wongsa Pala, was unable to persuade the people to return voluntarily to the original Halockhani camp. The Commander of the Ninth Infantry Division in Kanchanaburi, Major-General Chalong Chotikakham, then also made a statement that the Mons were not refugees, but illegal immigrants who must return to their homeland, and that "There is no war in this part of Burma now."[39]

Finally, on August 31, 1994, under command of the Ninth Infantry Division, the BPP denied access to the refugees' vital resource, the rice store, which contained 70,000 kilograms in supplies. This store was located "in Thailand," but within the area of old Halockhani. It was decided that the rice would be blockaded and access to it prevented until the people agreed to go back. According to refugee advocates and representatives, hunger thus became the tool of repatriation and, eventually, of resistance, for by holding out without rice as long as possible, the people demonstrated they were being "starved" back by the Thai government.[40] By September 9, the remaining population at the checkpoint site finally, albeit reluctantly, returned to the original Halockhani site. After returning, many shared houses, often moving in together at night and remaining in the section of the camp closest to the Thai checkpoint.[41]

---

[35] "Mon 'Illegal Immigrants' Urged to Return Home," *Bangkok Post*, August 13, 1994, p. 7.

[36] "Military Officer to Visit Area," *The Nation*, August 21, 1994, p. A2.

[37] "New Deadline Set for Return to Burma," *The Nation*, August 20, 1994, p. A4; "Officers Reassure Mon Refugees on Return to Burma," *The Nation*, August 23, 1994, p. A4.

[38] "Military Officer to Visit Area," p. A2.

[39] "Army Official Calls Mon 'Illegal Immigrants'," *The Nation*, August 27, 1994, p. A4.

[40] Interviews, CCSDPT, Bangkok, and MNRC, Sangkhlaburi, September 20, 1995.

[41] Ibid.

The Commander of the Royal Thai Army's First Region, Lieutenant-General Chetta Thanajaro, summarized the situation conclusively on September 9:

> I can give assurances that we respect the opinions of the international community—the United Nations. Regarding the Mons, as I am in charge of the First Army Region, I can say that I had to follow the government's policy for various reasons. First, the entry of the Mons was illegal. Second, their presence affected the livelihood of Thai people along the border. Third, destruction of the environment—the forest—was unavoidable. Fourth, their continued presence would have affected national security. There were also other repercussions resulting from their presence. They therefore had to leave. Their departure was achieved humanely. They went to areas which are safe.
>
> I would add that if fighting erupts after their return and their safety is threatened, they can cross into Thailand again. They will have to return once the situation in their country becomes normal.[42]

By September 14, the makeshift shelters of "New Halockhani" had been destroyed at the request of officials from the BPP. Thai authorities then lifted the blockade on September 15, and the flow of supplies resumed, though the rice store remained under the control of Thai soldiers who had managed distribution during the transitional period.

Until the Halockhani incident, the UNHCR had maintained a minimal involvement with the border camps. Its representatives remained in Bangkok, with only "very sporadic monitoring missions, every third month or so."[43] Following the events at Halockhani, however, the UNHCR became somewhat more involved with the refugees on the Burmese border. The UNHCR's Bangkok regional representative, Ruprecht von Arnhim, formally expressed concerns about the safety of the Mon refugees to then-General Secretary of the NSC (National Security Council), General Charan Kullavanijaya, and the Ministry of Foreign Affairs. The UNHCR obviously failed to gain any substantive concessions regarding the return of the Mons to Halockhani in 1994, but, according to Mr. von Arnhim, a clear break from past practice in relation to the Burmese refugees was achieved (behind the scenes), as the UNHCR gained acceptance as a mediator in negotiations pertaining to the Burmese refugee situation.[44]

In sum, the ambiguous location of Halockhani ("on the border") made it possible to obscure in diplomatic pronouncements a practice that accomplished, in fact, the *refoulement* of the Mon refugees. Although at first the Thai authorities claimed that Halockhani was not in Burma, it later transpired that the people had been "sent back." Where was Halockhani after all? By September 1994 it was clearly in Burma. The incident precipitated by the July 21 attack established a concrete boundary across this once permeable borderland locale. And it seemed that, for all the ambiguity about the boundary, the line was being redrawn to the

---

[42] First Army Regional Commander Lt.-Gen. Chetta Thanacharo, Radio Thailand Network in Thai, Bangkok, September 9, 1994, quoted and translated in *Foreign Broadcast Information Service* (FBIS), FBIS-EAS-94-177, September 13, 1994, p. 67.

[43] Interview, Ruprecht von Arnhim, UNHCR Regional Representative, Bangkok, September 18, 1995.

[44] Ibid.

disadvantage of the refugee population sheltering there. Thai authorities effectively imposed both a physical boundary on a once vague and ill-defined place, and a parallel "moral" boundary that finally excluded the Mon from shelter in Thailand.

The Halockhani incident served to draw unprecedented attention to this previously remote, unpoliticized, and permeable section of the border, which was now more strictly mapped and defined in response to the flow of unwanted people. In doing so, the Halockhani incident cast into question Thailand's adherence to the international principle of non-*refoulement*.

THE REPATRIATION OF THE MON REFUGEES IN 1996

The prospects of continued sanctuary for the Mon refugees in Thailand had deteriorated with the frequent relocations of the camps and when the events at Halockhani in 1994 demonstrated that the Mon were unwelcome on the Thai side of the border. The Commander of the Ninth Division, Major-General Chalong, had also already hinted during the Halockhani incident that residents of the last remaining Mon camp at Pa Yaw would also be sent back.[45] Therefore, after the cease-fire reached between the NMSP and the SLORC in Moulmein on June 29, 1995, the deadline for the final repatriation of the Mon refugees was set for April 30, 1996.

Repatriation as a "Refugee Solution"

How did the Mon refugees fare, in terms of both international repatriation standards and the substantive conditions of the return? Repatriation is the globally preferred refugee solution, provided it takes place under minimally acceptable conditions to ensure that the arrangement is safe and durable. The ideal international standard advocated by the UNHCR is "voluntary repatriation in safety and dignity" to an environment in which "the causes of flight have been definitively and permanently removed."[46] In the normative framework of international law, repatriation is favored as a matter of principle because it reflects the right of a citizen to return to his or her own country.[47] When conditions permit, repatriation may build confidence in a peace process at home by "demonstrating in a very tangible manner that the peace process is moving forward and having tangible results."[48] The Cambodian refugees from Thailand, for example, were returned in time to participate in the national elections held in May 1993. Voluntary repatriation and a safe return can conclude the temporary or "palliative" role[49] of international refugee protection agencies, in which protection is explicitly conditional based on the risk that refugees face in their

---

[45] "Army Official Calls Mon 'Illegal Immigrants'."

[46] United Nations High Commissioner for Refugees, *The State of the World's Refugees: The Challenge of Protection* (London: Penguin, 1993), p. 104.

[47] Guy S. Goodwin-Gill, *The Refugee in International Law* (Oxford: Clarendon Press, 1996), p. 275.

[48] United Nations High Commissioner for Refugees, *The State of the World's Refugees*, p. 107.

[49] James C. Hathaway, "New Directions to Avoid Hard Problems: The Distortion of the Palliative Role of Refugee Protection," *Journal of Refugee Studies* 8,3 (1995): 288-294.

country of origin. And finally, repatriation is obviously the most desirable solution from the perspective of most host governments, who wish to reduce the number of, and limit their obligations to, refugees within their borders.

International principles of repatriation are outlined in a number of sources of international law. The 1951 Convention does not mention repatriation *per se*, but the UNHCR Statute specifically mentions voluntary repatriation in article 8(c). However, as Barbara E. Harrell-Bond notes, the 1951 Convention does refer to a kind of repatriation, indirectly and negatively, in article 31, which prohibits the expulsion or forcible return of refugees to their former homes (*refoulement*).[50] B. S. Chimni, among other scholars, argues that repatriation under duress may be tantamount to *refoulement*.[51] In this regard, voluntary return may be regarded as a necessary corollary of the principle of non-*refoulement* recognized in customary international law. There are also two key UNHCR Executive Committee Conclusions adopted in 1980 and 1985 dealing with repatriation. The first looks towards the facilitation rather than promotion of repatriation, while the 1985 text emphasizes that:

> . . . the voluntary and individual character of repatriation of refugees and the need for it to be carried out under conditions of absolute safety, preferably to the place of residence of the refugee in his country of origin, should always be respected.[52]

The UNHCR's standards and principles for voluntary repatriation are elaborated in its Handbook on Voluntary Repatriation.[53] The protection responsibilities of UNHCR require the agency to obtain the best available information regarding conditions in the country of origin and accurate analysis of the extent to which the causes of the refugee flows have modified or ceased. The UNHCR is also obliged to "refrain from *promotion* of repatriation where circumstances have not changed, or where instability and insecurity continue."[54] At the same time, the UNHCR acknowledges the problems of refugee repatriation in practice. In its 1997 document on "Repatriation Challenges," it notes that many refugee repatriations are undertaken in fragile and uncertain political conditions, where large questions remain concerning voluntariness of return, precipitous repatriation under pressure, and lack of safety or lack of a fundamental improvement in the original conditions that provoked refugee flight.[55]

---

[50] Barbara Harrell-Bond, "Repatriation: Under What Conditions is it the Most Desirable Solution for Refugees? An Agenda for Research," *African Studies Review* 32,1 (1989): 47.

[51] B. S. Chimni, "The Meaning of the Words and the Role of the UNHCR in Voluntary Repatriation," *International Journal of Refugee Law* 5,3 (1993): 454. For a critical view, see also Harrell-Bond, "Repatriation," pp. 41-69.

[52] See Goodwin-Gill, *The Refugee in International Law*, pp. 272-273. The text of "UNHCR Executive Committee Conclusion No. 40 (XXXVI) 1985" is found in Annex 3.

[53] United Nations High Commissioner for Refugees, *Handbook, Voluntary Repatriation: International Protection* (Geneva: UNHCR, 1996).

[54] Goodwin-Gill, *The Refugee in International Law*, p. 273 (emphasis in original).

[55] See UNHCR, Executive Committee of the High Commissioner's Programme, "Forty-Eighth Session Annual Theme: Repatriation Challenges," UN doc. A/AC.96/887, September 9, 1997. Reproduced in *International Journal of Refugee Law* 9,4 (1997): 679-687.

After the Cease-fire: Evaluating the Repatriation

The fundamental characteristics of the Mon repatriation by Thailand failed to meet the basic requirements outlined by international standards in three ways. First, the pressure applied by the host authorities prior to the final cross-border relocation of Pa Yaw camp in 1996 raised doubts that the refugees were, in fact, returning voluntarily. Second, the lack of voluntariness notwithstanding, the Mon refugees were simply returned across the border to resettlement areas within territory remaining under the administrative control of the NMSP, and not to the places of their original residence. The NMSP and the SLORC agreed to the resettlement of the refugees to nine new villages in four districts: Tavoy, Bee Ree in the Upper Ye River Valley, the Three Pagodas Pass area, and Mergui (a temporary site). When the cease-fire and accompanying repatriation were announced, the Mons living in Pa Yaw camp expressed a willingness to return only if they could resume their lives without fear in the places where their original homes were located. Otherwise, with very few exceptions, they remained resigned to moving to the interim cross-border resettlement areas until sustainable peace enabled them confidently to return to their home villages.[56] The MNRC expressed doubts about the conditions of the repatriation and noted the refugees' reluctance to move, and it appealed for adherence to international principles:

> The Mon refugees are now looking forward to returning home and are hoping to go back as early as possible. However, to attempt to return them prematurely without necessary protection and assistance would cause uncertainty among the Mon refugees as to their future existence in Burma, and this could lead them to flee back to Thailand once again in the future.[57]

The MNRC position in this regard differed from the position of the NMSP leadership, for those leaders had not identified a safe, sustainable, or monitored return as one of their highest priorities during the cease-fire negotiations. Also, the MNRC request for monitoring by the UNHCR was rejected by the SLORC authorities in Rangoon.[58] Consequently, the NMSP and the MNRC agreed in November 1995 to form the Mon Resettlement Committee[59] to take responsibility for repatriation and for monitoring the areas in which the returnees were to live.

Third, the conditions for the Mon returnees fell short of the ideal that states refugees ought to be returned to their homes only when the causes of flight have been permanently and definitively removed. The Mon repatriation occurred in the context of a purely military cease-fire reached between the NMSP and the SLORC

---

[56] Post-cease-fire visit to Pa Yaw camp, August-September 1995.

[57] Mon National Relief Committee, "Statement of the Mon National Relief Committee Regarding the Repatriation Program of Mon Refugees," unpublished statement, August 31, 1995.

[58] The UNHCR representative in Bangkok was concerned about the prospects of an unmonitored return of the Mon to the Burmese side of the border: "On the other side there is nobody to help them. The UNHCR has a word on this side of the border; it may not always be perfect, but we have a word . . . they must have assurances." Interview, Ruprecht von Arnhim, UNHCR Regional Representative, Bangkok, September 18, 1995. NMSP President, Nai Shwe Kyin, also later in April wrote to Ruprecht von Arnhim requesting monitoring.

[59] The Resettlement Committee was comprised of mainly members from the various NMSP administrative districts.

on June 29, 1995.[60] The cease-fire was the fifteenth such agreement between the SLORC and the insurgencies since 1989, when, beginning with the Communist Party of Burma, the SLORC embarked on a strategy of inviting "armed groups in the jungles to return to the legal fold in appreciation of the government's goodwill."[61] The NMSP first agreed to enter into dialogue with the SLORC in Moulmein in December 1993, but after two subsequent attempts at talks in March and July 1994, both sides failed to agree on either party's military, political, or economic demands. When the cease-fire was finally concluded, the government hailed it as "national reconciliation achieved through sincerity and mutual understanding."[62] At the same time, the NMSP acknowledged the limitations of a purely military—possibly temporary—agreement, noting: "This truce is just a military cease-fire" and the "arduous task of finding [a] satisfactory political solution is still in abeyance."[63]

The cease-fire primarily involved the renunciation of armed struggle by the NMSP (although the NMSP secured permission to retain their arms within their specified deployment areas) in exchange for "national development" under the auspices of the government's Central Committee for Development of the Border Areas and National Races. Discussions were held concerning funding for the restoration of the deteriorated roads between Thanbyuzayat and Three Pagodas Pass, as well as between Thanbyuzayat and Ye, for example.[64] On the matter of forced labor and portering services for the military, the SLORC authorities agreed in principle that these practices would eventually cease and that contracts would eventually be used to secure labor for infrastructure projects. At the same time, the SLORC could not promise that the army would cease conscripting porters so long as *tatmadaw* troops moved in and around the area in the immediate period subsequent to the cease-fire.[65] The NMSP also initiated negotiations to conduct business, such as import-export activities, logging, fishing, and other joint ventures, negotiations which were then scheduled to be continued in August in Rangoon.[66] Discussion concerning Mon participation in the political process was limited and resulted in nothing more than an agreement that the Mons would wait for the drafting of the future Constitution and that Mon representatives might possibly be granted

---

[60] The cease-fire was concluded at the Southeastern Regional Command headquarters in Moulmein, with senior members of NMSP led by Nai Tin (Vice-President) and Lt. Gen. Khin Nyunt (Secretary 1 of the SLORC) and eleven ministers in attendance to discuss "development" matters (health, education, roads, and so forth). There were also three mediators: Nai Khin Maung (a Mon MP from the Mon National Democratic Front, elected in 1990), Nai Pe Tin (a Mon merchant from Moulmein), and U Khun Myat (a Kachin businessman also involved in the SLORC-Kachin Independence Organization [KIO] cease-fire reached in 1993).

[61] Embassy of the Union of Myanmar, Bangkok, "New Mon State Party Becomes 15th Group to Realize True Attitude of the Government," *News Bulletin*, No. 16/95, July 7, 1995.

[62] "National Reconciliation Achieved through Sincerity, Mutual Understanding," *The New Light of Myanmar*, June 30, 1995.

[63] New Mon State Party, General Headquarters, Central Committee, "Statement on Ceasefire between the State Law and Order Restoration Council (SLORC) and the New Mon State Party (NMSP)," unpublished statement obtained from the NMSP, July 13, 1995.

[64] Personal discussion with NMSP officials, Bangkok and Sangkhlaburi, August 1995.

[65] Ibid.

[66] Letter, Nai Shwe Kyin, President of NMSP, to General Charan Kullavanijaya, Secretary General of the National Security Council, Thailand, dated August 1, 1998.

observer status at the SLORC's National Convention convened to draft the Constitution.[67] The mechanism for future communication and coordination with the government was established through a series of NMSP liaison offices located in Moulmein, Thanbyuzayat, Ye, Three Pagodas Pass, and Mergui.

The cease-fire agreement provided for twelve military "deployment areas" of five miles in radius under the control of the NMSP (with eight additional temporary areas established for an initial designated minimum period of six months). The NMSP requested that refugees be resettled in these areas of control, close to the Thai border, between November 1995 and April 1996. The proximity of the resettlement sites to Thailand allowed for the returnees to flee across the border in the advent of a breakdown in the cease-fire or a new outbreak of skirmishes. That is, Thailand did not "seal" the border against future refugee emergencies.

Overall, the agreements made at the time of the cease-fire, agreements which sought to repatriate the Mon refugees by 1996, were short-sighted and failed to provide a "durable solution" to the Mon refugee dilemma. The cease-fire necessarily addressed the immediate military dimension of violence for the war-weary combatant and civilian populations, but it did not resolve long-term problems of political reconciliation and peace. In furnishing the pretext for the return of the refugees, therefore, the military cease-fire reached in June 1995 did not engender confidence in the civilian populace for a durable return to a situation made tolerable by a lasting peace. Instead, the displaced Mons were returned, under sustained pressure from the host country and without international monitoring, to an interim arrangement in a politically fragile environment. They were also returning to an environment in the border areas marked by continuing (and sometimes growing) militarization, in which many of the original factors causing civilian displacement and flight persisted.

The Mon returnees completed their scheduled move to the resettlement areas by April 1996, and the authorities in Rangoon and Thailand permitted the CCSDPT to continue providing cross-border relief supplies,[68] which were stockpiled for the first year. Already in May 1996, however, camp committees in the resettlement areas of Halockhani and Tavoy reported new arrivals of displaced persons from neighboring Mon areas. They came to Halockhani from various villages in Ye township (Mon State), Kya Inn Seik Kyi township (Karen State), and Yebyu township (Tenasserim Division); they came to the Tavoy resettlement area from villages also in Yebyu township.[69]

---

[67] Personal discussion with officials from the NMSP, Bangkok and Sangkhlaburi, August 1995.

[68] These included rice, foodstuffs, general supplies (such as mosquito nets, mats, and blankets), medical supplies and also agricultural supplies (such as seeds, beans, and equipment including hoes, ploughs, etc.), in order to establish a degree of self-sufficiency. The returnees were encouraged to clear land for farms and cultivate their own rice (slash and burn cultivation) in the resettlement site areas. In 1996, however, efforts to grow rice were hampered by the need to construct new housing. A land dispute also erupted in April 1996 between Mon farmers planning to grow rice and Thai authorities in the Baleh Hnook area (close to Halockhani camp). For example, according the Mon National Relief Committee, *Monthly Report May 1996*, Thai authorities, including the military and the BPP, ordered approximately fifty Mon farmers out of the area.

[69] Mon National Relief Committee, *Monthly Report May 1996*, unpublished document, p. 3. New arrivals in May were reported as numbering forty-five families to Halockhani camp and forty families to the Tavoy area. The Burmese Border Consortium also noted the advent of new

Despite the cease-fire, civilians were still fleeing from the same locales which earlier refugees had abandoned in fear. They were not fleeing from the effects of direct fighting, but from the indirect effects of the war-zone that continued to surround them, where civilians remained targets for service as military porters, corvée laborers (mainly for the Ye-Tavoy railway and road), and were subject to ongoing arbitrary financial burdens.

As noted in Chapter Three, if we are considering civilian displacement, it is important to acknowledge that the cease-fire did improve the situation of the Mon in significant ways: fighting ceased, and the Burmese army no longer assumed a direct association between civilians and insurgents, so that civilians did not feel themselves constantly under suspicion as "rebel sympathizers." The cease-fire thus helped to alleviate the entrenched cycle of suspicion and fear connected to allegations of civilian support for the NMSP in the context of counter-insurgency campaigns. This applied to the former contested NMSP "black" and "brown" areas, and the cease-fire was clearly a necessary step towards peace in this regard. However, the original factors provoking flight encompassed both the direct and indirect effects of the civil war. The indirect consequences associated with the war, such as forced labor and portering, financial demands, and the cycle of periodic hiding and return, served to undermine and destabilize livelihoods and to threaten basic survival. A durable cease-fire and sustainable repatriation required the removal of both direct and indirect causes of flight. These requirements, however, remained clearly problematic in the post-cease-fire context.

Meanwhile, The War Goes On

Meanwhile, outside the small domain of resettlement sites and the NMSP cease-fire territories, and elsewhere in the eastern border regions of Burma, civil war continued with intensity. While the SLORC managed to seal fifteen cease-fire agreements with insurgent groups in 1995, not all insurgents were willing to negotiate. A major exception was the Karen National Union (KNU), the largest and longest-running ethnic insurgency, which continued to fight an increasingly formidable *tatmadaw* making substantial military gains into formerly rebel-held territories.

Already stripped of its large bases along the Thai-Burmese border,[70] the KNU came under sustained attack in two new major offensives against its positions in Karen State and Tenasserim Division beginning in February 1997. These positions were held by the KNU's 6th Brigade in Duplaya district (adjacent to Thai territory between Sangkhlaburi and Mae Sot) and its 4th Brigade, located in areas along the upper Tenasserim and Paw Kloh rivers in the Mergui-Tavoy district (opposite Thai territory from Sangkhlaburi to Prachuab Khirikhan). The offensives were large-scale, with some twenty thousand *tatmadaw* troops from six different Light Infantry Divisions deployed.[71] An estimated twenty thousand

arrivals. Burmese Border Consortium, "Burmese Border Consortium 1996—Emergency/ Funding Update No. 2," private NGO correspondence, May 20, 1996.

[70] Notably, the *tatmadaw* captured KNU headquarters at Manerplaw in January 1995, followed by Kawmura (sixty kilometers south of Manerplaw) in February 1995.

[71] Karen Human Rights Group, "An Independent Report by the Karen Human Rights Group," KHRG No. 97/07, May 2, 1997, p. 3.

Karen refugees fled into Thailand in February 1997, while others remained trapped or internally displaced, as the government's capture of former-KNU border territories in some areas prevented access to Thailand. Moreover, the Burmese army initiated a large-scale conscription of civilian porters from Mon State, Karen State, and Tenasserim Division in its February 1997 offensives against the KNU. Each region had to contribute ten thousand porters, totaling thirty thousand people.[72] According to the Mon Information Service, into May 1997, an estimated five thousand civilians from towns and villages in Tenasserim Division (Yebyu, Tavoy, Launglon and Thayet Chaung townships) were conscripted during the first two weeks of May 1997, apparently at random, to work as frontline porters for over two thousand troops in the *tatmadaw*'s 33rd Infantry Division during its operation against the KNU, the All Burma Students' Democratic Front (ABSDF), and the Myeik-Dawei United Front (MDUF, a small ethnic Tavoyan armed group) in the KNU's 4th Brigade area.[73]

In view of continuing conflict in the southeastern border region of Burma as a whole, therefore, the Mon repatriation did not constitute an internationally acceptable or "durable" refugee solution. Benefits gained from the NMSP SLORC cease-fire and the subsequent repatriation of the Mon refugees in 1996 were confined to the narrow jurisdiction of the cease-fire areas and were, in fact, marginal in relation to the broader situation of ongoing conflict and civilian displacement elsewhere.

As indicated, militarization in the border areas of southeastern Burma, if not throughout the entire region of the Thai-Burmese border,[74] continued after the NMSP cease-fire. Militarization took the form of direct hostilities (notably between the *tatmadaw* and the KNU), consolidation of counterinsurgency campaigns (the army "secured" newly captured territories through depopulation and by cutting off supplies to the KNU in some areas and establishing permanent control in others), expansion of numbers of troops, and increased surveillance in particular regions.[75] According to one account, for example, two large relocations

---

[72] Personal communication, Mon Information Service, Thailand, February 1998. In addition to enduring the physical conscription of porters, households across the region were required to pay levies described as "emergency portering fees." In Moulmein alone, 250-300 persons recruited as porters were believed to have been detained daily in an all-weather stadium under "armed guard" of the 31st and 62nd Infantry Battalions. Mon Information Service (MIS), *Life in the Country: Continued Human Rights Violations in Burma* (Bangkok: MIS, July 1997), p. 19.

[73] Ibid.

[74] Counterinsurgency campaigns continued—at various stages, affecting all ethnic groups—in the border territories, from Tenasserim Division in the south to Shan State in the northeast. In central Shan State, for example, a forcible relocation program in the large rural areas of eleven townships was launched in March 1996, affecting at least 300,000 people. The program was intensified during 1997 and 1998. Villagers subject to relocation either moved to the relocation sites, fled into hiding in jungles nearby, or fled into Thailand as illegal migrants (an estimated eighty thousand). See Amnesty International, *Myanmar: Atrocities in the Shan State*, ASA 16/05/98 (London: Amnesty International, April 15, 1998); and The Shan Human Rights Foundation, *Dispossessed: Forced Relocation and Extra-judicial Killings in Shan State* (Chiang Mai: Shan Human Rights Foundation, April 1998).

[75] For instance, in Tenasserim Division it was estimated that, by 1996, five battalions comprising some two thousand government troops (LIBs 217, 282 and LIBs 404, 405, and 406) were exclusively associated with the security of the sixty-three-kilometer onshore stretch of the Yadana gas pipeline (running through portions of KNU-held areas). The new Coastal Region Military Command created in early 1996 in the south, headquartered in Mergui town and

were carried out under the new Coastal Region Military Command in Tenasserim in 1996.[76] Orders for the relocation of Karen and Mon villages in Kya Inn Seik Kyi township were also documented in September 1997.[77] In addition, since May 1997, over 270 villages in the townships of Thayet Chaung, Tavoy, and Launglon of Tenasserim Division were required to perform a twenty-four-hour "anti-guerrilla watch" for the Coastal Region Military Command and the local township Law and Order Restoration Councils.[78] Forced labor and extortion (including "portering fees") also continued in areas of Mon State and Tenasserim Division, from Kya Inn Seik Kyi township in the north to Yebyu township in the south, although villagers were granted some respite from work on the Ye-Tavoy railway.[79] Since 1996, male villagers were being conscripted as new recruits for the *tatmadaw* within the jurisdiction of the Coastal Region Command. It was reported that in 1996 each local battalion was required to make a quota of five new recruits per month, a total of sixty for 1996; and, in 1997, the quota was set at three recruits per month, a total of thirty-six recruits for the year in 1997.[80] Local sources in the Tavoy district also noted that new recruits were conscripted to undergo basic military training for the *tatmadaw* from villages in the area of Yebyu, Tavoy, and Thayet Chaung townships, under the Coastal Region Command, in May 1997. Each village, depending on its size, was required to provide from two to five young men to the army. [81]

The Mon repatriation in the resettlement area of the Mergui district was also disrupted by new fighting, as a small breakaway faction from the NMSP attempted to hold onto former NMSP territory, one of the temporary deployment areas under the cease-fire which was scheduled to be released to the *tatmadaw* in late 1996. The splinter group, known as the Mon Army Mergui District (MAMD), comprising less than two hundred troops, broke away from the NMSP on November 6, 1996.[82] It was met with a sustained *tatmadaw* offensive, however, beginning on

---

covering Tenasserim Division, was composed of twenty-seven battalions and two artillery units (11,400 armed forces) compared to only five battalions (some two thousand troops) in this region before 1988. ABSDF Documentation and Research Center, *Terror in the South* (Bangkok: ABSDF, November 1997), p. 20.

[76] Ibid., pp. 25-26.

[77] Mon Information Service, "Forced Relocation of Karen and Mon Villagers in Kya Inn Seik Kyi Township," unpublished statement, October 14, 1997. The statement indicated that officials from the NMSP attempted to intervene in the relocations, resulting in an agreement to halt the orders but mandating movement of some, not all.

[78] Mon Information Service, *What is Going on in Burma's Coastal Region? A News Report* (Bangkok: MIS, January 1998), p. 3.

[79] As noted in Chapter Three, the railway was completed and officially opened in March 1998, and *tatmadaw* soldiers had undertaken some of the construction work at various times since 1996.

[80] Mon Information Service, *What is Going On in Burma's Coastal Region?*, p. 2.

[81] A reported payment of 10,000 *kyats* was required as payment from those villages not willing to provide recruits. Mon National Relief Committee, *Monthly Report June 1997*, unpublished document, pp. 1-2.

[82] This information is based on discussions with former MAMD soldiers, Bangkok, February 1998. Since the cease-fire between the NMSP and the SLORC in June 1995, a number of small, regionally located Mon splinter groups have broken away from the NMSP. In addition to the MAMD, for instance, a small splinter group, formed in December 1995, began operating in Tavoy District, in the area south of Ye as well as in Yebyu township.

April 13, 1997, and heavy fighting broke out in the Chaung Kyi area opposite Thailand's Thap Sakae district in Prachuab Khirikhan province. A refugee village under the control of the MAMD was burned down, and several others in the area were destroyed during the offensive; several locally conscripted porters were also killed in landmine explosions. By April 26, the *tatmadaw* occupied the area and had established a base. Over eight hundred local villagers and returnees fled across the Thai border into Thap Sakae district.

Local Thai authorities initially provided these displaced persons with temporary shelter close to the BPP checkpoint, although the temporary nature of the arrangement was strongly emphasized. People were expected to return after the fighting had stopped or to move to Halockhani camp. The MAMD eventually surrendered to the SLORC on May 25, 1997, placing the refugees under pressure for an immediate return to the Chaung Kyi area. The villagers generally feared return to the newly occupied area, but at a meeting between the Commander of the Coastal Region Command and the Thai Ninth Infantry Division on May 30, they were committed to return.[83] On June 6, some five hundred people were repatriated, a process that was observed from the Thai side by the UNHCR and some media and non-governmental organizations. No independent monitoring was permitted on the Burmese side, and the MNRC complained that they had been handed into the direct control of the Burmese army. Following their return, the MNRC noted that the Burmese army established checkpoints around their villages, and some of the returnees were required to contribute to the construction of the local military encampments in the villages of the Chaung Kyi area.[84] The MNRC noted that, after the attempted seizure of villagers for use in the *tatmadaw's* continuing offensive in the nearby KNU 4th Brigade area in the second week of July, around four hundred people fled to Thailand again, the majority moving further into Thailand as illegal immigrants.[85]

In early 1997, the official terminology in Thailand referring to "displaced persons" shifted to the more restrictive designation of "displaced persons fleeing fighting"; this new phrase was employed by each of the relevant authorities. This term applied particularly to those seeking asylum in the border areas of the First Army's Ninth Infantry Division, as well as in some parts of the Third Army region (notably in the Umphang district of Tak province). New refugee camps were now referred to as "temporary sites," and many of these camps were more restrictive than before, with minimal physical structures and prohibitions against free entry,[86] so that a growing number of asylum seekers were living outside the camp structure. The new terminology emphasized "fleeing from fighting" as the defining

---

[83] The Ninth Infantry Division also met earlier with MNRC Chairman, Abbot Pra Wongsa Pala, and MAMD personnel to request the MAMD to surrender. Interview, Pra Wongsa Pala, Bangkok, March 2, 1998.

[84] Mon National Relief Committee, *Monthly Report June 1997*, unpublished document, p. 4.

[85] Ibid., p. 2.

[86] In early 1997, the Karen camps of Htam Hin and Don Yan (housing some 7,400 and 1,500 people respectively) in Kanchanaburi province, for example, were not permitted to build structures with thatched roofs or sleeping platforms. Instead, they were permitted only plastic sheeting, despite the onset of the rainy season. On her visit to Htam Hin in October 2000, the chief of the UNHCR, Sadako Ogata, said that she was "shocked" at the crowded conditions she witnessed in the camp. "UN Chief Shocked at Camp Conditions," Associated Press, October 17, 2000.

character of displacement and the condition for sanctuary ·in Thailand. The policy and practice in some areas echoed the policies of "humane deterrence" which had been adopted by Thailand in the 1980s when it faced the growing burden of the Indochinese refugees. The assumption was that once the fighting stopped, the people should return to their homes. In this respect, the broader context and complexities of displacement were not acknowledged. The new restrictions on the Karen asylum seekers culminated in a highly publicized *refoulement* in Umphang district of Tak province in November 1997. The UNHCR judged this to be an act of *refoulement*, and the newly elected Chuan Leekpai government in Thailand intervened, promising that such an action would not be repeated.[87] The formal 1998 statement by the Royal Thai Government inviting the UNHCR to take on a active role in border situations demonstrated an evolving response on the part of Thailand and due consideration to the serious protection concerns it continued to confront.

SHIFTING SANCTUARY

In the case of the Mons, the contingencies of a shifting sanctuary endangered refugee protection. A detailed look at the Mon refugees' situation showed how these people became increasingly vulnerable to the political vicissitudes that unsettled their cross-border sanctuary in Thailand, culminating in an involuntary repatriation to Burma in 1996 which did not satisfy minimum refugee protection standards. To understand the dilemmas faced by the Mon refugees is not to understand the whole refugee predicament along the border, as responses in different areas have varied over time, from locale to locale, and across the agencies dealing with refugee politics. Yet the response to the Mons needs to be considered carefully in view of the remaining camps along the border. For the Burmese refugees in Thailand, sanctuary has been negotiated at the edge of refugee protection, which, in the case of the Mons, finally excluded them from protection altogether. The following chapter extends the examination of the political contingencies shaping sanctuary further in relation to the fluid context of the borderlands' geography, in which the Burmese refugees have lived and continue to live.

---

[87] Personal discussion, Jack Dunford, Chairman, Burma Border Consortium, CCSDPT, Bangkok, February 26, 1998; and Khun Wannida Boonpracong, Chief, Displaced Persons and Illegal Immigrant Affairs Subdivision, Ministry of Interior, Bangkok, March 9, 1998.

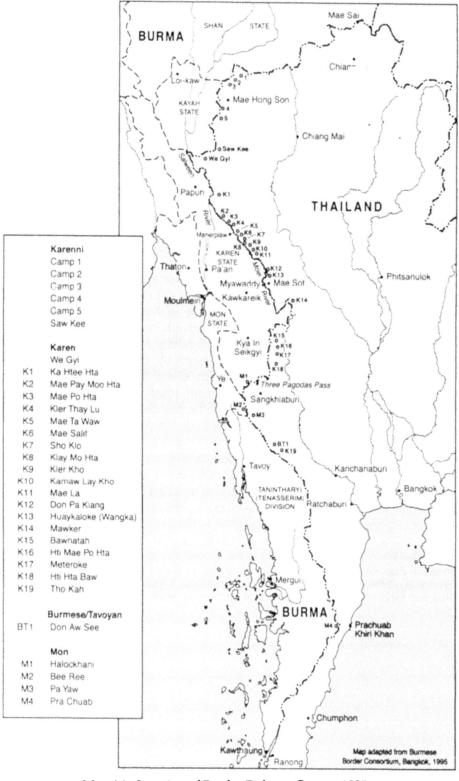

Map 6.1   Location of Border Refugee Camps, 1995

CHAPTER SIX

REFUGEES AND THE BORDER

What the map cuts up, the story cuts across.

Michel de Certeau, 1994[1]

INTRODUCTION

Of all the villagers I talked with during my stay at the Pa Yaw refugee camp, very few described their flight into the Thai borderland as the crossing of an international border. Their border crossing was described as a trek that brought them from fear to the comparative safety of the "relief village" at Pa Yaw. Yet it was the location of the camps across the international boundary into Thai jurisdiction that made this sanctuary possible, and in various ways, the evolving military and political geography of the borderland affected the fortunes of their sanctuary. Borders are "political membranes"[2] encompassing symbolic, military, legal, cultural, and economic phenomena, and they function variously as places of separation and regulation, of interaction, passage, and opportunity. The opportunity provided by the Thai borderland as a sanctuary for refugees cannot be understood separately from the various components that infuse and have an impact upon it.

In this chapter, the shifting contingencies that have shaped and reconfigured refugee sanctuary are further illuminated through an elaboration of historical and contemporary aspects of the Thai-Burmese border. The first historical section outlines the traditional notion of borders in the precolonial polity in Thailand (where territoriality was of less consequence to population migrations) and how it contrasted with the"territorialization" of today's modern body politic and its geographic boundaries (where territorial borders matter for refugee protection). The second, larger section of the chapter then examines some of the salient features of contemporary border politics—the changing configuration of Thai-Burmese relations and the borderland over time, especially since 1988—and explores how this unfolding context has affected the fortunes of refugee sanctuary. Finally, particular attention is directed to the implications of the transformation in the security landscape of the border in 1995, when cross-border raids on the Karen refugee camps began and the refugee population itself came to feature more prominently in the deteriorating borderlands' security environment.

---

[1] Michel de Certeau, *The Practice of Everyday Life*, trans. Steven F. Rendall (Berkeley: University of California Press, 1984), p. 129.

[2] Thomas M. Wilson and Hastings Donnan, "Nation, State and Identity at International Borders," in *Border Identities: Nation and State at International Frontiers*, ed. Thomas M. Wilson and Hastings Donnan (Cambridge: Cambridge University Press, 1998), p. 9.

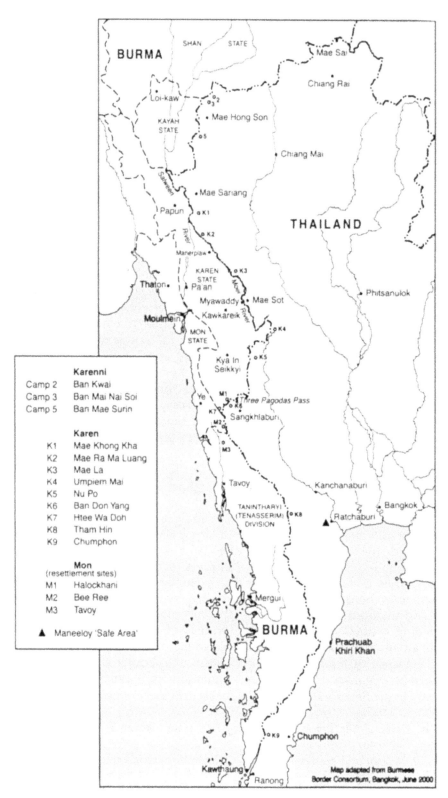

Map 6.2   Location of Border Refugee Camps, 2000

Borders

In political geography, the concept of the border combines two phenomena: boundary and borderland. Boundaries denote a precisely defined political-territorial line on a map dividing two contiguous states. In Ladis K. D. Kristof's classic formulation, "the boundary indicates certain well established limits (the bounds) of the given political unit" and as such functions to exert an arbitrary limit separating two jurisdictions.[3] The concept of borderlands, on the other hand, does not carry the same cartographic precision. Instead, borderlands (or frontiers), as "zones or territories flanking and straddling international land boundaries,"[4] are a more fluid ecumene, encompassing a confluence of political, military, cultural, and economic interactions.[5] The characteristic distinction in political geography is therefore between the boundary as a definite line of separation and the frontier or borderland as a zone of contact and interaction. For Kristof, the disciplinary orderliness of the boundary contrasts with the frontier, for the frontier is "characteristic of rudimentary socio-political relations; relations marked by rebelliousness, lawlessness, and/or absence of laws."[6] In comparison, the boundary

> . . . has no life of its own, not even a material existence . . . Also, the boundary is not tied inextricably to people—people teeming, spontaneous, and unmediated in their daily activities on, along, or athwart the border . . . It is . . . abstracted and generalized in the national law, subjected to the tests of international law, it is far removed from the changing desires and aspirations of the inhabitants of the borderlands.[7]

But while a boundary is set up to establish a blunt distinction, enabling officials to exert the authority of national and international law inside designated territories, the sovereign state is always subject to the persistent flows that traverse the borderlands' environment. The authority of the boundary is not (and cannot) be strictly or entirely imposed according to Krisof's formulation. Modern boundaries are often the arbitrary products of history, in particular colonialism and imperialism, while the borderland is a lived and negotiated political phenomenon, flowing across the boundary in different forms.

Here, the Thai-Burmese border is conceptualized as combining these two notions. Although a discrete international boundary has been mapped (albeit with many points of unclear or disputed demarcation), a borderlands environment flourishes there as well. And this political geography entails substantial

---

[3] Ladis K. D. Kristof, "The Nature of Frontiers and Boundaries," *Annals of the Association of American Geographers* 49,3 (1959): 270-273. For a review discussion of boundaries and frontiers, see also J. R. V. Prescott, *Boundaries and Frontiers* (London: Crook & Helm, 1978).

[4] Carl Grundy-Warr, "Coexistent Borderlands and Intra-state Conflicts in Mainland Southeast Asia," *Singapore Journal of Tropical Geography* 14,1 (1993): 45.

[5] Dennis Rumley and Julian V. Minghi, "Introduction: The Border Landscape Concept," in *The Geography of Border Landscapes*, ed. Dennis Rumley and Julian V. Minghi (London: Routledge, 1991), p. 4.

[6] Kristof, "The Nature of Frontiers and Boundaries," p. 281.

[7] Ibid., p. 272.

consequences for the fortunes of the refugees. In Burma, half a century of armed rebellion and counterinsurgency has created a violently contested and fractured frontier geography, which in turn affects both sides of the boundary. From the perspective of the refugees sheltered in Thailand, the boundary has been a form of physical protection, and the borderland has made it possible for them to respond flexibly to threats by periodically fleeing from their neighboring war-zone homelands. However, the borderlands' environment has been in a state of transition, influencing, and, most recently, complicating, the refugees' situation vis-à-vis their cross-border haven. How this has occurred is examined in the second part of this chapter.[8] The borders of the precolonial state, however, were managed differently, with different consequences for migrant people.

HISTORICAL DIMENSIONS

As Thongchai Winichakul shows in his book, *Siam Mapped*,[9] Thailand's modern territorial form of sovereignty emerged as recently as the 1870s. The official representation of a "bounded Siam" first appeared in 1893, with only the boundary and map of the western front between Siam and Burma completed.[10] Boundaries—continuous lines on a map "demarcating an exclusive sovereignty wedged between other sovereignties"—are a recent invention and legacy of European imperialism in the region for Thailand, Burma, and other Southeast Asian polities, indeed throughout much of the non-Western world.[11] Traditional conceptions of political administration and space, in which the traditional polity was generally defined more by its center than its boundaries, were directly and indirectly transformed in the wake of European colonialism.

The Traditional Polity

Traditionally, Southeast Asian kingdoms were composed of "galactic polities" or "central planets" surrounded by an attenuated field of satellite tributary states whose number and allegiances fluctuated according to the military and political strength of the center.[12] Political and administrative control was vertically organized in a patron-client structure, situated around a core ruler, while effective power outside the center was generally weaker and more diffuse. Also, traditional statecraft as it functioned in Burma, Siam, Cambodia, and Java was oriented towards the control of people—for the collection of taxes and levies, conscripted

---

[8] This discussion of borderland politics is largely focused on the Siamese/Thai side, with an emphasis on the borderlands' context of sanctuary in Thailand.

[9] Thongchai Winichakul, *Siam Mapped: A History of the Geo-body of a Nation* (Chiang Mai: Silkworm Books, 1994). Siam was renamed Thailand in 1941.

[10] Ibid., p. 128.

[11] See Benedict Anderson, *Imagined Communities: Reflections on the Origins and Spread of Nationalism* (London: Verso, 1991), p. 172.

[12] See Victor B. Lieberman, "Ethnic Politics in Eighteenth-Century Burma," *Modern Asian Studies* 12,3 (1978): 458. See also, Robert E. Elson, "International Commerce, the State and Society: Economic and Social Change," in *The Cambridge History of Southeast Asia*, Vol. 2, ed. Nicholas Tarling (Cambridge: Cambridge University Press, 1992), pp. 131-132.

labor service, and mobilization for war—rather than towards the control of land or territory as such.[13]

In Siam, according to the cosmological worldview of the court, the king occupied the focal role as the divine monarch residing at the center of a sacred space, with power emanating outward and downward from him.[14] At the core of the royal domain, the direct administration of the king prevailed, spatialized by an apparatus of cosmologically oriented palaces, courts, and chambers. Beyond the royal domain was a series of provinces, tributary states, and small hill principalities, acknowledging varying degrees of obligation, sanction, and allegiance vis-à-vis the Siamese dynasty.[15] Thus, in the early nineteenth-century "Siam was a small kingdom exercising loose control over a large hinterland."[16] The network of local rulers throughout the realm frequently juggled their allegiances with several overlapping, competing neighboring empires. Siamese kings did not and could not impose any form of close rule over the far-flung hinterland territories which are today included in country maps of Thailand.[17] Rather, the center aimed to secure from the hinterland supplies of valuable forest goods (as tax or tribute), trade routes, supplies of people for labor and warfare, and the loyalty of local rulers so that they would be allies, not enemies, in times of war.

"Territorializing" the Traditional Polity

But by the mid-nineteenth century, the traditional polity had entered an era of substantial transformation, or "revolution in government."[18] This began in the 1860s under King Mongkut (1851-68), who recognized that "the independence of his realm depended on understanding the mentality of those behind Western colonial

---

[13] David Joel Steinberg, ed., *In Search of Southeast Asia: A Modern History* (Honolulu: University of Hawai'i Press, 1987), p. 30. As Desmond Ball points out, military strategy was not about territory. See Desmond Ball, "Strategic Culture in the Asia-Pacific Region," *Security Studies* 3,1 (1993): 48.

[14] Charles F. Keyes, *Thailand: Buddhist Kingdom as Modern Nation-State* (Boulder, CO: Westview Press, 1987), p. 52. For further discussion of the cosmological world view and its influence on the organisation of government in the traditional polity, see also Fred W. Riggs, *Thailand: The Modernization of a Bureaucratic Polity* (Honolulu: East-West Center Press, 1966), pp. 66-79.

[15] For further elaboration on the nature of tributary relationships, see Thongchai, *Siam Mapped*, pp. 81-83. See also O. W. Wolters, *History, Culture, and Region in Southeast Asian Perspectives* (Singapore: Institute of Southeast Asian Studies, 1982), pp. 16-33.

[16] Pasuk Phongpaichit and Chris Baker, *Thailand: Economy and Politics* (New York: Oxford University Press, 1995), p. 211. In the early to mid-nineteenth century, the area directly ruled from Bangkok was confined to the rice basin extending about 100 kilometers north-south through the Chrao Phraya Delta, with border outposts to the west (Kanchanaburi and Tak) and east (Korat and Prachin). For a more detailed description of the outer provinces, Siamese tributary states, and the small hill principalities, see ibid., pp. 212-215.

[17] Ibid., pp. 4, 44. By the end of 1851, principalities in what are today northern Thailand, Laos, the southernmost part of Yunnan, the sultanates on the Malay peninsula, and the kingdom of Cambodia were all under the suzerainty of Bangkok. Charles F. Keyes, "Cultural Diversity and National Identity in Thailand," in *Government Policies and Ethnic Relations in Asia and the Pacific*, ed. Michael E. Brown and Sumit Ganguly (Cambridge, MA: MIT Press, 1997), p. 198.

[18] Pasuk and Baker, *Thailand: Economy and Politics*, p. 221.

expansion,"[19] and it intensified in the 1880s and 1890s during the reign of King Chulalongkorn (1868-1910). Internal reforms in Siam aimed to extend and protect the trading hinterland of the royal domain and to assert effective authority in view of the growing threat of European colonial expansion in the region. European powers had moved into the region earlier. In the period 1786 to 1826, the British had moved into Siam's frontier areas, into the Malay sultanates, and into Burma on the Tenasserim peninsula (1826), although with little impact on the Siamese court thus far.[20] By the mid-nineteenth century, the threat loomed greater, however, when—shortly after the second Anglo-Burmese war (1852) —Britain added all of neighboring Lower Burma to its colonial empire. The Siamese court exercised skillful diplomacy with the British in this situation, proceeding with the timely strategy of opening its doors to international trade in recognition of colonial trading interests.[21] Mongkut was simultaneously under pressure from the French, who in the 1860s established their presence in Cambodia and southern Vietnam, resulting in a series of treaties in which Siam recognized the status of France in the region as well. During the 1880s, the British and French further extended their control over territories in Burma and Indochina. By 1886, following the annexation of Upper Burma, Britain controlled all the former royal domains of Burma, and France had extended its rule over central and northern Vietnam. By 1888, France was advancing into northwestern Laos.

In response to this threat, the Siamese court was quick to grasp the need for reform of the traditional polity in order to consolidate effective authority over the realm and protect it from external encroachment. In doing so, the court effectively reformulated the governmental structure of the kingdom to resemble the "western standards" of a territorial state. As indicated above, the most dramatic innovations occurred after the 1870s with Chulalongkorn, who reorganized and enlarged the bureaucracy that, at the time, only directly governed the small core domain in close proximity to Bangkok. In the 1870s, he also appointed commissioners (these were military appointments) in the frontier areas, hitherto regions only loosely tied to Bangkok.[22] Their task was to protect and extend these hinterland regions, a concept Chulalongkorn termed "protection over territory" (*thesaphiban*).[23] The king designed these new appointments after several trips abroad to study colonial systems of provincial administration, including those of

---

[19] Keyes, "Cultural Diversity and National Identity in Thailand," pp. 206-207. Keyes notes that King Mongkut had gained significant insights into this mentality through his interactions with Western missionaries during his previous twenty-five years as a Buddhist monk. Then, as king, he sponsored the introduction of Western education at the court.

[20] Ibid., p. 206.

[21] Riggs, *Thailand: The Modernization of a Bureaucratic Polity*, pp. 28-29. He contrasts the Siamese and Burmese responses to imperialist expansion, attributing Siam's preservation of independence to the success of its effective internal reforms of administration, as much as to the "buffer" that it provided between the British and French empires. See ibid., pp. 22-44.

[22] See Pasuk and Baker, *Thailand: Economy and Politics*, p. 224.

[23] See Thongchai, *Siam Mapped*, p. 103. D. R. SarDesai points to the connection between British conquests into Burma and a reassertion by the ruling Burmese dynasty of the reach of its empire's borders, echoing tactics of "protection over territory" employed by Siam. D. R. SarDesai, *Southeast Asia: Past and Present* (London: Westview Press, 1989), p. 105. On the prelude to empire, annexation, and frontier issues in Burma, see Dorothy Woodman, *The Making of Burma* (London: The Cresset Press, 1962).

Java, Malaya, Burma, Singapore, and India. The king's decision to dispatch Siamese commissioners to the hinterlands—first to the vulnerable principality of Chiang Mai in 1874—anticipated the later reforms of 1892 in provincial administration and the creation of the Ministry of Interior, headed by the king's half-brother, Prince Damrong Rajanubhab.

The cosmologically organized palace administration was transformed according to a European bureaucratic model, with separate ministries for finance, defense, interior, foreign affairs, justice, and so forth; Chulalongkorn appointed his brothers, half-brothers, and close associates as departmental heads. For instance, the two preeminent departments of Mahatthai and Kalahom—which traditionally performed essentially the same functions (administration and taxation of the populace), but in two different parts of the kingdom (the northern and southern regions, respectively)—were redefined as functional ministries. Mahatthai became the Ministry of Interior, and Kalahom became the Ministry of Defense.[24] Under Prince Damrong, appointed as Minister of Interior, government administration was systematically centralized, and the provincial administration and tax system reorganized. The old networks of local autonomy were replaced with "an apparatus of centrally appointed and rotated officials," responsive to Bangkok and the Ministry of Interior and capable of enforcing new rules in the territories throughout the hinterland.[25] Hereditary rulers in the outer territories, who previously exercised the prerogative of *kin muang* ("eat the realm," or self-remuneration),[26] were now paid regular salaries as civil servants. These changes did not occur without resistance in the provinces, however, and Prince Damrong discovered during his journeys that "the hinterland was almost as far from the capital, psychologically and politically, as the foreign countries he visited."[27] Thus, the new administrative structure developed slowly and unevenly across the country, hindered by lack of resources and by opposition from local powers.[28] The whole kingdom was sub-divided into eighteen *monthon* (circles)[29] and eighty-three *changwat* (provinces); the *changwat* were further sub-divided into *amphoe* (districts), headed by district officers (*nai amphoe*) sent out by the Ministry of Interior.[30]

---

[24] Keyes, *Thailand: Buddhist Kingdom as Modern Nation-State*, p. 52.

[25] Riggs, *Thailand: The Modernization of a Bureaucratic Polity*, p. 135

[26] See Ibid, p. 20. Similarly, in Burma the term *myosas* ("town eaters") applied to royal princes and high officials of the bureaucracy. For an account of the traditional system of local administration in Burma, see Michael Aung-Thwin, "Principles and Patterns of the Precolonial Burmese State," in *Tradition and Modernity in Myanmar*, ed. Uta Gärtner and Jens Lorenz (Berlin: Fakultätsinstitut für Asien- und Afrikawissenshaften, Humbolt Universität zu Berlin, 1994), pp. 32-33.

[27] Riggs, *Thailand: The Modernization of a Bureaucratic Polity*, p. 134.

[28] Pasuk and Baker, *Thailand: Economy and Politics*, p. 226.

[29] Chalong Soontravanich notes that the administrative model for *monthon thesaphiban* (administrative circles), introduced by Prince Damrong, was also the system of British colonial administration in Burma. Chalong Soontravanich, "Research on Thai-Myanmar Historical Relations in Thailand," in *Comparative Studies on Literature and History of Thailand and Myanmar*, ed. Withaya Sucharithanarugse (Bangkok and Yangon: Institute of Asian Studies, Chulalongkorn University and Universities' Historical Research Centre, 1997), p. 96.

[30] Wolf Donner, *The Five Faces of Thailand: An Economic Geography* (London and Hamburg: C. Hurst and Company/Institute of Asian Studies, 1978), p. 45.

With the "revolution in government" emerged a new sense of nationalism bounded by territorial borders. The adoption of modern cartography, in the form of Mercatorian mapping, another significant reform, mapped the "geo-body" and gave the elite a sense of its place in relation to their Siam and to the world beyond.[31] The territorial boundaries of European cartography were unknown in Siam prior to the 1850s; instead, the sovereign limits represented on traditional maps (cosmographic or profane)[32] reflected the power structures of the traditional polity. Thongchai distinguishes between traditional and European conceptions of boundary, contrasting the sense of passage in "the golden, silver paths, free for traders" with the fixed lines of modern maps. He points to the Three Pagodas Pass as one such historically noted passage which permitted travel, trade, and warfare to cross between Siam and Burma, and he observes that the three pagodas were not pagodas as such but "huge piles of stones intentionally constructed" to mark a frontier limit.[33] In sum, Thongchai shows how, while Siam escaped colonization, it came to accept European mapping practices and the colonial alignment of boundaries.[34] Once these boundaries were defined, the notions of *chat* (the people) and *prathet* (territory, country) were combined (*prathetchat*) to signal a common people living together within the defined geographical space of the nation. In 1911, the government passed the Nationality Act to classify those born within the national boundaries as Thai.[35] Thus, historically, the transformation of the traditional polity into a modern country was a process in which state power was "territorialized."[36]

Mapping the Modern Boundary

The modern boundary demarcation between Thailand and Burma proceeded along two main divisions, north and south of the confluence of the Salween and Thaungyin (Moei) rivers. To the south, the section contiguous with the Tenasserim peninsula was negotiated between Siam and the British East India Company following the first Anglo-Burmese war in 1826. Here, the boundary was largely thought to be well defined according to features of the physical geography, following the crest of the Bilauktaung and Dawna ranges from Victoria Point to the pass just east of Mae Sot on the old trade route from Sukhothai to the Gulf of Martaban.[37] The boundary was then extended northwards following British annexation of Lower Burma in 1852.[38]

---

[31] Thongchai, *Siam Mapped*, pp. 37-61. See also, Anderson, *Imagined Communities*, Chapter 10: "Census, Map, Museum," especially pp. 170-178; and for a critique of Thongchai, see Gehan Wijeyewardene, "The Frontiers of Thailand," in *National Identity and its Defenders: Thailand 1939-89*, ed. Craig Reynolds (Melbourne: Centre for Southeast Asian Studies, Monash University, 1991), especially pp. 157-170.

[32] Cosmographic maps were a symbolic representation of the worlds of Buddhist cosmology, and profane maps were diagrammatic guides for military campaigns and shipping.

[33] Thongchai, *Siam Mapped*, pp. 73-76.

[34] Thongchai, *Siam Mapped*, pp. 68-80.

[35] Pasuk and Baker, *Thailand: Economy and Politics*, p. 234.

[36] Peter Vandergeest and Nancy Lee Peluso, "Territorialization and State Power in Thailand," *Theory and Society* 24,3 (1995): 385-426.

[37] Alistair Lamb, *Asian Frontiers: Studies in a Continuing Problem* (Melbourne: Australian Institute of International Affairs, 1968), p. 163. Lamb notes that the story of the Tenasserim

To the north of the confluence, the frontier was much wider, and both Britain and Siam argued over the rights of the small indigenous states straddling the Salween River.[39] The final stretch of boundary from the Salween to the Mekong was demarcated in 1892-93, following British annexation of Upper Burma (1886), and formally recognized in the exchange of maps in 1894.[40] It cut through regions inhabited by the Karens and, further north, divided the Shan states from Chiang Mai, with which many Shan groups maintained close political and cultural relations.[41] In this region to the north, therefore, the boundary cut through areas where, during the precolonial period, Siam and Burma still actively competed for influence. Siam and Burma repeatedly sought authority over the Shan plateau, for instance; and Burma in particular used the region as a staging area and base for attacks on Thai territory.[42] During World War II, the Japanese actually "transferred" the Shan tracts of Kengtung and Mongpan to Thai administration. Alistair Lamb observes that, with the boundary mapped, Thailand "secured" its western flank, and finally "Bangkok gained a stable border with Burma which, for the first time in centuries, was free from the danger of Burmese military incursions."[43] However, as discussed in the second part of this chapter, the process of modern border politics is more complex than Lamb's observation implies.

The Mons: Early Flights and the Traditional Polity

The strength of precolonial statecraft was therefore largely predicated on the control of population rather than territory, with a decline in population marking a weakening of the kingdom, and an increase marking the strengthening of the kingdom. Wars were fought for the control of people more than the conquest of

---

strip could well have been otherwise, since at one point the British considered handing Tenasserim "back" to Siam and at another considered placing Tenasserim under the rule of an indigenous Mon dynasty (descendants of whom could not be found, however). He speculates on the possible implications, noting "the almost accidental process of Asian boundary evolution in the colonial era."

[38] It was only formally defined later in 1868, with the boundary line described in a table of fifty-one markers along 1,126 kilometers of territory. J. R. V. Prescott notes that comparison of these 1868 coordinates with modern maps showed that some measurements were shown as too far west. J. R. V. Prescott, *Map of Mainland Asia by Treaty* (Melbourne: Melbourne University Press, 1975), p. 384.

[39] For further detail on these politics, see ibid., pp. 385-387. The allegiances of these tributary states fluctuated according to the strength of the Burmese and Siamese kingdoms. The presence of the British at the mouth of the Salween after the first Anglo-Burmese war had repercussions to the north, when the Shans and the Karens began to hope for more autonomy from their Burmese overlords, while the palace at Ava also began an attempt to increase their authority over the Shans and Karens. Constance M. Wilson, "Thai-Shan Diplomacy in the 1840s," in *The Burma-Thailand Frontier over Sixteen Decades: Three Descriptive Documents*, ed. Constance M. Wilson and Lucien M. Hanks (Athens, OH: Center for International Studies, Ohio University, 1985), p. 10.

[40] Lee Yong Leng, *Southeast Asia: Essays in Political Geography* (Singapore: Singapore University Press, 1982), pp. 12-13.

[41] Lamb, *Asian Frontiers*, p. 164. Lamb also notes that by 1893 a number of the tributary relationships between the Shan *sawbwas* (chiefs) and Bangkok were effectively terminated.

[42] Wilson, "Thai-Shan Diplomacy in the 1840s," p. 9.

[43] Lamb, *Asian Frontiers*, p. 165.

territory alone. As James C. Scott emphasizes, the precolonial state aimed to achieve the "sedentarization" of its population through permanent, concentrated settlement, securing economic surplus, labor, and military service.[44] Rulers were always in need of population in order to enhance their position in relation to neighboring polities. Indeed, physical mobility was the historical basis of freedom.[45] In times of war, rulers and ambitious officials generally welcomed deserters from other jurisdictions, a practice that increased income, military personnel, and political influence for the host. In the wars between Burma and Siam, the winner also took as many captives as possible, resettling them near the captor's court.[46] In addition, the creation of large numbers of refugees was less likely because armies were heavily dependent upon the local populations to produce their food and provide logistical support, as well as warriors.[47] Basically, there were no camps that kept refugees in a state of suspension between states as modern day refugee camps do.

It was in this context that early flights of Mons into Siam occurred. Accounts of these early migrations of the Mons from Burma into Siam suggest that the migrants encountered an atmosphere of welcome in Siam, which was not the result simply of benevolence, but also of precolonial statecraft, as discussed above. R. Halliday records the words of the exiled Mons of Martarban in a letter to the king of Siam (Ayutthaya) around 1633, expressing appreciation of the hospitality they received: "The Lord of the golden *prasada*, the righteous king of Ayuthia, was the haven of the Mon race, and on every occasion saved the lives of the Mon people."[48] The rare scholarly articles on these migrations point out that the Mons were regarded as "desirable immigrants" who, in addition to augmenting the population of the kingdom, served as loyal soldiers and spies for Siamese military campaigns against the Burmese and sometimes rose to high positions in the Siamese court.[49]

While there are few documented reports of the arrivals of various Mon refugee movements into Siam, three main migrations are generally identified, stretching from the period of Ayutthaya in the sixteenth century to Thornburi-Bangkok in the late eighteenth century. These movements were relatively substantial for the time, and descendants of the immigrants form a small ethnic minority—now largely assimilated—in Thailand today.[50] The first flight of "considerable numbers" noted

---

[44] As Scott also points out, of course, the postcolonial state also had this aim in mind, but with superior means for achieving it. James C. Scott, "Freedom and Freehold: Space, People and State Simplifications in Southeast Asia," in *Asian Freedoms: The Idea of Freedom in East and Southeast Asia*, ed. David Kelly and Anthony Reid (Cambridge: Cambridge University Press, 1998), p. 50.

[45] Ibid.

[46] Ibid., p. 52.

[47] Michael R. Marrus, "Introduction," in *Refugees in the Age of Total War*, ed. Anna C. Bramwell (London: Unwin Hyman, 1988), p. 3.

[48] R. Halliday, "Immigration of the Mons into Siam," in *The Mons: Collected Articles from the Journal of the Siam Society*, ed. Michael Smithies (Bangkok: The Siam Society, 1986), p. 10. (Reprinted from the original published in the *Journal of the Siam Society* 10,3 (1913): 1-15.)

[49] Ibid.; see also Eric Seidenfaden, "Mon Influence on Thai Institutions," in *The Mons: Collected Articles from the Journal of the Siam Society*, pp. 29-30.

[50] Keyes records the Mon population (as a distinct minority) in Thailand today as sixty thousand, or 0.1 per cent, of the population. "Cultural Diversity and National Identity in Thailand," p. 212. However, such estimates and Mon demography in Thailand are subject to conjecture, largely due to various characteristics (language, genealogy, etc.) by which Mon

by Halliday occurred in the 1660s, following a Mon revolt in Martaban[51]; it is thought that some ten thousand people took refuge under King Narai at Ayutthaya.[52] The Siamese king sent his Mon officials to receive the Mon in Kanchanaburi province,[53] and these refugees were granted a "gracious audience" in the palace at Ayutthaya and allotted lands.[54] According to Halliday, the next general flight of Mons into Siam occurred in 1774, in the aftermath of the fall of the last Mon kingdom at Pegu (1757). He argues that there is no trace of an immediate outflow of people following the destruction of Pegu, as the Mons were "so paralysed by the slaughter which ensued that there could not be sufficient strength left for any general movement."[55] Also, after the defeat of Pegu, many Mons switched their allegiance and identified themselves as Burman in order to survive.[56] People who took part in the third major flight, which occurred in 1814–15, comprising some thirty to forty thousand Mons,[57] were also hospitably received in Siam. For example, the young Prince Phra Chom Klao (later to become King Mongkut) was sent by King Rama II to greet the Mons at Kanchanaburi so he could provide for their immediate needs and bring them to Bangkok.[58]

Mon settlement in Thailand was peaceful, partly due to their way of life and a social and religious background similar to, and compatible with, their host's. The majority of the Mon people who settled in Thailand were wet rice farmers, as they had been in Burma,[59] and this occupation added to the economic strength of their host kingdom. Today, the descendants of these early Mon refugee settlers are predominantly found in the vicinity of Bangkok, and in the provinces of Kanchanaburi, Ratchaburi, Samut Sakhon, Lopburi, Uthaithani, and beyond.[60]

---

identity is measured. See Christian Bauer, "Language and Ethnicity: The Mon in Burma and Thailand," in *Ethnic Groups Across National Boundaries in Mainland Southeast Asia*, ed. Gehan Wijeyewardene (Singapore: Institute of Southeast Asian Studies, 1990), pp. 23-31.

[51] Halliday, "Immigration of the Mons into Siam," p. 9.

[52] The Mon captured and took with them the uncle of the Ava King Pindale (the viceroy of Martaban), and handed him over to the King Ayutthaya. An angry Burmese King Pindale is recorded to have sent orders from Ava for his army to pursue the Mon into Thai territory by way of the Three Pagodas Pass. Damrong Rajanubhab, *Journey Through Burma in 1936* (Bangkok: River Books, 1991), p. 52.

[53] Niyaphan Pholwaddhana, "Ethnic Relations in Thailand: The Mon-Thai Relationship" (PhD dissertation, University of Kansas, 1986), p. 50.

[54] G. E. Harvey, *Outline of Burmese History*, 2nd edition (Bombay: Longmans, Green and Co., 1929), p. 119.

[55] Halliday, "Immigration of the Mons into Siam," p. 10.

[56] Victor Lieberman, *Burmese Administrative Cycles: Anarchy and Conquest, c. 1580-1760* (Princeton: Princeton University Press, 1984), p. 249. Michael Adas argues that some historians have exaggerated the number of Mon migrants from Lower Burma to Siam during this period, pointing out that the decline in the "Mon population" is attributable more to the Burman policy of suppressing the Mon language than the Mons' death rate or mass migration. Michael Adas, "Imperialist Rhetoric and Modern Historiography: The Case of Lower Burma Before and After Conquest," *Journal of Southeast Asian Studies* 3,2 (1972): 189.

[57] Niyaphan, "Ethnic Relations in Thailand," p. 52.

[58] Halliday, "Immigration of the Mons into Siam," p. 11.

[59] Brian L. Foster, "Ethnicity and Economy: The Case of the Mons in Thailand" (PhD dissertation, University of Michigan, 1972), p. 13.

[60] Ibid., p. 12. See also, Brian L. Foster, "Ethnic Identity of the Mon in Thailand," in *The Mons: Collected Articles from the Journal of the Siam Society*, pp. 59-82.

Twentieth-century Mon Migrations

The next Mon migrations occurred in the post-World War II era, with a periodic trickle of migrants settling permanently in Thailand, augmented by temporary, seasonal displacements of people due to the outbreak of persistent civil war in Burma in 1949. Sangkhlaburi, in the area southeast of Three Pagodas Pass, has been one such place of settlement. Theodor Stern, writing in the 1970s, described Sangkhlaburi as a polyethnic "frontier post" town.[61] Bertil Lintner, who traveled through the region in 1981, described his journey from Kanchanaburi to Sangkhlaburi as "a grueling, ten-hour journey along a narrow, winding road through dense forest . . . 225 kilometers further up the river."[62] In the 1990s, the trip would have been much smoother, on well-paved bitumen roads. Living in Sangkhlaburi are contiguous communities of Karens, Mons, some Burmans, and Thais (generally officials and their families who have moved from elsewhere in Thailand). The Mon community, in particular, has grown quite substantially over the years, and their village within Sangkhlaburi (or Wangka, as it is locally known) forms a distinct sector of the town. In this Mon community stands a large, attractive monastery under the patronage of the renowned Mon abbot, Luang Phor Uttama.[63]

Elderly Mon villagers living in Wangka recall the early settlement of the area by war refugees from Burma, noting that the first migrants arrived in the mid-1940s, initially fleeing World War II-related conflicts (this area is close to the infamous Thailand-Burma Railway), and later the outbreak of civil war. Wangka began with approximately thirty households, and a consistent trickle of newcomers, hearing it was a safe place to settle, joined the small village over the years, establishing their own rice fields and a village infrastructure. It was the abbot Luang Phor Uttama who first migrated to the area in the 1940s, after an earlier exploratory trip to discover a suitable place for war refugees to live. Since this time, he has played a remarkable role as a "firm foundation stone" for the village and as a negotiator between the Mon villagers and the Thai authorities. Advocating the struggle for Mon self-determination in Burma, he apparently told the Thai authorities that he had no intention of returning to Burma until this was achieved, nor should the Mon people be forced back. Luang Phor Uttama also conducted humanitarian relief work along the border, distributing rice and other provisions to displaced persons sheltered in the nearby border areas and successfully mobilizing his religious followers in Thailand to provide such supplies. On occasion, he personally rode elephant-back, distributing relief items and checking on the situation of the various displaced groups in the areas (including Mon, Karen, and Tavoyan peoples). In the early 1980s, when the Thai government dammed waterways in the Sangkhlaburi region (for the Khao Laem

---

[61] Theodor Stern, "A People Between: The Pwo Karen of Western Thailand," in *Ethnic Adaptation and Identity: The Karen on the Thai Frontier with Burma*, ed. Charles F. Keyes (Philadelphia: Institute for the Study of Human Issues, 1979), p. 73.

[62] Bertil Lintner, *Burma in Revolt: Opium and Insurgency Since 1948* (Boulder, CO and Bangkok: Westview Press and White Lotus, 1994), p. ix.

[63] This section is based on information from interviews with senior residents of Wangka, Sangkhlaburi, September 1995.

dam), he traveled to meet with the Thai king and personally asked him to grant the Mon people permission to remain in the area.

It is evident that this early Mon settlement in the remote borderland of the Thai "geobody" was flexibly accommodated over the years. In 1979, the Ministry of Interior attempted to register all non-citizens living in the area; pre-1976 arrivals were eligible to register as permanent residents in Thailand and were issued "pink cards" known as "displaced persons cards." Identification as a "displaced person" permitted the card holder access to ownership of a small piece of land in the Sangkhlaburi area and the right to own a house, for example. In the mid-1990s, with a population of over one thousand households, the Mon village of Wangka is the largest long-term Mon settlement of its kind in the Thai borderland. Further, this settlement contrasts considerably with the refugee camps established after the fall of the NMSP (New Mon State Party) headquarters at Three Pagodas Pass in 1990 because it does not arouse the same political sensitivities or pose the same difficulties as a refugee camp. Rather, it is the presence of the refugee camps that has politicized this part of the border for Thailand. This reaction was evident in the case of the Mon camps southwest of Three Pagodas Pass, examined in the previous chapter, where the borderland haven was finally eliminated when the Thai government imposed stricter boundaries at Halockhani, an action that effectively removed those Mon refugees from Thailand altogether. Using Kristof's characterization, we can say that the Thai state has sought to impose a stricter boundary in a more fluid borderlands environment.

In historical terms, therefore, the modern border was mapped in the context of regional imperial and colonial discourse and practices, both of which reformed the traditional state according to the techniques of modern statecraft and in the direction of centralized, territorial regulation. Whereas the strength of the traditional polity generally involved the control of people, and movements of people were often a welcome addition to the country, modern refugee migrations have more often presented security and foreign policy complications for both sending and host states. These complications are explored below.

CONTEMPORARY BORDER POLITICS

The politics of the modern Thai-Burmese border involve a multi-layered array of actors and relationships, operating across a variety of political, military, and economic dimensions, and occurring at various local, national, regional, and transnational levels. This makes the characterization of the Thai-Burmese border a difficult and sometimes elusive task. There is also considerable differentiation along the borderlands; Gehan Wijeyewardene has described the borderland region as "a mosaic, or perhaps a string of beads of different shapes and sizes, each one of which possesses its own distinct, and sometimes unique characteristics."[64] The neighboring Burmese borderlands, beset by armed insurrection and government counterinsurgency since independence, also show unique characteristics in the midst of a fractured and contested military and political geography.

Border politics have always been a crucial feature of modern Thai-Burmese relations. Today, Thailand and Burma share a 2,401-kilometer boundary—flanked

---

[64] Gehan Wijeyewardene, "More on Thai Borders," *Thai-Yunnan Project Newsletter* 16 (March 1992): 2.

by a physical borderland geography that is, in many places, isolated, rugged, and richly forested—with a political-military geography that is in a process of remarkable transition. The transition in the Burmese borderland is particularly striking, as the *tatmadaw* has successfully gained and consolidated a permanent military foothold in virtually all of the formerly "rebellious" (to use Kristof's word) borderland peripheries of the Burmese body politic. The secure position of the *tatmadaw* here is a relatively new phenomenon that was originally made possible by the large counterinsurgency campaigns of the mid-1980s, and that neared completion after the capture of Manerplaw and Kawmura in early 1995.

Previously, the Burmese borderland comprised a mosaic of territories under the *de facto* control of various insurgent armies fighting against the central government in Rangoon. This change in the military geography of the Burmese borderland has, of course, had significant consequences for Thailand. Previously, Thailand undertook a delicate balancing act in its relations with Burma, as it dealt with the various ethnic insurgent groups settled along the borderlands at the practical local level, while attempting a cautious, though somewhat distant, official relationship with Rangoon. As Wijeyewardene has noted elsewhere, "Until very recently one could say that though the Thai have not satisfied any of the parties concerned, they had not unduly offended them either."[65] But this is a general characterization since, in the past, Thailand's cross-border relationship at a practical substantive level was focused largely, albeit unofficially, on supporting the various non-communist opposition groups in Burma. More recently, however, Thailand has in many ways reoriented its border politics towards the authorities in Rangoon (as well as towards Burma's regional military commands), particularly since the reestablishment of Thai-Burmese official relations starting in 1988.

Several aspects of contemporary border politics—particularly in view of this transition—warrant special consideration if we wish to understand the status of refugee sanctuary in Thailand today. Obviously, the success of the *tatmadaw*'s military campaigns in eastern Burma has led to growing civilian displacement and increased numbers of refugees sheltering in Thailand, a phenomenon discussed in the previous three chapters. Additional, interrelated factors have also influenced the changing dynamics of the civil war in Burma's eastern borderland, factors which are of significance to Thailand and to refugee sanctuary. These include: 1) Thailand's abandonment of its previous "buffer" policy, which relied on the various non-communist opposition groups to act as a buffer separating Thailand from its historically hostile neighbor and to prevent cross-border links between the Thai and Burmese communist insurgencies; 2) diplomatic rapprochement with Rangoon and pursuit of a "constructive engagement" policy, the foreign policy concomitant of Thailand's closer business and military relationships with the SLORC, cultivated since 1988; and 3) a new security environment in which the *tatmadaw* is now Thailand's immediate neighbor and cross-border incursions by the renegade Democratic Karen (Kayin) Buddhist Army (DKBA) have complicated the security of the refugee camps and the surrounding territories within the Thai borderland.

---

[65] Wijeyewardene, "The Frontiers of Thailand," pp. 174-175.

The Thai-Burmese Border Relationship Prior to 1988

Before elaborating on these changes, it is worth reflecting briefly on some aspects of Thai-Burmese relations prior to 1988. The relationship between Thailand and Burma is frequently viewed in terms of its long history of mutual suspicion and enmity, dating back to the Burmese conquest of Ayutthaya in 1767. As noted above, between the mid-sixteenth and early nineteenth century, a continuous stream of invading armies traveled to and fro between these regions in a succession of wars. Sunait Chutintaranond describes the depiction of "the Burmese as archenemy" in Thai historiography and literature, noting that the sacking of Ayutthaya (then the center of the Thai political, economic, and spiritual world) by the Burmese "implanted fear and hatred into the minds of the Thai ruling class."[66] He argues that, with the emergence of Thai nationalism in the mid-nineteenth century, Burma was constructed as a hostile and threatening neighbor.[67] This negative historical image is considered to have exercised a strong hold on Thai consciousness, influencing modern Thai foreign policy towards Burma. In addition, Robert H. Taylor points out that Burmese perceptions of this anti-Burmese component of Thai nationalism have in turn intensified the level of distrust on their part.[68] However, the past fifty years of relations between the two countries—official diplomatic relations were established on August 24, 1948—have fluctuated between conflict and cooperation, with varying degrees of bilateral interaction, and a renewed emphasis on cooperation after 1988.

Various patterns of cooperation and conflict marked the relationship between the two countries prior to 1988. Overall, cooperative relations were generally "cool" rather than amicable.[69] A formal agreement on border arrangements and cooperation was signed in Rangoon on May 17, 1963.[70] The treaty aimed to "give full and practical effect to the maintenance of peace and security along the common border,"[71] providing for the establishment of a High-Level Committee to meet on border security matters (co-chaired by each country's respective Foreign Minister). But the agreement and various other diplomatic interactions throughout the period failed to alleviate many of the problems and tensions that strained relations between the two countries.[72]

---

[66] Sunait Chutintaranond, *On Both Sides of the Tenasserim Range: History of Siamese-Burmese Relations* (Bangkok: Chulalongkorn University, 1995), p. 5.

[67] Ibid., pp. 16-17.

[68] Robert H. Taylor, "Burma's Foreign Relations since the Third Indochina Conflict," *Southeast Asian Affairs 1983* (Singapore: Institute of Southeast Asian Studies, 1983), p. 105.

[69] Corrine Phuangkasem, *Thailand's Foreign Relations, 1964-80* (Singapore: Institute of Southeast Asian Studies, 1984), p. 21.

[70] See "Thailand and Burma. Agreement (with Annexes) on Border Arrangements and Cooperation. Signed at Rangoon, on 17 May 1963." (No. 6779). In United Nations, *Treaty Series: Treaties and International Agreements Registered or Filed and Recorded with the Secretariat of the United Nations*, Volume 468 (New York: United Nations, 1964), pp. 320-329.

[71] Ibid., p. 320.

[72] Although the treaty provided for semi-annual meetings of the High-level Committee, it should be noted that cooperation on this basis occurred only in 1964, 1972, and 1973. Phuangkasem, *Thailand's Foreign Relations, 1964-80*, p. 22. For an account of Thai-Burmese relations in this period, see Chi-shad Liang, *Burma's Foreign Relations: Neutralism in Theory and Practice* (New York: Praeger, 1990), pp. 97-105.

A key source of conflict was official Burmese displeasure concerning the use of Thailand by various anti-Rangoon ethnic forces as an "insurgent sanctuary" for the passage—in and out of Burma—of arms and income derived from the lucrative black market and smuggling trade, a trade which saw a dramatic rise after 1963.[73] Thailand, however, repeatedly attempted to assure Rangoon that it did not permit these activities, which were seen as harmful to bilateral relations.[74] Tensions increased when U Nu, the former prime minister of Burma who had been exiled, left India and was granted political asylum in Bangkok, in November 1969, on the condition that he did not engage in political activities. U Nu did engage in political activities, however, using Thailand as a base for his insurgent Parliamentary Democracy Party (PDP), which aimed to overthrow the Rangoon regime.[75] But this source of tension was removed and relations improved in 1973 when, following a visit by Ne Win to Bangkok, the Thai government terminated U Nu's political asylum and forced him to leave the country. Burma also officially admonished Thailand about lax border security through a general statement by Burmese Prime Minister U Sein Win at the non-aligned summit in 1976; on this occasion, U Sein Win noted that Southeast Asian countries should "faithfully undertake not to provide one's territory as a springboard of attack on its neighbors both covert and overt."[76] Declarations concerning the refugees were also made in Thailand. For example, in 1977 governors of the border provinces were provided with new guidelines by the Thai Ministry of Interior, urging them "to prevent the refugees from using Thai territory to stage hostile or subversive acts against their home countries and to maintain good relations between Thailand and neighboring countries."[77] It was not only officials in Rangoon who found the border tensions exasperating and wished their neighbor would exert better control. *Tatmadaw* intrusions into Thai territory also occurred from time to time, and they resulted in the killing or injuring of Thai citizens and the destruction of their property.[78] These events angered the Thai government.

---

[73] A two-way black market economy flourished between 1962 and 1988, with a 5 to 10 percent levy on the value of the numerous goods crossing the border (via KNU, NMSP, etc., customs gates), a levy which provided a substantial source of income to the ethnic armies. As Lintner writes: "Consumer goods, textiles, machinery, spare parts for vehicles and medicine went from Thailand to Burma and teak, minerals, jade, precious stones and opium in the opposite direction. The total value of these unofficial transactions has never been thoroughly researched, but it is fair to say that Thailand owes much of its rapid economic growth and development to the thriving cross-border trade with Burma." Lintner, *Burma in Revolt*, p. 180.

[74] For instances of such assurances during the 1970s and 1980s, see Liang, *Burma's Foreign Relations*, pp. 99-101; and Taylor, "Burma's Foreign Relations Since the Third Indochina Conflict," pp. 104-106, for an account of official Burmese efforts to share information and coordinate on these matters.

[75] On U Nu's PDP, see Martin Smith, *Burma: Insurgency and the Politics of Ethnicity* (London: Zed Books, 1993), Chapter 14; and Lintner, *Burma in Revolt*, p. 423. Lintner notes that the PDP's armed wing, the Patriotic Liberation Army (PLA), established bases in Mon and Karen territory and had more than 3,000 armed personnel in the early 1970s.

[76] Albert D. Moscotti, "Current Burmese and Southeast Asian Relations," *Southeast Asian Affairs 1978* (Singapore: Institute of Southeast Asian Studies, 1978), p. 88.

[77] Ibid.

[78] Moscotti describes one such incident in March 1977, when Burmese troops in combat with the KNU near Wangka, opposite Mae Sot district, fired into Thai territory and killed some fifty villagers, wounded others, and caused extensive damage to the village. Ibid.

The "Buffer" Arrangement

Some countries, under the pretext of border problems, usually encourage the insurgents of their neighbors who have taken up strongholds on the border. Their motive is to make the border their buffer zone. Some countries make contacts with their neighbous' insurgents on the border for their economic gains.[79]

From Rangoon's perspective, the key source of tension bedeviling Thai-Burmese relations was Thailand's toleration of the various non-communist ethnic insurgencies operating up and down the border and Thailand's quiet manipulation of these insurgencies to create a strategic "buffer" between itself and Burma.[80] The buffer arrangement assumed further importance during the period of Burma's economic stagnation and isolation under "The Burmese Way to Socialism" after 1962, and became even more important when the communist insurgencies on both sides of the border posed a growing security threat beginning in the early 1970s.[81] Strategically, the non-communist insurgent armies in control of the contiguous Burmese borderlands acted to thwart possible links between the Communist Party of Thailand (CPT) and the Communist Party of Burma (CPB). Their position, described by KNU (Karen National Union) leader General Bo Mya—who said that his own organization acted as a kind of "foreign legion" for Thailand[82]—was one whereby the non-communist insurgencies "guarded" the long porous frontier, provided Bangkok with important cross-border intelligence, and sometimes even fought the CPT within Thailand.[83] The ethnic insurgent leaders were recruited for this work, and the policy was supported and partly funded by the American CIA (Central Intelligence Agency). Into the early 1980s, liaisons with the ethnic minority armies from Burma were coordinated by Thailand's Internal Security Operation Command (ISOC).[84] Thailand worked with the National Democratic Front (NDF), the umbrella organization of the major anti-Rangoon ethnic

---

[79] Sithu Aung, "Internal Insurgency and Outside Interference," *Working People's Daily*, March 8, 1993.

[80] Bertil Lintner dates the origins of Thailand's "buffer" policy along this western border to a relatively minor event in October 1953, when a *tatmadaw* aircraft bombed a Thai village, mistaking it for a KMT military camp. This event is said to have revived enmity towards Burma and resulted in the first secret negotiations between senior Thai officials and various ethnic insurgent leaders. Bertil Lintner, "Building New Bridges with a Former Foe," *Jane's Defence Weekly*, September 9, 1995, p. 46.

[81] At its peak in 1979, the Communist Party of Thailand had an estimated ten thousand armed members. Pasuk and Baker, *Thailand: Economy and Politics*, p. 311.

[82] Smith, *Burma: Insurgency and the Politics of Ethnicity*, p. 297.

[83] Lintner, "Building New Bridges with a Former Foe," p. 46.

[84] In 1974, ISOC replaced its predecessor, the Communist Suppression Operation Command (CSOC), which was established in 1965 as a combined military and police counterinsurgency organization. The name change reflected diplomatic consideration for China. ISOC was officially organized under the Prime Minister, but *de facto* control rested with the Army Chief. See Suchit Bunbongkarn, *The Military in Thai Politics, 1981-86* (Singapore: Institute of Southeast Asian Studies, 1987), pp. 49-53.

insurgencies, which was established in 1976 at KNU headquarters in Manerplaw on the northern Moei River opposite Ban Tha Song Yang. The various NDF members—including the KNU, NMSP, Karenni National Progressive Party (KNPP), and the Kachin Independence Organization (KIO)—each maintained close personal ties with senior Thai intelligence, police, and army officers. The Thais also attached special agents to Karen and Mon units as observers and advisers.[85] In sum, the buffer arrangement provided mutual benefit for both Thai security interests and the ethnic forces, much to the irritation of Rangoon. The buffer diminished the threat of communism to Thailand, while the ethnic forces gained access to Thailand and, as a result, access to trade, the regional black market (which provided arms, ammunition, communications equipment, and other supplies), secure places for "rebel" families to live, and hospitals for wounded combatants. As Lintner notes, in many ways the NDF needed the tacit support of Thailand's security agencies for its survival.[86]

But the buffer policy became increasingly less relevant by the early 1980s. By mid-1983, ISOC had claimed "total victory" over the CPT insurgency,[87] and the crucial buffer role once played by the Karen, Mon, and other minority forces diminished in importance. The Thai organizational structure that maintained cross-border liaisons with the minorities also shifted in the early 1980s from the national level to the local level, with a number of locally based Task Forces along the border now responsible for such liaisons.[88] Meanwhile, on the Burmese side of the border, it was not long before the *tatmadaw* launched its large, sustained offensives against ethnic oppositions, for these began during the dry season of 1983–84. At this stage, Thailand continued to provide covert support to the ethnic oppositions, although this began to change after 1988.

Thus, developments on both sides of the border combined to transform the military configuration in the area, so that the once favorable position enjoyed by the ethnic insurgencies began to decline. As noted in Chapter Two, opposition-held areas became more vulnerable as the *tatmadaw* waged larger and more successful counterinsurgency campaigns, which sent growing numbers of refugees fleeing to Thai-based camps. At the same time, the Thai authorities revised their alliances with both the ethnic insurgencies and the *tatmadaw* as their reliance on the non-communist "buffer" groups decreased. Although these changes were varied, elusive, and often ambiguous across different borderland areas, a gradual reorientation occurred from the mid- to late-1980s in Thailand away from a position of support for the insurgencies.

---

[85] Lintner, *Burma in Revolt*, p. 241. Lintner also describes the kind of "private army" involved with border issues at the time: "Border issues and 'special operations,' however, were in the hands of Sudsai Hasdin...In the aftermath of the 1973 uprising [in Thailand], he had founded what in effect amounted to a private army, named the Krathing Daeng, or the Red Gaurs....Many of his men were also mercenaries recruited from among Burma's many ethnic minorities." Ibid., p. 240.

[86] Ibid., p. 240.

[87] Pasuk and Baker, *Thailand: Economy and Politics*, p. 313.

[88] Border security, of course, remained crucial although, according to Lintner, liaison with ethnic forces became less so. See Lintner, "Building New Bridges with a Former Foe," p. 49; and "Special Army Force Tightens Noose on Khun Sa's Empire," *The Nation*, January 13, 1995, p. A7.

The Borderland in Transition Since 1988

The Thai and Burmese nations arranged a diplomatic rapprochement in 1988, underscored by the official cultivation of business-oriented diplomacy (with military connections). As Mya Maung observes, "The Thailand-Burma relationship . . . developed in terms of a political brotherhood between the military élites of the two countries . . . encouraged by Thailand's ambition for economic expansion in Southeast Asia."[89] In 1988, in the wake of the crackdown on the pro-democracy uprising in Burma, Thailand was the first state to develop positive official ties with the SLORC. The emergence of this relationship was intimately tied to business opportunities (i.e. the exploitation of natural resources) in the border areas. For instance, following a visit to Rangoon in December 1988 by Thailand's acting Supreme Commander General Chavalit Yongchaiyut (and his delegation of over eighty people), some twenty initial logging concessions were contracted by SLORC to Thai timber companies; significantly, sixteen of these were in insurgent-held areas.[90] Thai Prime Minister Chatichai Choonhavan explained the rationale for his government's foreign policy (towards Burma and Indochina in general) as one in which "politics will take second place to economics."[91] Chatichai is also well-known for his often-cited concept of "turning Indochina from a battlefield to a trading market."[92] From the SLORC's perspective, with the Burmese economy nearing bankruptcy—due in part to large foreign debts, very low foreign reserves, and negligible foreign exchange—it could derive significant benefits from a timely rapprochement with its neighbor.[93]

Thailand's policy response to Burma after 1988—and that of ASEAN more generally—came to be known as "constructive engagement." The policy advocated political coexistence rather than enforced isolation (or indeed criticism) of Burma

---

[89] Mya Maung, "The Burma Road from the Union of Burma to Myanmar," *Asian Survey* 30,6 (1990): 620.

[90] Carl Grundy-Warr and Ananda Rajah, "Security, Resources and People in a Borderlands Environment: Myanmar-Thailand," in *International Boundaries and Environmental Security: Frameworks for Regional Cooperation*, ed. G. Blake, L. Chia, C. Grundy-Warr, M. Pratt, C. Scholfield (Amsterdam: Kluwer Law International, 1997), p. 182.

[91] This quote is from a speech at the Foreign Correspondent's Club in Bangkok on December 22, 1988. Marc Innes-Brown and Mark J. Valencia, "Thailand's Resource Diplomacy in Indochina and Myanmar," *Contemporary Southeast Asia* 14,4 (1993): 334. In the same address, Chatichai also observed that "where the lines dividing friends and foes are no longer self-evident or clear-cut, diplomacy has become the art and science of...managing relationships with both friends and adversaries across all issue areas, to ensure that one's interests are protected and enhanced." Quoted in Khatharya Um, "Thailand and the Dynamics of Economic and Security Complex in Mainland Southeast Asia," *Contemporary Southeast Asia* 13,3 (1991): 245.

[92] Paisal Sricharatchanya, "A Lack-lustre Line-up," *Far Eastern Economic Review*, August 18, 1988, p. 25.

[93] See David I. Steinberg, "International Rivalries in Burma: The Rise of Economic Cooperation," *Asian Survey* 30,6 (1990): 596; Hamish McDonald, "The Generals Buy Time," *Far Eastern Economic Review*, February 22, 1990, p. 16. One of the first legislative initiatives of the newly installed SLORC involved its liberalization of the Foreign Direct Investment law, promulgated on November 30, 1988 and marking a major departure from its former closed policy stance towards external investment. See Mark Mason, "Direct Foreign Investment in Burma: Trends, Determinants, and Prospects," in *Burma: Prospects for a Democratic Future*, ed. Robert I. Rotberg (Cambridge MA and Washington, DC: World Peace Foundation/Harvard Institute for International Development and Brookings Institution Press, 1998), pp. 209-229.

as the most effective means to influence positive change in that country. The policy also promoted Thai and ASEAN economic and strategic interests by disregarding sensitive issues in the short term (including international condemnation of the SLORC's human rights record).[94] As Amitav Acharya points out, while the nature and scope of "constructive engagement" is somewhat obscure, the political restraint it embraced was "consistent not only with the ASEAN principle of non-interference in the internal affairs of a state, but was also a pragmatic move," allowing Thailand and other ASEAN states quietly to increase economic and military links with the SLORC.[95]

Thailand's recognition and exploitation of the enormous resource and economic potential in the Burmese border region (a phenomenon described as "resource diplomacy")[96] and the interests of the SLORC therefore converged in the period after 1988. As indicated above, the relationship furthered Thailand's broader ambition to establish a strong economic position in the region, potentially supported by the extraction of the vast natural resources in neighboring Indochina and Burma.[97] It also coincided with a severe domestic crisis in Thailand's own natural resource base, particularly after a nation-wide logging ban was instituted in November 1988, effectively closing Thailand's own forest frontier and necessitating a search for alternative sources to sustain the burgeoning timber industry. When Thailand turned to Burma in 1989–90, further logging concessions were issued by Burma, encompassing as much as 18,000 square kilometers granted to Thai companies (some closely affiliated with the Thai government).[98] The official connection in these deals was made evident in a Burmese Timber Corporation document: "In furtherance of the friendly and cordial relations existing between the two countries, Timber Corp. enters into contracts with Thai firms which are recommended by the Thai authorities concerned."[99] For Burma's SLORC, the logging deals contributed favorably to their economic and military goals. They not only helped to alleviate the serious foreign exchange shortfall mentioned earlier, with the sale of timber (mainly teak) accounting for 42 percent of all export income in 1989-90,[100] but logging in the border areas was also particularly important in terms of the *tatmadaw*'s military campaign against the insurgencies. As Raymond L. Bryant observes, although the significance of logging as an aid to military control of these areas should not be exaggerated, it did contribute to such control

---

[94] For a critique of the approach, see Leszek Busynski, "Thailand and Myanmar: The Perils of 'Constructive Engagement'," *The Pacific Review* 11,2 (1998): 290-305.

[95] Amitav Archarya, "Human Rights and Regional Order: ASEAN and Human Rights Management in Post-Cold War Southeast Asia," in *Human Rights and International Relations in the Asia-Pacific Region*, ed. James T. H. Tang (London: Pinter, 1995), p. 175.

[96] Innes-Brown and Valencia, "Thailand's Resource Diplomacy."

[97] This role involved the resurrection of the Thai vision of *suwannaphum*, the "golden land" that was Southeast Asia, with Thailand at the heart of the "nucleus of regional plentitude." Khatharya Um, "Thailand and the Dynamics of Economic and Security Complex in Mainland Southeast Asia," p. 246.

[98] Raymond L. Bryant, "The Politics of Forestry in Burma," in *The Politics of Environment in Southeast Asia: Resources and Resistance*, ed. Philip Hirsch and Carol Warren (London: Routledge, 1998), p. 113.

[99] Quoted in Hamish McDonald, "Partners in Plunder," *Far Eastern Economic Review*, February 22, 1990, p. 17.

[100] Bryant, "The Politics of Forestry in Burma," p. 116.

and played a part in the changing dynamic of the civil war between Rangoon and the insurgencies.[101] For the anti-Rangoon insurgencies, the borderland forests were a long-term strategic haven, a valuable source of revenue and taxation, indeed a symbolic site of (contested) sovereignty, particularly after the insurgents were pushed into these remote regions in the 1970s.[102]

Therefore, while resource diplomacy advanced Thai-Burmese business and military interests, it conflicted with the interests of the insurgencies. Clearly the SLORC's decision to grant logging concessions in the Mon, Karen, Karenni, and Shan opposition-held areas were motivated, in part, by its counterinsurgency strategy, as it sought to undermine the ethnic opposition's borderland economic dealings with Thailand and gain a stronger military position in those areas. Not only did the SLORC achieve new access to revenue from teak extraction (teak can be worth as much as US$25,000 per tree)[103] and the concomitant erosion of the opposition's resource base, but the logging activities helped to transform security conditions in the border areas. As Bryant has written:

> As the SLORC stepped up its campaign to eliminate the ethnic insurgent (especially Karen) forces along the Thai-Burmese border, the logging issue became intertwined as never before with the military conflict. The deals were thus designed in part to facilitate the Burmese army's anti-insurgency campaign insofar as the construction of a network of logging roads as well as clearcut logging practices simultaneously deprived Karen forces of strategic forest cover and facilitated Burmese troop mobility in the contested areas.[104]

In order to attain high volume teak extraction, Thai concession holders contributed to the clearing of logging routes between the concession areas and the Thai-Burmese border, and this facilitated the advance of the Burmese army. The "collaboration" not only opened the way for loggers, it subsequently contributed to changing the dynamic of the war.[105]

The "teak war" involved an additional layer of conflict between Thai loggers operating under SLORC sanction and the insurgencies. In some instances, the opposition could only acquiesce to the incursions of the logging companies, as Bryant points out was the case for the KNU. Since the loggers were supported by elements

---

[101] Ibid., p. 114.

[102] The importance of the forests was reflected in the power of the KNU's Forestry Department, which rose from just a few officials in the 1950s and 1960s, to 463 forest officials working in its various forestry districts in the 1990s. This sector constituted the major source of KNU income. Raymond L. Bryant, *The Political Ecology of Forestry in Burma, 1824-1994* (Honolulu: University of Hawai'i Press, 1997), pp. 166-168.

[103] Raymond L. Bryant, "Asserting Sovereignty through Natural Resource Use," in *Resources, Nations and Indigenous Peoples: Case Studies from Australasia, Melanesia and Southeast Asia,* ed. Richard Howitt, John Connell, and Philip Hirsch (Melbourne: Oxford University Press, 1996), p. 38.

[104] Bryant, *The Political Ecology of Forestry in Burma,* p. 178.

[105] See, for example, Em Marta, Karen National Union, and Democratic Alliance of Burma, "The War of Annihilation against the Indigenous Peoples of Burma and the Raping of their Heritage Forests," statement presented to the United Nations Working Group on Indigenous Peoples, Geneva, July 23, 1990. See also, Robert Birsel, "New Winners in Burma's Teak War," *Cultural Survival Quarterly* 13,4 (1989): 36-37.

of the Thai military, there was little that could be done to stop their advance without risking the wrath of Thai authorities.[106] There were acts of resistance and conflict, however, as illustrated by an instance concerning a Thai concessionaire operating in the Mon areas around Three Pagodas Pass. This particular case involved Thai businessman Sunthorn Rasmeererkset, better known as Khun Sia Huk, the director of Pathumthani Tangkakarn, a logging company with concessions to the north and south of Three Pagodas Pass, a man said to be well connected with General Chavalit, the local Thai authorities, and the local Burmese army.[107] Some of Khun Sia's activities in this area provoked the ire of the NMSP. First, senior leaders of the NMSP claimed that in January 1990 his trucks were used to transport Burmese troops (not only through Burmese, but also Thai, territory) during the *tatmadaw*'s successful offensive against the Mon and Karen stronghold at Three Pagodas Pass.[108]

This allegation set the scene for a hostile relationship between the two parties, and the hostility was exacerbated as Khun Sia developed close relations with the local *tatmadaw* commander subsequently installed at Three Pagodas Pass. Thus, when in April 1991 the NMSP found a Sia Huk truck using a road the company had built through a sensitive Mon-controlled area—improvements to the road were made in return for the SLORC-sanctioned logging concession in the area— NMSP representatives were outraged. Claiming that they had repeatedly warned the company not to trespass into Mon-controlled forest reserves, and angry that the company had built the road providing military access for *tatmadaw* supplies, Mon troops seized one truck and torched it. A large damages fee (1.4 million *baht*) was then demanded of the NMSP and the delivery of food and medical supplies to the Mon National Relief Committee's refugee camps was threatened.[109] A local relief worker from the area also associated the relocation of Baleh Hnook refugee camp with retribution for this incident.[110] Another truck owned by Pathumthani Tangkakarn was destroyed by the NMSP in November 1991 after Khun Sia refused to pay a standard tax for logging in an NMSP-controlled area. Shortly after this incident, three senior NMSP officials[111] were arrested and imprisoned in December on "illegal immigration" charges. The arrest was orchestrated through the Sangkhlaburi District Office under the pretext of a dinner invitation to resolve the Pathumthani-NMSP conflict; according to the NMSP, this was a act of retaliation for the destruction of the Sia Huk truck.[112] The NMSP became increasingly nervous and hostile towards Thai-Burmese "resource diplomacy," which appeared to bestow strategic advantages on the *tatmadaw*. The MNRC (Mon National Relief Committee) described this souring of local relations in *The Nation* as follows: "It is

---

[106] Moreover, because they claim they needed to acquiesce in this way, in 1989-93 the KNU abandoned its previously disciplined sustainable forest management practices and permitted over-cutting in an attempt to maintain forest-based revenues. Bryant, "Asserting Sovereignty through Natural Resource Use," p. 38.

[107] Interviews, NMSP and MNRC, Sangkhlaburi, August 1995.

[108] Ibid.

[109] Interview, Mon National Relief Committee, Sangkhlaburi, August 1995.

[110] Ibid.

[111] These were NMSP General Secretary Nai Rot Sar, Secretary Nai Hong Sar, and Commander of the Mon National Liberation Army, General Htaw Mon.

[112] Interview, Mon National Relief Committee, Sangkhlaburi, August 1995.

regrettable that our leaders have been arrested by the Thai authorities. . . . The Mon[s] and Thailand have enjoyed close relations for thirty years."[113] The forests were already a contested resource in the shadow of military conflict in Burma, and now the involvement of Thai loggers became more important.

The conflict between Thai loggers and the insurgencies arose in part from the scale of logging activities underway at the time. The new demand for high volume teak extraction altered the profitable, black market business relationships once enjoyed by the ethnic insurgent armies. Illegal logging practices in opposition-controlled areas could no longer satisfy the increased demand for logs by Thai companies. Yet, at the same time, some Thai companies continued surreptitiously to purchase logs from opposition areas. Consequently, a further layer of conflict often emerged when the situation did not always proceed to the satisfaction of the SLORC. Some of the continued illegal logging activities in these areas vexed the Burmese authorities, and "logging diplomacy" between Thailand and Burma soured by mid-1993. In June 1993, the SLORC announced that it would terminate all cross-border logging concessions by the end of the year, apparently in response to illegal and unsustainable practices on the part of Thai companies.[114] A comment by then Forestry Minister Lieutenant-General Chit Swe illustrates the SLORC's frustration:

> In an attempt to attract investment we made a foolish mistake in 1989 by granting thirty-six Thai companies forty-two timber concessions in the Manerplaw and Three Pagodas Pass border areas. We couldn't cut the timber there because of the Mon and Karen insurgencies, so we gave five-year concessions to the Thais. We canceled them after three years because they produced no tangible benefit to the government or the people along the border.[115]

By this time the SLORC could afford to impose such measures since logging was no longer crucial to its long-term financial survival, particularly in view of new and potentially lucrative foreign direct investment in offshore oil and gas exploration.

By the mid-1990s, the focus of resource diplomacy shifted to oil and gas exploration, especially with the construction of the Yadana natural gas pipeline from Burma's Gulf of Martaban through a sixty-three kilometer stretch in Tenasserim Division, and extending from Nat Ei Taung (Ban-I-Tong in Thai) on the border into Ratchaburi province in Thailand. Oil and gas quickly became the largest foreign investment sector in Burma,[116] and the Yadana pipeline the major project, with an estimated revenue source of US $400 million per annum. While the SLORC had invited multinational companies to purchase oil and gas exploration licenses much earlier, it was not until June 1994 that the discovery of two major

---

[113] Korkhet Chanthalertlak, "Crackdown on Mons Sours Ties," *The Nation*, December 22, 1991, p. B2.

[114] Bertil Lintner, "Soft Option on Hardwood: Rangoon to Scrap Thai Logging Deals on Border," *Far Eastern Economic Review*, July 22, 1993, p. 25. See Bryant, *The Political Ecology of Forestry in Burma*, pp. 179-180.

[115] Quoted in Grundy-Warr and Rajah, "Security, Resources and People in a Borderlands Environment," p. 185.

[116] Mya Maung, "Burma's Economic Performance Under Military Rule: An Assessment," *Asian Survey* 38,6 (1997): 522.

offshore gas fields (Yadana and Yetagun)[117] with massive proven reserves prompted substantial investment.[118] The Yadana project was the result of a US$1 billion joint-venture contract signed in February 1995 between the Myanma Oil and Gas Enterprise (MOGE), a private subsidiary of the Petroleum Authority of Thailand (PTT), the French multinational oil company Total, and the US Unocal Corporation. The thirty-year contract for the export of gas (an estimated 525 million cubic feet per day along the 669-kilometer pipeline) to the Ratchaburi power plant was considered vital to satisfy Thailand's projected future demands for electrical power.[119] Total was actively involved in the supervision of the sixty-three-kilometer overland pipeline route from the coast in Burma to Nat Ei Taung, a pipeline which in some places necessitated construction through contested territory or territory vulnerable to armed opposition attack.

The route of the pipeline through some Mon, Karen, and Tavoyan opposition areas posed a security problem for the various interested parties. How would the pipeline be constructed in the contested areas where stability remained in question? In this way, the intentions of the SLORC and the pipeline beneficiaries clashed with those of the armed oppositions, as the pipeline project became a new site for contesting control, attempting resistance, and stirring up controversy. The achievement of physical (or military) security in the area along the route was clearly in the interests of both the SLORC and the pipeline consortium; and it was agreed that the SLORC would provide for the security of the Yadana project.[120] Meanwhile, in the months prior to and during the pipeline construction, Mon and Karen forces had been active in some nearby areas.[121] And the KNU, the NMSP, and other forces saw that the *tatmadaw* would seek to increase its military control in these areas where the pipeline venture required enhanced security. The KNU issued statements opposed to the presence of business ventures that strengthened the SLORC's counterinsurgency aims.[122] Before the cease-fire, the NMSP expressed

---

[117] The Yetagun Gas Sales Agreement was signed in Rangoon on March 13, 1997. For details of the agreement, see Maung Lu Zaw, "Another Important Milestone in Myanmar-Thai Economic Cooperation," *Myanmar Perspectives* 3 (March 1997). Accessed online at www.myanmar.com/gov/perspec/97mar/thai3-97.html [February 4, 1998].

[118] These reserves were estimated at six trillion cubic feet of natural gas. Beginning in 1989, a number of multinational companies bought exploration licenses—generally for onshore concessions in government-controlled areas of central Burma—but they did not renew these licenses due to poor discoveries, high operating costs, etc. Article 19, *Paradise Lost? The Suppression of Environmental Rights and Freedom of Expression in Burma* (London: Article 19, 1994), pp. 16-17.

[119] The Yadana project involved a thirty-year sales contract to the Petroleum Authority of Thailand. It was originally scheduled for online completion by mid-1998, but impediments such as the 1997 financial crisis in Thailand, as well as human rights and environmental controversies (including a law suit against Unocal in the United States), have delayed the process. For details of the Yadana Project, see Unocal, *Myanmar: The Yadana Project*. Accessed online at www.unocal.com/ogops/yadtoc.htmp [February 3, 1997]; see also, Anonymous, "Myanmar's Upstream Sector Hobbled by Controversy," *Oil and Gas Journal*, June 26, 2000.

[120] EarthRights International, *EarthRights News* 1,4 (1996): 4.

[121] For instance, the pipeline was to be built through the KNU's Mergui-Tavoy District (Fourth Brigade).

[122] For example, Karen National Union, Office of the Supreme Headquarters, Kawthoolei, "Statement by KNU Foreign Affairs Department on Burma-Thailand Natural Gas Pipeline," unpublished statement, February 24, 1995.

similar concerns and explicitly threatened to disrupt the construction. The pipeline was thus subject to opposition threats of sabotage, some of which were carried out in 1995 and 1996.

The SLORC attempted to achieve security for the construction of the pipeline by augmenting its already growing military presence in these areas. According to local Mon reports, Total's French field managers were accommodated in Ohnbingkwin and Hpaungdaw villages in Yebyu Township under substantial armed guard provided by the *tatmadaw*'s local 405th and 273rd Light Infantry Battalions (LIBs) assigned there.[123] Wire, bunkers, trenches, and a large armed security contingent reportedly enclosed the Total field camp near Ohnbingkwin.[124] The security implications, however, extended well beyond these locales. A number of LIBs were introduced into militarily important or vulnerable areas along the route. For instance, LIBs 408, 409, and 410 constructed camps in the Kaleinaung area, reportedly with the intention of preparing for an indefinite stay in the immediate vicinity of the pipeline construction, and they were reinforced by LIBs 401, 406, and 407. By some estimations, around five to seven thousand troops were stationed in the region in connection with the pipeline,[125] and this introduction of troops apparently coincided with offensives throughout the eastern part of the route near Nat Ei Taung.[126] What's more, increased militarization produced the hazards associated with a military presence elsewhere in Burma; suspicious military personnel stationed in the areas alleged that the local population was assisting the insurgent groups and punished local people for insurgent attacks. Mon sources noted the military's response to an armed attack (by an unspecified Karen militia group) on a *tatmadaw* column moving with a pipeline survey team in March 1995, an attack that resulted in the deaths of five Burmese employees. It was reported that the commander of LIB 408 subsequently accused local people in the region of failing to warn the *tatmadaw* of the attack and ordered compensation from six villages in Yebyu Township of 100,000 *kyat* each.[127] Although such specific demands for retributions may have been rare, the looming threat of opposition attack and the counter-threat of government retaliation served to perpetuate the now familiar civil war cycle of suspicion and hazard implicating the local population.

Some have argued that the multinational corporations involved in the pipeline project were careful to minimize the effects of the project on the local population. The multinationals involved explicitly distanced themselves from the forced labor and forced relocation practices generally associated with growing militarization. In the International Labor Organization (ILO) inquiry into Burma, for example, Total stated that no forced labor was undertaken in association with

---

[123] Mon Information Service, *French Total Co.'s and American Unocal Corp.'s Disastrous Gas Pipeline Project in Burma's Gulf of Martaban* (Bangkok: MIS, May 1996), p. 1.

[124] Karen Human Rights Group, "Effects of the Gas Pipeline Project," KHRG No. 96-21, May 23, 1996, p. 5.

[125] EarthRights International (ERI) and Southeast Asian Information Network (SAIN), *Total Denial: A Report on the Yadana Pipeline Project in Burma* (Chiang Mai: ERI and SAIN, 1996), pp. 13-14.

[126] Karen Human Rights Group, "Effects of the Gas Pipeline Project," p. 5.

[127] Mon Information Service, "French Total Co.'s and American Unocal Corp.'s Disastrous Gas Pipeline Project," p. 4.

the gas pipeline project.[128] Elsewhere in public statements, the companies denied any complicity in this regard.[129] But while the corporations themselves did not conscript forced labor (indeed the daily rate of 200 *kyat*, or less than $US2, is not a large expense), they were not in a position to control (and unwilling to admit to) the broader consequences resulting from the dynamic of militarization in the region. Opposition groups, on the other hand, pointed to instances in which local people were exploited by the *tatmadaw* in the area to perform work related to the pipeline infrastructure, such as the construction of supporting roads and the preparation of military outposts.[130] The oil companies also claimed that they did not rely on the Ye-Tavoy railroad intersecting the pipeline, emphasizing that the project would not and could not use the railroad.[131] But others argued that the railroad was generally linked to the project because *tatmadaw* deployment along the railway permitted the army to strengthen its general presence in the region, making it more difficult for ethnic forces to move between the coastal and land areas between Ye and Tavoy.

In addition to logging and gas, various other sub-regional development business ventures between Thailand and Burma were scheduled for the Tenasserim Division. Notable among these was the western seaboard scheme, particularly the construction of a deep-sea port at Tavoy, of significant commercial value for Thailand (since it saved shipping transportation time to India, Europe, and the Mediterranean),[132] and the associated development of a large industrial estate. Each of these projects involved major Thai investments. To facilitate this scheme, a concession for the construction of a 110-kilometer highway linking Bongti (in Sai Yok district, just south of Three Pagodas Pass) in Kanchanaburi with Tavoy was agreed to.[133] A further container port at Thanbyuzayat in Mon State was also

---

[128] International Labour Organization, *Forced Labour in Myanmar (Burma), Report of the Commission of Inquiry appointed under Article 26 of the Constitution of the International Labour Organization to Examine the Observance by Myanmar of the Forced Labour Convention, 1930 (No. 29)* (Geneva: ILO, 1998), p. 130.

[129] For instance, in one interview John Imle, Unocal President, claimed that: "Everyone who has done work on this project or on the roads supporting this project has been paid. There have been no relocations of villages to accommodate this pipeline. Period." See "Sanctions Hurts People: Unocal Tries to Defend a Controversial Project," *Asiaweek*, February 21, 1997, p. 24. On its internet website, Unocal provides a number of discussion articles in defense of its "reputation and the integrity of the Yadana project." The corporation states that the Yadana project "has brought significant benefits in health care, education and economic opportunity to more than 40,000 people living in the pipeline area . . . " See Unocal, "Unocal in Myanmar (Burma): The Story You Haven't Heard About . . . ," accessed online at http://www.unocal.com/myanmar/00report/index.htm [May 22, 2000].

[130] EarthRights International and Southeast Asian Information Network, *Total Denial*, pp. 36-38. When Unocal's John Imle was questioned on the matter of opposition to the pipeline project, he curiously admitted to a dynamic of militarization: "If you threaten the pipeline there's gonna be more military. If forced labour goes hand and glove with the military, yes, there will be more forced labour. For every threat to the pipeline there will be a reaction." Ibid., p. 19.

[131] Unocal, *Myanmar: The Yadana Project*. The Yadana Project brief asserted that the railroad was physically incapable of transporting the large, heavy equipment needed for the pipeline:

[132] Supunnabul Swannaku, "Thai-Burma Link Could Speed Exports," *The Nation*, May 17, 1997.

[133] This joint venture is reportedly between the Kanchanaburi Tavoy Development Company and its Burmese partner, the KLM Company. Preecha Srisathan, "Call for Border Opening," *Bangkok Post*, October 5, 1998, p. 4.

proposed, with a concession for road construction connecting the port to Thailand from Three Pagodas Pass also granted. The Thai entrepreneur closely involved in the NMSP cease-fire negotiations, Khun Xuwicha Hiranpreuk, is reportedly a shareholder in this road, with the NMSP assigned responsibility for security.[134] This area is envisaged as a future hub of economic activity (including fishing, logging, property development, and construction) which will directly benefit Thailand's western provinces of Kanchanaburi, Ratchaburi, Prachuab Khirikhan, and Ranong. Business interests and the provincial authorities have also campaigned to establish official Thai-Burmese border passes, including passes at Ban Bongti and Three Pagodas Pass, to facilitate these economic activities.[135] Khun Sia Huk has also remained involved in this region of the border, both by pursuing his continuing interests in rubber, logging, and wood products, and in his capacity as an advisor to the Kanchanaburi Industrial Council.[136]

The pursuit of Thai business diplomacy has not only required military stability in the border regions for success; it is also, to some extent, implicated in the achievement of this objective. It is not my intention here to evaluate this relationship as such, but rather to point to the convergence of interests in official Thai-Burmese relations concerning the establishment of a "peaceful" borderland free of insurgency and military instability. This convergence of interests is evident in the NMSP-SLORC cease-fire of June 1995. In the case of the Mons, the cease-fire negotiations occurred under pressure from both the SLORC and Thailand. Khun Xuwicha Hiranpreuk, the Thai entrepreneur mentioned above, was the central interlocutor in the Mon cease-fire process between late 1993 and June 1995. In his capacity as an advisor to the then Secretary General of Thailand's National Security Council (NSC), he moved between NSC meetings in Bangkok, liaisons with the NMSP Central Committee based at the border, and discussions with senior SLORC personnel. Working in this way, he vigorously promoted the NMSP cease-fire dialogue from behind the scenes. In a private meeting subsequent to the cease-fire, Khun Xuwicha reiterated Chatichai's 1988 vision of "turning battlefields into marketplaces" by suggesting that the NMSP Central Committee members seated at the table were just such agents for change, and that they had been converted from soldiers and revolutionaries into businessmen. Referring to Thailand's unofficial buffer policy, he noted that, in the past, the gentlemen seated around the table were used by Thailand to prevent the spread of communism, but this was no longer the case.[137] The fate of the Mon refugees in the Thai-based camps was located at the intersection of these developments.

This returns us to the theme of the borderland in transition, and the way in which official Burmese and Thai interests have converged in the pursuit of attaining a "peaceful" borderland. As Carl Grundy-Warr observes, *de facto* control by opposition groups in the Burmese borderlands, tacit cross-border links with Thai officials, and informal trading ties have produced high degrees of cross-border interaction, even in the absence of a conducive state-to-state diplomatic environment. Indeed, the lack of central control in parts of these borderlands has

---

[134] Interviews, Sangkhlaburi, February 1998.

[135] Preecha Srisathan, "New Drive to Promote Regional Trade Links," *Bangkok Post*, April 5, 1998.

[136] Preecha Srisathan, "Call for Border Opening," p. 4.

[137] Private meeting, including the author, Bangkok, August 1995.

enabled flourishing, informal cross-border linkages.[138] Essentially, in examining the "coexistent borderlands" relationship, we are most concerned with the shift from informal and tacit trans-border relationships between Thailand and the opposition groups to the development of formal inter-state interactions.[139]

Thus, to sum up, the *tatmadaw* finally imposed control over many of Burma's once "rebellious" borderland peripheries, and the achievement of unprecedented military control in various contested areas coincided with several key developments on the Thai side of the border. These included Thailand's cessation of its old, anti-communist buffer policy, a degree of official rapprochement between the two countries, the pursuit of resource diplomacy, and concomitant support for the cease-fires, which transpired successfully in the case of the NMSP and concluded with the return of the refugees from Thailand. At the same time, the advance of the *tatmadaw*'s military campaigns in these border areas left ethnic forces increasingly dependent on Thailand—not only for military supplies, but also humanitarian sanctuary—just when, in the case of the Mons, the position of Thailand had become less receptive to these needs. The political tide of shifting alliances between ethnic opposition movements, Thailand, and the Burmese authorities—a tide that worked to the disadvantage of the opposition movements—has therefore fundamentally shaped the evolving context for refugees sheltered along the Thai border.

A Note on Cooperation, Conflict, and Ambiguity

Despite this growth in official Thai-Burmese relations, the two nations have not escaped considerable tensions and ambiguities. On the one hand, various mechanisms and forms of border cooperation (active since the early 1990s) have been developed. These include the most effective cooperative arrangement between the two militaries, the Regional Border Committee (RBC) and its local township counterparts along the border.[140] The RBC structure was initiated by Thailand's General Sanan Kajornklam in 1989, and he modeled it after the Thailand-Malaysia border committee. Meetings, chaired by the respective Army area commanders, are hosted in alternate countries approximately twice a year, and they focus on border security matters (including displaced persons).[141] At the civilian level, there are the Joint Commission for bilateral cooperation (JC) and the Joint Boundary Commission (JBC). The JC, jointly chaired by the two countries' foreign ministers,[142] is generally concerned with economic cooperation. The JBC, co-

---

[138] Grundy-Warr, "Coexistent Borderlands and Intra-state Conflicts in Mainland Southeast Asia," pp. 43-45.

[139] Ibid. Grundy-Warr borrows the "coexistant borderlands" concept from models developed in Oscar J. Martinez, "The Dynamics of Border Interaction: New Approaches to Border Analysis," in *Global Boundaries: World Boundaries Series*, Vol. 1, ed. Clive H. Schofield (London: Routledge, 1994), pp. 2-3.

[140] Many issues are dealt with at the local township to township level (between Myawaddy and Mae Sot, for instance), with five contact points along the border between Mae Sai in the north and Ranong in the south.

[141] Interview, General Sanan Kajornklam, Special Expert [on Myanmar], Office of the Permanent Secretary and Spokesman for the Ministry of Defense, Bangkok, April 7, 2000.

[142] Established after 1988, this is the main bilateral mechanism for "foreign relations." Interview, Director, Division 2, National Security Council, Bangkok, March 10, 1998.

chaired at the deputy foreign minister level, first met in 1993 and agreed to demarcate the long and disputed 2,401-kilometer boundary; prior to this meeting, only fifty-eight kilometers of the border had been formally determined. The JBC oversees three permanent border checkpoints,[143] as well as other official projects, such as the Thai-funded "Myanmar-Thai Friendship Bridge" between Mae Sot and Myawaddy. The emphasis in these official cooperative arrangements is, however, on maintaining trust in the military relationship: the most "comfortable" and productive relations have taken place at a "straight-talking" military-to-military level.[144]

On the other hand, the official relationship between the two nations has fluctuated, and tensions have continued to plague it. A range of border problems have complicated matters; these problems include, for instance, Rangoon's continued dissatisfaction with Thailand as an "insurgent sanctuary," boundary disputes,[145] illegal fishing across maritime boundaries, and periodic retaliatory border closures, imposed by Burma to stop Thai trade. From Thailand's perspective, the periodic cross-border incursions since 1995 by renegade DKBA forces into refugee camps and the surrounding border areas have been of particular concern. Most recently, the large drug flow into Thailand, involving especially methamphetamines, has been equally worrisome.[146] Infusing these border tensions is also a sense of ambiguity, simmering at the edge of mutual distrust, in the relationship.

After all, on the one hand, the various anti-Rangoon oppositions continue to rely on (curtailed) access to Thailand, much to the displeasure of the Burmese authorities; while on the other hand, the consequences of the *tatmadaw*'s military campaigns in eastern Burma continue to spill over into Thailand. On this latter point, it is interesting to note that Thailand's official 1996 Defense White Paper specifically identifies the "suppression of minorities by the Myanmar government" as a security threat.[147] And Rangoon has remained perturbed about Bangkok's periodically inconsistent approach. For example, without referring to Thailand in particular, an article in the Burmese *Working People's Daily* in 1993 observed: "There are also cases of fence-straddling, that is, a country that is maintaining smooth relations with both the government and the insurgents in a neighboring

---

[143] These are: Mai Sai-Tachilek, Mae Sot-Myawaddy, and Ranong-Kawthaung. In addition to these three major checkpoints, since May 1997 there are a total of sixteen official "points of entry" along the Burmese side of the border. See Aaron Stern and Lawrence W. Crissman, *Maps of International Borders Between Mainland Southeast Asian Countries and Background Information Concerning Population Movements at these Borders* (Bangkok: Asian Research Center for Migration, Chulalongkorn University, 1998), pp. 30-31.

[144] Interview, Director, Division 2, National Security Council, Bangkok, March 10, 1998.

[145] Among the many sites in dispute, there are five major locations. These are at Mai Sai, the Moei River (north and south of Mae Sot), Three Pagodas Pass, Hill 491 in Chumphon, and Ban-I-Tong.

[146] By 2000, the narcotics production and trafficking issue was a key security issue for Thailand. Thailand faced an estimated flow of 600 million methamphetamines from factories in Burma in 2000. "Burmese Troops 'Live off the Land'," *Far Eastern Economic Review*, May 18, 2000, p. 10.

[147] Ministry of Defence, *The Defence of Thailand 1996* (Bangkok: Strategic Research Institute, National Institute of Defence Studies, Supreme Command Headquarters, 1996), p. 8.

country."[148] Yet somehow a path of bilateral relations has been cleared through the different, tangled layers of the relationship, even cutting through those aspects of conflict which have a complex, non-linear character[149]—and, as the next section shows, the refugees have become an increasingly prominent political component in the unfolding story.

SANCTUARY IN PERIL: THE CROSS-BORDER RAIDS ON THE REFUGEE CAMPS

From early 1995, following the fall of the opposition strongholds of Manerplaw and Kawmura, a new dimension of the ongoing military conflicts in the Burmese borderlands directly affected Thailand. This happened when the newly established DKBA, a breakaway faction of the KNU formed on December 21, 1994, began conducting cross-border raids on the hitherto stable Karen refugee camps in Tak and Mae Hong Son provinces. Whereas in the past the security of the camps did not present a significant problem, now a number of camps were subject to regular, frequently violent, raids, creating chaos and complicating the refugees' once secure haven. The safety of cross-border sanctuary for the refugees was under threat, as the armed intruders designated the refugee camps as support bases for the KNU and, therefore, as targets for intimidation. For Thailand, the civil war was "spilling" across the border in the most dramatic manifestation to date. As well as creating terror in the camps, DKBA forces also endangered local Thai citizens and security personnel; some Thai citizens were killed.

The formation of the DKBA began with the open revolt of some four hundred Buddhist KNLA (Karen National Liberation Army) troops against the KNU. Dissatisfied with the senior KNU leadership and aggrieved by the harsh conditions they had endured so long and by their sense that the KNU revolution had failed, they gathered under the spiritual and organizational patronage of the venerated Abbot (or Sayadaw) U Baddanta Thuzana. They also received financial and military backing and supplies (as well as sanction) from the *tatmadaw*.[150] The DKBA combined religious and supernaturalist elements in its ethno-nationalist program for the reunification of the Karen under their leadership, a cause which it

---

[148] Sithu Aung, "Internal Insurgency and Outside Interference," *Working People's Daily*, March 8, 1993.

[149] Personal communication, Directorate of Army Intelligence, Royal Thai Army Headquarters, Bangkok, April 4, 2000.

[150] The role of the *tatmadaw* as an accessory to the activities of the DKBA is suggested in the government's publication, *Whither KNU?* For instance, the publication states that "...there is no longer any reason to refuse should the DKBA come to seek military help. The DKBA has said that Kayin nationals will prosper only when there is no Nga Mya or KNU. Sanghas have also begun to ask the Tatmadaw for help." A Resident of Kayin State, *Whither KNU?* (Yangon: The News and Periodicals Enterprise, 1995), p. 35. (*Whither KNU?* is a compilation of a series of articles chronicling the 1994-95 military campaigns against the KNU published in the official newspaper, *The New Light of Myanmar*, at that time.) In March 1995, the Commander of Thailand's Task Force Unit 34, Colonel Direk Yaemngamreap, pointed to *tatmadaw* collusion in DKBA incursions, saying Burmese forces were also involved in the incidents. "Task Force Accuses Burmese Junta of Border Mayhem," *The Nation*, March 3, 1995. A non-governmental report in 1998 noted that cartridges, mortar casings, ammunition boxes, and shells recovered after the 1997 and 1998 attacks on the refugee camps were Burma Army supplies. Images Asia and Borderline Video, *A Question of Security: A Retrospective on Cross-border Attacks on Thailand's Refugee and Civilian Communities along the Burmese Border since 1995* (Chiang Mai: Images Asia and Borderline Video, May 1998), p. 7.

believes the KNU has failed to achieve.[151] The DKBA played a decisive role in the *tatmadaw*'s capture of Manerplaw at the end of January 1995, as it provided crucial guidance at an operational level based on inside information concerning strategic routes into the formidable terrain and reportedly shared other military secrets about the KNU as well.[152] Furthermore, it was also heavily involved in the subsequent assault and occupation of Kawmura in February. The DKBA is thus a proxy army for the government in Rangoon in some areas and a nationalist Karen splinter faction pursuing its own concerns in other areas.

The headquarters of the DKBA were established at Myaing Gyi Ngu (known as Khaw Taw in Karen) on the Salween River in northeastern Pa'an District by Sayadaw U Thuzana, with the backing of the SLORC, as a "refuge" to attract people from the KNU/KNLA. Since 1995, U Thuzana has called for Karen villagers and refugees to move to this DKBA settlement, where they would be free of the portering and taxation demands of both the KNU and the SLORC, and where most families would be required to provide one volunteer member to the DKBA, thereby contributing to its civilian support base. Organizationally, the DKBA is structured into four military brigades, known simply as 333, 555, 777, and 999 (of which 999 is the largest and most active), although it is believed that the overall command structure remains weak: local DKBA groups tend either to act independently or, more often, to function as small militia units attached to *tatmadaw* battalions.[153] Familiar with the local areas and villagers from their KNU days, DKBA personnel frequently serve as guides, sometimes pointing out "suspects" to the *tatmadaw*. However, the activities of various DKBA groups—and their behavior towards the local villagers—have varied from area to area. The DKBA has been operating predominantly in the Pa'an, Papun, Nyaunglebin, and Thaton districts of Karen State, opposite Thailand's Tak and Mae Hong Son provinces. They also moved into some areas of the KNU's Sixth Brigade area south of Kawkareik in 1996, and were present in small numbers in western and southwestern Duplaya District in the southern part of Karen State and around the "white" areas of Mon State by 1998. The DKBA also occupied the territory projecting eastward into Thailand in Duplaya District and the narrow strip of territory along the Moei River northward to Myawaddy on the border.

Prior to the first cross-border raids, the DKBA distributed leaflets in the Thai-based camps in February 1995, warning all refugees to return to Burma and threatening to destroy the camps if they refused. The leaflets reportedly promised

---

151 Announcement No. 2/94, as reproduced in *Whither KNU?*, declared "that our organization will form different levels...with the aim of setting the people free from all social sufferings and establish peaceful state [sic]..." Democratic Kayin Buddhist Organization, December 28, 1994, in *Whither KNU?*, p. 20. For further background on the DKBA, see Hsaingt Seetsar, "Facets of a Buddhist Army: Part 1," *Burma Issues* 8,7 (1998): 2-3; and Hsaingt Seetsar, "Facets of a Buddhist Army: Part 2," *Burma Issues* 8,8 (1998): 2-3.

152 Desmond Ball and Hazel Lang, *Factionalism and the Ethnic Insurgent Organisations*, Working Paper No. 356 (Canberra: Strategic and Defence Studies Centre, Australian National University, 2001).

153 On the DKBA, see Desmond Ball and Hazel Lang, "Factionalism and the Ethnic Insurgent Organisations," in *Danger Line: People, Sovereignty and Security Along the Burma-Thailand Border*, ed. Carl Grundy-Warr, Desmond Ball, and Hazel Lang (Bangkok: White Lotus Books, 2002).

returnees land, rice, and "tranquillity."[154] In early February, armed intruders from the DKBA also began sneaking across the Moei River into various Thai camps, abducting senior KNU officials and seizing refugees for return to DKBA areas in Burma. One person abducted was Pado Mahn Yein Sein, a senior Buddhist KNU leader and Chairman of Pa'an District, on February 9. By April 1995, the attacks had escalated, and several long-established camps were completely destroyed and abandoned.

Refugee security was now seriously at risk in Thailand. The Karen refugee camps in Thailand became targets for intimidation, viewed by the DKBA and the *tatmadaw*, variously, as "hardcore villages and base villages," "rear bases," and "permanent safe havens" for the KNU.[155] In this new outbreak of cross-border attacks, the DKBA, with *tatmadaw* collusion, aimed to drive the "KNU refugee camp" populations out of Thailand and into their own locales of control within Burma.[156] Moreover, suspicions flowed in both directions. For instance, those people who had lived at Myaing Gyi Ngu were now no longer accepted by the refugee camp administration in Thailand because they were considered potential agitators or spies; this left many people trapped in hiding, caught between the camps and the DKBA.[157]

For Thailand, beginning in 1995, the phenomenon of cross-border raids became a regular factor complicating the security landscape along this stretch of the border in the Third Army Region. One source estimates that there were some 152 cross-border incursions between January 1995 and April 1998.[158] (See Map 6.1 for the locations of the refugee camps in 1995.) The attacks subsided during the wet season of 1995 (June to October), only to resume again in November with increased banditry by DKBA forces.[159] In January 1997, a number of major attacks, some carried out simultaneously, occurred again. In late January, DKBA forces raided and burned three camps—at Huay Kaloke (ten kilometers north of Mae Sot, destroying 80 percent of the dwellings) and Don Pa Kiang (twenty kilometers north of Mae Sot, also losing 80 percent of its buildings) on the night of January 28, and at Mae La (sixty-two kilometers north of Mae Sot) on the morning of January 29. (Thai

---

[154] "Rebel Faction Running Campaign of Fear Among Karen Refugees," *Bangkok Post*, February 15, 1995.

[155] *Whither KNU?*, pp. 103, 119, 128-129.

[156] During all the chaos of the cross-border raids, some refugees "returned" to DKBA base areas in Burma, although figures on the number of these "returnees" are not reliable. The SLORC in its publication *Whither KNU?* claimed that by March some nine thousand people had returned. See ibid., p. 123. In a March edition of the official News Bulletin of the Embassy of the Union of Myanmar, Bangkok, it was claimed that ten thousand "so-called refugees" had returned to Myaing Gyi Ngu village under the patronage of U Thuzana. The news article also recorded a visit to the village by Secretary 2 of the SLORC, Lieutenant-General Tin Oo, and other ministers on March 7, 1995, where they "paid obeisance to . . . U Thuzana. The Sayadaw then requested the need for assistance to be given to the families which have returned to Myaing Gyi Ngu village. The Secretary (2) made supplications on providing assistance under short-term and long-term projects, to meet the food, clothing and shelter needs of the families which fled to Thailand due to the KNU's bullying and have now returned about 10,000 so-called refugee"[sic]. Embassy of the Union of Myanmar, Bangkok, "Secretary (2) Lieutenant-General Tin Oo Visits Kayin State," *News Bulletin*, No. 4/95, March 3, 1995, p. 1.

[157] Karen Human Rights Group, "Inside the DKBA," KHRG No. 96-14, March 31, 1996, p. 5.

[158] Images Asia and Borderline Video, *A Question of Security*, p. 2.

[159] Karen Human Rights Group, *Inside the DKBA*, p. 7.

security forces that engaged the attackers outside the camp perimeter were not successful in halting the raid.) Earlier on January 4, Sho Klo camp (110 kilometers north of Mae Sot) was shelled.[160] (Sho Klo was closed in February 1998, and its more than seven thousand residents moved to Mae La.) Other camps, such as Maw Ker (fifty kilometers south of Mae Sot) and Mae Kong Kha (further north in Mae Hong Son province), were also threatened, sending people fleeing into nearby jungles in fear.[161] Major assaults on the refugee camps continued into 1998. In March 1998, three camps were affected, with Huay Kaloke raided, Mae La (situated nine kilometers away from the border) shelled, and Maw Ker also attacked.[162] One resident of Huay Kaloke reported that the attackers ordered all refugees to return to Burma: "They told us, 'Don't run, we will shoot you and kill you all.' They asked, 'Have you seen any Kawthoolei [KNLA soldiers]?'"[163]

The incursions prompted Thai authorities to consolidate many of the smaller camps into larger camps. Subsequently, the population of the Mae La camp rose from some five thousand in 1995 to around 25,000 by 1996, making it the largest camp on the border. By the year 2000, there were just twelve camp locations in Thailand, compared with more than thirty at the beginning of 1995.[164] The Thai security presence around the camps was increased in an attempt to defend Thailand from persistent incursions into its territory, for Thai citizens were being caught up in the chaos. Banditry and harassment emerged as a regular source of danger along a 250-kilometer stretch of the border. Thai defenses in this long, porous border area were seriously challenged, and the deployment of additional security forces to engage the intruders was found to be an insufficient deterrence. The Thai army was under pressure to respond more effectively. RTA Commander-in-Chief, General Chetta Thanajaro, met with Army commanders from the regions to discuss improvements to intelligence gathering and coordination,[165] and local region commanders were told they would be held responsible for border violations.[166] Although persistent attacks at times tested the patience of the Thai authorities and a flurry of diplomatic and military responses were communicated to the Burmese authorities, Thailand was publicly reluctant to attribute responsibility for the intrusions directly to the Burmese government. For example, in January 1997, General Chetta responded cautiously in this regard: "We cannot blame the Burmese

---

[160] These attacks are listed in a Karen Refugee Committee press release, Mae Sot, January 29, 1997; and described in detail (with interviews) in Karen Human Rights Group, "Attacks on Karen Refugee Camps," KHRG No. 97-05, March 18, 1997, pp. 1-16.

[161] Ibid., p. 1. Further north, an attack on a Karenni camp six kilometers inside Thai territory in Mae Hong Son province on January 3, sending two thousand of its inhabitants into nearby mountains, was attributed by one source directly to the *tatmadaw*'s 302nd Light Infantry Battalion. The All Burma Students' Democratic Front (ABSDF), also residing in this Karenni camp, made this allegation. "Burmese Troops Gun Down Karenni Refugees," *The Nation*, January 4, 1997.

[162] For details of these March 1998 attacks, see KHRG documentation, including interviews with camp residents in Karen Human Rights Group, "Attacks on Karen Refugee Camps: 1998," KHRG No. 98-04, May 29, 1998.

[163] This interview is cited in ibid., p. 6.

[164] Burmese Border Consortium, *Refugee Relief Programme: Programme Report for the Period January to June 2000* (Bangkok: Burmese Border Consortium, August 2000), p. 1.

[165] "Intelligence Work to be Upgraded," *Bangkok Post*, February 24, 1997, p. 4.

[166] Wassana Nanuam, "Military Reshuffle Imminent," *Bangkok Post*, March 17, 1997.

government. . . . They say [the attack] was not carried out by their soldiers. This is true. The DKBA is a militant minority that has broken off from the [other] Karen group."[167] If Thailand was reluctant to attribute blame, the SLORC was most adamant in exonerating itself. In a letter to *The Nation*, the Burmese embassy in Bangkok claimed "that the abduction of Pado Mahn Yein Sein by the DKBA [in February 1995] was not an action backed by the Government. The Government could neither control nor restrict the activities of the DKBA since the DKBO has not yet officially come into the legal fold."[168] Later, in one of its official "Information Sheets," referring to the raids in March 1998, the Burmese government noted:

> The recent incident which took place are [sic] merely interfactional conflicts within separatist KNU movement which had been waging a war on successive central government [sic] beginning from the era of the Parliamentary Democracy Government. It is not the policy the Myanmar Government to encourage any faction of the KNU to violate the sovereignty of a neighbouring country.[169]

Nevertheless, Thai patience frayed, and a range of Thai government sources issued stern warnings from the Foreign Ministry to the military. For example, after the March 1998 attacks, General Chetta was reportedly "enraged" and "ordered the Third Army to use all kinds of military means in countering the aggression."[170] Moreover, Thai authorities acknowledged that a lapse in security allowed the attack on Huay Kaloke in March 1998. In relation to this security concern, the General Secretary of the National Security Council was quoted as saying, "we accept we were inactive" and that "it [security] should have been stronger, particularly in our intelligence gathering."[171] Following the shelling of Mae La, the Thai army responded with cross-border artillery fire, resulting in the deaths of a number of DKBA troops.[172] It should be noted that these cross-border attacks occurred during the time of the *tatmadaw*'s large-scale 1997 counterinsurgency offensives against the KNU in neighboring Burmese territories. The KNLA sought to retaliate against these cross-border attacks, which were designed to undermine the KNU, by destroying several DKBA camps in four counterattacks; all the time, the *tatmadaw*/SPDC was its real target.[173]

In sum, since 1995, cross-border raids have increased militarization and danger along the border. The incursions have complicated the refugee predicament in

---

[167] "Thai General Absolves Burma for Raids," UPI, January 30, 1997. Accessed online at www.soros.org/burma/thaiabso.html [February 17, 1997].

[168] Embassy of the Union of Myanmar, "Cordial Meeting Over Border," *The Nation*, February 21, 1995. DKBO: Democratic Karen Buddhist Organization.

[169] Myanmar Information Committee, "Information Sheet 1998," No. A-0365(I), March 26, 1998, Myanmar Infoweb. Accessed online at www.myanmarinformation.net/infosheet/1998/980326/htm [April 2, 1998].

[170] "Army Told to Protect Border at all Costs," *Bangkok Post*, March 24, 1998.

[171] "NSC Admits Security Lapse Led to Refugee Camp Attack," *Bangkok Post*, March 21, 1998.

[172] "Thai Army Kills 7 Rangoon Allies," *The Nation*, March 18, 1998, p. A6.

[173] Karen National Union, "KNU: Statement Regarding Retaliation Against SPDC Troops and their Followers," unpublished statement, April 1, 1998. Supamart Kasem and Wassana Nanuam, "Reprisal Raid Kills 10 Karens," *Bangkok Post*, March 18, 1998.

Thailand in two principle ways. First, refugee security in this once stable sanctuary was now in jeopardy. The extension of violence against refugee populations—refugees living in the Thai camps were characterized by the DKBA and the *tatmadaw* alike as rebel (KNU) sympathizers—resembled the dynamics that have generally troubled civilians living in conflict areas inside Burma. Just as the military conflict at home has blurred the status of civilian and "rebel collaborator," these conflations were now transferred into the cross-border camp setting. The refugee camps were not viewed as neutral havens,[174] but instead had become targets for attack. Second, due to the violence and security violations taking place across its sovereign border, Thailand was directly confronted by the political and military conflict occurring within the contiguous Burmese borderlands. Not only was Thailand host to growing numbers of people displaced from their homelands, but border security was now also under constant threat, with refugees deliberately characterized as military targets.

In this regard, Thailand, as the refugees' host state, has inevitably become further entwined in the conflicts of its neighbor. The camps along the Thai-Burmese border have always been under the control and administration of the armed oppositions. Now, however, the camps inside Thailand, which for so long were characterized by low-key local administration and provided secure havens to displaced persons, are threatened by the changing security environment of the borderlands. In this new scenario, Thailand found itself under pressure due to both this deterioration in border security and its obligation to protect the refugees.

CONCLUSIONS

The story of the refugees is intertwined with the evolving political and military context of the border, and it is not possible to understand the refugee predicament without a detailed consideration of this context in which sanctuary is configured.

First, the mapping of the boundary, arising from the colonial era, and the historical task of securing the outer reaches of the hinterland, marked a transition from earlier forms of political authority by "territorializing" the limits of sovereign authority. Yet until recent times the boundary—as a notion of a fixed and abstract territorial division—was simply not (and could not be) strictly enforced; in practice, it was subsumed by a more fluid sense of borderland. Second, until the early 1980s, and operating according to the current political context, this borderland functioned for Thailand as a buffer zone where a string of non-communist, anti-Rangoon insurgencies held control of Burmese territory. During this era, Thailand was generally in a position that allowed it flexibly to accommodate displaced persons sheltering in the border areas, provided that their presence remained unobtrusive. However, since 1988 in particular, the dynamics of border relations between Thailand and Burma were reoriented towards greater official interaction (however uneven), with a form of diplomatic rapprochement and a convergence of interests in business diplomacy. Also, the vicissitudes of the military geography in the Burmese borderland shifted substantially in favor of the regime in Rangoon and increasingly weakened the insurgencies, all at a time

---

[174] One Burmese commented that "the so-called refugee camps are in fact the KNU rear camps." Resident of Kayin State, *Whither KNU?*, p. 103.

when Thailand had also become less receptive to the insurgents. At the same time, Thailand has found itself with a growing refugee burden, facing increased border insecurity arising from post-1995 developments in the neighboring Burmese territories, especially the intensification of the *tatmadaw*'s counterinsurgency campaigns and the violent cross-border forays of the DKBA.

Third, cross-border sanctuary is an interactive process in which the borders delineating safety and danger shift along with the unfolding political context. The refugee populations themselves have "mapped" their story onto the borderland, and they are actively present as a quasi-permanent feature of the border landscape. Yet the transformation of the borderlands has reconfigured the circumstances of refugee sanctuary. Since 1995, safe havens for the refugees have been in serious jeopardy, with the margins outlining safety and danger more volatile, and the pressure on both the refugee populations and their host greater than ever.

To complicate matters, Burmese refugees seeking asylum in Thailand are not concentrated exclusively along the borderlands. Apart from the growing presence of illegal Burmese migrant workers scattered throughout Thailand, there is another group of political exiles from Burma, mainly located in Bangkok, whose sanctuary adds a further dimension to the refugee predicament involving these two countries. This situation is explored in the next chapter.

CHAPTER SEVEN

ASYLUM IN BANGKOK

INTRODUCTION

Non-Burman minority refugees have found sanctuary in the border camps, but the students and political exiles of 1988 have encountered new kinds of fear in Thailand. Burmese "students" and political dissidents, based mainly in Bangkok, form the other major group of Burmese asylum-seekers in Thailand. These exiles fled Burma in the aftermath of the deployment of the military's strike forces to crush the 1988 pro-democracy uprising, and in Thailand they have been characteristically active in opposition politics against the Burmese regime. They contrast with the border population in that they conform to the definition of "activist" refugee[1] contained in the classic 1951 UN Convention, and consequently they have had access to recognition from the Office of the United Nations High Commissioner for Refugees in Bangkok on an individual, case-by-case basis. The "Burmese students" are an all-encompassing category by which the 1988 student and political activist generation are identified (by themselves and others), sometimes irrespective of actual former and/or current student status.

This chapter looks at why and how the situation for this group of exiles has been politically contentious, uncertain, and punctuated by tensions. As political activists, the Burmese students in Bangkok have been entangled in a fundamental tension with their host authorities, for the two parties hold divergent expectations about the conditions of their asylum. On the one hand, the students view political activism as their key task in exile, while, on the other hand, Thailand insists that they submit to the requirement that their protection is conditional on the agreement that they refrain from such activities. In an attempt to manage this noisy group of asylum-seekers, the Thai authorities transferred the refugee protection apparatus to a holding center outside Bangkok referred to as the "Safe Area." The problem, however, is that the facility has been unable to—and until recently, could not, in sheer logistical terms—include and accommodate all the activist Burmese asylum-seekers, and therefore the arrangement has been unsatisfying. Further, despite the formal protection mechanism in place, asylum-seekers and even recognized refugees in Bangkok more often than not negotiate their survival as if they were "ordinary" illegal immigrants.

The chapter begins with a brief description of the flight of Burmese students and dissidents to the Thai border following the events of 1988 in Burma, when pro-democracy uprisings spread across the nation and the SLORC military government

---

[1] Aristride R. Zolberg, Astri Suhrke, and Sergio Aguayo, *Escape from Violence: Conflict and the Refugee Crisis in the Developing World* (New York: Oxford University Press, 1989), p. 30.

was installed. The evolution of the Thai response to their presence is then considered and detailed attention devoted to the security predicaments faced by this group of asylum-seekers in Bangkok; we will consider the formal protection apparatus available to them and the mutual dissatisfaction experienced by both the students and their Thai host authorities. Finally, we will examine the establishment of the Safe Area camp as an institutional response to the dilemma, as well as the patterns of everyday life—in which the distinction between "refugee" and "illegal immigrant" is blurred—to which many Burmese have been exposed, irrespective of their status under formal protection arrangements.

THE STUDENTS FLEE

Most of the eight to ten thousand Burmese students and other activists who left the towns and cities of Burma after September 1988 fled eastwards to the Thai border areas controlled by the Karen, Mon, and Karenni insurgencies. By October 1988, at the KNU camp at Thi Baw Bo opposite Tak province, for example, some 1,900 students and activists had converged, all in need of food and shelter.[2] Smaller numbers also turned up in the Pa-O areas further north in Shan State, in the Kachin Hills opposite the Chinese border, and in India (in Mizoram, Manipur, and beyond) and southeastern Bangladesh to the west.[3]

Many of the students held high hopes and expectations of the battle they could wage—with foreign support, arms and ammunition—against the regime from the border area.[4] At Three Pagodas Pass, over a thousand Mon students and activists turned up, and many joined the New Mon State Party (NMSP). They undertook military training, albeit under adverse conditions, considerably increasing the ranks of the NMSP.[5] However, as a result of the rigors and difficulties of jungle survival in the border areas—including diseases such as malaria, skin, respiratory and other infections, and a lack of food[6]—the initial large numbers of recruits soon subsided, as many students either returned home or moved further into exile in Bangkok. Those students remaining on the border, still a sizable number at around 2,500 or more, formed their own political organization and army, the All Burma Students' Democratic Front (ABSDF). The ABSDF was born in early November 1988 after lengthy debates and meetings at the KNU base of Kawmura and organized into a series of "battalions" along the border, from the Mawdaung Pass opposite Prachuab Khirikhan province in the south to the Pai River near Mae Hong Son in

---

[2] Rodney Tasker and Bertil Lintner, "Food Before Fighting: Dissident Students Regroup with Rebels on the Border," *Far Eastern Economic Review*, October 20, 1988, p. 38.

[3] Bertil Lintner, *Outrage: Burma's Struggle for Democracy* (Bangkok: White Lotus, 1990), p. 147.

[4] Ibid., p. 149.

[5] As Lintner notes, "They were trained as guerilla soldiers—but the drills were carried out with bamboo sticks instead of rifles since the NMSP had no resources to arm all the new recruits." Ibid., p. 157.

[6] Lintner writes that "food had been a problem all along...the remote camps at Three Pagodas Pass and other bases on the Thai-Burma frontier were hardly havens for gourmets. The urban youths in their new environment soon found themselves eating snakes, lizards, dogs, trunks of banana trees, and whatever they could forage for in the jungle." Bertil Lintner, *Burma in Revolt: Opium and Insurgency since 1948* (Boulder, CO and Bangkok: Westview Press and White Lotus, 1994), p. 290.

the north.[7] The arrival of these educated, urban-based refugees on this scale to the border areas was a new phenomenon. Until then, exposure to the civil war and life in the border areas had generally been remote from the lives of most of the urban Burmese population,[8] and the ethnic insurgent groups were not involved in the 1988 pro-democracy uprising. This conjunction of circumstances now provided an opportunity for a new alliance between the opposition ethnic and the democracy forces, first realized in the establishment of the Democratic Alliance of Burma (DAB) on November 18, 1988, a coalition of twenty-three anti-government groups.[9]

The 1988 Pro-democracy Uprising

The students first fled the Burmese heartland in the wake of the final military crackdown on the pro-democracy demonstrations and the installation of the State Law and Order Restoration Council (SLORC) on September 18, 1988. The tumultuous year of 1988 saw massive "people power"-style antigovernment demonstrations against one-party authoritarian rule and economic mismanagement, which spread across the country.[10] The political spark that ignited the uprising was a seemingly isolated incident in a teashop on March 12, 1988. It began as a local "town versus gown" confrontation-cum-brawl between students from the Rangoon Institute of Technology (RIT) and local youths at the "Sanda Win" teashop in Rangoon's Gyogon West neighborhood, culminating in the stabbing of a student (for which the culprit was later arrested).[11] However, the student response to the incident grew into a violent protest when the *Lon Htein* (riot police) responded with gunfire, resulting in the death of twenty-three-year-old Maung Phone Maw at the scene.[12]

---

[7] Bertil Lintner, "Running for Cover: Students Flee Cities in Wake of Army Suppression," *Far Eastern Economic Review*, September 7, 1988, p. 27. Battalions 101 and 102 were located within NMSP territory; 201 through to 211 in KNU areas; 303 in the Karenni National Progressive Party (KNPP) area; 601 with the Pa-O National Organization. Battalions 701 and 702 operated in the Kachin Independence Organization area; 801 with the Shan State Liberation Organization (SSLO); and 901 with the National Unity Front of Arakan (NUFA) in the northwest of Burma.

[8] Further, as Priyambudi Sulistiyanto notes, the students had absorbed substantial anti-minority propaganda during their lives under the military government. "However, by living alongside the ethnic minority villages, the students finally discovered that those stories were not true. They discovered the suffering of the ethnic people, which the students now experienced also." Priyambudi Sulistiyanto, "Burma: The Politics of an Uncertain Transition, 1988-1994" (MA thesis, Flinders University, 1995), p. 90.

[9] Ibid., pp. 158-159.

[10] The antecedent of the large-scale outpouring of discontent in 1988 was the government's demonetization of up to 80 percent of the Burmese currency on September 5, 1987. In "Ordinance No. 1" it was announced that from that day forward twenty-five, thirty-five and seventy-five *kyat* notes ceased to be legal tender, leaving many people suddenly destitute. See Lintner, *Burma in Revolt*, pp. 273-274.

[11] For accounts of the events of the 1988 uprising, see, for instance, Lintner, *Outrage*; Maureen Aung-Thwin, "Burmese Days," *Foreign Affairs* 68,2 (1989): 143-161; Moksha Yitri, "The Crisis in Burma: Back from the Heart of Darkness?," *Asian Survey* 29,6 (1989): 543-558; *Burma Debate* 5,3 (Summer 1998) (special issue on 1988). For the regime's perspective, see A Tatmadaw Researcher, *A Concise History of Myanmar and the Tatmadaw's Role, 1948-1988*, Vol. 1 (Yangon: News and Periodicals Enterprise of the Ministry of Information of the Government of the Union of Myanmar, 1991), pp. 88-153.

[12] See Lintner, *Outrage*, pp. 1-12.

Student unrest then gathered momentum, and the anti-government movement spread to Rangoon University, but again on March 16 the riot police struck back violently with clubs against hundreds of students trapped on the "White Bridge," leaving scores of students and school children killed and wounded. The students' anger was compounded further when the government refused to acknowledge the massacre at the "White Bridge." In the official account of the "1988 disturbances," there is also no mention of fatalities on March 16.[13] The government did, however, agree to an investigation of a subsequent event that occurred on the night of March 18, in which forty-one young people suffocated to death in an overcrowded police van destined for Insein jail. The finding of the inquest—"that those prisoners had died as a result of tear gas they had inhaled earlier in the day and also of suffocation in the over-loaded lock-up"—was only made public on July 19 "for fear," according to the authorities, "of fueling further violence."[14] In April and May, due primarily to the harsh crackdown, the country returned to a "tottering 'normalcy,'"[15] although when the universities and colleges reopened in June, a mass, pro-democracy movement emerged, growing to include hundreds of thousands of people by the time of the "8-8-88" National General Strike on August 8, 1988.

As Marc Purcell writes, students have historically been "a barometer of the nation" and "the vanguard of protest" in Burma.[16] And in the 1988 pro-democracy demonstrations, university students again took a leading role as "instigators, a vanguard, and networkers."[17] Purcell identifies earlier eras of student activism, notably in the 1930s, when student leaders recast themselves as politicians in the wider community, and also in the crescendo of the nationalist struggle of 1945–48, and, later, in the post-independence period following General Ne Win's military coup of March 2, 1962. On July 7, 1962, students were confronted by the *Lon Htein* and Ne Win's Fourth Burma Rifles outside the Rangoon University Student Union, a confrontation that resulted in a large number of deaths, as the army opened fire, providing a deadly warning to opponents of the regime.[18] Then in November and December of 1963, the students involved themselves in the ethnic "peace parley" protests. Large-scale student protest did not occur again until the U Thant unrest in 1974.[19] From the 1960s, the Burmese government refused to tolerate the political involvement of students in public life, so that the sphere of their activities was transferred into "small underground cells and amorphous discontent."[20] But in 1988,

---

[13] The account of this day reads " . . . the People's Police had to intervene and disperse the crowd. One hundred and fifty four students were detained and not one was killed." A Tatmadaw Researcher, *A Concise History of Myanmar*, p. 91.

[14] Ibid., p. 92.

[15] Yitri, "The Crisis in Burma," p. 545.

[16] Marc Purcell, "Putting the Genie Back in the Bottle: Reflections on Burmese Student Activism: 1921-1938 and 1954-1968" (MA thesis, Monash University, 1996), p. 4.

[17] Ibid., p. 4.

[18] Writing about that confrontation, Purcell observes: "Finally they had come face to face— students with a proud tradition of anti-authoritarianism and the *tatmadaw* who had proved themselves the most powerful force in the state." Ibid., p. 194.

[19] See Andrew Selth, *Death of a Hero: The U Thant Disturbances in Burma, December 1974*, Research Paper No. 49 (Brisbane: Centre for the Study of Australian Asian Relations, Griffith University, 1989).

[20] Purcell, "Putting the Genie Back in the Bottle," p. 249.

the students again emerged at the forefront of protest, as Aung San Suu Kyi noted in her August 26 speech to a mass rally at the Shwedagon Pagoda in Rangoon:

> It is the students who have paved the way to the present situation where it is possible to hold such a rally. The occasion has been made possible because the recent demonstrations have been spearheaded by the students and even more because they have shown a willingness to sacrifice their lives.[21]

In the lead up to the "8-8-88" General Strike, in the crescendo of discontent and protest, students participated in the proliferation of local strike committees formed around the country—organizations comprised of students, monks and other professionals who administered local order and distributed food supplies as government administration crumbled.

After renewed street demonstrations in June 1988, the government announced the "Extraordinary Party Congress" of the Burmese Socialist Program Party (BSPP), held on July 23-25, 1988, in which a resolution was adopted "permitting Party Chairman U Ne Win and Vice Chairman U San Yu to retire from the Party."[22] In his resignation speech, Ne Win stated that he felt "indirectly responsible for the distressing incidents of March and June,"[23] though he also uttered his now infamous warning: " . . . if in the future there are mob disturbances, if the army shoots, it hits—there is no firing in the air to scare."[24] Despite the threat, from July 28 to August 2 mass demonstrations occurred again, spreading from the precincts of Shwedagon Pagoda out into the city. On August 3, the authorities responded with the installation of a "Military Administration," warning the "rioters" with loud-speakers all over the city "to cease disturbing the peace" or face the consequence "that the Military Administration would unavoidably have to open fire."[25] The official history notes that "[t]he *Tatmadaw* stepped in only to protect the people from all the dangers and perils and had no inclination, as a People's *Tatmadaw*, to bully the people,"[26] although it proceeds to document those occasions over the ensuing period when it "had to resort to shooting."[27] Nevertheless, the National General Strike of 8-8-88 went ahead, with hundreds of thousands of people from all walks of life taking to the streets in Rangoon and in the cities and townships around Burma. Late at night in Rangoon, after the day of demonstrations, the military resorted to widespread, indiscriminate shooting when the crowds of people in the Sule Pagoda region of downtown Rangoon refused to disperse. The killings and violence continued over the following days, and the country descended into chaos—suspected government agents and police were killed (some were beheaded) and state properties looted—as the "government machinery ceased to

---

[21] Aung San Suu Kyi, *Freedom From Fear and Other Writings* (London: Penguin Books, 1991), p. 198.

[22] A Tatmadaw Researcher, *A Concise History of Myanmar*, p. 105.

[23] Yitri, "The Crisis in Burma," p. 547.

[24] U Sein Lwin was appointed as the successor to the position of BSPP Chairman (he was in charge of the 1962 Rangoon University massacre and again responsible for suppressing the protests in March and June 1988). Lintner, *Burma in Revolt*, p. 276.

[25] A Tatmadaw Researcher, *A Concise History of Myanmar*, p. 107.

[26] Ibid.

[27] For instance, ibid., pp. 109-110.

function."[28] On August 24, Dr. Maung Maung (who had become President following Ne Win's ouster) broadcast an announcement that the Military Administration was withdrawn, and he appealed for calm.[29] However, the discontent and chaos continued and spread, until the severe clampdown of September 18, 1988.

On September 18, with some 300,000 people marching in the streets, the *tatmadaw* staged a "nominal coup d'état,"[30] resulting in a further massive death toll and the installation of the State Law and Order Restoration Council (SLORC).[31] The SLORC, in its "Announcement 1/88" on this date, proclaimed that its goal was to "effect a timely halt to the deteriorating conditions on all sides all over the country,"[32] and it promised to hold democratic multi-party elections in the future. According to the official account, the *tatmadaw* could not escape its "historic duty," which was "to protect national solidarity and sovereignty."[33] Of course, other accounts of events in 1988 do not portray the actions of the SLORC so positively, but rather view the crackdown as a violent suppression of dissent. For example, Moksha Yitri writes:

> That city dwellers were finally being subjected to the kind of treatment that had been commonplace in the ethnic-minority operational zones for decades was borne out by the readiness, the alacrity with which the army shot and killed people. . . . It was a full-blown military suppression pursued with a vengeance, naked military force used against unarmed or poorly armed civil disobedience, and the result was carnage . . . Burma awoke to find itself occupied by its own army...[34]

Following the September crackdown and its aftermath—when many of the leaders and participants of the uprising were now in danger of arrest, torture, imprisonment, and even death—students and activists fled to the border areas.

THE THAI RESPONSE

While formal provisions for granting refugee status to particular groups of asylum seekers have existed in Thailand, the situation of the Burmese exiles in Thailand has evolved under considerable tension. Responding to the first arrival of about 250 Burmese students in the border town of Mae Sot on September 20, 1988,

---

[28] Yitri, "The Crisis in Burma," p. 551.

[29] Ibid., pp. 114-115.

[30] Aung-Thwin, "Burmese Days," p. 143.

[31] For a detailed account of September 18, 1988 and the SLORC, see Lintner, *Outrage*, pp. 131-145.

[32] "Announcement No. 1/88 of the State Law and Order Restoration Council, 18 September 1988," in *Democracy and Politics in Burma: A Collection of Documents*, ed. Marc Weller (Bangkok and Manerplaw: National Coalition Government of the Union of Burma, 1993), p. 142.

[33] A Tatmadaw Researcher, *A Concise History of Myanmar*, p. 153. Also, for an analysis of the official press during the 1988 pro-democracy uprising, see Jan Becka, "The Military and the Struggle for Democracy in Burma: The Presentation of the Political Upheaval of 1988 in the Official Burmese Press," *Archiv Orientalni* 61,1 (1993): 63-80.

[34] Yitri, "The Crisis in Burma," pp. 552-553.

Thais initially welcomed the students and granted them temporary asylum.[35] On November 22, 1988, the Thai cabinet decided to offer asylum to Burmese student dissidents, but swiftly changed its policy with the establishment of the Tak Repatriation Center, which became operational on December 22, at the provincial airport of Mae Sot.[36] Meanwhile, the Burmese authorities had set up twenty-seven official reception centers along their borders with Thailand, India, and Bangladesh, to which the students were required to return by November 18 (this deadline was repeatedly extended) or be "treated as insurgents."[37] During the life of the Tak Repatriation Center, over three hundred students were sent back into the hands of the authorities in Rangoon aboard Burmese airforce planes. The Tak facility was closed down in February 1989 following allegations of instances of forced return (*refoulement*).[38]

The movement of Burmese asylum seekers into Bangkok began after the closure of the Tak center, and from 1989 the Bangkok office of UNHCR (United Nations High Commission for Refugees) began dealing with a major new group of non-Indochinese asylum seekers. At this time, the UNHCR implemented a process to determine the status of those Burmese who directly participated in the 1988 uprising and could demonstrate they were unable to return home; those who qualified were recognized as "Persons of Concern to the UNHCR." It also provided them with a monthly financial allowance, as well as social, health, and educational support services. But, as we discuss below, documentation of their status has remained an uncertain form of protection for these refugees since the inception of the process. In 1990, the situation of Burmese asylum seekers in Bangkok became increasingly sensitive, particularly in the wake of the hijacking by Burmese students of a Thai Airways flight on route from Bangkok's Don Muang airport to Rangoon on November 10, 1990.[39] This was the second hijacking by Burmese students—the first occurred in October 1989, when two students hijacked a

---

[35] United States Committee for Refugees, *"The War is Growing Worse and Worse": Refugees and Displaced Persons on the Thai-Burmese Border* (Washington, DC: USCR, 1990), p. 2.

[36] Asia Watch, *Abuses Against Burmese Refugees in Thailand* 4,7 (New York: Asia Watch, 1992), p. 2. Bertil Lintner perceives the change in approach (a crackdown on the students) as an outcome of the official visit of General Chavalit Yongchaiyut to Rangoon on December 14, 1988. Bertil Lintner, "Less Than Welcome: Thais Get Tough with Fugitive Burmese Students," *Far Eastern Economic Review*, January 12, 1989, p. 13.

[37] Lintner, *Outrage*, p. 160; Bertil Lintner, "A Darkening Scene: Military Government Resorts to Repression to Curb Dissent," *Far Eastern Economic Review*, November 24, 1988, p. 40. For an official account of the *tatmadaw*'s "consultations with the Royal Thai Army" and the reception camps for "absconders," see Nawrahta, *Destiny of the Nation* (Yangon: The News and Periodicals Enterprise, 1995), pp. 64-65.

[38] Asia Watch, *Abuses Against Burmese Refugees in Thailand*, p. 3; see also United States Committee for Refugees, *"The War is Growing Worse and Worse,"* p. 3. The USCR lists occasions between 1988 and 1990 on which it considers *refoulements* to have occurred (p. 9). That *refoulements* occurred in this early period was acknowledged during an interview with the UNHCR regional representative. Interview with Ruprecht von Arnhim, UNHCR Regional Representative, Bangkok, September 18, 1995.

[39] As Khin Nyunt has explained in detail, "twenty-five minutes after it was airborne and as soon as it had entered Myanmar air space," the plane was hijacked by "terrorists . . . brandishing the handmade bomb." Lieutenant-General Khin Nyunt, "How Some Western Powers Have Been Aiding and Abetting Terrorism Committed by Certain Organizations Operating under the Guise of Democracy and Human Rights by Giving Them Assistance in Both Cash and Kind," unpublished statement by SLORC Secretary (1), Rangoon, June 1997, p. 4.

Rangoon-bound Myanmar Airways flight from Kawthaung. The November 1990 hijacking, in particular, intensified Thailand's doubts concerning the activities of Burmese students located inside its borders. The Ministry of Interior responded by establishing a committee to expedite inchoate plans for a holding center for Burmese students in Thailand as a way to restrict their political activities.[40] Human rights organizations at the time noted that, in view of these heightened sensitivities, formal recognition as a "person of concern to the UNHCR" ironically increased the vulnerability of Burmese students to arrest and surveillance.[41]

From Thailand's perspective, therefore, the presence of this politically active group of asylum seekers in Bangkok has generated a constant sense of conflict. As in Burma—where the students were agitators and organizers for change—these same activists now carry out their pro-democracy struggle from exile in Thailand, discomfiting both the Thai and Burmese governments. The students are even mentioned in Thailand's 1996 Defense White Paper:

> ... Burmese students opposed to the government in Rangoon and taking refuge in Thailand have caused many problems for the Thai government by making unfair demands and causing bodily harm to Thai government officials looking after them.[42]

In this way, the students have carried with them some of the conflict from which they have fled, and the situation has placed many genuine asylum seekers in need of effective refugee protection. What, then, has been the quality of protection for this group in the context of the tensions provoked by their presence in Thailand?

REFUGEE STATUS AND PROTECTION

Although the Royal Thai Government has not acceded to the 1951 Refugee Convention or its 1967 Protocol, it allows UNHCR a specific role in the "care, maintenance, and protection"[43] of the Burmese asylum seekers in Bangkok. In legal terms, because Thailand is not a signatory to the UN refugee instruments, the UNHCR in Thailand acts in accordance with its 1950 Statute. Also, because the

---

[40] Thammasak Lamaiphan et al., "Burmese Dissidents Face 'Crackdown,'" *The Nation*, November 13, 1990, p. A1. The committee contained representatives from the Ministry of Foreign Affairs, National Security Council, National Intelligence Agency, Immigration Bureau, and Joint Security Command of the Supreme Command headquarters. Tom Kramer, "Thai Foreign Policy Towards Burma, 1987-1993" (MA thesis, Universiteit van Amsterdam, 1994), p. 130.

[41] According to one report, for instance, beginning in 1991, several students even requested to withdraw their UNHCR registration, preferring to stay in Thailand as illegal immigrants, which could afford them greater anonymity and flexibility to negotiate their own asylum with local police and authorities. Asia Watch, *Abuses against Burmese Refugees in Thailand*, p. 6. Amnesty International, *Thailand: Concerns about Treatment of Burmese Refugees*, ASA 39/15/91 (London: Amnesty International, 1991), p. 3.

[42] Ministry of Defense, *The Defence of Thailand, 1996* (Bangkok: Strategic Research Institute, National Institute of Defence Studies, Supreme Command Headquarters, 1996), p. 8.

[43] Daniel E. Conway, UNHCR Representative in Thailand, "Burmese Students and the Safe Area Established by the Royal Thai Government: Statement to the Parliamentary Committee on Justice and Human Rights," unpublished statement, Bangkok, February 18, 1993, p. 1.

political situation is sensitive and complex, the UNHCR has used the phrase "persons of concern," rather than "refugees,"[44] to refer to these displaced persons, although individual status determination proceeds according to the traditional refugee criteria set by the agency. The formal refugee protection apparatus in Bangkok thus entails a collaborative relationship between the Thai Ministry of Interior and the UNHCR, in which the UNHCR is permitted to perform its functions: determining the status of particular individuals and then assisting this group of political refugees. In principle, the arrangement has aimed to identify from among the broader population of illegal immigrants in the capital those people who should be exempted from punishment for illegal immigration because of their history as "activists." This group of urban-based Burmese asylum seekers was first officially recognized in the Thai Cabinet decision of September 24, 1991 that authorized the Minister of Interior to grant them a temporary stay under Article 17 of the 1979 Immigration Act.[45]

In 1989 and 1990, the small staff of the UNHCR office in Bangkok was overwhelmed with applications for asylum. By the end of 1991, the Burmese caseload comprised a total of 3,630 asylum seekers registered with the UNHCR, with 1,864 recognized as "persons of concern" (the majority of whom were students), another 535 applications pending, and 1,232 rejections.[46] In addition to an "NI" number (indicating "non-Indochinese"), successful applicants for status as "persons of concern" with the UNHCR received a letter identifying them as such. The Cabinet decision of September 1991 also formalized the plan for a holding camp for the Burmese students in Thailand. It was to this camp that the formal protection apparatus was eventually transferred.

The "Safe Area" Camp

The Ministry of Interior opened the "Safe Area for Burmese Students" (also known as the "Burmese Students' Center") in December 1992. Officially, the broad purpose of the camp was to provide material facilities and a temporary safe haven for the students pending their return, pursuant to political improvements in their home country.[47] Politically, the purpose of the camp was to manage the Burmese students who have frequently been regarded as "troublemakers." Or, following Malkki, the Safe Area constitutes an institution of "regulation and care" for "people out of place."[48] It was set up at the old Pak Thor Border Patrol Police headquarters in the small village of Maneeloy, Pak Thor district, Ratchaburi province, some 130 kilometers southwest of Bangkok. The Ministry of Interior (MOI) has maintained responsibility for the overall administration of the camp at

---

[44] Discussions with legal officers, UNHCR, Bangkok, March 1998.

[45] Interview, Ruprecht von Arnhim, UNHCR Regional Representative, Bangkok, September 18, 1995.

[46] United States Committee for Refugees, *World Refugee Survey 1992* (Washington, DC: USCR, 1992), p. 66. For further discussion on this period, see also Therese Caouette, "Burmese Asylum Seekers in Thailand," *Refugee Participation Network* 13 (1992): 26-27.

[47] Interview, Khun Wannida Boonpracong, Chief, Displaced Persons and Illegal Immigrant Affairs Subdivision, Ministry of Interior, Bangkok, March 9, 1998.

[48] Liisa Malkki, "National Geographic: The Rooting of Peoples and the Territorialization of National Identity Among Scholars and Refugees," *Cultural Anthropology* 7,1 (1992): 34.

the Bangkok level; the Ratchaburi Governor has input at the provincial level; and various other local MOI staff members operate the center on an everyday basis.[49]

In accordance with the September 1991 Cabinet decision, Burmese students seeking asylum in Thailand were now technically permitted to stay in the Kingdom by the Minister of Interior under Article 17 of the Immigration Act. However, with the establishment of the Safe Area, this grant of stay was now contingent on their residence at the camp and concomitant compliance with the rules.[50] In February 1992, a initial group of 516 students holding MOI registration cards were informed that they had to register and transfer from Bangkok to the camp—deadlines were issued—or face the consequences of illegal immigration. The MOI announcement (from the Operations Center for Displaced Persons) pertaining to the September deadline noted:

> Those who do not report to the Operations Center or travel to the Safe Area within the above-mentioned period shall be considered as if they do not want protection and assistance from the Government and shall be treated as illegal immigrants . . . and after the legal action is completed shall be deported out of the Kingdom of Thailand.[51]

Yet even as the camp was due to open, only fifteen students had entered the center at Maneeloy.[52] By the end of 1993, there was still a meager population of less than 150 people registered and fewer actually in residence.

Students in Bangkok resisted being transferred to the Safe Area from its inception. They complained both that their safety and protection in the camp was not assured and that the location of the camp would curtail opportunities for political activism. Burmese student representatives wrote to the Minister of Interior expressing concerns about their "internment in the safe area" and their "foreboding and anxiety, born out of the knowledge and realization that our professed endeavors to answer the call of duty to our country and people came under restrictions and bondage."[53] But from the perspective of the Thai authorities, the "Safe Area" provided an opportunity to reduce political activism by Burmese students in Thailand by providing a safe haven for them that was specifically conditional on their disengagement from political activities. The point of contention was obviously that the students themselves viewed their task in exile as the pursuit of just such activism. Strongly discordant perspectives, punctuated with conflict, have therefore marked debates about how the students should live in Thailand.

---

[49] On the ground, staff at the center include the Camp Commander, appointed by the governor, who is in charge of the everyday decisions pertaining to the camp and its residents, several clerks from MOI, a pool of security officers from the local village militia, health and education personnel (including those from voluntary agencies), and a part-time UNHCR protection officer.

[50] Detailed ministerial regulations concerning the conditions of stay in the camp were issued on September 9, 1992, supplemented by further provincial regulations and rules in May 1995.

[51] Police-General Pao Sarasin, Minister of Interior, "Announcement of the MOI. Subject: Extension Period for Burmese Students to Report for Admittance into the Safe Area," unpublished statement, September 25, 1992.

[52] United States Committee on Refugees, *World Refugee Survey 1993*, p. 86.

[53] The representatives formed a group called the "Burmese Students Committee for Handling of [the] Closed Camp." Letter to Minister of Interior, Royal Thai Government, September 9, 1992.

The UNHCR broadly accepted the concept of a Safe Area for the Burmese students in the absence of other options besides "a fugitive existence in Thailand."[54] The agency stated in November 1992 that "on balance, they [students] will be more secure in the Safe Area than living illegally in Bangkok, subject to arrest and deportation." The Commission was also satisfied that the camp complied with internationally acceptable standards for such a facility, announcing that it would transfer the assistance payments for students to the Safe Area.[55] However, as noted above, the influx of students into the Safe Area proceeded slowly and reluctantly, so that, in practice, many "persons of concern" continued to live in Bangkok, with financial assistance, until the UNHCR itself eventually implemented a more stringent system of compliance concerning the Safe Area in mid-1995. In stricter accord with government policy, the UNHCR issued letters to registered "persons of concern" not yet resident at the Maneeloy camp (the letters were sent in monthly batches according to NI number), informing them of these new arrangements: "your status, pursuant to the policy of the Royal Thai Government, can be legalized in the Safe Area, whereas this is not the case if you remain in Bangkok."[56] In June 1995, the UNHCR announced:

> Please be advised that UNHCR can no longer provide protection or assistance in Bangkok to Myanmar nationals who are recognized as Persons of Concern to the office. Protection and assistance will instead be provided in the Maneeloy Burmese Student Center (Safe Area) . . . UNHCR has determined that the Safe Area meets accepted international standards for the protection and welfare of refugees.[57]

Slowly, although only after substantial resistance, the population of the camp grew, until it reached its capacity and was actually "closed" to new arrivals in mid-1996. At this time, the official population stood at 762.[58] By 1998, an additional and growing population of other Burmese displaced persons (numbering over five hundred) was also residing illegally in the camp.

Thus, eventually the Safe Area developed into a fully functioning institution to which the protection apparatus and material assistance for Burmese students and political activists in Thailand were transferred. However, social life in the camp has been problematic, characterized by boredom (notwithstanding educational activities provided by voluntary agencies), uncertainty about the future, general mistrust, serious problems such as drug abuse, and diseases, including HIV/AIDS in some instances. Since October 1993, intermittent confrontations (sometimes physical) have occurred between students and camp security personnel and/or the

---

[54] Daniel E. Conway, "Burmese Students and the Safe Area Established by the Royal Thai Government," p. 2.

[55] United Nations High Commission for Refugees, "UNHCR Position on the Safe Area for Burmese in Thailand," press release, November 30, 1992.

[56] Quoted from a letter to a Burmese "person of concern" from the UNHCR, September 1, 1995.

[57] UNHCR Branch Office in Thailand, "Notice to Asylum Seekers/Persons of Concern to UNHCR (Myanmar Nationals)," unpublished statement, June 1, 1995.

[58] UNHCR, Executive Committee of the High Commissioner's Programme, "Update on Regional Developments in Asia and Oceania," Standing Committee 4th Meeting, UN doc. EC/46/SC/CRP.44, 1996, paragraph 9(a).

camp commander within the center and in the surrounding Maneeloy village community, as well as between groups of residents within the camp. In January 1995, for example, following a late-night incident between students and security personnel, a group of some 150 students marched out of the compound in protest, claiming the camp to be unsafe and demanding its closure, and provoking the ire of both the Thai authorities and the UNHCR.[59]

Until late 1999 there were no high fences to keep people within the camp perimeter, and the shelter operated as a "semi-open camp,"[60] run by the Thai authorities and monitored via regular visits by a Bangkok-based UNHCR officer. It operated as a semi-open camp because, under the rules, residents were able to apply for permission from the MOI to leave (for up to one week per month) for trips outside the provincial boundary.

However, since October 1999, after the dramatic twenty-six-hour take-over of the Burmese embassy in Bangkok by the radical student faction calling itself the Vigorous Burmese Student Warriors (VBSW), some members of which were registered with the Safe Area, a general clampdown on the movement of Burmese students was implemented. After the embassy siege, the VBSW received a safe passage by Thai helicopter to the Burmese border (opposite Thailand's Ratchaburi province), where members took shelter in territory controlled by the hitherto little-known Karen splinter group, the millenarian God's Army.[61] Although Thailand avoided declaring this action "terrorist," the reputation of Burmese students as a group suffered from the incident, which led more Thais to perceive activist students as "troublemakers." In mid-November, security within the Safe Area also deteriorated after a series of violent altercations that erupted between several students and camp authorities. The semi-open style of the holding camp ended; barbed-wire fences were raised around the perimeter and much tighter security regulations imposed. An even tougher Thai approach to the students came some three months later, when in January 2000, heavily armed hostage-takers from the VBSW and their God's Army counterparts seized the Ratchaburi provincial hospital in Thailand.[62] This time the Thai authorities did not show the restraint that marked their response to the earlier embassy drama; the ten gunmen were treated as serious terrorists and shot dead by Thai security forces.

The Safe Area has also served as a holding center for persons awaiting ultimate "exit permission" from the MOI for third country resettlement to the West (mainly the United States, Australia, Canada, New Zealand, and northern Europe). After the two hostage-taking episodes of October 1999 and January 2000, which intensified misunderstanding and mistrust associated with "Burmese

---

[59] Interview, Ruprecht von Arnhim, UNHCR Regional Representative, Bangkok, September 18, 1995.

[60] UNHCR, Executive Committee of the High Commissioner's Programme, "UNHCR Activities Financed by Voluntary Funds: Thailand," UN doc. A/AC.96/846/Part II/7, August 2, 1995, Section 7—"Thailand," paragraph 1.

[61] The God's Army was formed around twin nine-year old brothers, Luther and Johnny Htoo, in 1997, when the Karen National Liberation Army's 4th Brigade abandoned Karen villagers during a *tatmadaw* offensive in Tenasserim Division.

[62] The siege of the hospital, which grabbed the attention of Thai and international media, was an ill-conceived attempt to call attention to the desperate situation faced in the God's Army area opposite Thailand's Ratchaburi province. Sheltering the VBSW at this time, the God's Army faction had become a prime target.

students" in Thailand, speculation circulated that the Safe Area would be closed down and relocated. The Chuan Leekpai government sought to expedite the resettlement of the students, and closure of the camp (not yet closed at the end of 2001) was announced in September 2000.[63]

But while the Safe Area became the key site for the regulation and care of Burmese students in Thailand, still larger numbers (including many "persons of concern") have attempted to forge their own survival in various ways in Bangkok.

THE BLURRED BOUNDARY BETWEEN "REFUGEE" AND "ILLEGAL IMMIGRANT"

For Burmese asylum seekers remaining in Bangkok, the legal boundary that distinguishes an individual as a "refugee" rather than an "illegal immigrant" is frequently blurred in everyday life. The protection apparatus exists in principle, but many asylum seekers negotiate their stay in the country as though they were effectively illegal immigrants. Of course, this is not unique to the Burmese in Thailand; as Guy S. Goodwin-Gill notes, there has been a general, persistent, international trend, such that refugees more often find themselves treated as illegal aliens by the authorities in their host country, a problem linked to the overall decline in the availability of durable solutions for refugees.[64] This has been the case both prior and subsequent to the establishment of the Safe Area in Thailand and the UNHCR/Thai decree that Burmese activists would only be recognized as "persons of concern" if they resided in that Safe Area. Even students holding "persons of concern" documentation have often negotiated their existence as if they were simply illegal immigrants in the capital. While sometimes the local authorities have recognized this identification appropriately, more often apprehended students have needed to negotiate their way out of arrest and detention for illegal immigration (usually by paying money), and these negotiations have not always been successful. The following discussion applies to the caseload of such persons recognized by the UNHCR—it includes approximately 2,500 persons—as well as to exiles rejected for UNHCR-status and others who live an otherwise undocumented (or falsely documented) existence.

Everyday Life and Survival

Individual refugees trying to survive in Thailand find themselves in many different local situations. While some of the luckier Burmese are able to avoid the police and negotiate their asylum through local interactions, others seem to suffer a more precarious existence of continual encounters with police surveillance and arrest. There are, of course, situations where sympathetic local residents, employers, and sometimes individual police are indeed helpful with accommodation and other practical arrangements. Long-term relationships and marriages are sometimes formed between Burmese asylum seekers and Thai nationals. There has also been a small but growing number of successful Burmese applicants for third country resettlement. Some "persons of concern" have been able

---

[63] "Maneeloy to be Shut Down Next Year," *The Nation*, September 29, 2000, p. A8.

[64] Guy S. Goodwin-Gill, "International Law and the Detention of Refugees and Asylum Seekers," *International Migration Review* 20,2 (1986): 193-194.

to pursue their studies in Bangkok with UNHCR and other scholarships, and others have found themselves with stable jobs. Students also usually live together in small groups, sustained by their activism, a sense of camaraderie, and a supportive network of friends. However, the overall, more general experience of exile in Bangkok is more often characterized by a persistent fear of arrest and other vulnerabilities associated with everyday life as an "illegal."

Everyday life and survival for Burmese in Bangkok typically involves a familiar cycle of fear/hiding-arrest-detention-deportation-return. The students live in hiding because they fear arrest by Thai police, as noted by one Burmese woman:

> We have so many difficulties in Bangkok. We are afraid everywhere, outside along the way, and also when we are at home. The most trouble for us is the Thai police. We are afraid of them. On the street, the police riding their motorcycles are always checking with suspicious eyes. We dare not look at them. . . . We are more afraid to be arrested on the street than in our apartment. If we are arrested while we walk alone on the street, then nobody will know. When we are arrested at home, we have some friends who can know that we have been arrested.
>
> We are from Burma with no identity. . . . Whenever we go out, we are always afraid. Sometimes when the neighbors find out that we are not Thai citizens, they inform the Thai police, and they come to our apartment. We were arrested this way once, in May 1992.[65]

Out on the street, students adopt various simple techniques to prevent possible identification as Burmese, including, for example, dressing in the "Thai style" (in jeans, with a sense of "Bangkok fashion"), walking "Thai style," and carefully avoiding certain areas where immigration police may be particularly active. Living arrangements may be quite unstable, as people find that they need to keep moving from place to place to avoid detection and arrest. Some landlords are cooperative, although others are reluctant to accept "illegal" Burmese, and still others take the opportunity to charge high rents to insecure refugees. Some students are lucky enough to find steady accommodation, while others are constantly on the run. The most politically active students and exiles are the most likely targets for surveillance and arrest by Thai police at their places of residence, and some arrange physical escape routes in the event of a knock at the door. Asylum seekers without financial assistance are also vulnerable to unscrupulous employers who exploit their uncertain status as illegal immigrants. A pyscho-social study of Burmese political dissidents in Thailand conducted in 1992–93 by the Harvard Program in Refugee Trauma from a sample of 104 registered "persons of concern" reported a high level of overall depressive symptoms associated with exile in Bangkok. The study noted "the most common trauma events were difficulty finding adequate shelter, forced separation from family members, and threat of deportation."[66]

---

[65] Interview, Burmese refugee, Bangkok, September 1995.

[66] Kathleen Allden, et al., "Burmese Political Dissidents in Thailand: Trauma and Survival among Young Adults in Exile," *American Journal of Public Health* 86,11 (1996): 1565. The study concluded that "this group of young adult exiles is in a state of chronic hypervigilance, constantly on guard, and fearful of arrest and other threats...Their traumatic experiences began

The detection of Burmese students by police typically involves either an informal monetary payment for release (often equivalent to the UNHCR monthly allowance, or more, per person) or arrest and detention for illegal immigration. Burmese exiles complain that they are frequently used as "ATMs" (automatic teller machines) for the Thai police. A student described one such incident: "In the police station they kept us in the lockup. They asked us whether we had 30,000 *baht* [for six people]. If we could pay them 30,000 they would release us. But we had no money—we couldn't pay them. Because of that they sent us to IDC [the Immigration Detention Center]."[67]

While "persons of concern" apprehended by the police can technically appeal for protection by invoking their UNHCR status (and/or calling the regional office), usually this identification is not effective in preventing arrest. One student, who is a documented "person of concern," related this typical story of arrest: "I pleaded with them to release me. I showed them the papers and pleaded again. Yet I was still arrested and taken to the IDC. The police didn't listen to me."[68] Another student explained:

> UNHCR cannot protect us. The document did not protect us. That document cannot do anything. We can show it to the police officer and use it to beg him—that is all. When we meet an honest policeman, we can be free. When we meet with a bad policeman, we will be arrested.[69]

Moreover, many students prefer to withhold their identification and negotiate the system more flexibly as "ordinary" illegal immigrants. The technical explanation for this, explained by the UNHCR field officer working at Bangkok's Immigration Detention Center, is that "persons of concern" must usually face a prolonged (possibly indefinite) period of detention because the authorities are required to consider the dangers these refugees will face if they are deported to the border.[70] This was a particular problem after the Safe Area became "full" in 1996, though even the availability of the Safe Area didn't eliminate the problem, since, as indicated earlier, many students resisted being sent there. Detention as an ordinary illegal immigrant, rather than as a "person of concern," often results in a more expeditious release, deportation to the border, and eventual return to Bangkok, options not available to a documented "refugee."

Immigration Detention

According to many Burmese exiles, "IDC is hell." The IDC headquarters is located in Soi Suan Phlu, off South Sathorn Road in Bangkok. IDCs in Thailand are administered by the Immigration Bureau, under the Royal Thai Police department

---

as the perils of a revolutionary student movement, shifted to the hardships of a jungle escape, and now have been transformed into conditions of violence and insecurity that are characteristic of the lives of illegal immigration" (p. 1568).

[67] Interviews with "persons of concern" living in Bangkok, September 1995.

[68] Ibid.

[69] Ibid.

[70] Discussion with UNHCR field officer at the Immigration Detention Center (IDC), Bangkok, March 20, 1998.

(within the Ministry of Interior), and do not come under the regular criminal prison system.[71] Those detained in IDC are held there in administrative detention for contravening the 1979 Immigration Act, either for overstaying a visa or because they lack any documentation at all. False documentation (such as holding a fake passport or visa) usually carries a heavier penalty in the regular prison system. Reference to the IDC headquarters as "hell" describes the overall experience of incarceration within the Center and conditions there. The Center is known for its chronic overcrowding, poor sanitation, and the violence associated with the dynamics of power and control among the detainees and the "room leaders." Thus, the experience of being detained in the IDC resembles prison experiences elsewhere, particularly in view of this violence. The IDC headquarters in Bangkok contains ten rooms, of which two are reserved for women and children.[72] The eight remaining large rooms each measures sixteen meters by six meters and are occupied by over one hundred people at any time, per cell, with sometimes 200 and more.

Persons incarcerated in the IDC confront two different systems of control: one is the official state system of sentencing for illegal immigration, and the other involves "underworld" system of the IDC run by corrupt inmates within the rooms of the Center itself (in collusion with some IDC personnel). The state conducts the court hearing and determines the fine and incarceration period (in lieu of the payment of the fine, at a rate of seventy *baht* per day). There are varying periods of detention imposed for illegal immigration, generally ranging from forty days and upwards. In the initial procedure for admission to IDC, detainees are interviewed by the immigration police and the MOI officials working at the Center in order to obtain basic information, such as bio-data, date of arrival in Bangkok, and a record of fingerprints, which is imprinted onto an IDC Identification Card. Induction into the "informal" system of the IDC "underworld" then begins with assignment to a room by the wardens. New arrivals are required to present themselves to the room leadership for interrogation and a "briefing" and the payment of their "entry fee" (in cash or in kind). They are then informed of the rules, as described by one Burmese man (a "person of concern") who spent nine months in IDC:

> As soon as we arrived at room number one, a man who looked like the leader of the room ordered us in Thai language, "Sit down! Listen! Take anything that you have—gold, money, pens—off your body and put it in front of you. For anything you hide, you will be beaten." They gave us a briefing: "When you

---

[71] The other detention institution in Bangkok is known as the Special Detention Center (SDC), located at the Metropolitan Police Training School in Bangkhen. It is not routine for Burmese asylum-seekers to find themselves kept here because this facility is reserved for the most pugnacious and "hardcore" of the political activists. Small numbers of Burmese activists have been apprehended and held here at times coinciding with crackdowns by the Thai authorities on their anti-Rangoon political activities. As noted by a U.S. State Department report, in 1996, for example, there were twelve Burmese students ("persons of concern") held at the SDC (four of whom were held for periods ranging between twenty-two and thirty months). U.S. Department of State, *Thailand: Report on Human Rights Practices for 1996* (Washington, DC: Bureau of Democracy, Human Rights and Labor, January 30, 1997, p. 3.

[72] There is also a special room (known as "10A" in early 1998) set aside for UNHCR "persons of concern" (all nationalities) who are contained on a list held with IDC as such—but discussion here does not refer to this room as it has rarely been used by Burmese "persons of concern" in detention. Visit to the IDC, March 1998.

stay outside, that is outside. When you are inside, we have our own rules." We had to pay 300 *baht* each for a place in the room.[73]

Then over the following days, weeks, and months (or even more prolonged periods), life in detention proceeds according to the IDC system, governed by room dictators and other cliques organized by nationality. Conditions have often been so overcrowded within the rooms that inmates must develop a system of sleeping in shifts in order to arrange for sufficient space to stretch out. Detainees are provisioned with two meals a day; other supplies must be brought in from relatives, friends, and support networks outside. (These supplies usually become IDC "currency" within the rooms and may be confiscated by the leaders.) The rooms feature concrete floors, small windows for ventilation above, a rudimentary bathroom and toilets, and another small, partitioned-off section which is occupied in comparative comfort by the room leaders and their cohorts. Fans and lights are turned on twenty-four hours a day. Detainees are forbidden to leave the rooms during the period of incarceration. The women's rooms operate with a similar system, also governed by room leaders and cliques, and there have been reports of women detainees being harassed and abused by immigration officers, guards, and police associated with the IDC.[74] In some cases, room leaders remain in the IDC for prolonged periods of time, operating their "business" of accumulation through extortion, before perhaps being "overthrown" in a leadership change, or until they can purchase an illegal passport and leave the system.

As noted, asylum seekers, even "persons of concern," detained in the IDC generally do not admit their status so that they may be released more expeditiously and deported along with other illegal aliens. This is the next component in the typical cycle of illegal immigration. Once the period of detention has been served in the Bangkok IDC, Burmese nationals are deported to a "safe area" of the Thai-Burmese border. Deportees may specify to which places they prefer to be deported; favored destinations usually include places around Ranong, Sangkhlaburi, Mae Sot, and Mai Sai. Many deportees choose the Mon refugee camp at Halockhani, near Sangkhlaburi in Kanchanaburi province, as their preferred site for reasons of relative safety and distance (this is the shortest trip, with the cheapest deportation "fare").[75] Once it is time for release—the time may be served or detainees may leave by stealth, having traded their IDC identification cards with other inmates due for release—a fare is paid and deportation occurs. At the

---

[73] Interviews, Burmese "persons of concern," Bangkok, September 1995.

[74] See Asia Watch/Women's Rights Project, *A Modern Form of Slavery: Trafficking of Burmese Women and Girls into Brothels in Thailand* (New York: Asia Watch/Women's Rights Project, 1993), pp. 91-94. One former IDC (male) inmate told me about one incident: "I have seen so many things in IDC. Women, be careful . . . When I was in room number five, at midnight two or three police who were on night duty brought some young and beautiful women prisoners to the spare room next to room number six. After twenty or thirty minutes they were sent back. The first time I was shocked. But the older prisoners told me—that is just the way of IDC police." Interview, personal account of a stay in the IDC, Bangkok, August 1995.

[75] The problem with return to Halockhani has been the requirement of a further stay (sometimes it is a stopover of a week, sometimes up to one month) in the Kanchanaburi police lock-up, which serves as an IDC, where conditions are poorer than in the Bangkok facility (although it is possible to walk around the compound there). Personal communication with former IDC deportees, Bangkok and Kanchanaburi, 1995. From Kanchanaburi, illegal immigrants are loaded in standing position onto "IDC trucks."

drop-off point on the border, the dreary "round trip" of the illegal immigration cycle proceeds as usual. Following payment of the fare, most deportees simply undertake their return journey once again. Some will only remain in the border area for a few days, until they can arrange their transportation with brokers, police, and friends. A young Mon man (a "person of concern") explained the process of the "round trip" back to Bangkok:

> There are two ways for me to return to Bangkok: friends and police. I tried to contact my friends so that they could send me money for the car fee. When they sent the money I could hire a car [through a broker] to go back to Bangkok. Or there is a police car. Sometimes they take people back to Bangkok—you have to pay money, about 2,000 *baht* [each]. . . . So you go with the police and when you arrive in Bangkok you can go to your friends and collect the money to pay the police. . . We went back in the police car.[76]

This is the basic pattern of life as an illegal immigrant, irrespective of refugee status.

PROTECTION?

In sum, the UNHCR can only protect those "persons of concern" who identify themselves as such, but most do not identify themselves in this way, and therefore most negotiate their existence and face the hazards to which ordinary illegal immigrants are exposed, as if the protection apparatus did not exist. The experience of Burmese asylum seekers in the immigration detention system highlights the practical difficulties associated with the effective functioning of the protection apparatus for refugees in Bangkok and shows how the distinctions between "refugee" and "illegal immigrant," outlined in international law, are blurred in actuality. In this regard, refugee protection in Bangkok falls short of the international standard contained in the 1986 UNHCR EXCOM Conclusion No. 44 on the "Detention of Refugees and Asylum-Seekers" which "[s]tressed the importance for national legislation and/or administrative practice to make the necessary distinction between the situation of refugees and asylum-seekers, and that of other aliens."[77]

For Burmese students and exiles in Bangkok, the boundaries between "refugee" and "illegal immigrant" have been routinely blurred, irrespective of the formal protection apparatus in place. While the protection apparatus has existed under which eligible asylum-seekers are recognized as "persons of concern to the UNHCR," in practice most asylum-seekers (even those with status as "persons of concern") were left to negotiate their everyday lives as if they were illegal immigrants. As a result, this group of exiles has lived at the edge of refugee protection, continually uncertain about the effectiveness of their UNHCR status.

---

[76] Interview, Burmese "person of concern," Bangkok, September 1995.

[77] UNHCR, Executive Committee of the High Commissioner's Programme, "No. 44 (XXXVII) 1986-Detention of Refugees and Asylum-Seekers, Report of the 37th Session," UN doc. A/AC.96/688, 1986, paragraph 128.

With refugee protection restricted to the Safe Area holding camp in formal terms, Burmese asylum-seekers have been transferred there in greater numbers to await their opportunity for third country resettlement or simply to endure a life in waiting.

CHAPTER EIGHT

CONCLUSION

THE NATURE AND CAUSES OF DISPLACEMENT

The Burmese language expression for refugee is *dukkha-the*, "the one who has to bear *dukkha*, suffering."[1] A comprehensive approach to understanding the *dukkha* that characterizes the Burmese refugee predicament in Thailand must include a multifaceted analysis of the specific root and precipitating causes of displacement, the politically contingent contexts of sanctuary in the host state, and reference to the broad framework of international protection norms. The cycles of fear and sanctuary for the borderland refugees have arisen from the ways in which civilian populations have become the targets in the struggles for control over the modern territorialized state. War and insecurity prevailing within Burma have cast, and continue to cast, their shadows across the border into Thailand, and this book has examined how.

The long-term root causes are found in Burma's protracted imbroglio of ethnopolitical conflict and civil war, of which the borderlands' refugees are the human casualties. From the mid-1980s, the growing efficacy of the *tatmadaw*'s counterinsurgency campaigns against its ethnopolitical opponents in the eastern border regions produced the cross-border flow of displaced persons which, since 1984, has created a semi-permanent refugee presence encamped along that border. Dominated by its military government, modern Burma is essentially ruled as an ethnocratic state. In fixing its claim for legitimacy, the *tatmadaw* has ideologically invested itself with historic responsibility as the ultimate protector and defender of national unity and state sovereignty, in accordance with a form of state nationalism founded on the notion of "holding the country together." In pursuing such aims for the country by military means, the *tatmadaw* implemented the "Four Cuts" counterinsurgency strategy in an attempt to cut the insurgents off from their support system in the civilian population. The Four Cuts strategy was first adopted in 1968, but was applied to the ethnic-minority (insurgent) dominated border regions after 1975 and with greater intensity to those areas contiguous with Thailand since the mid-1980s.

The experiences of protracted insurgency and counterinsurgency served to reinforce and entrench the convictions of the belligerents in the absence of an otherwise sustainable political solution or reconciliation. On the one hand, successive *tatmadaw*-dominated regimes in Rangoon have emphasized the

---

[1] Aung San Suu Kyi, "Towards a True Refuge," Eighth Joyce Pearce Memorial Lecture delivered by Dr. Michael Aris on May 19, 1993 at the University of Oxford, Queen Elizabeth House, p. 13.

unrelenting threat of "disintegration" posed by the rebellions, while on the other hand, the ethnonationalist forces have characterized the regime as one bent on their cultural and political destruction. As a consequence of this impasse, the fundamental political grievances of the protagonists remain unresolved. This means that the political environment, which must accommodate negotiation between the chief parties if the root causes of the conflict are ever to be eliminated, remains fundamentally contentious. This scenario leaves open to question the potential sustainability of the military cease-fire agreements between the regime in Rangoon and its former rebel opponents as the basis upon which to forge long-term and durable solutions for the refugee problem.

FEAR: THE FRONTLINE AND THE "HOME FRONT"

However, the displaced persons are not simply the by-products of the conflict: in important ways, they are at the center of this war-zone setting. The nature of insurgency and counterinsurgency warfare—shaped in part by the root causes of the civil conflict—has mercilessly entangled the civilian population, leading to consequent insecurity and displacement. The "low-intensity" nature of this conflict has been played out in the midst of everyday life, and the civilian populations living in the affected regions have, therefore, become the "battlefield" of the conflict itself.

In short, insurgency implicates entire populations, and counterinsurgency punishes entire populations. To understand the precipitating causes of civilian displacement, therefore, we need to understand how the nature of both insurgency and counterinsurgency has involved civilian populations by effectively blurring the distinction between combatants and noncombatants. Insurgency in the form of guerrilla struggle blurs this distinction by identifying the civilian population closely with its own cause, a practice that often exposes civilians to the risks of war, or even "invites" the enemy to attack. Typically, the insurgents' guerrilla struggle also relies on the civilian population to provide its crucial support base, a situation that further muddles any distinction between insurgent combatants and non-combatants and their respective properties, or territories, within a shared social and geographic space. And counterinsurgency blurs the (rebel) soldier/civilian distinction *because* the civilian base is crucial for the opposition guerrillas. Indeed, counterinsurgency strategy essentially seeks to break this link, to deprive the opposition of its support and to undermine the political will of the civilian population. In the course of counterinsurgency, civilian noncombatants (as potential rebel collaborators), as well as combatants, become the generalized opponent and the deliberate targets for attack. The government army's suspicions of all civilians as potential rebel collaborators threaten people's daily lives and livelihoods. As a result, fear pervades everyday life, latent as an invisible violence and, consequently, as a tool of control over civilian populations. This pattern of suspicion and fear is further reinforced when civilians run and flee, perpetuating the whole cycle. The impact of "low-intensity" conflict is pervasive and destructive. This book shows how, in this kind of setting, violence is perpetrated in the midst of civilian life. In other words, the boundary dividing the frontline (where combatants engage in battle) from the "home front" (where noncombatants ideally pursue their everyday lives) is fundamentally blurred.

Civilian displacement, however, is not only caused by active armed hostilities, as experiences in the Mon areas have demonstrated. While many of the refugees flee direct hostilities and attacks by counterinsurgency troops, others flee the more indirect effects of war, such as militarized surveillance and military control. In the case of the Mon refugees, both the direct and indirect effects of the conflict provoked civilian displacement. Insecurity arose from the combined consequences of the cycles of fear and suspicion outlined above and the effects of a steady stream of other demands on the local populations (including taxes and "fees," forced labor and forced portering for the military). These insecurities exacted a significant toll on survival and livelihoods. People's fears that they would be seized for forced labor and portering prompted them to flee, and, as a result, they became caught up in the pattern of flight, dislocation, and impoverishment. Many of the Mon refugees from Pa Yaw camp cited this combination of fear and deprivation as the final precipitating cause of their displacement. It is therefore necessary to consider both the direct and indirect impacts of war and militarization as the constituent causes of civilian displacement.

Thus, the nature and causes of refugee displacement ultimately need to be addressed with this complex mix of direct and indirect factors in mind. These factors that precipitate displacement, and occur in the midst of everyday life, must be studied in conjunction with analysis of the nature of internal, "low-intensity" war that blurs the boundary between the "home front" and the frontline.

After the Fighting Stops?

What happens, then, when the fighting stops? What does an end to armed hostilities mean for the cycle of civilian displacement and insecurity? This study has shown that, in the case of the military cease-fire reached between the NMSP (New Mon State Party) and the SLORC (State Law and Order Restoration Council) in June 1995, an end to active fighting provided a necessary, but substantially insufficient, step towards the resolution of the causes of civilian displacement. By halting the overt armed conflict, the cease-fire was an important essential first step toward peace (and an event allegorized by the authorities as the achievement of "peace"). But while the cease-fire served to alleviate the entrenched cycle of suspicion and fear characteristic of insurgency and counterinsurgency warfare, the indirect effects of militarized control in the Mon region continued to prevail. The cease-fire may have allayed the violence of combat, but it failed meaningfully to address the range of constituent elements, direct and indirect, precipitating displacement, much less the antagonisms and grievances that constituted the root causes of the conflict. To this extent, the end to fighting did not significantly improve prospects for the local populations in the former war zones, who hoped they could live more secure lives after the cease-fire was implemented.

Thus, the cease-fire agreement reached between former foes in 1995, presaging the repatriation of the Mon refugees from camps in Thailand, only partially addressed the problems producing civilian displacement. For this reason, observers questioned whether this "calmer" situation—where active combat had ceased, but certain kinds of military aggressions persisted—qualified as a sufficiently secure, and sustainable, basis for the repatriation of the cross-border population. In fact, residents of the Mon camps were returned to Burma, pursuant to a purely military cease-fire, in an insecure environment where the root and precipitating causes of displacement were insufficiently addressed. In the case of the Mons, neither the cease-fire nor the repatriation gave the refugee population enough confidence to motivate them to return to their original homes. Instead, the camps were simply transferred into the designated cease-fire areas within Burma under the management of the NMSP. This constituted an interim arrangement in the context of a politically unresolved and potentially fragile military environment. In this way, repatriation on the basis of the military cease-fire disaggregates the indirect causes precipitating displacement from the direct causes.

Following a less than comprehensive resolution of the underlying causes that provoked the refugees to flee from their homes, the 1996 repatriation shifted the Mon camps from their cross-border havens in Thailand into resettlement sites within Burmese territory, leaving the larger story of Mon refugees unfinished. After this period of unsettled sanctuary in Thailand, the repatriation of the Mons effectively transformed their status from "unrecognized" refugees into internally displaced persons (IDPs). While the refugees were returned to safe sites across the border, the repatriation was far from a durable solution. Khalid Koser and Richard Black, writing on this general issue, have argued that, by converting refugees into IDPs, state authorities in some cases aim to strengthen government-held, as opposed to rebel-held, areas, and this contributes to the consolidation of government control.[2] In the case of the Mon returnees, the resettlement sites were autonomous—not administered by authorities in Rangoon—but the Burmese government still publicized (and manipulated) the repatriation of the refugees as a component in its "victory" over insurgency. Moreover, the government treated repatriation as a goal in itself rather than as a substantive step towards a durable solution and future security for the Mons.

THE POLITICAL CONTINGENCIES OF SANCTUARY

The second part of this book explored the way in which refugee protection has been negotiated and configured within a fluid landscape of political possibilities that helped some refugees and hurt others.

For the borderland refugees sheltering in Thailand, their status as people who were "unrecognized" in formal terms did not generally have an adverse impact on their sanctuary, for in practice Thailand maintained a flexible approach that accommodated the asylum-seekers in accord with international protection principles. As outlined in the introduction to this study, a flexible approach by receiving states to a growing number of "non-classic" refugees in global terms is necessary in order to overcome the limitations of the original 1951 Convention-based definition of a refugee. Indeed, the Thai authorities have not signed the 1951/1967 instruments because they have determined that the 1951 definition and the gamut of obligations under the Convention are inappropriate and impractical if applied to the actual situations of the non-classic refugees whom they host. Technically, asylum-seekers in Thailand are all "illegal immigrants." But in practice the Burmese refugees along the border have been accorded a form of *prima*

---

[2] Richard Black and Khalid Koser, "The End of the Refugee Cycle?" in *The End of the Refugee Cycle? Repatriation and Reconstruction*, ed. Richard Black and Khalid Koser (New York: Berghahn Books, 1999), p. 8.

facie recognition, even while formally "unrecognized" by Thailand. In addition, the low-key, village-style atmosphere of the camps—the hallmark of the Thai response—has been appropriate to the circumstances of displacement. The model of refugee sanctuary and administration on the Thai-Burmese border since 1984 was "localized" in a way that helped preserve traditional patterns of community, with minimal external intervention in the management of humanitarian relief, for instance. (This contrasted with the large-scale manipulation of aid that occurred with the Cambodian refugees.)

The case of the Mon border camps in Thailand was different, however, and the Thai response to the Mons less accommodating. Their sanctuary in Thailand was politically contingent, and at last their steadily declining welcome in the host-state culminated in the post-cease-fire repatriation. For the Mons, cross-border sanctuary within Thai jurisdiction was, at last, effectively terminated, and the burden of the Mon refugee camps shifted out of Thai territory. The return of the Mons did not accord with the ideal of repatriation as a durable solution for refugees because there was no convincing evidence that a fundamental change had taken place in the original conditions that provoked refugee flight—this is especially true if the indirect effects of war and militarized surveillance are taken into account. Moreover, the Mon repatriation was carried out under substantial pressure from the host authorities, demonstrating the way in which Thailand's diminishing welcome related to shifting political contingencies in the nation. The Mon refugees' vulnerability and their loss of sanctuary in Thailand thus involved two key elements—their delicately negotiated position as "unrecognized" refugees and the vicissitudes of borderland relations between Thailand and Burma. The Mon refugees were ultimately unprotected when the political pressure compelling them to return to Burma was applied. In this case, the delicately negotiated status of their sanctuary in the host state and the evolving context of borderland politics converged to undermine Thailand's adherence to the basic principle of non-*refoulement*.

The Shifting Borderlands Context

An analysis of sanctuary for the Burmese refugees in Thailand cannot be understood without reference to the politico-military context of the border, for sanctuary has often been reconfigured in the shifting context of borderlands' politics. To understand the situation, we must conceptualize "borderland" as a combination of "boundary"—a distinct line separating two jurisdictions on a map—and "borderland," that is, a living and negotiated political phenomenon that flows across the boundary in different forms. As power in the modern body politic is "territorialized," its sovereign authority marked by boldly drawn boundaries on a map, refugees are presented with both opportunities and limits. While states are concerned to regulate the flows of people across their borders—sometimes imposing strict limits that threaten asylum—the physical boundary of the state also provides the opportunity for asylum-seekers to flee to safety.

A focus on the evolving borderlands' geography showed the role it has played in influencing, reconfiguring, and complicating that sanctuary. In the case of the Mon refugees, for instance, their repatriation was influenced by the growing level of official interaction (centered on a convergence of interests in "resource diplomacy") between Thailand and Burma throughout the borderlands. In the pursuit of a certain (business-oriented) diplomatic rapprochement, Thailand played an informal role as an interlocutor between the parties in the cease-fire agreement reached between the NMSP and the SLORC in June 1995. In this way, the Mon refugees were caught up in the evolving borderland realities that threatened their asylum and heralded the end of their stay in Thailand.

Further, the actions of the refugees themselves can alter the security environment of the borderlands. The formation of the DKBA (Democratic Karen Buddhist Army) as a breakaway faction of the KNU (Karen National Union)—and proxy of the *tatmadaw*—complicated the borderland environments in both Burma and Thailand, and the DKBA's cross-border raids, beginning in 1995, jeopardized the stability of the Karen camps within Thailand. The raids effectively caught the Thai-based camps in the net of the civil war occurring across the border in Burma. Although the Karen refugee camps in Thailand were always associated with the insurgent KNU—local administration was handled by former and current KNU personnel—they were not previously designated as a direct target for military attack. Beginning in 1995, however, these camps were explicitly targeted as KNU support bases, extending the confusion and violence that typify a modern civil war—where non-combatants are so often treated as collaborators, or even rebel soldiers—into the cross-border setting.

The consequences of this dramatic "spilling" of the war across the border have created contending pressures for Thailand in terms of the refugees. On the one hand, Thailand has been placed under greater pressure to end the refugee predicament on its western border, particularly in view of the security implications of this cross-border chaos. At the same time, the attacks have also heightened the need for greater physical and political protection of the refugees. The raids have shown how refugees who have taken sanctuary across the border are inextricably linked to the security situations in their home state, and how the host state can be come embroiled in conflict. The problem for the receiving state is that the root and precipitating causes of conflict and chaos in the sending state continue to prevail.

The "Activist" Asylum-seekers

Away from the borderlands' environment, sanctuary has also been negotiated in Bangkok, another place where national politics affect the status and situation of refugees. For the post-1988 Burmese asylum-seekers in Bangkok, the question of protection raised distinct concerns and issues. These students, who sought sanctuary in an urban setting, fit the classical conception of the "activist" refugee contained in the 1951 UN Convention. Accordingly, the formal protection apparatus developed there provides for the recognition of Burmese asylum-seekers who qualify under the traditional UNHCR (United Nations High Commission for Refugees) criteria on an individual case-by-case basis. Thus, the problem for this group of asylum-seekers has not been their "unrecognized" status in formal and institutional terms, but their actual situation relative to the Thai authorities in charge of immigrants. Many of these people live and are treated as if they were illegal immigrants, irrespective of formal refugee status. The blurred boundary between "refugee" and "illegal immigrant" for the Bangkok caseload of asylum-seekers highlights the practical difficulties associated with the effective functioning of the protection apparatus.

In contrast to the displaced persons in the border camps, the Bangkok exiles have been characterized by their political activism: an intense, seemingly indomitable, struggle against the regime in Burma from which they have fled. This sometimes vociferous struggle for democracy in exile, which has provoked diplomatic problems for their host country, has generated persistent tension between the refugees and the Thai authorities. Thailand is reluctant to remain the haven, or indeed platform, for a group of outspoken Burmese activists in Bangkok. In addition, the official provision for asylum in the Safe Area at Maneeloy holding camp in Ratchaburi province is (over)full and on the verge of closure. The student exiles have become a long-term presence in Thailand. They face growing tensions and the frustration of restricted opportunities, or, if they venture outside the camp, few alternatives to a life in hiding.

THE FUTURE PROSPECTS FOR THE BORDERLAND REFUGEES

Thailand clearly cannot and does not want to remain host to a perpetual refugee burden along its western border. Yet this burden has become a long-term, semi-permanent feature of the border for Thailand, and it has been growing, not declining. For example, in the immediate aftermath of the *tatmadaw*'s large-scale offensives against the KNU in 1997, a further twenty thousand displaced persons fled to the Thai-based camps, and in early April 2000, more than four thousand Karen refugees, who had been encamped in the Mae La Po Hta settlement along the river on the Burmese side of the border, fled into Thailand's Tha Song Yang district, in Tak province.[3] The negative consequences of the deteriorating security in the borderlands affecting Thailand directly are clearly vexing. Thai policy makers in the National Security Council and Ministry of Defense, as well as policy makers at the highest levels in other agencies, are seriously contemplating the future prospects for the refugees with a view to their return to Burma. Since the late 1990s, public declarations that the refugees must return to their own country soon ("the sooner the better"[4]) have appeared at frequent intervals. However, with the exception of those selected regions administered under the terms of the NMSP-SLORC cease-fire agreement and other territories occupied by government forces, many substantial areas of the Burmese eastern borderland opposite Thailand remain either contested or in a state of war.

Since 1995, the politico-military scene within the eastern borderlands region of Burma has also been complicated by the emergence of new armed splinter groups. Numerous factions of the ethnic insurgent organizations abound in the border regions, including Mon, Karenni, and Karen breakaway groups and a plethora of other groups (including those associated with drug trafficking) operating in Shan State.[5] After the Mon cease-fire between the NMSP and the SLORC in 1995, a number of small regionally based splinter factions broke off from the NMSP, vowing to fight on in contravention of the cease-fire. These splinter armies

[3] Visit to the area, March-April 2000.

[4] NSC Secretary-General, Kachadpai Burusapatana, quoted in Marisa Chimprabha, "Red Cross Access to Burmese Labour Camp 'Positive'," *The Nation*, March 11, 2000, p. A6.

[5] For further details, see Desmond Ball and Hazel Lang, *Factionalism and the Ethnic Insurgent Organisations*, Working Paper No. 356 (Canberra: Strategic and Defence Studies Centre, Australian National University, 2001).

operated in those familiar locales that, before the NMSP-SLORC cease-fire, had been targeted for counterinsurgency and that remain targeted for military suppression because of the continuing activities of the armed rebels. The activities of the splinter factions not only threaten the cease-fire agreement by opposing and challenging it and also creating trouble for the NMSP, but they also cause further suffering to local villagers inhabiting the areas in which these groups are active.[6]

In addition, within Burma the problem of internally displaced persons (IDPs) has continued to grow, presenting possibly the most difficult, as well as invisible and inaccessible, challenge threatening effective protection. An examination of the nature and the substantive content of internal displacement in the eastern borderlands' region was beyond the scope of this study, but it is imperative that this particularly complicated dimension of human insecurity be addressed by those seeking overall solutions to forced displacement in Burma. As the UN Representative of the Secretary-General on Internally Displaced Persons, Francis M. Deng, has noted with respect to internal displacement:

" . . . the primary responsibility to provide protection and assistance rests with the State. And yet, paradoxically, the State is often the principal source of their insecurity and deprivation, viewing the displaced not as persons to be protected, but as part of the enemy to be targeted, oppressed or eliminated, thereby creating a protection gap."[7]

Despite the cease-fire, for example, local Mon commentators estimate the figure of Mon IDPs to be as high as forty thousand.[8] The number of IDPs elsewhere within the eastern border areas of Burma is estimated to be as large as 500,000 persons (particularly within the Shan, Karen, and Karenni States),[9] which includes both those people forced to enter relocation sites under the control of the army and those who are dispersed and hiding in the jungle.[10] IDPs are also vulnerable to

---

[6] The subject of the Mon splinter groups is a very sensitive matter for the NMSP. The NMSP emphasizes their lack of sophistication and strength, as well as their unpopularity among the region's people. As one NMSP official noted, "these armies have no discipline; their rules are in their mouths, their power is in their mouths only." At the same time, the faction commanders and members (who keep a low profile) express their determination to fight on. Personal communication with NMSP and splinter faction leaders, Sangkhlaburi, Thailand, June and November 1999.

[7] United Nations High Commissioner for Human Rights, *Statement by Representative of the Secretary-General on Internally Displaced Persons, Dr. Francis M. Deng*, (Fifty-fifth session, United Nations Commission on Human Rights, Geneva, March 22-April 30, 1999, item 14(c): Specific Groups and Individuals; Mass Exoduses and Displaced Persons), April 16, 1999, p. 1.

[8] Personal communication, Mon National Relief Committee, Sangkhlaburi, Thailand, June 28, 1999.

[9] In 2000, the estimated numbers of IDPs in the eastern border areas of Burma comprised the following: as noted, about 40,000 Mons; around 200,000 Karens; about 20–30,000 Karennis (in relocation sites and in hiding); and about 200,000 IDPs affected by the relocations in the central Shan State since 1996. Interviews with Mon, Karen, Karenni, and Shan refugee leaders, Thai-Burmese border, February-March 2000.

[10] See also, United Nations Commissioner on Human Rights, *Question of the Violation of Human Rights and Fundamental Freedoms in Any Part of the World. Situation of Human Rights in Myanmar. Report of the Special Rapporteur, Mr Rajasoomer Lallah, Submitted in Accordance with Commission on Human Rights Resolution 1998/63*, UN doc. E/CN.4/1999/35, January 22, 1999, p. 10.

identification as "rebel collaborators" because they generally hide (and move around) within opposition-held areas. Further, as Roberta Cohen and Francis M. Deng note, states are generally not inclined to admit to the existence of IDPs and may want to conceal the extent to which their own policies or actions have contributed to war and displacement.[11] As with external displacement, the long-term impact of internal displacement extends beyond the frame outlined by available statistics and requires us to consider both the plight of those immediately affected and the broader, indirect costs incurred by these civil disruptions.[12]

The forced migration of people across the border does not always stop in the refugee camps; there are also indeterminable numbers of people who are regularly added to the ranks of the estimated 700,000 illegal migrant workers who have crossed from Burma into Thailand. The numbers of migrant workers in the border provinces alone are remarkable: one knowledgeable observer in Mae Sot, for example, noted that in 1999 some 130,000 persons from Burma were working in the Mae Sot, Mae Ramat, Tha Song Yang, and Umphang districts of Thailand's Tak province alone.[13] The approximate number of illegal Mon migrants working in Thailand is thought to be as high as 200,000.[14] Thus, the consequences of military, political, and economic insecurity in Burma flow powerfully into Thailand, flooding beyond the refugee camps on the border.

The problem of Burmese refugees in Thailand will persist so long as the underlying factors of *dukkha* and displacement continue in the sending state. So long as fear and insecurity exist in Burma, Thailand is bound to receive flows of forced migrants across its western border. Meanwhile, concerned parties must seek to define and implement appropriate forms of protection which would be responsive to the specific realities of displacement examined in this book, at the same time that Thailand is persuaded to continue to adhere to the broad principles of refugee protection. The difficult question of "under what conditions should the refugees be returned to Burma in the future?" remains open to discussion and hinges on developments within Burma.

THE REPATRIATION PREDICAMENT

Repatriation is a necessarily complex issue, but the process of repatriating Burmese refugees cannot be initiated until there is a fundamental change in the underlying causes of displacement. This book has sought to define and analyze these causes and suggest that the problem of Burmese refugees in Thailand can only

---

[11] Roberta Cohen and Francis M. Deng, *Masses in Flight: The Global Crisis of Internal Displacement* (Washington, DC: Brookings Institution Press, 1998), p. 7.

[12] See further ibid., pp. 23-26, 35-36.

[13] Illegal migrant workers residing in Thailand confront many problems associated with the vulnerabilities of this status, including exploitation at the hands of unscrupulous employers and local authorities, debt bondage to brokers, and health problems (including dangerous "backyard" abortions for women). Discussion with Dr. Cynthia Maung, Mae Tao Clinic, Mae Sot, Thailand, June 5, 1999.

[14] Personal communication, Sangkhlaburi, Thailand, June 1999.

be resolved if the parties involved pay attention to this complexity.[15] "Repatriation" refers to a series of steps: the preparation for return, the process of return, and the reception and arrangements for integration provided immediately after refugees have arrived back in their home country.[16] Repatriation can contribute to confidence-building in the reconciliation and peace process at home, and it is obviously the most desirable solution from the perspective of most host governments.

The international standard that defines "ideal" repatriation requires "voluntary repatriation in safety and dignity" to an environment in which "the causes of flight have been definitively and permanently removed."[17] Guy S. Goodwin-Gill argues that repatriation—involving issues of change, human rights, and change in status from "refugee" to "citizen"—is by definition a protection exercise.[18] Repatriation can conclude the "temporary" or "palliative" role of international protection,[19] in which protection is explicitly conditional on the risk that refugees face in their country of origin. And a voluntary repatriation to a safe and secure environment is the hope of the refugees on this border: "We want to go back, to work hard, without war and fighting and running."[20]

Contending Agendas

Politically, repatriation is also a highly charged issue involving a complicated mix of key players with contending agendas and vital stakes in the matter; these include the host country, the country of origin, the UNHCR (now a formal participant on the Burmese border), and the refugees' representatives and their advocates. From the perspective of the host country, not only in Thailand, but also globally, refugees are increasingly viewed as a burden or a potential threat to national security and stability. This is particularly true when asylum conditions deteriorate and political pressures to return the refugees to their homes mount in the host country. The security of Thailand's own citizens has been disrupted by the situation of the refugees in the borderlands. But while Thailand would like to repatriate the refugees, senior policy-makers and practitioners recognize that a safe and voluntary repatriation is possible only when conditions of peace and security prevail. Senior military officers, for example, promise that Thailand will not push the displaced persons back until the conditions are acceptable, so that the problem "as a whole" is resolved "to serve all parties" (Thailand, the Burmese

---

[15] See Hazel Lang, *The Repatriation Predicament of Burmese Refugees in Thailand: A Preliminary Analysis,* New Issues in Refugee Research Working Paper No. 46 (Geneva: United Nations High Commissioner for Refugees, July 2001).

[16] Rosemary Preston, "Researching Repatriation and Reconstruction: Who is Researching What and Why?," in *The End of the Refugee Cycle?,* p. 25.

[17] United Nations High Commission for Refugees, *The State of the World's Refugees: The Challenge of Protection* (London: Penguin Books, 1993), p. 104.

[18] Guy S. Goodwin-Gill, "Refugee Identity and the Fading Prospect of Protection," in *Refugee Rights and Realities: Evolving International Concepts and Regimes,* ed. Frances Nicholson and Patrick Twomey (Cambridge: Cambridge University Press, 1999), p. 243.

[19] James C. Hathaway, "New Directions to Avoid Hard Problems: The Distortion of the Palliative Role of Refugee Protection," *Journal of Refugee Studies* 8,3 (1995): 288-294.

[20] Interviews, Thai-Burmese border, February-April 2000.

authorities, and the minorities).[21] Some senior members of the Royal Thai Army emphasize the need to assess issues having to do with repatriation in the broader "non-linear" context of war, ethnic conflict, and border security as a whole. From this perspective, the problem is multi-faceted and requires an appropriately integrated response. Other key persons in the Ministry of Defense also recognize that the solutions to Thailand's security problems along the border are to be found in Burma, but they describe the resolution process differently. One key general, for instance, notes that Thailand needs to acknowledge the reality of "Myanmar as a military state" which is loath to discuss or address key problems raised by perceived insurgents—that is, refugees, minorities, and pro-democracy activists—with its neighbor, Thailand.[22] Other Thai agencies are also actively contemplating the conditions for a future repatriation. According to the Ministry of Interior, Thailand "cannot consider repatriation without security, although we are thinking about repatriation."[23]

Of course, the priorities of the country of origin affect and politicize the repatriation issue and process. It is essential to understand the attitude of the home government towards the displaced persons and towards the political, military, and security situation in their nation as a whole. On the one hand, the absence of a country's nationals can be damaging to the government's legitimacy—the existence of the refugee camps provides a visible reminder of the precarious situation inside the country. As a visible reminder, the refugee presence may embarrass the country of origin. In international relations, refugees represent a rupture in the bond between the citizen and the state. Indeed, displaced persons are ultimately the responsibility of the sending state. The SPDC (State Peace and Development Council) has been unwilling to acknowledge responsibility for the refugees encamped along the Thai border, although in March and October 2000 government officials in Rangoon agreed to permit respective visits by the UNHCR Assistant High Commissioner and the UNHCR chief from Geneva. At the same time, the junta has proven unwilling to accept the return of its displaced persons, and their resistance must be taken into consideration if we wish to comprehend the whole situation. According to other senior Thai military sources, Rangoon is unwilling to discuss the matter of repatriation with its Thai counterparts. At the biannual Regional Border Committee meetings between the two militaries, for instance, the official Burmese response stipulates that (a) it can only accept back "Myanmar citizens," and (b) that they "already have twenty reception centers around the country" [for this purpose].[24] Thailand's Deputy Foreign Minister Sukhumbhand Paribatra has stated that "Burma must have reaffirmed a willingness to receive the displaced persons."[25] In practice, however, it is unlikely that the Burmese

---

[21] Personal communication, Royal Thai Army Headquarters, Bangkok, April 2000.

[22] Interview, General Sanan Kajornklarn, Special Expert [on Myanmar], Office of the Permanent Secretary and Spokesman for the Ministry of Defence, Bangkok, April 7, 2000.

[23] Khun Wannida Boonpracong, Chief, Displaced Persons and Illegal Immigrant Affairs Subdivision, Ministry of Interior, speaking at a seminar, Re-thinking Policies Toward Burmese Refugees and Students in Thailand, held at Chulalongkorn University, Bangkok, November 8, 1999.

[24] Interviews, Ministry of Defense, Bangkok, April 2000.

[25] Don Pathan and Marisa Chimphrabha, "Burma Agrees to UNHCR Monitor," *The Nation*, March 17, 2000, p. A1.

regime will want to take back refugees until it has secured cease-fire surrenders (on its own terms) and/or complete control over the minority forces and their border territories. Because the aim of the *tatmadaw's* counterinsurgency strategy is to undermine and eliminate the civilian support base for the insurgents, the regime is unlikely to accept back people of whom it is suspicious.

While UNHCR's mandate places the highest priority on insuring secure and lasting protection for refugees internationally, there has been concern that the UNHCR's official presence in the region effectively promotes repatriation as the solution to the Burmese refugees' dilemma. In its "Thai/Myanmar mission statement," the UNHCR lists repatriation as one objective: " . . . the UNHCR aims to ensure preparedness for repatriation by keeping close contact with refugees and by monitoring the situation in the country of origin."[26] Although the UNHCR has been criticized by some commentators, both in Thailand and elsewhere, for promoting repatriation in the short-term rather than facilitating repatriation when conditions have become conducive, the UNHCR in Bangkok has emphasized that the agency cannot "act on its own" and can only promote repatriation when the conditions allow it. The Bangkok office notes that until it has access to those relevant (war-affected) areas in Burma, it is not in a position to promote an organized repatriation.[27]

Overall, representatives who speak for the refugees advocate change in Burma and call for a durable peace that would make repatriation possible. One such representative commented: "If they [SPDC] declare peace today, we would not even have to wait for tomorrow, we would go back today."[28] Their agenda is necessarily influenced by the status of the politico-military struggles across the border. In many cases, the representatives of the refugees are closely associated with, if not members of, the ethnic insurgent organizations still fighting in Burma. Refugee leaders administering the camps frequently cooperate with, and even identify with, their respective opposition armies. Not only are the refugee committees reliant on insurgent groups for information; their work is fundamentally entwined with the circumstances and dynamics of the wider military and political context. Also, the refugees who seek safe haven in their camps have generally fled those regions where the government has gained control or where control remains contested, so that the refugees are by implication identified with the insurgencies. At the same time, we should beware of exaggerating the links between camp administrators and active insurgents, for the views of the refugee representatives do not always echo the views of their armed ethnic organization counterparts. For instance, one independently minded refugee leader stated:

> As civilians we would have to watch the . . . cease-fire, and if it only benefits the [ethnic] leaders, then that would be no good . . . . If such an agreement is just a leaders' agreement, and not for the well-being of the people, then it would not be acceptable. If the KNPP and the SPDC came to an agreement, we would still need to think [about it], observe the conditions . . . We civilians would

---

[26] UNHCR, 1999 Mid-Year Progress Report—Thailand and Myanmar, "Initial Objectives." Accessed online at www.unhcr.ch/fdrs/my99/th.htm [December 8, 1999].

[27] Interview, J. de Riedmatten, UNHCR Deputy Regional Representative and Head of Legal Section, Bangkok, March 23, 2000.

[28] Interview, Karen Refugee Committee representatives, Mae Sot, February 2000.

watch these conditions, actually, we'd suggest that the leaders and their families go first, not the civilians![29]

Human Security and Essential Pre-conditions

Repatriation as a refugee solution cannot just be a means to an end: it is necessary to approach a future repatriation in the context of the problem as a whole. The achievement of human security is necessary if future repatriation is to be a durable solution for the refugees.

The achievement of genuine human security requires interested parties to focus on the quality of life of individuals whose security has been threatened and on the people who collectively make up a society or polity.[30] If we ask, "security for whom?," the individual is the primary referent. But the conception of human security is not intended to clash with the interests of states so much as generate the protection—through developing norms, strengthening institutions, and implementing strategies—for those who are most vulnerable.[31] Proponents of this approach argue that state security ultimately depends on the security of the individual human being, and security of the individual depends on the security of the state, among other things.[32] Policy makers who consider human security broadly and who think in terms of a people-based notion of security will be concerned with, as Richard Falk describes, "the social and human dimensions of unresolved conflicts" which are "more in touch with the actual circumstances of conflict . . . [and] more closely attuned to the emerging political situation . . . "[33] Although it is beset by major political machinations and obstacles, a human security approach is most likely to permit the resolution of the refugee predicament as a whole, for it will embrace a variety of concerns, including the problems confronting Thailand as the host state and the needs of the displaced persons and their communities, while at the same time looking into the future, toward post-conflict repatriation and reconstruction/reconciliation within Burma.

For the achievement of human security in the Thai-Burmese borderlands, certain conditions must be met before a future repatriation is possible, and these combine three elements. They involve a voluntary return, a fundamental change in the underlying causes of displacement, and the achievement of safety and security within Burma. First, as an international standard, the principle of voluntariness (though frequently overlooked in practice) essentially means that the return of the refugees to their homeland is free from pressure and that the returnees are kept

---

[29] Interview, Mae Hong Son, February 2000.

[30] Ramesh Thakur, "From National to Human Security," in *Asia-Pacific Security: The Economics-Politics Nexus*, ed. Stuart Harris and Andrew Mack (St. Leonards, NSW: Allen & Unwin in association with the Department of International Relations, ANU, 1997), p. 53; Roxanne Lynn Doty, "Immigration and the Politics of Security," *Security Studies* 8,2/3 (1998/99): 81-82.

[31] Astri Suhrke, "Human Security and the Interests of States," *Security Dialogue* 30,3 (1999): 273.

[32] See also Kanti Bajpai, "Human Security: Concept and Measurement," Occasional Paper #19: OP:1, Joan B. Kroc Institute for International Peace Studies, University of Notre Dame, August 2000.

[33] Richard Falk, "An Alternative to Geopolitics," *Peace Review* 11,3 (1999): 374.

fully informed throughout the process.[34] The second element of a fundamental change of circumstances in the country of origin relates to the root and precipitating causes of displacement in the conflict-affected areas elaborated in this book. A substantial level of insecurity in Burma's eastern borderlands, however, continues to uproot people due to the direct and indirect consequences of war and military control. For example, according to members of a new group of Karenni displaced persons who arrived in the Thai-based "Camp 2" in March 2000, harassment and economic hardships continue to make life impossible: " . . . they [troops of the Burmese army] are going to kill everyone in the village if they hear just one gunshot near the village."[35] Third, the condition that there be safety and security within Burma involves legal safety, as well as physical and material security.[36] To insure the returnees' legal safety, there would have to be arrangements, such as a tripartite memorandum between the country of origin, country of asylum, and the UNHCR, with the option that non-state entities might act as a fourth party in the process. Also, formal guarantees, such as amnesties, peace agreements, and guarantees for the requisition of nationality, as well as guarantees for the refugees' safety, would have to be provided.[37] Physical security requires that such matters as the anti-personnel (AP) landmines problem be addressed. The reestablishment of material security would involve the rebuilding of damaged infrastructures, reinstitution of community services, and agriculture and economic development. The large-scale AP landmine problem alone presents a major, immediate challenge that must be solved before a sustainable repatriation would be possible. In 2000, the number of casualties produced by these weapons in Burma exceeded the number of casualties in mine-afflicted Cambodia, and neither the *tatmadaw* nor the insurgent forces have demonstrated any intention of restricting their use.[38] In some cases, landmines cause displacement; in others they inhibit return home or make life difficult after return.

Finally, all parties committed to solving this problem must consider how the refugees themselves would be involved in building a firm and lasting peace for their homeland. The return of the refugees will in the future contribute to the long-term process of reconstruction and reconciliation in Burma. As the UNHCR's

---

[34] The principle of voluntariness relates to the situation in the country of asylum (permitting a free choice) and the conditions in the country of origin (calling for an informed decision). See United Nations High Commission for Refugees, *Handbook, Voluntary Repatriation: International Protection* (Geneva: UNHCR, 1996), pp. 10-11.

[35] Visit to the Karenni camps, Mae Hong Son, March 2000.

[36] These elements are elaborated in United Nations High Commission for Refugees, *Handbook*, p. 33.

[37] The requisition of nationality is a concern for refugees and the country of asylum alike. Such provisions for thousands of people who were born in the Thai-based camps, and those without Burmese national identity cards will be a necessary future precondition for return. Rangoon's present position is that it will only take back those with Burmese identity cards and this may be a means on the part of the home government to prevent repatriation.

[38] Andrew Selth, *Landmines in Burma: The Military Dimension*, Working Paper No. 352 (Canberra: Strategic and Defence Studies Centre, Australian National University, November 2000), p. 1.

Sadako Ogata has noted on the relationship between refugees and peace-building, "peace-building requires just solutions for refugees and displaced persons ... Ending suffering should be regarded as both a humanitarian and a political imperative: it is a function of peace-building."[39]

---

[39] Sadako Ogata, United Nations High Commissioner for Refugees, "Opening Address," in *Healing the Wounds of War: Refugees, Reconstruction and Reconciliation*, Conference Proceedings, UNHCR and International Peace Academy, June 30-July 1, 1996, pp. 4-5.

ACRONYMS

ABSDF	All Burma Students' Democratic Front. Burmese insurgent organization of student activists founded in November 1988.
AFPFL	Anti-Fascist People's Freedom League
ASEAN	Association of Southeast Asian Nations
BBC	Burmese Border Consortium. A consortium of NGOs assisting Karen refugees in Thailand.
BDA	Burma Defense Army
BIA	Burma Independence Army
BNA	Burma National Army
BPP	Border Patrol Police (Thailand). Established in 1953 to gather intelligence and maintain security in the remote border regions of the country.
BSPP	Burmese Socialist Program Party. The party established by the Revolutionary Council (RC), declared to be the only legal political party in Burma by the military dictator, Ne Win.
CCSDPT	Coordinating Committee for Services to Displaced Persons. An umbrella group made up of all the agencies assisting Indochinese refugees in Thailand.
CPA	Comprehensive Plan of Action. Plan adopted by seventy-seven nations in June 1989 to confront the growing Indochinese refugee problem.
CPB	Communist Party of Burma
CPPSM	Committee for the Promotion of People's Struggle in Monland
CPT	Communist Party of Thailand
DAB	Democratic Alliance of Burma. A coalition of twenty-three anti-government groups formed on November 18, 1988.
DDSI	Directorate of Defense Services Intelligence
DKBA	Democratic Karen (Kayin) Buddhist Army. A Karen armed splinter faction that broke away from the KNU in December 1994 and which has served as a proxy army for the *tatmadaw*.
Dobama Asiayone	"We Burma" Association
DPPU	Displaced Persons Protection Unit
EXCOM	Executive Committee of the High Commissioner's Program (United Nations High Commissioner for Refugees).

I B	Infantry Battalion
IDC	Immigration Detention Center (Thai)
IDPs	Internally Displaced Persons
ISOC	Internal Security Operations Command (Thailand). Thai governmental office that acted as liaison with Burmese ethnic minority armies.
JC	Joint Commission. A commission made up of Thai and Burmese representatives, chaired by the two countries' foreign ministers, assigned to oversee and promote economic cooperation between the two nations.
JBC	Joint Boundary Commission. A civilian committee, co-chaired by the deputy foreign ministers of Burma and Thailand, assigned to demarcate officially the boundary between the two nations.
KHRG	Karen Human Rights Group
KIO	Kachin Independence Organization
KNDO	Karen National Defense Organization
KNLA	Karen National Liberation Army
KNPP	Karenni National Progressive Party
KNU	Karen National Union
KNUP	Karen National Unity Party. A Karen group allied to the Communist Party of Burma's front, the National Democratic United Front.
KRC	Karens Refugee Committee, a relief agency formed by the Karens in 1989 to administer camps of Karenni refugees in Thailand.
LBC	Local Border Committee
LIB	Light Infantry Battalion. Mobile battalions that make up the Burma Army's Light Infantry Division.
LID	Light Infantry Division. Burma Army division made up of Light Infantry Battalions (LIBs). Introduced in mid-1966, these mobile "strike forces" were formed to combat communist and ethnic insurgencies.
MAMD	Mon Army Mergui District. Splinter group that refused to abide by the NMSP's 1996 cease-fire agreement with the Burmese army.
MDUF	Myeik-Dawei United Front, a small ethnic Tavoyan armed group.
MFA	Ministry of Foreign Affairs (Thai)
MFL	Mon Freedom League
MIS	Mon Information Service
MNDO	Mon National Defense Organization. Formed in 1948, following the attainment of Burmese independence, the organization initiated armed insurrection against the new government, hoping to establish an independent Mon state.
MNLA	Mon National Liberation Army. The armed wing of the NMSP, founded in 1971.

MNRC	Mon National Relief Committee. A relief agency formed by the Mons after 1984 to aid and support Mon refugees in Thailand.
MOC	Military Operational Command
MOI	Ministry of Interior (Thailand)
MOGE	Myanma(r) Oil and Gas Enterprise. A Burmese agency that contracted with the Petroleum Authority of Thailand and other international companies in a joint oil and gas extraction venture involving the construction of a pipeline through contested Burmese territory.
MPF	Mon People's Front. The organization formed in 1953 from the union of Mon cultural, political, and guerrilla organizations.
MUF	Mon United Front
NDF	National Democratic Front. The umbrella organization constituted of major anti-Rangoon ethnic insurgent groups.
NDUF	National Democratic United Front. An alliance of political and ethnic groups that attempted to negotiate with Burma's dictatorship in 1963. Front for the CPB.
NGO	Non-government organization.
NIA	National Intelligence Agency (Thailand)
NMSP	New Mon State Party. Insurrectionary party formed after the surrender and consequent dissolution of the Mon People's Front in 1958.
NSC	National Security Council (Thailand). The most powerful civilian decision-making body in the RTG directly concerned with refugee policy.
NUFA	National Unity Front of Arakan
NULF	National United Liberation Front
PBF	Patriot Burmese Forces
PDP	Parliamentary Democracy Party. An insurgent political party founded by the exiled former prime minister of Burma, U Nu, who sought to overthrow the Rangoon regime.
PLA	Patriotic Liberation Army
PRK	People's Republic of Kampuchea. The Cambodian government installed by Vietnam in 1978.
PTT	Petroleum Authority of Thailand
RBC	Regional Border Committee. Committee representing the Burmese and Thai militaries, chaired by the respective army commanders, focusing on border security matters.
RC	Revolutionary Council. Military oligarchy that ruled Burma from 1962 to 1974.
RIT	Rangoon's Institute of Technology
RTA	Royal Thai Army
RTG	Royal Thai Government
SLORC	State Law and Order Restoration Council. The military regime that ruled Burma from 1988 to 1997, when its name was changed to the State Peace and Development Council.

SPDC	State Peace and Development Council. The new title adopted by the SLORC regime in November 1997.
SSLO	Shan State Liberation Organization
TBC	Township Border Committee
TOC	Tactical Operations Command
UMA	United Mon Association
UNBRO	United Nations Border Relief Organization. United Nations organization assigned to assist Cambodian refugees seeking sanctuary in Thailand. 1982-1991.
UNHCR	United Nations High Commission for Refugees
UNHRC	United Nations Human Rights Commission
UNTAC	United Nations Transitional Authority in Cambodia. A United Nations body granted the authority to govern Cambodia following the Paris Peace Agreement, signed October 23, 1991.
USCR	United States Committee for Refugees
VBSW	Vigorous Burmese Student Warriors. Radical student faction that briefly took over the Burmese embassy in Bangkok in October 1999.

BIBLIOGRAPHY

BOOKS

Agnew, John, and Stuart Corbridge. *Mastering Space. Hegemony, Territory and International Political Economy.* London and New York: Routledge, 1995.

Aleinikoff, T. Alexander. "State-centred Refugee Law: From Resettlement to Containment." In *Mistrusting Refugees,* ed. E. Valentine Daniel and John Chr. Knudsen. Berkeley: University of California Press, 1995.

Allott, Anna. *The End of the First Anglo-Burmese War: The Burmese Chronicle Account of How the 1826 Treaty of Yandabo Was Negotiated.* Bangkok: Chulalongkorn University Press, 1994.

Anderson, Benedict. *The Spectre of Comparisons: Nationalism, Southeast Asia, and the World.* London: Verso, 1998.

―――. *Imagined Communities: Reflections on the Origin and Spread of Nationalism.* London: Verso, 1991.

Anzaldua, Gloria. *Borderland/La Frontera: The New Mestiza.* San Francisco: Aunt Lute Books, 1987.

Appadurai, Arjun. "The Production of Locality." In *Counterworks: Managing the Diversity of Knowledge,* ed. Richard Fardon. London and New York: Routledge, 1995.

―――. "Global Ethnoscapes: Notes and Queries for a Transnational Anthropology." In *Recapturing Anthropology: Working in the Present,* ed. R. G. Fox. Sante Fe, NM: School of American Research Press, 1991.

Archarya, Amitav. "Human Rights and Regional Order: ASEAN and Human Rights Management in Post-Cold War Southeast Asia." In *Human Rights and International Relations in the Asia-Pacific Region,* ed. James T. H. Tang. London: Pinter, 1995.

Arendt, Hannah. *The Origins of Totalitarianism,* 3rd edition. London: George Allen and Unwin, 1967.

Asia Watch/Women's Rights Project, *A Modern Form of Slavery: Trafficking of Burmese Women and Girls into Brothels in Thailand.* New York: Asia Watch/Women's Rights Project, 1993.

Aung San Suu Kyi. *Letters from Burma.* London: Penguin Books, 1997.

―――. *The Voice of Hope.* London: Penguin Books, 1996.

———. *Towards a True Refuge (The Eighth Joyce Pearce Memorial Lecture).* Oxford: The Refugee Studies Programme, Queen Elizabeth House, 1993.

———. *Freedom From Fear and Other Writings.* London: Penguin Books, 1991.

Aung Saw Oo. *Burma's Student Movement: A Concise History.* Chiang Mai: Chiang Mai University, 1993.

Aung-Thwin, Michael. "Principles and Patterns of the Precolonial Burmese State." In *Tradition and Modernity in Myanmar,* ed. Uta Gärtner and Jens Lorenz. Berlin: Fakultätsinstitut für Asien- und Afrikawissenshaften, Humbolt Universität zu Berlin, 1994.

Ayoob, Mohammed. "State Making, State Breaking, and State Failure." In *Managing Global Chaos,* ed. Chester A. Crocker, et al. Washington, DC: United States Institute of Peace Press, 1996.

Bajpai, Kanti. "Human Security: Concept and Measurement." Occasional Paper #19:OP:1, Joan B. Kroc Institute for International Peace Studies, University of Notre Dame, August 2000.

Ball, Desmond. *Burma's Military Secrets: Signals Intelligence (SIGINT) from 1941 to Cyber Warfare.* Bangkok: White Lotus, 1998.

Ball, Desmond, and Hazel Lang. *Factionalism and the Ethnic Insurgent Organisations.* Working Paper No. 356. Canberra: Strategic and Defence Studies Centre, Australian National University, 2001.

Ball, Nicole. "The Challenge of Rebuilding War-Torn Societies." In *Managing Global Chaos,* ed. Chester A. Crocker, et al. Washington, DC: United States Institute of Peace Press, 1996.

Barnes, R. H., A. Gray, and B. Kingsbury, eds. *Indigenous Peoples of Asia.* Ann Arbor, MI: Association for Asian Studies, 1995.

Barth, F. *Ethnic Groups and Boundaries.* London: Allen and Unwin, 1969.

Bauer, Christian. "Language and Ethnicity: The Mon in Burma and Thailand." In *Ethnic Groups Across National Boundaries in Mainland Southeast Asia,* ed. Gehan Wijeyewardene. Singapore: Institute of Southeast Asian Studies, 1990.

Bedjaoui, Mohammed. Modern Wars: *The Humanitarian Challenge. A Report for the Independent Commission on International Humanitarian Issues.* London: Zed Books, 1986.

Benjamin, Walter. "Theses on the Philosophy of History." In *Illuminations,* trans. Harry Zohn, ed. Hannah Arendt. New York: Schocken Books, 1968.

Black, Richard, and Khalid Koser. "The End of the Refugee Cycle?" In *The End of the Refugee Cycle? Refugee Repatriation and Reconstruction,* ed. Richard Black and Khalid Koser. New York: Berghahn Books, 1999.

Black, Richard, and Vaughan Robinson, eds. *Geography and Refugees: Patterns and Processes of Change.* London and New York: Belhaven Press, 1993.

Brandon, John J., ed. *Burma/Myanmar: Towards the Twenty-first Century: Dynamic of Continuity and Change*. Bangkok: Open Society/Chulalongkorn University, 1997.

Bray, John. *Burma: The Politics of Constructive Engagement*, RIIA Discussion Paper 58. London: Royal Institute of International Affairs, 1995.

Brown, David. *The State and Ethnic Politics in Southeast Asia*. London: Routledge, 1994.

Brown, Michael E. "Introduction." In *The International Dimensions of Internal Conflict*, ed. Michael E. Brown. Cambridge, MA: MIT Press, 1996.

———. "Causes and Implications of Ethnic Conflict." In *Ethnic Conflict and International Security*, ed. Michael E. Brown. Princeton: Princeton University Press, 1993.

Bryant, Raymond L. "The Politics of Forestry in Burma." In *The Politics of Environment in Southeast Asia: Resources and Resistance*, ed. Philip Hirsch and Carol Warren. London: Routledge, 1998.

———. *The Political Ecology of Foresty in Burma, 1824-1994*. Honolulu: University of Hawai'i Press, 1997.

———. "Asserting Sovereignty through Natural Resource Use." In *Resources, Nations and Indigenous Peoples: Case Studies from Australasia, Melanesia and Southeast Asia*, ed. Richard Howitt, John Connell, and Philip Hirsch. Melbourne: Oxford University Press, 1996.

Butler, Judith, and Joan Scott, eds. *Feminists Theorize the Political*. New York and London: Routledge, 1992.

Butwell, Richard. *U Nu of Burma*. Stanford: Stanford University Press, 1969.

Cady, John F. *A History of Modern Burma*. Ithaca, NY: Cornell University Press, 1958.

Callahan, Mary P. "Cracks in the Edifice? Military-Society Relations in Burma since 1988." In *Burma/Myanmar: Strong Regime, Weak State?*, ed. Morten B. Pedersen, Emily Rudland, and R. J. May. Adelaide: Crawford House Publishing, 2000.

———. "The Sinking Schooner: Murder and the State in Independent Burma, 1948-58." In *Gangsters, Democracy, and the State in Southeast Asia*, ed. Carl A. Trocki. Ithaca, NY: Cornell Southeast Asia Program Publications, 1998.

Carey, Peter, ed. *Burma: The Challenge of a Divided Society*. London: Macmillan, 1997.

Carsten, Janet. "Borders, Boundaries, Tradition and State on the Malaysian Periphery." In *Border Identities: Nation and State at International Frontiers*, ed. Thomas M. Wilson and Donnan Hastings. Cambridge: Cambridge University Press, 1998.

Castillo, Manuel Angel and James C. Hathaway. "Temporary Protection." In *Reconceiving International Refugee Law*, ed. James C. Hathaway. The Hague: Martinus Nijhoff Publishers, 1997.

Chaliand, Gerard. *Minority Peoples in the Age of Nation States*. London: Pluto Press, 1989.

Chalong Soontravanich. "Research on the Thai-Myanmar Historical Relations in Thailand." In *Comparative Studies on Literature and History of Thailand and Myanmar*, ed. Withaya Sucharithanarugse. Bangkok and Yangon: Institute of Asian Studies, Chulalongkorn University and Universities' Historical Research Centre, 1997.

Chao-Tzang Yawnghwe. "Burma: The Depoliticization of the Political." In *Political Legitimacy in Southeast Asia: The Quest for Moral Authority*, ed. Muthiah Alagappa. Stanford: Stanford University Press, 1995.

Chimni, B. S. *From Resettlement to Involuntary Repatriation: Towards a Critical History of Durable Solutions to Refugee Problems*, New Issues in Refugee Research Working Paper No. 2. Geneva: United Nations High Commissioner for Refugees, May 1999.

Christie, Clive J. "Anatomy of Betrayal: The Karens of Burma." In *A Modern History of Southeast Asia: Decolonization, Nationalism, Separatism*. London and New York: I. B. Tauris Publishers, 1996.

Clifford, James, and George E. Marcus, eds. *The Poetics and Politics of Ethnography*. Berkeley: University of California Press, 1986.

Coates, Austin, "The Proud Mon (reproduced from a 1953 essay)." In *Inroads Into Burma: A Travellers' Anthology*, ed. Gerry Abbott. Kuala Lumpur: Oxford University Press, 1997.

Coedès, George. *The Indianized States of Southeast Asia*, ed. Walter F. Vella, trans. Susan Brown Cowing. Canberra: Australian National University Press, 1975.

———. *The Making of Southeast Asia*, trans. H. M. Wright. London: Routledge and Kegan Paul, 1966.

Cohen, Roberta, and Francis M. Deng. *Masses in Flight: The Global Crisis of Internal Displacement*. Washington, DC: Brookings Institution Press, 1998.

Coles, Gervase. "Approaching the Refugee Problem Today." In *Refugees and International Relations*, ed. Gil Loescher and Laila Monahan. Oxford: Oxford University Press, 1989.

Connor, Walker. *Ethnonationalism: The Quest for Understanding*. Princeton: Princeton University Press, 1994.

Cultural Survival, ed. *Southeast Asian Tribal Groups and Ethnic Minorities*. Cambridge, MA: Cultural Survival, 1987.

Dalby, Simon. "Crossing Disciplinary Boundaries: Political Geography and International Relations after the Cold War." In *Globalization: Theory and Practice*, ed. Eleonore Kofman and Gillian Youngs. London: Pinter, 1996.

Daniel, E. Valentine, and John Chr. Knudsen, eds. *Mistrusting Refugees*. Berkeley: University of California Press, 1995.

Darby, Phillip, ed. *At the Edge of International Relations: Postcolonialism, Gender and Dependency*. London and New York: Pinter, 1997.

de Certeau, Michel. *The Practice of Everyday Life*, trans. Steven F. Rendall. Berkeley: University of California Press, 1984.

Deng, Francis M. *Protecting the Dispossessed: A Challenge for the International Community*. Washington, DC: The Brookings Institution, 1993.

Deudney, Daniel. "Ground Identity: Nature, Place, and Space in Nationalism." In *The Return of Culture and Identity in IR Theory*, ed. Yosef Kratochwil and Friedrich Lapid. Boulder, CO and London: Lynne Rienner Publishers, 1996.

Donner, Wolf. *The Five Faces of Thailand: An Economic Geography*. London and Hamburg: C. Hurst and Company/Institute of Asian Studies, 1978.

Donnison, F. S. V. *Burma*. London: Eernest Benn Limited, 1970.

Ellen, R. F., ed. *Ethnographic Research: A Guide to General Conduct*. London: Academic Press, 1984.

Elson, Robert. "International Commerce, the State and Society: Economic and Social Change." In *The Cambridge History of Southeast Asia, Volume Two*, ed. Nicholas Tarling. Cambridge: Cambridge University Press, 1992.

Enloe, Cynthia H. *The Morning After: Sexual Politics at the End of the Cold War*. Berkeley: University of California Press, 1993.

————. "When Ethnicity in Militarized: The Consequences for Southeast Asian Communities." In *Southeast Asian Tribal Groups and Ethnic Minorities*, ed. Cultural Survival. Cambridge, MA: Cultural Survival Inc., 1987.

————. *Ethnic Soldiers: State Security in Divided Societies*. Harmondsworth: Penguin Books, 1980.

Eriksen, Thomas Hylland. *Ethnicity and Nationalism: Anthropological Perspectives*. London/Boulder, Colorado: Pluto Press, 1993.

Evans, Grant, ed. *Asia's Cultural Mosaic: An Anthropological Introduction*. New York: Prentice Hall, 1993.

Falk, Richard, Friedrich Kratochwil, and Saul H. Mendlovitz, eds. *International Law: A Contemporary Perspective*. Boulder, CO: Westview Press, 1985.

Ferris, Elizabeth, ed. *Refugees and World Politics*. New York: Praeger, 1985.

Foster, Brian L. "Ethnic Identity of the Mon in Thailand." In *The Mons: Collected Articles from the Journal of the Siam Society*, ed. Michael Smithies. Bangkok: The Siam Society, 1986.

Foucault, Michel. *Power/Knowledge: Selected Interviews and Other Writings 1972-1977*, ed. Colin Gordon. New York: Pantheon Books, 1980.

Fredholm, Michael. *Burma: Ethnicity and Insurgency*. Westport, CN: Praeger, 1993.

Furnivall, J. S. *Colonial Policy and Practice: A Comparative Study of Burma and Netherlands India*. New York: New York University Press, 1956.

———. *The Fashioning of Leviathan: The Beginnings of British Rule in Burma.* Canberra: Economic History of Southeast Asia Project and Thai-Yunnan Project, 1991. Reproduced from the *Journal of the Burma Research Society* 29,1 (1938).

Gahl-Madsen, Atle. *The Status of Refugees in International Law, Vol. II.* Leiden: A. W. Sijthoff, 1972.

Girling, J. S. *Thailand: Society and Politics.* Ithaca and London: Cornell University Press, 1981.

Gooden, Christian. *Three Pagodas: A Journey Down the Thai-Burmese Border.* Halesworth: Jungle Books, 1996.

Goodwin-Gill, Guy S. "Refugee Identity and the Fading Prospect of Protection." In *Refugee Rights and Realities: Evolving International Concepts and Regimes,* ed. Frances Nicholson and Patrick Twomey. Cambridge: Cambridge University Press, 1999.

———. *The Refugee in International Law.* Oxford: Clarendon Press, 1996.

Green, Linda. *The Routinization of Fear in Rural Guatemala,* Occassional Paper No. 2. Saskatchewan: Department of History, University of Saskatchewan, 1995.

Grundy-Warr, Carl, Desmond Ball, and Hazel Lang, eds. *Danger Line: People, Sovereignty and Security Along the Burma-Thailand Border.* Bangkok: White Lotus, 2002.

——— and Ananda Rajah. "Security, Resources and People in a Borderlands Environment: Myanmar-Thailand." In *International Boundaries and Environmental Security: Frameworks For Regional Cooperation,* ed. G. H. Blake, L. Chia, C. Grundy-Warr, M. Pratt, and C. Scholfield. Amsterdam: Kluwer Law International, 1997.

Guest, Iain, and Francoise Bouchet-Saulnier. "International Law and Reality: The Protection Gap." In *World in Crisis: The Politics of Survival at the End of the Twentieth Century,* ed. Medecins San Frontieres. London and New York: Routledge, 1997.

Guidieri, Remo, and Francesco Pellizzi. "Introduction: 'Smoking Mirrors'—Modern Polity and Ethnicity." In *Ethnicities and Nations: Processes of Interethnic Relations in Latin America, Southeast Asia and the Pacific,* ed. Remo Guidieri and Francesco Pellizzi, et al. Austin, TX: Rothko Chapel/University of Texas Press, 1988.

Guillon, Emmanuel. *The Mons: A Civilization of Southeast Asia,* trans. by James V. Di Crocco. Bangkok: The Siam Society under Royal Patronage, 1999.

Gurr, Ted Robert. *Minorities at Risk: A Global View of Ethnopolitical Conflicts.* Washington, DC: United States Institute of Peace Press, 1993.

Gurr, Ted Robert and Barbara Harff. *Ethnic Conflict in World Politics.* Boulder, CO: Westview Press, 1994.

H. R. H. Prince Damrong Rajanubhab. *Journey Through Burma in 1936.* Bangkok: River Books, 1991.

Haliday, Robert. *The Talaings*. Rangoon: Superintendant, Government Printing, Burma, 1917.

Hall, Kenneth, and John K Whitmore, eds. *Explorations in Early Southeast Asian History: The Origins of Southeast Asian Statecraft*. Ann Arbor, MI: Center for South and Southeast Asian Studies, University of Michigan, 1976.

Halliday, R. "Immigration of the Mons into Siam." In *The Mons: Collected Articles from the Journal of the Siam Society*, ed. Michael Smithies. Bangkok: The Siam Society, 1986.

Hampton, Janie, ed. *Internally Displaced People: A Global Survey*. London: Norwegian Refugee Council and Earthscan Publications, 1998.

Hannum, Hurst. *Autonomy, Sovereignty, and Self-determination: The Accomodation of Conflicting Rights*. Philadelphia: University of Pennsylvania Press, 1990.

Harrell-Bond, Barbara E. *Imposing Aid: Emergency Assistance to Refugees*. Oxford/New York/Nairobi: Oxford University Press, 1986.

Harvey, G. E. *Outline of Burmese History*, 2nd edition. Bombay: Longmans, Green and Co., 1929.

Hathaway, James C. "Preface." In *Reconceiving International Refugee Law*, ed. James C. Hathaway. The Hague: Martinus Nijhoff Publishers, 1997.

———. "Reconceiving Refugee Law as Human Rights Protection." In *Human Rights in the Twenty-first Century: A Global Challenge*, ed. Kathleen E. Mahoney and Paul Mahoney. Dordrecht: Martinus Nijhoff Publishers, 1992.

———. *The Law of Refugee Status*. Toronto: Butterworths, 1991.

Heine-Geldern, Robert. *Conceptions of State and Kingship in Southeast Asia*. Ithaca, NY: Southeast Asia Program, Cornell University, 1956.

Hilsdon, Anne-Marie. *Madonnas and Martyrs: Militarism and Violence in the Philippines*. St. Leonards: Allen and Unwin, 1995.

Hindess, Barry. *Discourses of Power: From Hobbes to Foucault*. Oxford: Blackwell, 1996.

Hirsch, Philip. "Thailand and the New Geopolitics of Southeast Asia: Resource and Environmental Issues." In *Counting the Costs: Economic Growth and Environmental Change in Thailand*, ed. Jonathan Rigg. Singapore: Institute of Southeast Asian Studies, 1995.

Hitchcox, Linda. *Vietnamese Refugees in Southeast Asian Camps*. Basingstoke and London: St. Antony's/Macmillan, 1990.

Howitt, Richard, John Connell, and Philip Hirsch. "Introduction." In *Resources, Nations and Indigenous Peoples: Case Studies from Australasia, Melanesia and Southeast Asia*, ed. Richard Howitt, John Connell and Philip Hirsch. Melbourne: Oxford University Press, 1996.

Htin Aung. *A History of Burma*. New York and London: Columbia University Press, 1967.

Ireland, Allyene. "The People of Burma." In *The Province of Burma: A Report on Colonial Administration in the Far East*. Boston and New York: Houghton, Mifflin and Company, 1907.

Jackson, Michael. *Paths Toward a Clearing: Radical Empiricism and Ethnographic Inquiry*. Bloomington and Indianapolis: Indiana University Press, 1989.

Jannuzi, Frank S. "The New Burma Road (Paved by Polytechnologies)?" In *Burma: Prospects for a Democratic Future*, ed. Robert I. Rotberg. Washington, DC and Cambridge, MA: World Peace Foundation/Harvard Institute for International Development and Brookings Institution Press, 1998.

Jean, Francois. "The Plight of the World's Refugees: At the Crossroads of Protection." In *World in Crisis: The Politics of Survival at the End of the Twentieth Century*, ed. Medecins Sans Frontieres. London and New York: Routledge, 1997.

Jean, Francois, ed. *Populations in Danger 1995: A Medicins Sans Frontieres Report*. Australian. Rushcutters Bay, NSW: Halstead Press, 1995.

Jeshurun, Chandran, ed. *Governments and Rebellions in Southeast Asia*. Singapore: Institute of Southeast Asian Studies, 1985.

Joo-Jock, Lim, and Vani S., eds. *Armed Separatism in Southeast Asia*. Singapore: Institute of Southeast Asian Studies, 1984.

Keyes, Charles F. "Cultural Diversity and National Identity in Thailand." In *Government Policies and Ethnic Relations in Asia and the Pacific*, ed. Michael E. Brown and Sumit Ganguly. Cambridge, MA: MIT Press, 1997.

———. *Thailand: Buddhist Kingdom as Modern Nation-State*. Boulder, CO: Westview Press, 1987.

———. "Introduction." In *Ethnic Adaptation and Identity: The Karen on the Thai Frontier with Burma*, ed. Charles F. Keyes. Philadelphia: Institute for the Study of Human Issues, 1979.

Koenig, William J. *The Burmese Polity 1752-1819: Politics, Administration and Social Organization in the Early Konbaung Period*. Ann Arbor, MI: Center for South and Southeast Asian Studies, University of Michigan, 1990.

Kofman, Eleonore, and Gillian Youngs, eds. *Globalization: Theory and Practice*. London and New York: Pinter, 1996.

Kratochwil, Friedrich. "Citizenship: On the Border of Order." In *The Return of Culture and Identity in IR Theory*, ed. Yosef Krotochwil and Friedrich Lapid. Boulder, CO and London: Lynne Rienner Publishers, 1996.

Kristeva, Julia. *Nations Without Nationalism*, trans. Leon S Roudiez. New York: Columbia University Press, 1993.

Kunstadter, Peter, ed. *Southeast Asian Tribes, Minorities, and Nations*. Princeton: Princeton University Press, 1967.

Lake, David A., and Donald Rothchild. *Ethnic Fears and Global Engagement: The International Spread and Management of Ethnic Conflict*. San Diego: Institute on Global Conflict and Cooperation, University of California, 1996.

Lamb, Alistair. *Asian Frontiers: Studies in a Continuing Problem.* Melbourne: Australian Institute of International Affairs, 1968.

Lang, Hazel. *The Repatriation Predicament of Burmese Refugees in Thailand: A Preliminary Analysis.* New Issues in Refugee Research Working Paper No. 46. Geneva: United Nations High Commissioner for Refugees, July 2001.

Lawson, Stephanie. *The Politics of Authenticity: Ethnonationalist Conflict and the State.* Canberra: Peace Research Centre, Australian National University, 1992.

Leach, Edmund. "The Political Future of Burma." In *Futuribles*, Volume 1. Geneva: Droz, 1963.

Lee Yong Leng. *Southeast Asia: Essays in Political Geography.* Singapore: Singapore University Press, 1982.

———. *The Razor's Edge. Boundaries and Boundary Disputes in Southeast Asia.* Singapore: Institute of Southeast Asian Studies, 1980.

Lehman, F. K. "Ethnic Categories in Burma and the Theory of Social Systems." In *Southeast Asian Tribes, Minorities, and Nations,* ed. Peter Kundstadter. Princeton: Princeton University Press, 1967.

Lian Kwen Fee, and Ananda Rajah. "The Ethnic Mosaic." In *Asia's Cultural Mosaic: An Anthropological Introduction,* ed. Grant Evans. New York: Prentice Hall, 1993.

Liang, Chi-shad. *Burma's Foreign Relations: Neutralism in Theory and Practice.* New York: Praeger, 1990.

Lieberman, Victor B. *Burmese Administrative Cycles: Anarchy and Conquest, c.1580-1760.* Princeton: Princeton University Press, 1984.

Lintner, Bertil. *Burma in Revolt: Opium and Insurgency Since 1948.* Boulder, CO and Bangkok: Westview Press and White Lotus, 1994.

———. "The Internationalization of Burma's Ethnic Conflict." In *Internationalization of Ethnic Conflict,* ed. K. M. de Silva and R. J. May. London: Pinter, 1991.

———. *Outrage: Burma's Struggle for Democracy.* Bangkok: White Lotus, 1990.

———. *The Rise and Fall of the Communist Party of Burma.* Ithaca, NY: Southeast Asia Program, Cornell University, 1990.

Lissak, Moshe. *Military Roles in Modernization: Civil-military Relations in Thailand and Burma.* Beverly Hills: Sage Publications, 1976.

Lobe, Thomas, and David Morell. "Thailand's Border Patrol Police: Paramilitary Political Power." In *Supplementary Military Forces: Reserves, Militias, Auxilaries,* Volume 8, ed. Louis A. Zurcher and Gwyn Harries-Jenkins. Beverly Hills: Sage Publications, 1978.

Loescher, Gil, and Laila Monahan, eds. *Refugees and International Relations.* New York: Oxford University Press, 1989.

Loescher, Gil. *Beyond Charity: International Cooperation and the Global Refugee Crisis*. New York and Oxford: Oxford University Press, 1993.

———. *Refugee Movements and International Security*. London: Brassey's for the International Institute for Stategic Studies, 1992.

Long, Lynellyn D. *Ban Vinai: The Refugee Camp*. New York: Columbia University Press, 1993.

MacMillan, John, and Andrew Linklater, eds. *Boundaries in Question: New Directions in International Relations*. London and New York: Pinter Publishers, 1995.

Manz, Beatriz. *Refugees of a Hidden War: The Aftermath of Counterinsurgency in Guatemala*. Albany, NY: State University of New York Press, 1988.

Marrus, Michael R. "Introduction." In *Refugees in the Age of Total War*, ed. Anna C. Bramwell. London: Unwin Hyman, 1988.

Martinez, Oscar J. "The Dynamics of Border Interaction. New Approaches to Border Analysis." In *Global Boundaries: World Boundaries Series*, Volume 1, ed. C. H. Schofield. London: Routledge, 1994.

Mason, Mark. "Direct Foreign Investment in Burma: Trends, Determinants, and Prospects." In *Burma: Prospects for a Democratic Future*, ed. Robert I. Rotberg. Cambridge, MA and Washington, DC: World Peace Foundation/Harvard Institute for International Development and Brookings Institution Press, 1998.

Maung Aung Myoe. *Building the Tatmadaw: The Organisational Development of the Armed Forces in Myanmar, 1948-98*, Working Paper No. 327. Canberra: The Strategic and Defence Studies Centre, Australian National University, 1998.

McCormack, Gavan, and Hank Nelson. *The Burma-Thailand Railway: Memory and History*. St. Leonards, NSW: Allen and Unwin, 1993.

McNamara, Dennis. "The Origins and Effects of 'Humane Deterrence' Policies in Southeast Asia." In *Refugees and International Relations*, ed. Gil Loescher and Laila Monahan. New York: Oxford University Press, 1989.

McVey, Ruth. "Separatism and the Paradoxes of the Nation-State in Perspective." In *Armed Separatism in Southeast Asia*, ed. Lim Joo-Jock and Vani S. Singapore: Institute of Southeast Asian Studies, 1984.

Mellor, Roy E. H. *Nation, State, and Territory: A Political Geography*. London and New York: Routledge, 1989.

Minh-ha, Trinh T. *Woman, Native Other: Writing Postcoloniality and Feminism*. Bloomington and Indianapolis: Indiana University Press, 1989.

Mirante, Edith T. "Ethnic Minorities of the Burma Frontiers and their Resistance Groups." In *Southeast Asian Tribal Groups and Ethnic Minorities*, ed. Cultural Survival. Cambridge, MA: Cultural Survival, 1987.

Mohanty, Chandra Talpade. "Under Western Eyes: Feminist Scholarship and Colonial Discourses." In *Third World Women and the Politics of Feminism*, ed. Chandra Talpade, Ann Russo and Torres Lourdes. Bloomington and Indianapolis: Indiana University Press, 1991.

Moscotti, Albert D. "Current Burmese and Southeast Asian Relations."In *Southeast Asian Affairs 1978*. Singapore: Institute of Southeast Asian Studies, 1978.

Mya Than. "Economic Transformation in Southeast Asia: The Case of Myanmar." In *Burma/Myanmar: Towards the Twenty-First Century: Dynamic of Continuity and Change*, ed. John J. Brandon. Bangkok: Open Society/Chulalongkorn University, 1997.

Neptnapis Nakavachara, and John Rogge. "Thailand's Refugee Experience." In *Refugees: A Third World Dilemma*, ed. John Rogge. Totowa, NJ: Rowman and Littlefield, 1987.

Newland, Kathleen. "Ethnic Conflict and Refugees." In *Ethnic Conflict and International Security*, ed. Michael E. Brown. Princeton: Princeton University Press, 1993.

Nicolson, Frances and Patrick Twomey, eds. *Refugees Rights and Realities: Evolving International Concepts and Regimes*. Cambridge: Cambridge University Press, 1999.

Nietschmann, Bernard. "The Fourth World: Nations Versus States." In *Reordering the World: Geopolitical Perspectives on the Twenty-first Century*, ed. George J. Demko and William B. Wood. Boulder, CO: Westview Press, 1994.

Nordstrom, Carolyn. *A Different Kind of War Story*. Philadelphia: University of Pennsylvania Press, 1997.

———. "Creativity and Chaos." In *Fieldwork Under Fire: Contemporary Studies of Violence and Survival*, ed. Carolyn Nordstrom and Antonius C. G. M. Robben. Berkeley: University of California Press, 1995.

Nordstrom, Carolyn, and Antonius C. G. M. Robben. *Fieldwork Under Fire: Contemporary Studies of Violence and Survival*. Berkeley: University of California Press, 1995.

———. *Rape: Politics and Theory in War and Peace,* Working Paper No. 146. Canberra: Peace Research Centre, Research School of Pacific and Asian Studies, Australian National University, 1994.

———. *Warzones: Cultures of Violence, Militarisation and Peace*, Working Paper No. 145. Canberra: Peace Research Centre, Research School of Pacific and Asian Studies, Australian National University, 1994.

———. "Contested Identities and Essentially-Contested Powers." In *War and Peace Making: Essays on Conflict and Change*, ed. Ed Garcia. Quezon City: Claretian Publications, 1994.

———. "The Backyard Front." In *The Paths to Domination, Resistance, and Terror*, ed. Carolyn Nordstrom and JoAnn Martin. Berkeley: University of California Press, 1992.

Nordstrom, Carolyn, and JoAnn Martin. *The Paths to Domination, Resistance, and Terror*. Berkeley: University of California Press, 1992.

O'Connor Sutter, Valerie. *The Indochinese Refugee Dilemma*. Baton Rouge: Louisiana State University Press, 1990.

Ogata, Sadako. "Human Rights, Humanitarian Law and Refugee Protection." In *Human Rights and Humanitarian Law: The Quest for Universality*, ed. Daniel Warner. The Hague/Boston/London: Martinus Nijhoff Publishers, 1997.

Panitan Wattanayagorn. "Thailand: The Elite's Shifting Conceptions of Security." In *Asian Security Practice: Material and Ideational Influences*, ed. Muthiah Alagappa. Stanford: Stanford University Press, 1998.

Paolini, Albert. "Globalization." In *At the Edge of International Relations: Postcolonialism, Gender and Dependency*, ed. Phillip Darby. London and New York: Pinter, 1997.

Parnwell, Mike. *Population Movements and the Third World*. London and New York: Routledge, 1993.

Pasuk Phongpaichit, and Chris Baker. *Thailand: Economy and Politics*. New York: Oxford University Press, 1995.

Peterson, Spike, ed. *Gendered States: Feminist (Re)Visions of International Relations Theory*. Boulder, CO: Lynne Rienner, 1992.

Pettman, Jan Jindy. "Border Crossings/Shifting Identities: Minorities, Gender, and the State in International Perspective." In *Challenging Boundaries: Global Flows, Territorial Identities*, ed. Michael J. Shapiro and Hayward R. Alker. Minneapolis and London: University of Minnesota Press, 1996.

———. *Worlding Women: A Feminist International Politics*. St. Leonards, NSW: Allen and Unwin, 1996.

Phuangkasem, Corrine. *Thailand's Foreign Relations, 1964-80*. Singapore: Institute of Southeast Asian Studies, 1984.

Phuwadol Songprasert. *Thailand: A First Asylum Country for Indochinese Refugees*, Asian Monographs no. 38. Bangkok: Institute of Asian Studies, Chulalongkorn University, 1988.

Plender, Richard. "The Legal Protection of Refugees." In *Human Rights for the 1990s: Legal, Political and Ethical Issues*, ed. Robert Blackburn and John Taylor. London and New York: Mansell, 1991.

Prescott, J. R. V. *Political Frontiers and Boundaries*. London: Allen and Unwin, 1987.

———. *Boundaries and Frontiers*. London: Crook & Helm, 1978.

———. *Map of Mainland Asia by Treaty*. Melbourne: Melbourne University Press, 1975.

Prescott, J. R. V., H. J. Collier, and D. F. Prescott. *Frontiers of Asia and Southeast Asia*. Melbourne: Melbourne University Press, 1977.

Preston, Rosemary. "Researching Repatriation and Reconstruction: Who is Researching What and Why?" In *The End of the Refugee Cycle? Repatriation and Reconstruction*, ed. Richard Black and Khalid Koser. New York: Berghahn Books, 1999.

Purcell, Marc. "'Axe Handles or Willing Minions?': International NGOs in Burma." In *Strengthening Civil Society in Burma: Possibilities and Dilemmas for*

International NGOs, ed. Burma Center Netherlands and Transnational Institute. Chiang Mai: Silkworm Books, 1999.

Rajah, Ananda. "Ethnicity, Nationalism, and the Nation-State: The Karen in Burma and Thailand." In *Ethnic Groups across National Boundaries in Southeast Asia*, ed. Gehan Wijeyewardene. Singapore: Institute of Southeast Asian Studies, 1990.

Rapport, David C. *The Importance of Space in Violent Ethno-Religious Strife*, Policy Paper No. 21. Davis, CA: Institute on Global Conflict and Cooperation, University of California, Davis, 1996.

Renard, Ronald D. "Minorities in Burmese History." In *Ethnic Conflict in Buddhist Societies: Sri Lanka, Thailand and Burma*, ed. K. M. de Silva, et al. London: Pinter Publishers, 1988.

Reynell, Josephine. *Political Pawns: Refugees on the Thai-Kampuchean Border.* Oxford: Refugee Studies Program, Oxford University, 1989.

Riggs, Fred W. *Thailand: The Modernization of a Bureaucratic Polity.* Honolulu: East-West Center Press, 1966.

Robinson, Court. *Double Vision: A History of Cambodian Refugees in Thailand.* Bangkok: Asian Research Center for Migration, Institute of Asian Studies, Chulalongkorn University, 1996.

Rodley, Nigel. "Can Armed Opposition Groups Violate Human Rights?" In *Human Rights in the Twenty-first Century: A Global Challenge*, ed. Kathleen E. Mahoney and Paul Mahoney. Dordrecht: Martinus Nijhoff Publishers, 1992.

Rosaldo, Renato. *Culture and Truth: The Remaking of Social Analysis.* Boston: Beacon Press, 1993.

Rotberg, Robert I., ed. *Burma: Prospects for a Democratic Future.* Cambridge, MA and Washington, DC: The World Peace Foundation/Harvard Institute for International Development and Brookings Institution Press, 1998.

———. *Vigilance and Vengeance: NGOs Preventing Ethnic Conflict in Divided Societies.* Washington, DC and Cambridge, MA: Brookings Institution Press and The World Peace Foundation, 1996.

Rumley, Dennis, and Julian V. Minghi. "Introduction: The Border Landscape Concept." In *The Geography of Border Landscapes*, ed. Dennis Rumley and Julian V. Minghi. London: Routledge, 1991.

Rupesinghe, Kumar. "Governance and Conflict Resolution in Multi-ethnic Societies." In *Ethnicity and Power in the Contemporary World*, ed. Kumar Rupesinghe and Valery A. Tishkov. Tokyo: United Nations University Press, 1996.

———. "The Disappearing Boundaries Between Internal and External Conflicts." In *Internal Conflict and Governance*, ed. Kumar Rupesinghe. New York: St. Martin's Press, 1992.

Rupesingh, Kumar, with Sanam Naraghi Anderlini. *Civil Wars, Civil Peace: An Introduction to Conflict Resolution.* London/Sterling, Virginia: Pluto Press, 1998.

Said, Edward W. *Culture and Imperialism.* London: Vintage, 1993.

———. "Nationalism, Human Rights and Interpretation." In *Freedom and Interpretation,* ed. Barbara Johnson. New York: Basic Books, 1992.

SarDesai, D. R. *Southeast Asia: Past and Present.* London: Westview Press, 1989.

Scarry, Elaine. *The Body in Pain: The Making and Unmaking of the World.* New York: Oxford University Press, 1985.

Scheper-Hughes, Nancy. *Death Without Weeping: The Violence of Everyday Life in Brazil.* Berkeley: University of California Press, 1992.

Scott, James C. "Freedom and Freehold: Space, People and State Simplifications in Southeast Asia." In *Asian Freedoms: The Idea of Freedom in East and Southeast Asia,* ed. David Kelly and Anthony Reid. Cambridge: Cambridge University Press, 1998.

———. *Domination and the Arts of Resistance: Hidden Transcripts.* New Haven and London: Yale University Press, 1990.

Seidenfaden, Eric. "Mon Influence on Thai Institutions." In *The Mons: Collected Articles from the Journal of the Siam Society,* ed. Michael Smithies. Bangkok: The Siam Society, 1986.

Selth, Andrew. *Landmines in Burma: The Military Dimension,* Working Paper No. 352. Canberra: Strategic and Defence Studies Centre, Research School of Pacific and Asian Studies, Australian National University, November 2000.

———. *Burma's Order of Battle: An Interim Assessment,* Working Paper No. 351. Canberra: Strategic and Defence Studies Centre, Research School of Pacific and Asian Studies, Australian National University, 2000.

———. *Burma's Secret Military Partners,* Canberra Papers on Strategy and Defence No. 136. Canberra: Strategic and Defence Studies Centre, Research School of Pacific and Asian Studies, Australian National University, 2000.

———. "The Armed Forces and Military Rule in Burma." In *Burma: Prospects for a Democratic Future,* ed. Robert I. Rotberg. Washington, DC and Cambridge, MA: World Peace Foundation/Harvard Institute for International Development and Brookings Institution Press, 1998.

———. *Burma's Intelligence Apparatus,* Working Paper No. 308. Canberra: Strategic and Defence Studies Centre, Research School of Pacific and Asian Studies, Australian National University, 1997.

———. *Transforming the Tatmadaw: The Burmese Armed Forces Since 1988.* Canberra: Strategic and Defence Studies Centre, Research School of Pacific and Asian Studies, Australian National University, 1996.

———. *Death of a Hero: The U Thant Disturbances in Burma, December 1974,* Research Paper No. 49. Brisbane: Centre for the Study of Australian Asian Relations, Griffith University, 1989.

Shapiro, Michael J., and Hayward R. Alker, eds. *Challenging Boundaries: Global Flows, Territorial Identities*. Minneapolis: University of Minnesota Press, 1996.

Shwe Lu Maung. *Burma, Nationalism and Ideology: An Analysis of Society, Culture and Politics*. Dhaka: Dhaka University Press, 1989.

Silverstein, Josef. "Fifty Years of Failure in Burma." In *Government Policies and Ethnic Relations in Asia and the Pacific*, ed. Michael E. Brown and Sumit Ganguly. Cambridge, MA: The MIT Press, 1997.

———. "Minority Problems in Burma Since 1962." In *Military Rule in Burma Since 1962*, ed. F. K. Lehman. Singapore: Marugen Asia, 1981.

———. *Burmese Politics: The Dilemma of National Unity*. New Brunswick: Rutgers University Press, 1980.

———. *Burma: Military Rule and the Politics of Stagnation*. Ithaca, NY: Cornell University Press, 1977.

———. "Part Two: Burma." In *Governments and Politics of Southeast Asia*, ed. George McTurnan Kahin. Ithaca, NY: Cornell University Press, 1969.

Singh, Balwant. *Independence and Democracy in Burma, 1945-1952: The Turbulent Years*, Michigan Papers on South and Southeast Asia No. 40. Ann Arbor, MI: Center for South and Southeast Asian Studies, University of Michigan, 1993.

Sivard, Ruth Leger. *World Military and Social Expenditures 1993*, 15th edition. Washington, DC: World Priorities, 1993.

Smith, Anthony D. "The Ethnic Sources of Nationalism." In *Ethnic Conflict and International Security*, ed. Michael E. Brown. Princeton: Princeton University Press, 1993.

———. *The Ethnic Revival*. Cambridge: Cambridge University Press, 1981.

Smith, Donald Eugene. *Religion and Politics in Burma*. Princeton: Princeton University Press, 1965.

Smith, Martin. "A State of Strife: The Indigenous Peoples of Burma." In *Indigenous Peoples of Asia*, ed. R. H. Barnes, A. Gray and B. Kingsbury. Ann Arbor, MI: Association for Asian Studies, 1995.

Smith, Martin. *Ethnic Groups in Burma: Development, Democracy and Human Rights*. London: Anti-Slavery International, 1994.

———. *Burma: Insurgency and the Politics of Ethnicity*. London: Zed Books, 1993.

Snow, Donald M. *Uncivil Wars: International Security and the New Internal Conflicts*. Boulder, CO: Lynne Rienner Publishers, 1996.

Soguk, Nevzat. "Transnational/Transborder Bodies: Resistance, Accommodation, and Exile in Refugee and Migration Movements on the US-Mexican Border." In *Challenging Boundaries: Global Flows, Territorial Identities*, ed. H. Alker and M. Shapiro. Minneapolis: University of Minnesota Press, 1996.

Sollenberg, Margareta, and Peter Wallenstein. "Major Armed Conflicts." In *SIPRI Yearbook 1997: Armaments, Disarmament and International Security*. Stockholm: Stockholm International Peace Research Institute, 1997.

State Law and Order Restoration Council. "Announcement No. 1/88 of the State Law and Order Restoration Council, 18 September 1988." In *Democracy and Politics in Burma: A Collection of Documents*, ed. Marc Weller. Bangkok and Manerplaw: National Coalition of the Union of Burma, 1993.

Stavenhagen, Rodolfo. *The Ethnic Question: Conflicts, Development, and Human Rights*. Tokyo: United Nations University Press, 1990.

Stein, Barry N. "The Nature of the Refugee Problem." In *Human Rights and the Protection of Refugees Under International Law*, ed. A. Nash. Halifax: Institute for Research on Public Policy, 1988.

Steinberg, David I. "A Void in Myanmar: Civil Society in Burma." In *Strengthening Civil Society in Burma: Possibilities and Dilemmas for International NGOs*, ed. Burma Center Netherlands and Transnational Institute. Chiang Mai: Silkworm Books, 1999.

———. "The Road to Political Recovery: The Salience of Politics in Economics." In *Burma: Prospects for a Democratic Future*, ed. Robert I. Rotberg. Cambridge, MA and Washington, DC: The World Peace Foundation/Harvard Institute for International Development and Brookings Institution Press, 1998.

———. "The Burmese Political Economy: Opportunities and Tensions." In *Burma/Myanmar: Towards the Twenty-First Century: Dynamic of Continuity and Change*, ed. John J. Brandon. Bangkok: Open Society/Chulalongkorn University, 1997.

———. "Constitutional and Political Bases of Minority Insurrections in Burma." In *Armed Separatism in Southeast Asia*, ed. Lim Joo-Jock and Vani S. Singapore: Institute of Southeast Asian Studies, 1984.

———. *Burma: A Socialist Nation in Southeast Asia*. Boulder, CO: Westview Press, 1982.

Steinberg, David Joel, ed. *In Search of Southeast Asia: A Modern History*. Honolulu: University of Hawaii Press, 1987.

Stern, Aaron, and Lawrence W. Crissman. *Maps of International Borders Between Mainland Southeast Asian Countries and Background Information Concerning Population Movements at these Borders*. Bangkok: Asian Research Center for Migration, Chulalongkorn University, 1998.

Stern, Theodor. "A People Between: The Pwo Karen of Western Thailand." In *Ethnic Adaptation and Identity: The Karen on the Thai Frontier with Burma*, ed. Charles F. Keyes. Philadelphia: Institute for the Study of Human Issues, 1979.

Stockholm International Peace Research Institute. *SIPRI Yearbook 1997*. Oxford: Oxford University Press, 1997.

Suchit Bunbongkarn. *State of the Nation: Thailand*. Singapore: Institute of Southeast Asian Studies, 1996.

———. *The Military in Thai Politics, 1981-86*. Singapore: Institute of Southeast Asian Studies, 1987.

Suhrke, Astri. "The 'High Politics' of Population Movements: Migration, State and Civil Society in Southeast Asia." In *International Migration and Security*, ed. Myron Weiner. Boulder, CO: Westview Press, 1993.

Sukhumbhand Paribatra, and Chai-Anan Samudavanija. "Factors Behind Armed Separatism: A Framework for Analysis." In *Armed Separatism in Southeast Asia*, ed. Lim Joo-Jock and Vani S. Singapore: Institute of Southeast Asian Studies, 1984.

Sunait Chutintaranond. *On Both Sides of the Tennasserim Range: History of Siamese-Burmese Relations*. Bangkok: Chulalongkorn University, 1995.

Supang Chanatavanich, et al. *The Lao Returnees in the Voluntary Repatriation Programme from Thailand*, Occasional Paper Series No./003. Bangkok: Indochinese Refugee Information Center, Institute of Asian Studies, Chulalongkorn University, 1992.

Tanet Charoenmuang. "Living Meaningfully with the Wolves: The World and Thailand Toward Burma." In *Burma/Myanmar: Towards the Twenty-First Century: Dynamic of Continuity and Change*, ed. John J. Brandon. Bangkok: Open Society/Chulalongkorn University, 1997.

Taylor, Peter J. *Political Geography: World-Economy, Nation-State and Locality*. New York: Longman Scientific and Technical, 1993.

Taylor, Robert H. "The Military in Myanmar (Burma): What Scope for a New Role?" In *The Military, the State, and Development in Asia and the Pacific*, ed. Viberto Selochan. Boulder, CO: Westview Press, 1991.

———. *The State in Burma*. Honolulu: University of Hawaii Press, 1987.

———. "Government Responses to Armed Communist and Separatist Movements: Burma." In *Governments and Rebellions in Southeast Asia*, ed. Chandran Jeshurun. Singapore: Institute of Southeast Asian Studies, 1985.

———. "Burma." In *Military-Civilian Relations in Southeast Asia*, ed. Zakaria Haji Ahmad and Harold Crouch. Singapore: Oxford University Press, 1985.

———. "Burma's Foreign Relations since the Third Indochina Conflict." In *Southeast Asian Affairs 1983*. Singapore: Institute of Southeast Asian Affairs, 1983.

———. *An Undeveloped State: The Study of Modern Burma's Politics*, Working Paper No. 28. London: Department of Economics and Political Studies, School of African and Oriental Studies, University of London, 1983.

Thakur, Ramesh. "From National to Human Security." In *Asia-Pacific Security: The Economic-Politics Nexus*, ed. Stuart Harris and Andrew Mack. St. Leonards, NSW: Allen & Unwin in association with the Department of International Relations, ANU, 1997.

Thompson, Loren B. "Low-Intensity Conflict: An Overview." In *Low-Intensity Conflict: The Pattern of Warfare in the Modern World*, ed Loren B. Thompson. Toronto: Lexington Books, 1989.

Thompson, Robert. *Defeating Communist Insurgency: Experiences from Malaya and Vietnam*. London: Chatto and Windus, 1966.

Thongchai Winichakul. *Siam Mapped: A History of the Geo-body of a Nation*. Chiang Mai: Silkworm Books, 1994.

Tilley, Charles. *Coercion, Capital, and European States, AD 990-1990*. Oxford: Basil Blackwell, 1990.

Tin Maung Maung Than. "Myanmar: Preoccupation with Regime Survival, National Unity, and Stability." In *Asian Security Practice: Material and Ideational Influences*, ed. Muthiah Alagappa. Stanford: Stanford University Press, 1998.

———. "Myanmar Democraticization: Punctuated Equilibrium or Retrograde Motion?" In *Democratization in Southeast and East Asia*, ed. Anek Laothamatas. Singapore: Institute of Southeast Asian Studies, 1997.

Tinker, Hugh. *The Union of Burma*, 4th edition. London: Oxford University Press, 1967.

Trinh Minh-ha."The Undone Interval, Trinh T. Minh-ha in conversation with Annamaria Morelli." In *The Post-Colonial Question: Common Skies, Divided Horizons*, ed. Iain Chambers and Lidia Curti. London and New York: Routledge, 1996.

Tuathail, Gearoid O. *Critical Geopolitics: The Politics of Writing Global Space*. Minneapolis: University of Minnesota Press, 1996.

Turton, David. "Introduction: War and Ethnicity." In *War and Ethnicity: Global Connections and Local Violence*, ed. David Turton. San Marino: Center for Interdisciplinary Research on Social Stress and University of Rochester Press, 1997.

U Htin Aung. *A History of Burma*. New York: Colombia University Press, 1967.

U Maung Maung. *Burmese Nationalist Movements, 1940-1948*. Honolulu: University of Hawaii Press, 1989.

Umozurike, Oji. "International Dimensions of Humanitarian Law." In *International Dimensions of Humanitarian Law*, ed. Scientific and Cultural Organization United Nations Educational. Geneva: Henry Dunant Institute, 1988.

United Nations Development Programme. "New Dimensions of Human Security." In *Human Development Report 1994*. New York: Oxford University Press, 1994.

United Nations High Commissioner for Refugees. *The State of the World's Refugees 1997-98: A Humanitarian Agenda*. Oxford and New York: Oxford University Press, 1997.

———. *The State of the World's Refugees: In Search of Solutions*. Oxford: Oxford University Press, 1995.

———. *The State of the World's Refugees: The Challenge of Protection*. New York and London: Penguin Books, 1993.

Vitit Muntarbhorn. *The Status of Refugees in Asia*. Oxford: Clarendon Press, 1992.

Voutira, Eftihia, and Barbara Harrell-Bond. "The Search of the Locus of Trust: The Social World of the Refugee Camp." In *Mistrusting Refugees*, ed. E. Valentine Daniel and John Chr. Knudsen. Berkeley: University of California Press, 1995.

Walker, R. B. J., and Saul H. Mendlovitz. "Interrogating State Sovereignty." In *Contending Sovereignties: Redefining Political Community*, ed. R. B. J. Walker and Saul H. Mendlovitz. Boulder, CO and London: Lynne Rienner Publishers, 1990.

Walzer, Michael. "Guerilla War." In *Just and Unjust Wars: A Moral Argument with Historical Illustrations*. New York: Basic Books, 1977.

Warner, Daniel, ed. *Human Rights and Humanitarian Law*. The Hague/Boston/London: Martinus Nijhoff Publishers, 1997.

Warren, Kay B. "Introduction: Revealing Conflicts Across Cultures and Disciplines." In *The Violence Within: Cultural and Political Opposition in Divided Nations*, ed. Kay B. Warren. Boulder, CO: Westview Press, 1993.

Webb, Paul. *Escape from Burma*, Occasional Paper Series No. 2. Darwin: Centre for Southeast Studies, Northern Territory University, 1993.

Weller, Marc, ed. *Democracy and Politics in Burma: A Collection of Documents*. Bangkok and Manerplaw: National Coalition Government of the Union of Burma, 1993.

Wijeyewardene, Gehan. "The Frontiers of Thailand." In *National Identity and its Defenders: Thailand 1939-89*, ed. Craig Reynolds. Melbourne: Centre for Southeast Asian Studies, Monash University, 1991.

Wijeyewardene, Gehan, ed. *Ethnic Groups Across National Boundaries in Mainland Southeast Asia*. Singapore: Institute of Southeast Asian Studies, 1990.

Wilson, Constance M., and Lucien M. Hanks. "Thai-Shan Diplomacy in the 1840s." In *The Burma-Thailand Frontier Over Sixteen Decades: Three Descriptive Documents*, ed. Constance M. Wilson and Lucien M. Hanks. Athens, OH: Center for International Studies, Ohio University, 1985.

Wilson, Thomas M., and Hastings Donnan. "Nation, State and Identity at International Borders." In *Border Identities: Nation and State at International Frontiers*, ed. Thomas M. Wilson and Hastings Donnan. Cambridge: Cambridge University Press, 1998.

Wolters, O. W. *History, Culture, and Region in Southeast Asian Perspectives*. Singapore: Institute of Southeast Asian Studies, 1982.

Woodman, Dorothy. *The Making of Burma*. London: The Cresset Press, 1962.

Zolberg, Aristide R., Astri Suhrke, and Sergio Aguayo. *Escape From Violence: Conflict and the Refugee Crisis in the Developing World*. New York: Oxford University Press, 1989.

DISSERTATIONS

Barry, Lyndal. "The History of the Karen Revolutionary Movement: The Karen National Union and the Fall of Manerplaw." MA thesis, Latrobe University, 1995.

Callahan, Mary. "The Origins of Military Rule in Burma." PhD dissertation, Cornell University, 1996.

Fink, Christina Lammert. "Imposing Communities: Pwo Karen Experiences in Northwestern Thailand." PhD dissertation, University of California at Berkeley, 1994.

Foster, Brian Lee. "Ethnicity and Economy: The Case of the Mons in Thailand." PhD dissertation, University of Michigan, 1972.

French, Lindsay Cole. "Enduring Holocaust, Surviving History: Displaced Cambodians on the Thai-Cambodian Border, 1989-1991." PhD dissertation, Harvard University, 1994.

Harris, David W. "The Indochinese Refugee Problem in Thailand: A Political Analysis." PhD dissertation, George Washington University, 1994.

Jacobson, Karen. "The Response of Third World Governments to Mass Influxes of Refugees: A Comparative Policy Analysis of Thailand and Zimbabwe." PhD dissertation, Massachusetts Institute of Technology, 1992.

Kramer, Tom. "Thai Foreign Policy Towards Burma, 1987-1993." MA thesis, Universiteit van Amsterdam, 1994.

Maung Aung Myoe. "The Counterinsurgency in Myanmar: The Government's Response to the Burma Communist Party." PhD dissertation, Australian National University, 1999.

Niyaphan Pholwàddhana. "Ethnic Relations in Thailand: The Mon-Thai Relationship." PhD dissertation, University of Kansas, 1986.

Purcell, Marc. "Putting the Genie Back in the Bottle: Reflections on Burmese Student Activism: 1921-1938 and 1954-1968." MA thesis, Monash University, 1996.

Sulistiyanto, Priyambudi. "Burma: The Politics of an Uncertain Transition, 1988-1994." MA thesis, Flinders University, 1995.

JOURNAL ARTICLES

Adas, Michael. "Imperialist Rhetoric and Modern Historiography: The Case of Lower Burma Before and After Conquest." *Journal of Southeast Asian Studies* 3,2 (1972).

Allden, Kathleen, et al. "Burmese Political Dissidents in Thailand: Trauma and Survival among Young Adults in Exile." *American Journal of Public Health* 86,11 (1996).

Anonymous opinion. "The UNHCR Note on International Protection You Won't See." *International Journal of Refugee Law* 9,2 (1997).

Ashton, William. "Burma's Armed Forces: Preparing for the 21st Century." *Jane's Intelligence Review* 10,1 (1998).

Aung-Thwin, Maureen. "Burmese Days." *Foreign Affairs* 68,2 (1989).

Aung-Thwin, Michael. "Hierachy and Order in Pre-Colonial Burma." *Journal of Southeast Asian Studies* 15,2 (1984).

Ba Han. "The Emergence of the Burmese Nation." *Journal of the Burma Research Society* 48 (1965).

Badgley, John. "Myanmar in 1993: A Watershed Year." *Asian Survey* 34,2 (1994).

Ball, Desmond. "SIGINT Strengths Form a Vital Part of Burma's Military Muscle." *Jane's Intelligence Review* 10,3 (1998).

———. "Strategic Culture in the Asia-Pacific Region." *Security Studies* 3,1 (1993).

Becka, Jan. "Book Review: Taingyingtha Lumyomya Ayei hnin 1947 Acheihkan Upadei (The Nationalities Issue and the 1947 Constitution)." *Journal of Southeast Asian Studies* 24,2 (1993).

———. "The Military and the Struggle for Democracy in Burma: The Presentation of the Political Upheaval of 1988 in the Official Burmese Press." *Archiv Orientalni* 61,1 (1993).

Bennett, Jon. "Forced Migration Within National Borders: The IDP Agenda." *Forced Migration Review* 1 (1998).

Bhabba, Jacqueline. "Embodied Rights: Gender Persecution, State Sovereignty, and Refugees." *Public Culture* 9,1 (1996).

Birsel, Robert. "New Winners in Burma's Teak War." *Cultural Survival Quarterly* 13,4 (1989).

Bose, Sugata. "Safeguards for Minorities Versus Sovereignty of Nations." *The Fletcher Forum of World Affairs* 19,1 (1995).

Bowles, Edith. "From Village to Camp: Refugee Camp Life in Transition on the Thailand-Burma Border." *Forced Migration Review* 2 (1998).

Bronee, Stern A. "The History of the Comprehensive Plan of Action." *International Journal of Refugee Law* 5,4 (1993)

Burma Watcher. "Burma in 1988: There Came a Whirlwind." *Asian Survey* 29,2 (1989).

Busynski, Leszek. "Thailand and Myanmar: The Perils of 'Constructive Engagement'." *The Pacific Review* 11,2 (1998).

Callahan, Mary P. "Democracy in Burma: The Lessons of History." *Analysis* 9,3 (1998).

———. "Building an Army: The Early Years of the Tatmadaw." *Burma Debate* 4,3 (1997).

———. "Myanmar in 1994: New Dragon or Still Dragging?" *Asian Survey* 35,2 (1995).

Caouette, Therese. "Burmese Asylum Seekers in Thailand." *Refugee Participation Network* 13 (June 1992).

Chimni, B. S. "The Geopolitics of Refugee Studies: A View from the South." *Journal of Refugee Studies* 11,4 (1998).

———. "The Meaning of the Words and the Role of the UNHCR in Voluntary Repatriation." *International Journal of Refugee Law* 5,3 (1993).

Chowdhury, Subrata Roy. "A Response to the Refugee Problems in Post Cold War Era: Some Existing and Emerging Norms of International Law." *International Journal of Refugee Law* 7,1 (1995).

Clay, Jason. "States, Nations, and Resources: An Interdependent Relationship?" *The Fletcher Forum of World Affairs* 19,1 (1995).

Clemens, Walter C., Jr. and J. David Singer. "The Human Cost of War: Modern Warfare Kills More Civilians than Soldiers." *Scientific American* 282,6 (2000).

Cohen, Roberta. "Protecting the Internally Displaced." *World Refugee Survey* (1996).

Das, Veena. "Anthropological Knowledge and Collective Violence." *Anthropology Today* 1,3 (1985).

Davis, Anthony. "Thailand Tackles Border Security." *Jane's Intelligence Review*, March 2000.

Deng, Francis M. "The International Protection of the Internally Displaced." *International Journal of Refugee Law*, Special Issue (July 1995).

———. "Internally Displaced Persons." *International Journal of Refugee Law* 6,2 (1994).

Doty, Roxanne Lynn. "Immigration and the Politics of Security." *Security Dialogue* 30,3 (1999).

———. "The Double-Writing of Statecraft: Exploring State Responses to Illegal Immigration." *Alternatives* 21,2 (1996).

Dowty, Alan, and Gil Loescher. "Refugee Flows as Grounds for International Action." *International Security* 21,1 (1996).

Falk, Richard. "An Alternative to Geopolitics." *Peace Review* 11,3 (1999).

Farer, Tom J. "How the International System Copes with Involuntary Migration: Norms, Institutions and State Practice." *Human Rights Quarterly* 17,1 (1995).

Fieman, Colin Aldrin. "A State's Duty to Protect Refugees Under Customary International Law: A Case Study of Thailand and the Cambodian 'Displaced Persons'." *Columbia Human Rights Review* 21,1 (1989).

Gallagher, Dennis. "The Evolution of the International Refugee System." *International Migration Review* 23,3 (1989).

Goodwin-Gill, Guy S. "Who to Protect, How . . . , and the Future?" *International Journal of Refugee Law* 9,1 (1997).

———. "Asylum: The Law and Politics of Change." *International Journal of Refugee Law* 7,1 (1995).

———. "The Language of Protection." *International Journal of Refugee Law* 1,1 (1989).

———. "International Law and the Detention of Refugees and Asylum Seekers." *International Migration Review* 20,2 (1986).

Green, Linda. "Fear as a Way of Life." *Cultural Anthropology* 9,2 (1994).

Grundy-Warr, Carl. "Coexistant Borderlands and Intra-State Conflicts in Mainland Southeast Asia." *Singapore Journal of Tropical Geography* 14,1 (1993).

Grundy-Warr, Carl, Rita King, and Gary Risser. "Cross-border Migration, Trafficking and the Sex Industry: Thailand and its Neighbours." *Boundary and Security Bulletin* 4,1 (1996).

Gurr, Ted Robert. "Peoples Against States: Ethnopolitical Conflict and the Changing World System." *International Studies Quarterly* 38,3 (1994).

Harrell-Bond, Barbara. "Repatriation: Under What Conditions is it the Most Desirable Solution for Refugees? An Agenda for Research." *African Studies Review* 32,1 (1989).

Hathaway, James C., "Can International Refugee Law be Made Relevant Again?" *World Refugee Survey* (1996).

———. "New Directions to Avoid Hard Problems: The Distortion of the Palliative Role of Refugee Protection." *Journal of Refugee Studies* 8,3 (1995).

Hazelton, Joanna. "Mon Refugees Flee Halockhani Camp." *Thai-Yunnan Project Newsletter* 26 (September 1994).

———. "Some Observations on the Current Situation of Mon Refugees on the Thai-Burmese Border." *Thai-Yunnan Project Newsletter* 24 (March 1994).

Helton, Arthur C. "Displacement and Human Rights: Current Dilemmas in Refugee Protection." *Journal of International Affairs* 47,2 (1994).

———. "Refugee Determination under the Comprehensive Plan of Action: Overview and Assessment." *International Journal of Refugee Law* 5,4 (1993).

———. "What is Refugee Protection?" *International Journal of Refugee Law*, Special Issue (1990).

———. "Asylum and Refugee Protection in Thailand." *International Journal of Refugee Law* 1,1 (1989).

Hsaingt Seetsar. "Facets of a Buddhist Army: Part II." *Burma Issues* 8,8 (1998).

———. "Facets of a Buddhist Army: Part I." *Burma Issues* 8,7 (1998).

Innes-Brown, Marc, and Mark J. Valencia. "Thailand's Resource Diplomacy in Indochina and Myanmar." *Contemporary Southeast Asia* 14,4 (1993).

Jacquin-Berdal, Dominique. "Ethnic Wars and International Intervention." *Millennium: Journal of International Studies* 27,1 (1998).

"Special Issue: Refugee Studies and the Refugee Regime in Transition," *Journal of Refugee Studies* 11,4 (1998).

Khatharya Um. "Thailand and the Dynamics of Economic and Security Complex in Mainland Southeast Asia." *Contemporary Southeast Asia* 13,3 (1991).

Ko Ko Maung. "Benchmarks and Forced Labour." *Thai-Yunnan Project Newsletter* 29 (June 1995).

Kristof, Ladis. "The Nature of Frontiers and Boundaries." *Annals of the Association of American Geographers* 49,3 (1959).

Kusama Snitwongse. "Thailand in 1994: The Trials of Transition." *Asian Survey* 35,2 (1995).

Landgren, Karin. "The Future of Refugee Protection: Four Challenges." *Journal of Refugee Studies* 11,4 (1998).

Lang, Hazel. "Refugees on the Thai-Burma Border: An Update." *Thai-Yunnan Project Newsletter* 34 (September 1997).

————. "Women as Refugees: Perspectives from Burma." *Cultural Survival Quarterly* 19,1 (1995).

Leach, Edmund. "The Frontiers of 'Burma'." *Comparative Studies in Society and History* 3,1 (1960).

Lee Yong Leng. "Ethnic Differences and the State-minority Relationship in Southeast Asia." *Ethnic and Racial Studies* 6,2 (1983).

Levin, Burton. "Reminiscences and Reflections on 8-8-88." *Burma Debate* 5,3 (1998).

Lieberman, Victor B. "Political Consolidation in Burma." *Journal of Asian History* 30,2 (1996).

————. "Reinterpreting Burmese History." *Comparative Studies in Society and History* 29,1 (1987).

————. "Ethnic Politics in Eighteenth-Century Burma." *Modern Asian Studies* 12,3 (1978).

Linklater, Andrew. "The Evolving Spheres of International Justice." *International Affairs* 75,3 (1999).

Loescher, Gil. "The International Refugee Regime: Stretched to the Limit?" *Journal of International Affairs* 47,2 (1994).

Malkki, Liisa. "National Geographic: The Rooting of Peoples and the Territorialization of National Identity Among Scholars and Refugees." *Cultural Anthropology* 7,1 (1992).

Marx, Reinhardt. "Non-refoulement, Access to Procedures, and Responsibility for Determining Refugee Claims." *International Journal of Refugee Law* 7,3 (1995).

Mason, Elisa. "Sources of International Refugee Law: A Bibliography." *International Journal of Refugee Law* 8,4 (1996).

Maung Tha Hla. "Ethnic Communalism in Thailand and Burma." *Journal of the Burma Research Society* 56,1/2 (1973).

Mills, Kurt. "Permeable Borders: Human Migration and Sovereignty." *Global Society* 10,2 (1996).

Moksha Yitri. "The Crisis in Burma: Back from the Heart of Darkness?" *Asian Survey* 29,6 (1989).

Moller, Kay. "Cambodia and Burma: The ASEAN Way Ends Here." *Asian Survey* 38,12 (1998).

Morris, Nicholas. "Protection Dilemmas and UNHCR's Response: A Personal View from Within UNHCR." *International Journal of Refugee Law* 9,3 (1997).

Mya Maung. "Burma's Economic Performance Under Military Rule: An Assessment." *Asian Survey* 38,6 (1997).

———. "The Burma Road from the Union of Burma to Myanmar." *Asian Survey* 30,6 (1990).

Nietschmann, Bernard. "The Third World War." *Cultural Survival Quarterly* (Special Edition on "Militarization and Indigenous Peoples") 11,3 (1987).

Ogata, Sadako. "Statement by Mrs Sadako Ogata, United Nations High Commissioner for Refugees to the 53rd Session of the United Nations Commission on Human Rights (Geneva, April 1, 1997)." *International Journal of Refugee Law* 9,3 (1997).

———. "Interview. The Evolution of UNHCR, Mrs. Sadako Ogata, U. N. High Commissioner for Refugees." *Journal of International Affairs* 47,2 (1994).

Opondo, Enoch O. "Refugee Repatriation During Conflict: Grounds For Skepticism." *Disasters* 16,4 (1992).

Perry, Peter John. "Military Rule in Burma: A Geographical Analysis." *Crime, Law and Social Change* 19,1 (1993).

Pettman, Jan Jindy. "Nationalism and After." *Review of International Studies* 24,speical issue (December 1998).

Rajah, Ananda. "The Halockhani Incident and the Redefinition of a Boundary Issue between Burma and Thailand." *International Boundary and Security Bulletin* 2,3 (1994).

Roberts, Adam. "More Refugees, Less Asylum: A Regime in Transformation." *Journal of Refugee Studies* 11,4 (1998).

Roy Chowdhury, Subrata. "A Reponse to the Refugee Problems in Post Cold War Era: Some Existing and Emerging Norms of International Law." *International Journal of Refugee Law* 7,1 (1995).

Ruiz, Hiram A. "Emergencies: International Response to Refugee Flows and Complex Emergencies." *International Journal of Refugee Law* special issue (Summer 1995).

S. Chantavanich, and P. Rabe. "Thailand and the Indochinese Refugees: Fifteen Years of Compromise and Uncertainty." *Southeast Asia Journal of Social Sciences* 18,1 (1990).

Sandhaussen, Ulf. "Indonesia's New Order: A Model for Myanmar?" *Asian Survey* 35,8 (1995).

Scheper-Hughes, Nancy, and Margaret M. Lock. "The Mindful Body." *Medical Anthropology Quarterly* 1,1 (1987).

Selth, Andrew. "Burma's Intelligence Apparatus." *Intelligence and National Security* 13,4 (1998).

————. "Burma's Expanding Armed Forces: National Defence or National Disgrace?" *Current Affairs Bulletin* 73,3 (1996).

————. "The Myanmar Army Since 1988: Acquisitions and Adjustments." *Contemporary Southeast Asia* 17,3 (1995).

————. "Burma: 'Hidden Paradise' or Paradise Lost?" *Current Affairs Bulletin* 68,6 (1991).

————. "Race and Resistance in Burma, 1942-45." *Modern Asian Studies* 20,3 (1986).

Shacknove, Andrew. "From Asylum to Containment." *International Journal of Refugee Law* 5,4 (1993).

————. "Who is a Refugee?" *Ethics* 95,2 (1985).

Shapiro, Michael J. "Moral Geographies and the Ethics of Post-Sovereignty." *Public Culture* 6,3 (1994).

Silverstein, Josef. "Burma's Uneven Struggle." *Journal of Democracy* 7,4 (1996).

————. "Civil War and Rebellion in Burma." *Journal of Southeast Asian Studies* 21,1 (1990).

Smith, Anthony D. "Ethnic Nationalism and the Plight of Minorities." *Journal of Refugee Studies* 7,2/3 (1994).

————. "The Problem of National Identity: Ancient, Medieval and Modern?" *Ethnic and Racial Studies* 17,3 (1994).

Steinberg, David I. "Myanmar in 1992: Plus Ca Change . . . ?" *Asian* Survey 33,2 (1993).

————. "Myanmar in 1991: The Miasma in Burma." *Asian Survey* 32,2 (1992).

————. "International Rivalries in Burma: The Rise of Economic Competition." *Asian Survey* 30,6 (1990).

Stern, Aaron. "Thailand's Illegal Labor Migrants." *Asian Migrant* 9,4 (1996).

Suhrke, Astri. "Human Security and the Interests of States." *Security Dialogue* 30,3 (1999).

Surpong Posayanond. "Thailand's Policy on Myanmar Displaced Persons: The Challenges of Humanitarian Assistance." *UNHCR Newsletter*, Regional Office of Thailand, Cambodia and Vietnam (March 2000).

Takahashi, Saul. "The *UNHCR* Handbook on Voluntary Repatriation." *International Journal of Refugee Law* 9,4 (1997).

Tarzi, Shah M. "The Nation-State, Victim Groups and Refugees." *Racial Studies* 14,4 (1991).

Taylor, Robert H. "Myanmar: Military Politics and the Prospects for Democratisation." *Asian Affairs: Journal of the Royal Society for Asian Affairs* 29,1 (1998).

———. "Disaster or Release: J. S. Furnivall and the Bankruptcy of Burma." *Modern Asian Studies* 29,1 (1995).

———. "The Evolving Military Role in Burma." *Current History* 89 (1990).

———. "Perceptions of Ethnicity in the Politics of Burma." *Southeast Asian Journal of Social Science* 10,1 (1982).

Teitelbaum, Michael S. "Immigration, Refugees, and Foreign Policy." *International Organization* 38,3 (1984).

Thomas, Dorothy Q., and Regan E. Ralph. "Rape in War: Challenging the Tradition of Impunity." *SAIS Review: A Journal of International Affairs* 14,1 (1994).

Thomson, Curtis N. "Political Stability and Minority Groups in Burma." *The Geographical Review* 85,3 (1995).

Tin Maung Maung Than. "Burma's National Security and Defence Posture." *Contemporary Southeast Asia* 11,3 (1989).

Tint Way, Raymond. "Burmese Culture, Personality and Mental Health." *Australian and New Zealand Journal of Pyschiatry* 19 (1985).

UNHCR Executive Committee. "General Conclusion on International Protection, No. 81 (XLVIII), 1997." *International Journal of Refugee Law* 10,1/2 (1998).

UNHCR, Centre for Documentation on Refugees. "Special Issue on Refugee Women." *Refugee Survey Quarterly* 14, special issue (Summer 1995).

UNHCR. *Refugees*. Special Edition: The Internally Displaced, Geneva, 1996.

Vandergeest, Peter, and Nancy Lee Peluso. "Territorialization and State Power in Thailand." *Theory and Society* 24,3 (1995).

Wallenstein, Peter, and Margareta Sollenberg. "The End of International War? Armed Conflict 1989-95." *Journal of Peace Research* 33,3 (1996).

Watts, Michael. "Space for Everything (A Commentary)." *Cultural Anthropology* 7,1 (1992).

Weiner, Myron. "Bad Neighbours, Bad Neighborhoods: An Inquiry into the Causes of Refugee Flows." *International Security* 21,1 (1996).

———. "Ethics, National Sovereignty and the Control of Immigration." *International Migration Review* 30,1 (1996).

———. "Security, Stability, and International Migration." *International Security* 17,3 (1992/93).

Wichert, Tim. "Human Rights, Refugees and Displaced Persons: The 1997 UN Commission on Human Rights (Geneva, 10 March-18 April 1997)." *International Journal of Refugee Law* 9,3 (1997).

Wickham-Crowley, Timothy P. "Terror and Guerilla Warfare in Latin America, 1956-1970." *Comparative Studies in Society and History* 32,2 (1990).

Wijeyewardene, Gehan. "More on Thai Borders." *Thai-Yunnan Project Newsletter* 16 (March 1992).

Wood, William B. "Forced Migration: Local Conflicts and International Dilemmas." *Annals of the Association of American Geographers* 84,4 (1994).

Xenos, Nicholas. "Refugees: The Modern Political Condition." *Alternatives* 18,4 (1993).

Yitri, Moksha. "The Crisis in Burma: Back from the Heart of Darkness?" *Asian Survey* 29,6 (1989).

Zo Tum Hmung. "Burma: The Judicial Rights of the Idingenous Peoples and the Relation to the State and Non-Indigenous Population." *Indigenous Affairs* 4 (1995).

NEWSPAPER AND MAGAZINE ARTICLES

"139 Refugees Unwilling to Cross Over into Burma." *Bangkok Post*, October 11, 1993.

"Army Official Calls Mon 'Illegal Immigrants'." *The Nation*, August 27, 1994.

"Army Told to Protect Border at all Costs." *Bangkok Post*, March 24, 1998.

"Border Changes Forces Burmese, Thai Conflicts." *The Nation*, February 8, 2000.

"Burma: The Students Struggle On." *Asiaweek*, 1988.

"Burma to Seek Talks on Three Pagodas Dispute." *The Nation*, February 28, 1990.

"Burmese Poised to Strike at Karens, Mons." *The Nation Review*, November 29, 1984.

"Burmese Troops Gun Down Karenni Refugees." *The Nation*, January 4, 1997.

"Burmese Troops 'Live Off Land'." *Far Eastern Economic Review*, May 18, 2000.

"Intelligence Work to be Upgraded." *Bangkok Post*, February 24, 1997.

"Maneeloy to be Shut Down Next Year." *The Nation*, September 29, 2000.

"Military Officer to Visit Area." *The Nation*, August 21, 1994.

"Mon 'Illegal Immigrants' Urged to Return Home." *Bangkok Post*, August 13, 1994.

"Mon Refugees in Fear After Receiving Marching Orders." *The Nation*, October 12, 1993.

"National Reconciliation Achieved through Sincerity, Mutual Understanding." *The New Light of Myanmar*, June 30, 1995.

"New Deadline Set for Return to Burma." *The Nation*, August 20, 1994.

"NSC Admits Security Lapse Led to Refugee Camp Attack." *Bangkok Post*, March 21, 1998.

"Officers Reassure Mon Refugees on Return to Burma." *The Nation*, August 23, 1994.

"Rebel Faction Running Campaign of Fear Among Karen Refugees." *Bangkok Post*, February 15, 1995.

"Situation of Nation, Tatmadaw Clarified to Military Officers, Other Ranks." *The New Light of Myanmar*, February 20, 1998.

"Special Army Force Tightens Noose on Khun Sa's Empire." *The Nation*, January 13, 1995.

"Task Force Accuses Burmese Junta of Border Mayhem." *The Nation*, March 3, 1995.

"Thai Army Kills 7 Rangoon Allies." *The Nation*, March 18, 1998.

"Mon Base Overrun in Fierce Fighting." *Bangkok Post*, February 12, 1990.

"UN Chief Shocked at Camp Conditions." *Associated Press*, October 17, 2000.

New Light of Myanmar, March 29, 1998.

Anonymous, "Myanmar's Upstream Sector Hobbled by Controversy." *Oil and Gas Journal*, June 26, 2000.

Don Pathan and Marisa Chimphrabha. "Burma Agrees to UNHCR Monitor." *The Nation*, March 17, 2000.

Embassy of the Union of Myanmar. "Cordial Meeting Over Border." *The Nation*, February 21, 1995.

Ghosh, Amitav. "A Reporter at Large: Burma." *The New Yorker*, August 12, 1996.

Grilz, Almerigo, and Gian Micalessin. "Letter from Wangkha." *Far Eastern Economic Review*, November 1, 1984.

Grundy-Warr, Carl. "Shallow View of Security Ignores Border Realities." *The Nation*, February 20, 2000.

Karniol, Robert. "Burma Creates Improved Regional C2 Structure." *Jane's Defence Weekly*, May 29, 1996.

———. "Briefing: Thailand." *Jane's Defence Weekly*, September 9, 1995.

Korkhet Chanthalertlak. "Crackdown on Mons Sours Ties." *The Nation*, December 22, 1991.

Lintner, Bertil. "Burma: Velvet Glove." *Far Eastern Economic Review*, May 7, 1998.

———. "Building New Bridges with a Former Foe." *Jane's Defence Weekly*, September 9, 1995.

———. "Soft Option on Hardwood: Rangoon to Scrap Thai Logging Deals on Border." *Far Eastern Economic Review*, July 22, 1993.

———. "Neighbours' Interests: China and Thailand to Mediate in Burma's Civil War." *Far Eastern Economic Review*, April 1, 1993.

——. "Collective Insecurity: Series of Raids, Incursions Increase Border Tension." *Far Eastern Economic Review*, December 3, 1992.

——. "Less Than Welcome: Thais Get Tough with Fugitive Burmese Students." *Far Eastern Economic Review*, January 12, 1989.

——. "A Darkening Scene: Military Government Resorts to Repression to Curb Dissent." *Far Eastern Economic Review*, November 24, 1988.

——. "Running for Cover: Students Flee Cities in Wake of Army Suppression." *Far Eastern Economic Review*, September 7, 1988.

——. "Backs to the Wall." *Far Eastern Economic Review*, September 6, 1984.

Maha Thamun. "Taphet Naing-Ngan or Next-Door Country." *Working People's Daily*, March 7, 1993.

Marisa Chimprabha. "Red Cross Access to Burmese Labour Camp 'Positive'." *The Nation*, March 11, 2000.

McBeth, John. "A Test in the West. A General Says that Recent Advances by Burmese Forces Poses a Potential Security Threat to Thailand." *Far Eastern Economic Review*, August 18, 1983.

McDonald, Hamish. "Partners in Plunder." *Far Eastern Economic Review*, Febuary 22, 1990.

—— "The Generals Buy Time." *Far Eastern Economic Review*, February 22, 1990.

Nussara Sawatsawan. "Ogata Accepts Invitation." *Bangkok Post*, July 25, 1998.

Paisal Sricharatchanaya. "This Year's Big Push." *Far Eastern Economic Review*, May 10, 1984.

——. "A Lack-lustre Line-up." *Far Eastern Economic Review*, August 18, 1988.

Praisal Sricharatchanya, and Bertil Lintner. "Burma: Resentment Boils Over." *Far Eastern Economic Review*, March 31, 1998.

Preecha Srisathan. "Call for Border Opening." *Bangkok Post*, October 5, 1998.

——. "New Drive to Promote Regional Trade Links." *Bangkok Post*, April 5, 1998.

Said, Edward W. "The Mind of Winter: Reflections on Life in Exile." *Harpers*, 269,1612 (September 1984).

"Sanctions Hurts People: Unocal Tried to Defend a Controversial Project." *Asiaweek*, February 21, 1997.

Sithu Aung. "Internal Insurgency and Outside Interference." *Working People's Daily*, March 8, 1993.

Supamart Kasem, and Wassana Nanuam. "Reprisal Raid Kills 10 Karens." *Bangkok Post*, March 18, 1998.

Supunnabul Swannaku. "Thai-Burma Link Could Speed Exports." *The Nation*, May 17, 1997.

Tasker, Rodney. "Last Refuge: Report Outlines the Size of Country's Migrant Population." *Far Eastern Economic Review*, December 16, 1993.

Tasker, Rodney, and Bertil Lintner. "Second Coming. New Wave of Burmese Refugees Threatens Thailand." *Far Eastern Economic Review*, July 15, 1993.

———. "Burma: Food Before Fighting." *Far Eastern Economic Review*, October 20, 1988.

———. "Food Before Fighting: Dissident Students Regroup with Rebels on the Border." *Far Eastern Economic Review*, October 20, 1988.

Thammasak Lamaiphan, et al. "Burmese Dissidents Face 'Crackdown'." *The Nation*, November 13, 1990.

Thompson, Steve. "The New Burma Road Builders." *The Nation*, April 25, 1997.

Vatikiotis, Michael. "Border Burdens: Insurgent Defeat Poses Problems for Thai Army." *Far Eastern Economic Review*, March 6, 1997.

Wassana Nanuam. "Military Reshuffle Imminent." *Bangkok Post*, March 17, 1997.

———. "Someone Must Take on Some Responsibility." *The Nation*, May 7, 1995.

OFFICIAL SOURCES AND UNPUBLISHED MATERIAL

UN Commission on Human Rights and its Special Rapporteur on the situation in Myanmar (reports submitted since 1992);

UN General Assembly (since 1991); and the good offices of the Secretary-General (since 1993).

A Tatmadaw Researcher. *A Concise History of Myanmar and the Tatmadaw's Role, 1948-1988, Volume 1*. Yangon: News and Periodicals Enterprise of the Ministry of Information of the Government of the Union of Myanmar, 1991.

ABSDF Documentation and Research Center, *Terror in the South*. Bangkok: ABSDF, November 1997.

Amnesty International. *Myanmar: Atrocities in the Shan State*, ASA 16/05/98. London: Amnesty International, 1998.

———. *Thailand: Burmese and Other Asylum-seekers at Risk*, ASA 39/02/94. London: Amnesty International, 1994.

———. *Thailand: Concerns about Treatment of Burmese Refugees*, ASA 39/15/91. London: Amnesty International, 1991.

Article 19. *Paradise Lost? The Suppression of Environmental Rights and Freedom of Expression in Burma*. London: Article 19, 1994.

Asia Watch. *Abuses Against Burmese Refugees in Thailand*, Vol. 4, 7. New York: Asia Watch, 1992.

Aung San Suu Kyi. "Towards a True Refugee." Eighth Joyce Pearce Memorial Lecture delivered by Dr. Michael Aris on May 19, 1993 at the University of Oxford, Queen Elizabeth House.

Batdanta Palita. *The Mon Leader and the Golden Jubilee of Mon National Day*. Bangkok: n.p., 1997 [published in Mon language].

Burma Ethnic Research Group. *Forgotten Victims of a Hidden War: Internally Displaced Karen in Burma.* Chiang Mai: Friedrich Naumann Foundation, 1998.

Burma Frontier Areas Committee of Enquiry. *Report Presented to His Majesty's Government in the United Kingdom and the Government of Burma, volume 1.* Rangoon: Superintendent, Government Printing and Stationery, 1947.

Burmese Border Consortium. *Refugee Relief Programme: Programme Report for the Period January to June 2000.* Bangkok: Burmese Border Consortium, August 2000.

————. *Burmese Relief Programme Report for Period January to June 1997.* Bangkok: Burmese Border Consortium, 1997.

Chalerm Phromlert, Deputy Permanent Secretary of the Ministry of Interior. "Information from the MOI Regarding Policies for NGOs Dealing with Refugees and Displaced Persons in Thailand." Unpublished statement, Bangkok, May 23, 1994.

First Army Regional Commander Lt.-Gen. Chetta Thanacharo, Radio Thailand Network, September 9, 1994, quoted and translated by the Foreign Broadcast Information Service, FBIS-EAS-94-177, September 13, 1994.

Colonel Kyaw Thein. "An Analysis of the Return of the Armed Groups of National Races to the Legal Fold and the Renunciation of Armed Insurrection." In *Symposium on Socio-Economic Factors Contributing to National Consolidation.* Yangon: Ministry of Defence and Office of Strategic Studies, 1996.

Committee for the Promotion of People's Struggle in Monland. "Regular Use of Forced Labour/Porterage." Unpublished field report, Sangkhlaburi, August 15, 1995.

————. *Newsletter* 2,3 (October 1994).
————. *Newsletter* (August 1993).
————. "Ye-Tavoy Railway Construction." Unpublished field report, Bangkok, April 1994.

Committee on Foreign Affairs, U. S. House of Representatives. *Hearing and Markup Before the Subcommittees on Human Rights and International Organizations and on Asian and Pacific Affairs of the Committee on Foreign Affairs, House of Representatives, 101st Congress.* Washington, DC: U.S. Government Printing Office, 1989.

Conway, Daniel E., UNHCR Representative in Thailand. "Burmese Students and the Safe Area Established by the Royal Thai Government: Statement to the Parliamentary Committee on Justice and Human Rights." Unpublished statement, Bangkok, February, 18, 1993.

————. "Burmese Students Committee for Handling of [the] Closed Camp." Unpublished statement, Bangkok.

Coordinating Committee for Services to Displaced Persons in Thailand. "Notes of a Meeting of Mon Displaced Persons in Kanchanaburi Province." Unpublished meeting minutes, December 13, 1984.

————. "Notes on a Meeting Regarding Karen Situation, November 16, 1984." Unpublished meeting minutes.

———. "Karen Emergency: Notes on a meeting in Mae Sot, August 10, 1984." Unpublished meeting minutes.

Deng, Francis M. "Internal Displacement: A Global Overview," paper presented to "Workshop on Internal Displacement in Asia," Bangkok, February 22-24, 2000.

Dunford, Jack. "The Thai-Burmese Border: The Need for Humanitarian Assistance." Unpublished paper presented to the Australian Council for Overseas Aid (ACFOA) Burma Seminar, Sydney, May 28, 1993.

EarthRights International. *EarthRights News* 1,4 (1996).

EarthRights International (ERI) and Southeast Asian Information Network (SAIN). *Total Denial: A Report on the Yadana Pipeline Project in Burma.* Chiang Mai: ERI and SAIN, 1996.

Em Marta, Karen National Union, and Democratic Alliance of Burma. "The War of Annihilation against the Indigenous Peoples of Burma and the Raping of their Heritage Forests." Statement presented to the United Nations Working Group on Indigenous Peoples, Geneva, July 23, 1990.

Embassy of the Union of Myanmar, Bangkok. "New Mon State Party Becomes 15th Group to Realize True Attitude of the Government." *News Bulletin, No. 16/95,* July 7, 1995.

———. "Secretary (2) Lieutenant-General Tin Oo Visits Kayin State." *New Bulletin, No. 4/95,* March 3, 1995.

Enriquez, Major C. M. *Races of Burma (Handbooks for the Indian Army).* Delhi: Manager of Publications (Government of India), 1933.

"Further Reportage on Capture of Mon Headquarters," broadcast by Burmese state-run radio, February 13, 1990, recorded and translated by the Foreign Broadcast Information Service, *Daily Report: Southeast Asia,* FBIS-EAS-90-030.

Government of the Union of Burma. *Burma and the Insurrections.* Rangoon: Government of the Union of Burma, 1949.

Government of the Union of Burma, Director of Information. *Is Trust Vindicated? A Chronicle of the Various Accomplishments of the Government headed by General Ne Win During the Period of Tenure from November, 1958 to February 6, 1960.* Rangoon: Director of Information, Government of the Union of Burma, 1960.

Lieutenant-Colonel Hla Min. *Political Situation of Myanmar and its Role in the Region.* Yangon: Office of Strategic Studies, Ministry of Defense, August 2000.

Human Rights Watch/Asia. *Burma/Thailand. Unwanted and Unprotected: Burmese Refugees in Thailand.* New York: Human Rights Watch, 1998.

Images Asia and Borderline Video. *A Question of Security: A Retrospective on Cross-border Attacks on Thailand's Refugee and Civilian Communities along the Burmese Border since 1995.* Chiang Mai: Images Asia and Borderline Video, May 1998.

Immigration Act 1979. In *Royal Thai Gazette,* Vol 33, Nos 17-18, 20, June 30, 1979.

International Labour Organization. *Forced Labour in Myanmar (Burma), Report of the Commission of Inquiry appointed under Article 26 of the Constitution of the International Labour Organization to Examine the Observance by Myanmar of the Forced Labour Convention, 1930 (No. 29).* Geneva: ILO, 1998.

Kachadphai Burusapatana, Deputy Secretary of the National Security Council. "Displaced Persons and Illegal Immigrants." Presentation to workshop on the 1951 Convention Relating to the Status of Refugees. Cha-am, Thailand, November 6-9, 1992.

Karen Human Rights Group. "Dooplaya Under the SPDC: Further Developments in the SPDC Occupation of South-central Karen State." *KHRG No. 98-09,* 1998.

———. "Attacks on Karen Refugee Camps: 1998." *KHRG No. 98-04,* May 29, 1998.

———. "An Independent Report by the Karen Human Rights Group." *KHRG No. 97-07,* May 2, 1997.

———. "Attacks on Karen Refugee Camps." *KHRG No. 97-05,* March 18, 1997.

———. "Effects of the Gas Pipeline Project." *KHRG No. 96-21,* May 23, 1996.
———. "Inside the DKBA." *KHRG No. 96-14,* March 31, 1996.
———. "Ye-Tavoy Railway Area: An Update." *KHRG No. 95-26,* July 31, 1995.
———. "Summary of Types of Forced Portering." *KHRG No. 95-13,* April 11, 1995.

———. "Interview with an IDC Deportee" (Thailand, 1994).
———. "Torture of Karen Women by SLORC." February 16, 1993.

Karen National Union. Statement from the "Office of the Supreme Headquarters, Karen National Union, Kawthoolei," April 5, 2000.

Karen National Union. "KNU: Statement Regarding Retaliation Against SPDC Troops and their Followers." Unpublished statement, April 1, 1998.

Karen National Union, Office of the Supreme Headquarters. "Statement by KNU Foreign Affairs Department on Burma-Thailand Natural Gas Pipeline" Unpublished statement, February 24, 1995.

Brig.-Gen. Khin Nyunt, Secretary 1, State Law and Order Restoration Council. *The Conspiracy of Treasonous Minions Within the Myanmar Naing-Ngan and Traitorous Cohorts Abroad: Conspiracies and machinations to do great harm to the country perpetrated by party organizations, rightist forces, some diplomats, some foreign broadcasting stations, some foreign publications and anti-government forces outside the country who were carrying out both underground and above-ground activities using the students and simple and honest people as explained at the Special Press Conference held on 9-9-89. State Law and Order Restoration Council Secretary (1) Brig.-Gen. Khin Nyunt's Statement.* Yangon: Guardian Press of the News and Periodicals Enterprise, Ministry of Information of the Government of the Union of Myanmar, 1989.

"Large Ethnic Group Flees Across Burmese Border," Radio Thailand Network, recorded and translated by the Foreign Broadcast Information Service, *Daily Report: Southeast Asia,* FBIS-EAS-94-141, July 22, 1994.

Lt.-General Khin Nyunt. "How Some Western Powers have been Aiding and Abetting Terrorism Committed by Certain Organisations Operating Under the Guise of Democracy and Human Rights by giving them Assistance in both Cash and Kind." Unpublished statement by SLORC Secretary (1), Rangoon, June 1997.

Luce, G. H. "Mons of the Pagan Dynasty." Unpublished lecture delivered to the Rangoon University Mon Society, January 2, 1950.

Lt. Colonel Thein Han. "An Assessment of the Formulation and Implementation of Border Areas Development Project Strategies." In *Symposium on Socio-Economic Factors Contributing to National Consolidation.* Yángon: Ministry of Defence and Office of Strategic Studies, 1996.

Ministry of Defence. *The Defence of Thailand, 1996.* Bangkok: Strategic Research Institute, National Institute of Defence Studies, Supreme Command Headquarters, 1996.

Ministry of Defence, Office of Strategic Studies., *Symposium on Socio-economic Factors Contributing to National Consolidation.* Yangon: Office of Strategic Studies, Ministry of Defence, 1996.

Ministry of Interior, Operations Center for Displaced Persons. *Indochinese Refugees in Thailand, 1989-1992.* Bangkok: Ministry of Interior, 1992.

Mon Information Service. *What is Going On in Burma's Coastal Region? A News Report.* Bangkok: MIS, January 1998.

———. "Forced Relocation of Karen and Mon Villagers in Kya Inn Seik Kyi Township." Unpublished statement, October 14, 1997.

———. *Life in the Country: Continued Human Rights Violations in Burma.* Bangkok: MIS, July 1997.

———. *French Total Co.'s and American Unocal Corp.'s Disastrous Gas Pipeline Project in Burma's Gulf of Martaban.* Bangkok: MIS, May1996.

Mon National Relief Committee. *Monthly Report* (various years, 1990-1997). Unpublished documents.

———. "Statement of the Mon National Relief Committee Regarding the Repatriation Program of Mon Refugees." Unpublished statement, August 31, 1995.

———. *Mon Refugees: Hunger for Protection in 1994.* Bangkok: MNRC, 1994.

———. "Confidential Report of the Mon National Relief Committee." Unpublished statement, July 24, 1994.

———. "Emergency Report of Mon National Relief Committee." Unpublished statement, July 22, 1994.

Mon Unity League. *The Mon: A People Without a Country.* Bangkok: Mon Unity League, 1997.

Nawrahta. *Destiny of the Nation.* Yangon: The News and Periodicals Enterprise, 1995.

New Mon State Party. "Basic Political Policy and Constitution, 1992." December 15, 1992.

———. "The New Mon State Party's Military Statement Ending February 1990." Unpublished statement obtained from the NMSP.

———. "The New Mon State Party, Answers to Questionnaire on Mon Freedom Movement." Bangkok, 1985.

New Mon State Party, General Headquarters, Central Committee. "Statement on Ceasefire between the State Law and Order Restoration Council (SLORC) and the New Mon State Party (NMSP)." Unpublished statement, July 13, 1995.

"9th Division Command Changes Discussed," *Matichon*, June 7, 1994, pp. 1, 3, translated by the Foreign Broadcast Information Service, *Daily Report: Southeast Asia*, FBIS-EAS-94-145, July 28, 1994.

Office of the Special Representative of the Secretary General of the United Nations for Coordination of Cambodian Humanitarian Assistance Programmes. *Cambodian Humanitarian Assistance and the United Nations (1979-1991)*. Bangkok: United Nations, 1992.

Ogata, Sadako, United Nations High Commissioner for Refugees. "Opening Address." In *Healing the Wounds of War: Refugees, Reconstruction and Reconciliation*. Conference Proceedings, UNHCR and International Peace Academy, June 30-July 1, 1996.

Police-General Pao Sarasin, Minister of Interior. "Announcement of the MOI. Subject: Extension Period for Burmese Students to Report for Admittance into the Safe Area." Unpublished statement, Bangkok, September 25, 1992.

Resident of Kayin State. *Whither KNU? By a Resident of Kayin State*. Yangon: The News and Periodicals Enterprise, 1995.

Shan Human Rights Foundation. *Disposesssed: Forced Relocation and Extra-judicial Killings in Shan State*. Chiang Mai: Shan Human Rights Foundation, April 1998.

State Peace and Development Council. *The Announcement of State Peace and Development Council's Notification No. 1/97, The First Waning Day of Tazaungmon, 1359, M.E. 15th November 1997*. Yangon, 1997.

U Nu, "Promotion of Mon Culture."In *Forward With the People: Translation of Selected Speeches of the Hon. U Nu, Prime Minister of the Union of Burma, Delivered on Various Occasions Between 19th February 1953 and 1st June 1954*. Rangoon: Ministry of Information, Government of the Union of Burma, 1955.

United Nations Commission on Human Rights. *Question of the Violation of Human Rights and Fundamental Freedoms in any Part of the World. Situation of Human Rights in Myanmar. Report of the Special Rapporteur, Mr Rajasoomer Lallah, Submitted in Accordance with Commission on Human Rights Resolution 1998/63*. UN doc. E/CN.4/1999/35, January 22, 1999.

———. *Situation of Human Rights in Myanmar*, Fifty-third session. UN doc. E/CN.4/1997/64, February 6, 1997.

————. *Internally Displaced Persons, Report of the Representative of the Secretary-General, Mr. Francis M. Deng, Submitted Pursuant to Commission on Human Rights Resolution 1995-57.* UN doc. E/CN.4/1996/Add.2, 1996.

————. *Internally Displaced Persons: Report of the Representative of the Secretary-General, Mr. Francis M. Deng, Submitted Pursuant to Commission on Human Rights Resolutions 1993/95 and 1994/68.* UN doc. E/CN.4/1995/50, February 2, 1995.

————. *Report on the Situation of Human Rights in Myanmar, Prepared by the Special Rapporteur, Mr. Yozo Yokota.* UN doc. E/CN.4/1995/65, January 12, 1995.

United Nations Conference of Plenipotentiaries, *Convention Relating to the Status of Refugees (1951).* Geneva: 1951

United Nations High Commissioner for Regugees. *Handbook, Voluntary Repatriation: International Protection.* Geneva: UNHCR, 1996.

————. "UNHCR Position on the Safe Area for Burmese in Thailand." Press Release, November 30, 1992.

United Nations High Commissioner for Human Rights. *Statement by Representative of the Secretary-General on Internally Displaced Persons, Dr. Francis M. Deng, Fifty-fifth session, United Nations Commission on Human Rights, Geneva, 22 March-30 April 1999, item 14(c): Specific Groups and Individuals, Mass Exoduses and Displaced Persons,* April 16, 1999.

UNHCR Branch Office in Thailand. "Notice to Asylum Seekers/Persons of Concern to UNHCR (Myanmar Nationals)." Unpublished statement, Bangkok, June 1, 1995.

UNHCR, Executive Committee of the High Commissioner's Programme. "Forty-eighth Session, Annual Theme: Repatriation Challenges." UN doc. A/AC.96/887, September 9, 1997.

————. "Update on Regional Developments in Asia and Oceania." UN doc. EC/46/SC/CRP.44, 1996.

————. "UNHCR Activities Financed by Voluntary Funds: Thailand." UN doc. A/AC.96/846/Part II/7, August 2, 1995.

————. "Note on International Protection," Forty-fifth session. UN doc. A/AC.96/830, September 7, 1994.

————. "No. 44 (XXXVII)-1986 Detention of Refugees and Asylum-Seekers, Report of the 37th Session." UN doc. A/AC.96/688, 1986.

United Nations General Assembly. *Human Rights Question: Human Rights Situations and Reports of the special Rapporteurs and Representatives. Situation of Human Rights in Myanmar. Note by General Secretary, fifty-second session.* UN doc. A/52/484, October 16, 1997.

United Nations. "Thailand and Burma. Agreement (with Annexes) on Border Arrangements and Cooperation. Signed at Rangoon, on 17 May 1963. (No. 6779)." In *United Nations, Treaty Series: Treaties and International*

Agreements, Registered or Filed and Recorded with the Secretariat of the United Nations, Volume 468. New York: United Nations, 1963.

United States Committee for Refugees. *The Return of the Rohingya Refugees to Burma: Voluntary Repatriation or Refoulement?* Washington, DC: USCR, 1995.

———. *World Refugee Survey 1993.* Washington, DC: USCR, 1993.

———. *Refugee Reports.* Washington, DC: USCR, 1992.

———. *World Refugee Survey 1992.* Washington, DC: USCR, 1992.

———. *"The War is Growing Worse and Worse": Refugees and Displaced Persons on the Thai-Burmese Border.* Washington, DC: USCR, 1990.

———. *Cambodians in Thailand: People on the Edge.* Washington, DC: USCR, 1985.

United States Committee on Foreign Affairs, House of Representatives. *The Crackdown in Burma: Suppression of the Democracy Movement and Violations of Human Rights. Hearing and Markup Before the Subcommittees on Human Rights and International Organizations and on Asian and Pacific Affairs of the Committee on Foreign Affairs, House of Representatives, One Hundred First Congress, First Session on H. Con. Res. 185.* Washington, DC: September 13, 1989.

United States Department of State. *Thailand Country Report on Human Rights Practices for 1997.* Washington, DC: Bureau of Democracy, Human Rights and Labor, January 1998.
———. *Thailand: Report on Human Rights Practices for 1996.* Washington, DC: Bureau of Democracy, Human Rights and Labor, January 30, 1997.

Vitit Muntarbhorn. "Law and National Policy Concerning Displaced Persons and Illegal Immigrants in Thailand." Unpublished paper. Bangkok: Institute of Asian Studies, Chulalongkorn University, n. d.

WEBSITES AND INTERNET SOURCES

Maung Lu Zaw. "Another Important Milestone in Myanmar-Thai Economic Cooperation." *Myanmar Perspectives,* March 3, 1997. Online at http://www.myanmar.com/gov.perspec/97mar/thai3-97.html [accessed February 4, 1998].

Myanmar Information Committee. "Information Sheet 1998," No. A-0365(I), March 26, 1998. Myanmar Infoweb. Online at http://www.myanmarinformation.net/infosheet/1998/980326/htm [accessed April 2, 1998].

Myanmar Perspectives 3,12 (December 1997). Online at http://www.myanmar.com/gov.perspec/12-97/tra12-97.html [accessed April 2, 1998].

UNHCR Funding and Donor Relations, East Asia and the Pacific. *UNHCR 1999 Global Appeal—Thailand/Myanmar.* Online at http://www.unhcr.ch/fdrs/ga99/tha.html [accessed March 21, 1999].

UNHCR. "1999 Mid-Year Progress Report—Thailand and Myanmar, Initial Objectives." Online at http://www.unhcr.ch/fdrs/my99/th.htm [accessed December 8, 1999].

Regular editions of the BurmaNet News, subscribed from reg.burma@conf.igc.apc.org

BurmaNet News. "Special Report from Inside Halockhani Camp." Online at http://reg.burma@conf.igc.apc.org. Received August 13, 1994.

Unocal. *Myanmar: The Yandana Project.* Online at http://www.unocal.com/ogops/yadtoc.htm [accessed February 3, 1997].

Unocal. "Unocal in Myanmar (Burma): The Story You Haven't Heard About..." Online at http:/www.unocal.com/myanmar/00report/index.htm [accessed May 22, 2000].

"Thai General Absolves Burma for Raids." UPI, January 30, 1997. Online at http://www.soros.org/burma/thaiabso.html [accessed February 17, 1997].

INTERVIEWS AND PERSONAL COMMUNICATION

A great number of the interviews for this study were conducted on an unattributable basis. Those who consented to be identified are included in the following:

Interview, Director, Division 2, National Security Council, Bangkok, March 10, 1998.

Interview, Khun Wannida Boonprarong, Chief, Displaced Persons and Illegal Immigrant Affairs Subdivision, Ministry of Interior, Bangkok, March 9, 1998.

Personal communication, National Security Council, Government House, Bangkok, June 15, 1999.

Personal communication, Directorate of Army Intelligence, Royal Thai Army Headquarters, Bangkok, April 4, 2000.

Interview, General Sanan Kajornklarn, Special Expert [on Myanmar], Office of the Permanent Secretary and Spokesman for Ministry of Defence, Bangkok, April 7, 2000.

Personal communication, Dr. Cynthia Maung, Mae Tao Clinic, Mae Sot, Thailand, June 5, 1999, February 17, 2000.

Interviews, Burmese Border Consortium and the Coordinating Committee for Services to Displaced Persons in Thailand, Sangkhlaburi and Bangkok, September 1995, February 1998, June 1999.

Interviews, Mon National Relief Committee, Sangkhlaburi, Thailand, May-September 1995, February-March 1998, June 1999, November 1999.

Personal communication with members of the New Mon State Party, Thailand, May-September 1995, February-March 1998, June 1999, November 1999.

Personal communication with Mon splinter faction leaders, Sangkhlaburi, Thailand, June 1999.

Personal communication with Nai Shwe Kyin, President of the New Mon State Party, Pa Yaw refugee camp, Thailand, May-June 1995.

Personal communication, former MAMD soldiers, Bangkok, February 1998.

Personal communication, senior officials from the Karen National Union (KNU) and Karen National Liberation Army, Mae Sot, June 1999 and February 2000.

Personal communication, senior officials from the Karenni National Progressive Party, Mae Hong Son, February-March 2000.

Personal communication, Karenni National Relief Committee, Mae Hong Son, June 1999 and February-March 2000.

Personal communication, Shan Human Rights Foundation, March 2000.

Personal communication, Burma Relief Centre, Chiang Mai, March 2000.

Interview, UNHCR Protection Officers, Regional Office of the UNHCR, Bangkok, September 1995, March 1998, March 2000.

Interview, Ruprecht von Arnhim, UNHCR Regional Representative, Bangkok, September 18, 1995.

Personal communication, UNHCR field officer at the Immigration Detention Centre, Bangkok, March 20, 1998.

Personal communication, Mr. J. de Riedmatten, UNHCR Deputy Regional Representative and head of Legal Section, Bangkok, March 23, 2000.

Seminars, "Policy and Plans to Repatriate Undocumented Migrant Workers," Chulalongkorn University, Bangkok, March 13, 1998; "Re-thinking Policies Towards Burmese Refugees and Students in Thailand," Chulalongkorn University, Bangkok, November 8, 1999.

SOUTHEAST ASIA PROGRAM PUBLICATIONS
Cornell University

Studies on Southeast Asia

Number 32   *Fear and Sanctuary: Burmese Refugees in Thailand*, Hazel J. Lang. 2002. 204 pp. ISBN 0-87727-731-1.

Number 31   *Modern Dreams: An Inquiry into Power, Cultural Production, and the Cityscape in Contemporary Urban Penang, Malaysia*, Beng-Lan Goh. 2002. 225 pp. ISBN 0-87727-730-3.

Number 30   *Violence and the State in Suharto's Indonesia*, ed. Benedict R. O'G. Anderson. 2001. 247 pp. ISBN 0-87727-729-X.

Number 29   *Studies in Southeast Asian Art: Essays in Honor of Stanley J. O'Connor*, ed. Nora A. Taylor. 2000. 243 pp. Illustrations. ISBN 0-87727-728-1.

Number 28   *The Hadrami Awakening: Community and Identity in the Netherlands East Indies, 1900-1942*, Natalie Mobini-Kesheh. 1999. 174 pp. ISBN 0-87727-727-3.

Number 27   *Tales from Djakarta: Caricatures of Circumstances and their Human Beings*, Pramoedya Ananta Toer. 1999. 145 pp. ISBN 0-87727-726-5.

Number 26   *History, Culture, and Region in Southeast Asian Perspectives*, rev. ed., O. W. Wolters. 1999. 275 pp. ISBN 0-87727-725-7.

Number 25   *Figures of Criminality in Indonesia, the Philippines, and Colonial Vietnam*, ed. Vicente L. Rafael. 1999. 259 pp. ISBN 0-87727-724-9.

Number 24   *Paths to Conflagration: Fifty Years of Diplomacy and Warfare in Laos, Thailand, and Vietnam, 1778-1828*, Mayoury Ngaosyvathn and Pheuiphanh Ngaosyvathn. 1998. 268 pp. ISBN 0-87727-723-0.

Number 23   *Nguyễn Cochinchina: Southern Vietnam in the Seventeenth and Eighteenth Centuries*, Li Tana. 1998. 194 pp. ISBN 0-87727-722-2.

Number 22   *Young Heroes: The Indonesian Family in Politics*, Saya S. Shiraishi. 1997. 183 pp. ISBN 0-87727-721-4.

Number 21   *Interpreting Development: Capitalism, Democracy, and the Middle Class in Thailand*, John Girling. 1996. 95 pp. ISBN 0-87727-720-6.

Number 20   *Making Indonesia*, ed. Daniel S. Lev, Ruth McVey. 1996. 201 pp. ISBN 0-87727-719-2.

Number 19   *Essays into Vietnamese Pasts*, ed. K. W. Taylor, John K. Whitmore. 1995. 288 pp. ISBN 0-87727-718-4.

Number 18   *In the Land of Lady White Blood: Southern Thailand and the Meaning of History*, Lorraine M. Gesick. 1995. 106 pp. ISBN 0-87727-717-6.

Number 17   *The Vernacular Press and the Emergence of Modern Indonesian Consciousness*, Ahmat Adam. 1995. 220 pp. ISBN 0-87727-716-8.

Number 16   *The Nan Chronicle*, trans., ed. David K. Wyatt. 1994. 158 pp. ISBN 0-87727-715-X.

Number 15   *Selective Judicial Competence: The Cirebon-Priangan Legal Administration, 1680–1792*, Mason C. Hoadley. 1994. 185 pp. ISBN 0-87727-714-1.

Number 14   *Sjahrir: Politics and Exile in Indonesia*, Rudolf Mrázek. 1994. 536 pp. ISBN 0-87727-713-3.

Number 13   *Fair Land Sarawak: Some Recollections of an Expatriate Officer*, Alastair Morrison. 1993. 196 pp. ISBN 0-87727-712-5.

Number 12   *Fields from the Sea: Chinese Junk Trade with Siam during the Late Eighteenth and Early Nineteenth Centuries,* Jennifer Cushman. 1993. 206 pp. ISBN 0-87727-711-7.

Number 11   *Money, Markets, and Trade in Early Southeast Asia: The Development of Indigenous Monetary Systems to AD 1400,* Robert S. Wicks. 1992. 2nd printing 1996. 354 pp., 78 tables, illus., maps. ISBN 0-87727-710-9.

Number 10   *Tai Ahoms and the Stars: Three Ritual Texts to Ward Off Danger,* trans., ed. B. J. Terwiel, Ranoo Wichasin. 1992. 170 pp. ISBN 0-87727-709-5.

Number 9   *Southeast Asian Capitalists,* ed. Ruth McVey. 1992. 2nd printing 1993. 220 pp. ISBN 0-87727-708-7.

Number 8   *The Politics of Colonial Exploitation: Java, the Dutch, and the Cultivation System,* Cornelis Fasseur, ed. R. E. Elson, trans. R. E. Elson, Ary Kraal. 1992. 2nd printing 1994. 266 pp. ISBN 0-87727-707-9.

Number 7   *A Malay Frontier: Unity and Duality in a Sumatran Kingdom,* Jane Drakard. 1990. 215 pp. ISBN 0-87727-706-0.

Number 6   *Trends in Khmer Art,* Jean Boisselier, ed. Natasha Eilenberg, trans. Natasha Eilenberg, Melvin Elliott. 1989. 124 pp., 24 plates. ISBN 0-87727-705-2.

Number 5   *Southeast Asian Ephemeris: Solar and Planetary Positions, A.D. 638–2000,* J. C. Eade. 1989. 175 pp. ISBN 0-87727-704-4.

Number 3   *Thai Radical Discourse: The Real Face of Thai Feudalism Today,* Craig J. Reynolds. 1987. 2nd printing 1994. 186 pp. ISBN 0-87727-702-8.

Number 1   *The Symbolism of the Stupa,* Adrian Snodgrass. 1985. Revised with index, 1988. 3rd printing 1998. 469 pp. ISBN 0-87727-700-1.

SEAP Series

Number 19   *Gender, Household, State: Đổi Mới in Việt Nam,* ed. Jayne Werner and Danièle Bélanger. 2002. 153 pp. ISBN 0-87727-137-2.

Number 18   *Culture and Power in Traditional Siamese Government,* Neil A. Englehart. 2001. 130 pp. ISBN 0-87727-135-6.

Number 17   *Gangsters, Democracy, and the State,* ed. Carl A. Trocki. 1998. 94 pp. ISBN 0-87727-134-8.

Number 16   *Cutting across the Lands: An Annotated Bibliography on Natural Resource Management and Community Development in Indonesia, the Philippines, and Malaysia,* ed. Eveline Ferretti. 1997. 329 pp. ISBN 0-87727-133-X.

Number 15   *The Revolution Falters: The Left in Philippine Politics after 1986,* ed. Patricio N. Abinales. 1996. 182 pp. ISBN 0-87727-132-1.

Number 14   *Being Kammu: My Village, My Life,* Damrong Tayanin. 1994. 138 pp., 22 tables, illus., maps. ISBN 0-87727-130-5.

Number 13   *The American War in Vietnam,* ed. Jayne Werner, David Hunt. 1993. 132 pp. ISBN 0-87727-131-3.

Number 12   *The Political Legacy of Aung San,* ed. Josef Silverstein. Revised edition 1993. 169 pp. ISBN 0-87727-128-3.

Number 10   *Studies on Vietnamese Language and Literature: A Preliminary Bibliography*, Nguyen Dinh Tham. 1992. 227 pp. ISBN 0-87727-127-5.

Number 9   *A Secret Past*, Dokmaisot, trans. Ted Strehlow. 1992. 2nd printing 1997. 72 pp. ISBN 0-87727-126-7.

Number 8   *From PKI to the Comintern, 1924–1941: The Apprenticeship of the Malayan Communist Party*, Cheah Boon Kheng. 1992. 147 pp. ISBN 0-87727-125-9.

Number 7   *Intellectual Property and US Relations with Indonesia, Malaysia, Singapore, and Thailand*, Elisabeth Uphoff. 1991. 67 pp. ISBN 0-87727-124-0.

Number 6   *The Rise and Fall of the Communist Party of Burma (CPB)*, Bertil Lintner. 1990. 124 pp. 26 illus., 14 maps. ISBN 0-87727-123-2.

Number 5   *Japanese Relations with Vietnam: 1951–1987*, Masaya Shiraishi. 1990. 174 pp. ISBN 0-87727-122-4.

Number 3   *Postwar Vietnam: Dilemmas in Socialist Development*, ed. Christine White, David Marr. 1988. 2nd printing 1993. 260 pp. ISBN 0-87727-120-8.

Number 2   *The Dobama Movement in Burma (1930–1938)*, Khin Yi. 1988. 160 pp. ISBN 0-87727-118-6.

Translation Series

Volume 4   *Approaching Suharto's Indonesia from the Margins*, ed. Takashi Shiraishi. 1994. 153 pp. ISBN 0-87727-403-7.

Volume 3   *The Japanese in Colonial Southeast Asia*, ed. Saya Shiraishi, Takashi Shiraishi. 1993. 172 pp. ISBN 0-87727-402-9.

Volume 2   *Indochina in the 1940s and 1950s*, ed. Takashi Shiraishi, Motoo Furuta. 1992. 196 pp. ISBN 0-87727-401-0.

Volume 1   *Reading Southeast Asia*, ed. Takashi Shiraishi. 1990. 188 pp. ISBN 0-87727-400-2.

CORNELL MODERN INDONESIA PROJECT PUBLICATIONS
Cornell University

Number 75   *A Tour of Duty: Changing Patterns of Military Politics in Indonesia in the 1990s*. Douglas Kammen and Siddharth Chandra. 1999. 99 pp. ISBN 0-87763-049-6.

Number 74   *The Roots of Acehnese Rebellion 1989–1992*, Tim Kell. 1995. 103 pp. ISBN 0-87763-040-2.

Number 73   *"White Book" on the 1992 General Election in Indonesia*, trans. Dwight King. 1994. 72 pp. ISBN 0-87763-039-9.

Number 72   *Popular Indonesian Literature of the Qur'an*, Howard M. Federspiel. 1994. 170 pp. ISBN 0-87763-038-0.

Number 71   *A Javanese Memoir of Sumatra, 1945–1946: Love and Hatred in the Liberation War*, Takao Fusayama. 1993. 150 pp. ISBN 0-87763-037-2.

Number 70   *East Kalimantan: The Decline of a Commercial Aristocracy,* Burhan
             Magenda. 1991. 120 pp. ISBN 0-87763-036-4.

Number 69   *The Road to Madiun: The Indonesian Communist Uprising of 1948,*
             Elizabeth Ann Swift. 1989. 120 pp. ISBN 0-87763-035-6.

Number 68   *Intellectuals and Nationalism in Indonesia: A Study of the Following
             Recruited by Sutan Sjahrir in Occupation Jakarta,* J. D. Legge. 1988.
             159 pp. ISBN 0-87763-034-8.

Number 67   *Indonesia Free: A Biography of Mohammad Hatta,* Mavis Rose. 1987.
             252 pp. ISBN 0-87763-033-X.

Number 66   *Prisoners at Kota Cane,* Leon Salim, trans. Audrey Kahin. 1986. 112 pp.
             ISBN 0-87763-032-1.

Number 65   *The Kenpeitai in Java and Sumatra,* trans. Barbara G. Shimer, Guy Hobbs,
             intro. Theodore Friend. 1986. 80 pp. ISBN 0-87763-031-3.

Number 64   *Suharto and His Generals: Indonesia's Military Politics, 1975–1983,* David
             Jenkins. 1984. 4th printing 1997. 300 pp. ISBN 0-87763-030-5.

Number 62   *Interpreting Indonesian Politics: Thirteen Contributions to the Debate,
             1964–1981,* ed. Benedict Anderson, Audrey Kahin, intro. Daniel S. Lev.
             1982. 3rd printing 1991. 172 pp. ISBN 0-87763-028-3.

Number 61   *Sickle and Crescent: The Communist Revolt of 1926 in Banten,* Michael C.
             Williams. 1982. 81 pp. ISBN 0-87763-027-5.

Number 60   *The Minangkabau Response to Dutch Colonial Rule in the Nineteenth
             Century,* Elizabeth E. Graves. 1981. 157 pp. ISBN 0-87763-000-3.

Number 59   *Breaking the Chains of Oppression of the Indonesian People: Defense
             Statement at His Trial on Charges of Insulting the Head of State, Bandung,
             June 7–10, 1979,* Heri Akhmadi. 1981. 201 pp. ISBN 0-87763-001-1.

Number 58   *Administration of Islam in Indonesia,* Deliar Noer. 1978. 82 pp.
             ISBN 0-87763-002-X.

Number 57   *Permesta: Half a Rebellion,* Barbara S. Harvey. 1977. 174 pp.
             ISBN 0-87763-003-8.

Number 55   *Report from Banaran: The Story of the Experiences of a Soldier during the
             War of Independence,* Maj. Gen. T. B. Simatupang. 1972. 186 pp.
             ISBN 0-87763-005-4.

Number 52   *A Preliminary Analysis of the October 1 1965, Coup in Indonesia (Prepared
             in January 1966),* Benedict R. Anderson, Ruth T. McVey, assist.
             Frederick P. Bunnell. 1971. 3rd printing 1990. 174 pp.
             ISBN 0-87763-008-9.

Number 51   *The Putera Reports: Problems in Indonesian-Japanese War-Time Cooperation,*
             Mohammad Hatta, trans., intro. William H. Frederick. 1971. 114 pp.
             ISBN 0-87763-009-7.

Number 50   *Schools and Politics: The Kaum Muda Movement in West Sumatra
             (1927–1933),* Taufik Abdullah. 1971. 257 pp. ISBN 0-87763-010-0.

Number 49   *The Foundation of the Partai Muslimin Indonesia,* K. E. Ward. 1970. 75 pp.
             ISBN 0-87763-011-9.

Number 48   *Nationalism, Islam and Marxism,* Soekarno, intro. Ruth T. McVey. 1970.
             2nd printing 1984. 62 pp. ISBN 0-87763-012-7.

Number 43   *State and Statecraft in Old Java: A Study of the Later Mataram Period, 16th to 19th Century*, Soemarsaid Moertono. Revised edition 1981. 180 pp. ISBN 0-87763-017-8.

Number 37   *Mythology and the Tolerance of the Javanese*, Benedict R. O'G. Anderson. 2nd edition 1997. 104 pp., 65 illus. ISBN 0-87763-041-0.

Number 25   *The Communist Uprisings of 1926–1927 in Indonesia: Key Documents*, ed., intro. Harry J. Benda, Ruth T. McVey. 1960. 2nd printing 1969. 177 pp. ISBN 0-87763-024-0.

Number 7   *The Soviet View of the Indonesian Revolution*, Ruth T. McVey. 1957. 3rd printing 1969. 90 pp. ISBN 0-87763-018-6.

Number 6   *The Indonesian Elections of 1955*, Herbert Feith. 1957. 2nd printing 1971. 91 pp. ISBN 0-87763-020-8.

LANGUAGE TEXTS

INDONESIAN

Beginning Indonesian through Self-Instruction, John U. Wolff, Dédé Oetomo, Daniel Fietkiewicz. 3rd revised edition 1992. Vol. 1. 115 pp. ISBN 0-87727-529-7. Vol. 2. 434 pp. ISBN 0-87727-530-0. Vol. 3. 473 pp. ISBN 0-87727-531-9.

Indonesian Readings, John U. Wolff. 1978. 4th printing 1992. 480 pp. ISBN 0-87727-517-3

Indonesian Conversations, John U. Wolff. 1978. 3rd printing 1991. 297 pp. ISBN 0-87727-516-5

Formal Indonesian, John U. Wolff. 2nd revised edition 1986. 446 pp. ISBN 0-87727-515-7

TAGALOG

Pilipino through Self-Instruction, John U. Wolff, Maria Theresa C. Centano, Der-Hwa V. Rau. 1991. Vol. 1. 342 pp. ISBN 0-87727—525-4. Vol. 2. 378 pp. ISBN 0-87727-526-2. Vol 3. 431 pp. ISBN 0-87727-527-0. Vol. 4. 306 pp. ISBN 0-87727-528-9.

THAI

A. U. A. Language Center Thai Course Book 1, J. Marvin Brown. Originally published by the American University Alumni Association Language Center, 1974. Reissued by Cornell Southeast Asia Program, 1991. 267 pp. ISBN 0-87727-506-8.

A. U. A. Language Center Thai Course Book 2, 1992. 288 pp. ISBN 0-87727-507-6.

A. U. A. Language Center Thai Course Book 3, 1992. 247 pp. ISBN 0-87727-508-4.

A. U. A. Language Center Thai Course, Reading and Writing Text (mostly reading), 1979. Reissued 1997. 164 pp. ISBN 0-87727-511-4.

A. U. A. Language Center Thai Course, Reading and Writing Workbook (mostly writing), 1979. Reissued 1997. 99 pp. ISBN 0-87727-512-2.

KHMER

Cambodian System of Writing and Beginning Reader, Franklin E. Huffman. Originally published by Yale University Press, 1970. Reissued by Cornell Southeast Asia Program, 3rd printing 1992. 365 pp. ISBN 0-300-01314-0.

Modern Spoken Cambodian, Franklin E. Huffman, assist. Charan Promchan, Chhom-Rak Thong Lambert. Originally published by Yale University Press, 1970. Reissued by Cornell Southeast Asia Program, 3rd printing 1991. 451 pp. ISBN 0-300-01316-7.

Intermediate Cambodian Reader, ed. Franklin E. Huffman, assist. Im Proum. Originally published by Yale University Press, 1972. Reissued by Cornell Southeast Asia Program, 1988. 499 pp. ISBN 0-300-01552-6.

Cambodian Literary Reader and Glossary, Franklin E. Huffman, Im Proum. Originally published by Yale University Press, 1977. Reissued by Cornell Southeast Asia Program, 1988. 494 pp. ISBN 0-300-02069-4.

HMONG

White Hmong-English Dictionary, Ernest E. Heimbach. 1969. 7th printing 1997. 523 pp. ISBN 0-87727-075-9.

VIETNAMESE

Intermediate Spoken Vietnamese, Franklin E. Huffman, Tran Trong Hai. 1980. 3rd printing 1994. ISBN 0-87727-500-9.

* * *

Southeast Asian Studies: Reorientations. Craig J. Reynolds and Ruth McVey. Frank H. Golay Lectures 2 & 3. 70 pp. ISBN 0-87727-301-4.

Javanese Literature in Surakarta Manuscripts, Nancy K. Florida. Vol. 1, *Introduction and Munuscripts of the Karaton Surakarta.* 1993. 410 pp. Frontispiece, illustrations. Hard cover, ISBN 0-87727-602-1, Paperback, ISBN 0-87727-603-X. Vol. 2, *Manuscripts of the Mangkunagaran Palace.* 2000. 576 pp. Frontispiece, illustrations. Paperback, ISBN 0-87727-604-8.

Sbek Thom: Khmer Shadow Theater. Pech Tum Kravel, trans. Sos Kem, ed. Thavro Phim, Sos Kem, Martin Hatch. 1996. 363 pp., 153 photographs. ISBN 0-87727-620-X.

In the Mirror, Literature and Politics in Siam in the American Era, ed. Benedict R. O'G. Anderson, trans. Benedict R. O'G. Anderson, Ruchira Mendiones. 1985. 2nd printing 1991. 303 pp. Paperback. ISBN 974-210-380-1.

Milton Keynes UK
Ingram Content Group UK Ltd.
UKHW030608180124
436246UK00014B/328